Ride To The Top Of New England... *by Train!*

- ✿ **CLIMB...** to the highest peak in the Northeast on the world's first mountain-climbing cog railway! 3-hour guided round trip includes one hour at the summit.

- ✿ **ONLY...** cog railway operating in the US, located in the heart of New Hampshire's White Mountains.

- ✿ **NEW MUSEUM...** visit the new interactive Cog Railway Museum at the base!

- ✿ **CHOOSE** to take your trip with vintage coal-fired steam or eco-friendly biodiesel locomotives.

- ✿ **NOW...** offering one-way hiker tickets up or down.

Celebrating 150 years in 2019!

Daily specials and events! Join us for our 150th Anniversary party, Railway To The Moon Festival, Family Holiday Trains and more!

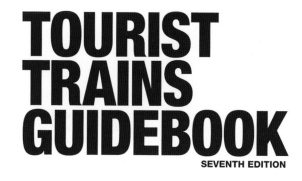

TOURIST
TRAINS
GUIDEBOOK

SEVENTH EDITION

Kalmbach
Media

Kalmbach Media
21027 Crossroads Circle
Waukesha, Wisconsin 53186
www.KalmbachHobbyStore.com

© 2019 Kalmbach Media
First edition published in 2007. Seventh edition in 2019.

Published in 2019
23 22 21 20 19   1 2 3 4 5

Printed in China

ISBN: 978-1-62700-589-0
EISBN: 978-1-62700-590-6

Front cover photo: Heber Valley Railroad by Dave Crosby
Back cover photo: White Pass & Yukon by Karl Zimmerman

Editor: Eric White
Book Design: Lisa Bergman

Library of Congress Control Number: 2018963695

Using the guidebook

Tourist Trains Guidebook describes 521 excursion trains, dinner trains, trolley rides, railroad museums, and historical depots across the United States and Canada. The sites are described in either full-page reviews or shorter listings.

Trains magazine staff and contributors reviewed 194 of the top attractions. Their reviews provide an in-depth look at each location. They describe what each train ride or museum offers and give you an idea of when to go for the best experiences. They also point out nearby activities that are worth doing and what you shouldn't miss to make your visit most enjoyable.

Another 327 unique attractions are presented in capsule descriptions that offer a concise look at each site and provide contact information.

We have included the most up-to-date details possible for every attraction. However, due to the many factors that can affect a tourist train or museum, we recommend that you contact any site before planning your visit. Steam engines may not be running, schedules and prices may change, and museums may be under renovation.

While almost every attraction has a website, many of them post their most current information and upcoming events on Facebook.

In this edition, the sites are organized into 12 geographic regions. Each region includes a list of sites and a handy locator map. You can browse a region's listings by state or province, where you'll find the shorter entries first followed by the full-page reviews. Each grouping is listed in alphabetical order. You can also look for an individual site using the index at the back of the book.

Contributors

The following people provided reviews of the tourist train sites: Kevin Andrusia, Bryan Bechtold, Marvin Clemons, Dave Crosby, Hayley Enoch, Justin Franz, Steve Glischinski, John Godfrey, Cody Grivno, Scott Hartley, Patrick Hiatte, David Hoge, Frank Keller, Tom Kline, G. Wayne Laepple, Robert LaMay, Elrond Lawrence, David Lustig, Rob McGonigal, Jackson McQuigg, Alexander Mitchell IV, Steve Patterson, Mark Perri, Mark Perry, Steve Smedley, Steve Sweeny, Jeff Terry, Ralcon Wagner, Jim Wrinn, and Karl Zimmermann.

Contents

Introduction

Welcome to a world of exploration, fun, and adventure. This guidebook will open a window into North American railway history, it will lead you to sacred places, and it will put you on board some of the oldest and coolest trains in some of the most beautiful locations around. Think of this guide as a key to unlocking something special.

I have used this guide for years to help find railroad attractions during business trips, while on vacation, and to make the most of my time. We've tried to provide as much helpful information as possible following in-the-field visits.

You'll be amazed at the number of venues and the wide range of experiences that are available. There are train rides that are about scenic wonders, train trips that are about bird watching, excursions that include cuisine as well as beverages, and even trains that take you to a gold mine.

Many venues include annual special events that bring Thomas the Tank Engine or the Polar Express to life. Some allow passengers to join the crew in the locomotive, and some even feature programs that put you in the engineer's seat.

Whatever you're looking for as far as a railroad attraction, it is probably in here. So, start turning pages. Get out those yellow sticky notes. And start planning. The train is ready and waiting. All aboard!

Jim Wrinn

Jim Wrinn, Editor
Trains magazine

REGION 1

Naugatuck Railroad, page 14

REGION 1

CONNECTICUT

1 Connecticut Antique Machinery Association
2 Connecticut Eastern Railroad Museum
3 Connecticut Trolley Museum
4 Danbury Railway Museum
5 Essex Steam Train
6 Naugatuck Railroad
7 Shore Line Trolley Museum
8 SoNo Switch Tower Museum

MAINE

9 Belfast & Moosehead Lake Railway
10 Boothbay Railway Village
11 Cole Land Transportation Museum
12 Downeast Scenic Railroad
13 Maine Narrow Gauge Railroad

14 Oakfield Railroad Museum
15 Seashore Trolley Museum
16 Wiscasset, Waterville & Farmington Railway Museum

MASSACHUSETTS

17 Berkshire Scenic Railway Museum
18 Cape Cod Central Railroad
19 Chatham Railroad Museum
20 Edaville USA
21 Lowell National Historical Park
22 Shelburne Falls Trolley Museum

NEW HAMPSHIRE

23 Ashland Railroad Station Museum
24 Café Lafayette Dinner Train
25 Conway Scenic Railroad
26 Gorham Historical Society Museum
27 Hobo Railroad
28 Mount Washington Cog Railway
29 Potter Place Railroad Station
30 Sandown Depot Museum
31 Silver Lake Railroad
32 White Mountain Central Railroad
33 Winnipesaukee Scenic Railroad

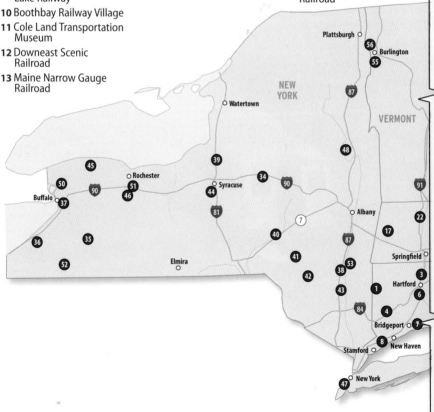

Edmundston ○

Presque Isle ○

14

95

MAINE

○ Orono
Bangor
11

12

9

26

91

93

28

32

27 **25**

24

31

23 **33**

89

29

○ Concord

NEW
HAMPSHIRE

30

Nashua ○

93 **95**

21

○ Boston

90

MA

2

84

RI

○ Providence

20

18 **19**

CT

95

54

5

49

Lewiston ○

95

16

10

Portland ○ **13**

15

NEW YORK

34 Adirondack Scenic
Railroad

35 Arcade & Attica Railroad

36 Brooks Alco Railroad
Display

37 Buffalo, Rochester
& Pittsburgh Depot
Museum

38 Catskill Mountain
Railroad

39 Central Square Station
Museum

40 Cooperstown & Charlotte
Valley Railroad

41 Delaware & Ulster
Railroad

42 Empire State Railway
Museum

43 Hyde Park Railroad
Station

44 Martisco Station Museum

45 Medina Railroad Museum

46 New York Museum of
Transportation

47 New York Transit Museum

48 North Creek Railway
Depot Museum

49 Railroad Museum of Long
Island

50 Railroad Museum of the
Niagara Frontier

51 Rochester & Genesee
Valley Railroad Museum

52 Salamanca Rail Museum

53 Trolley Museum of New
York

RHODE ISLAND

54 Newport & Narragansett
Bay Railroad

VERMONT

55 Shelburne Museum

56 Vermont Rail System

CONNECTICUT

Connecticut Antique Machinery Association

The association features an operating 3-foot-gauge railroad that is powered by a 1925 Baldwin locomotive that was used in the sugar cane fields of Hawaii. A variety of other locomotives and rolling stock fills out the collection. The site contains six other exhibits dedicated to antique industrial and agricultural machinery. It is open Wednesdays through Sundays, May through October.

LOCATION: 31 Kent-Cornwall Road (Route 7), Kent
PHONE: 860-927-0050
WEBSITE: ctamachinery.com
E-MAIL: form on website

Connecticut Trolley Museum

Founded in 1940, this museum offers a narrated 3-mile, round-trip trolley ride. Its collection contains passenger and freight streetcars, interurban cars, elevated railway cars, service cars, and other rail equipment. A fire equipment museum and motor coach museum are also on site. The museum is open April through October with Winterfest taking place in November and December.

LOCATION: 58 North Road, East Windsor
PHONE: 860-627-6540
WEBSITE: ceraonline.org
E-MAIL: form on website

Danbury Railway Museum

This museum contains about 70 pieces of equipment representing 13 different northeastern railroads and includes unique pieces such as a New Haven Railroad Mack FCD railbus. Vintage train rides in the yard include a spin around an operating turntable. The 1903 station features displays and a model layout of the Danbury yard. It is open year-round but closed on Mondays and Tuesdays from September through May and on most holidays.

LOCATION: 120 White Street, Danbury
PHONE: 203-778-8337
WEBSITE: danburyrailwaymuseum.org
E-MAIL: form on website

Shore Line Trolley Museum

The museum features a collection of nearly 100 vintage transit vehicles. A 3-mile round-trip trolley ride takes you along the area's scenic shore. Along the way, the trolley stops in the yard, where you can take a brief guided tour of the carbarn exhibits. You can also take a more comprehensive self-guided tour. The shop overlook allows you to view any restoration activities, and the station building contains additional exhibits. It is open Tuesday through Sunday, Memorial Day to Labor Day, with daily operations June to September.

LOCATION: 17 River Street, East Haven
PHONE: 203-467-6927
WEBSITE: shorelinetrolley.org
E-MAIL: info@shorelinetrolley.org

SoNo Switch Tower Museum

This 1896 New Haven Railroad switch tower has been restored, complete with an original armstrong 68-lever mechanical interlocking machine. Located next to Amtrak's Northeast Corridor main line, the unique museum is open Saturdays and Sundays May through October.

LOCATION: 77 Washington Street, South Norwalk
PHONE: 203-246-6958
WEBSITE: sonotower.org
E-MAIL: info@westctnrhs.org

Connecticut Eastern Railroad Museum

Robert A. LaMay

For anyone interested in seeing what happens in a 1900s-era railroad village, including devices such as this gallows signal, this would be the place to visit. Located on the original site of the Columbia Junction freight yard and roundhouse, the Connecticut Eastern Railroad Museum is one of the few railroad museums to have a roundhouse complete with an operating standard gauge 60-foot armstrong turntable.

CHOICES: The museum features a variety of restored buildings including a station, section house, freight house, and crossing shanties. It houses several diesel locomotives, various railcars, and a steam locomotive. The museum offers train rides along a section of the original Air Line Route. There is a new Kid's Area complete with scale size train and coal car to play and climb on. Also new is a 7½-inch scale train ride near the picnic area.

WHEN TO GO: The museum is open weekends from May into October. A variety of events takes place during the season, such as special events on opening day, a night photo shoot, Mothers ride free on Mothers' Day, Dads ride free on Fathers' Day, and the biggest event—Railroad Day on the first Saturday before Labor Day.

GOOD TO KNOW: With museum supervision, kids of all ages can ride on a replica 1850s pump car. You can also pretend you are the engineer and sit in the engineer's seat of a New Haven Railroad FL9 passenger diesel locomotive.

WORTH DOING: Willimantic is in the Last Green Valley, designated as the Quinebaug and Shetucket Rivers Valley National Heritage Corridor. The valley contains seven state forests and five state parks. During Walktober, there are more than 100 guided walks and special events, including one at the Connecticut Eastern Railroad Museum.

DON'T MISS: Train rides are available if there is demand for them. The fare for the round trip from Columbia Junction to Bridge Street is $3.

GETTING THERE: Willimantic is about 30 miles east of Hartford. The museum can be reached via state roads such as Routes 6, 66, 32, 195, and 2. Once downtown, turn onto Bridge Street (Route 32 South), cross the railroad tracks and take a quick right, and follow the railroad tracks down a dirt road to the museum entrance.

LOCATION: 55 Bridge Street, Willimantic
PHONE: 860-456-9999
WEBSITE: cteastrrmuseum.org
E-MAIL: info@cteastrrmuseum.org

Essex Steam Train & Riverboat

Karl Zimmerman

The Essex Steam Train, operated by the Valley Railroad Company, is unusual in offering a train ride that can be combined with a connecting riverboat excursion, providing scenic views of the Connecticut River from both rail and water. The 12-mile rail round trip from Essex station to Deep River and Haddam takes about an hour, while the rail-water package lasts 2.5 hours.

CHOICES: The Essex Steam Train is hauled by locomotive No. 40, which dates from 1920; No. 97, built in 1926; or the far newer Chinese-built No. 3025, while the *Becky Thatcher*, a replica of a three-deck Mississippi-style riverboat, handles the water excursion. A number of seasonal events take place, including a wildlife-viewing trip in February, as well as sunset cruises on Saturdays and a lunch train. On some weekends, a caboose is available for rides. Fall foliage steam specials now travel 4 miles north beyond the normal route as additional trackage has been restored.

WHEN TO GO: Trains operate from the historic 1892 Essex depot May through late October. Day Out with Thomas weekends take place in spring, and Santa Special (afternoons) and North Pole Express (evenings) trains run in November and December. Spring and fall are fine times to visit, with the leaves either a new green or in brilliant autumn colors.

GOOD TO KNOW: Essex is a historic seaport village, with lots of white-clapboard New England charm. The Victorian Goodspeed Opera House in nearby East Haddam presents productions of classic musical comedies.

WORTH DOING: Nearby Gillette Castle is a whimsical faux-medieval mountaintop estate built for actor and playwright William Gillette, most famous for his portrayal of Sherlock Holmes. Visit it on your own or as a train-ferry-hiking package offered by the railroad.

DON'T MISS: The diesel-hauled *Essex Clipper* Dinner Train operates seasonally and offers a four-course dinner. One of its dining cars is a special treat: the heavyweight Pullman parlor car *Wallingford*, built in 1927 for the New York, New Haven & Hartford.

GETTING THERE: Essex is located on Route 9 just 3 miles from I-95.

LOCATION: 1 Railroad Avenue, Essex
PHONE: 800-377-3987 or 860-767-0103
WEBSITE: essexsteamtrain.com
E-MAIL: info@essexsteamtrain.com

Naugatuck Railroad

Scott Hartley

Today's Naugatuck Railroad runs over 19.6 miles of former New Haven Railroad, between Waterbury and Torrington, a line built by the original Naugatuck in 1849. The tracks follow the railroad's namesake river for the entire route. The Naugatuck Railroad, part of the Railroad Museum of New England, offers regularly scheduled train service over a 9-mile portion of its line, and periodic special excursions over the whole route.

CHOICES: Departing the 1881 Thomaston station aboard 1920s heavyweight coaches or a 1950s streamlined Budd RDC, you cross two trestles over the Naugatuck River, see century-old New England brass mills, and roll high across the face of giant Thomaston Dam. Operating locomotives include U23B No. 2203 (the last domestic U-Boat built by General Electric) and EMD FL9 New Haven No. 2019 (the only FL9 still operating on original NH trackage).

WHEN TO GO: Excursions run on Saturdays and Sundays from Memorial Day through October. Fall colors peak in early- to mid-October, and this is the most popular time to ride the Naugatuck's trains. *Easter Bunny Express* trains run the weekend and the Saturday before Easter. *Northern Lights Limited* and *Santa Express* trains operate weekends late November through December. Specialty trains, including wine and bourbon tasting, BBQ, and Chocolate Decadence Tour trains, run throughout the year.

GOOD TO KNOW: Built in 1881 by the original Naugatuck Railroad, the brick Thomaston station is being restored. Pieces of the museum's extensive collection of historic New England railroad rolling stock are displayed on a track adjacent to the station.

WORTH DOING: Thomaston offers a pleasant New England downtown with historic mills, restaurants, and a picturesque opera house. Torrington has a thriving arts, culture, and dining scene. Nearby Litchfield has large 18th century homes, shops, and restaurants.

DON'T MISS: At Thomaston station, you can see an electro-pneumatic interlocking machine used by the New Haven, and 1920s semaphore signals, and board a former Boston & Maine SW1 locomotive.

GETTING THERE: Take I-84 to Waterbury and then Route 8 north to Exit 38.

LOCATION: 242 E. Main Street, Thomaston
PHONE: 860-283-7245
WEBSITE: rmne.org
E-MAIL: form on website

MAINE

Belfast & Moosehead Lake Railway

Excursion trains depart from City Point Railroad Museum in Belfast, run to Waldo, and return. You can enjoy the 70-minute trip aboard a coach, an open-air car, or a caboose. Special fall and pizza trains, and railcycle trips, are also available. Memorial Day weekend through October, with some midweek dates noted on the website.

LOCATION: 13 Oak Hill Road, Belfast
PHONE: 207-315-9410, 888-317-2142
WEBSITE: brookspreservation.org
E-MAIL: form on website

Boothbay Railway Village

A 2-foot-gauge steam train takes you around a re-created historic village with several stations and an engine house. A railbus also operates. Exhibits show the history of Maine's narrow gauge railroads, and various pieces of rolling stock and equipment are on display, as are more than 50 antique or classic vehicles. It is open daily from Memorial Day weekend through mid-October.

LOCATION: 586 Wiscasset Road, Boothbay
PHONE: 207-633-4727
WEBSITE: railwayvillage.org
E-MAIL: form on website

Cole Land Transportation Museum

The museum houses 200 antique land transportation vehicles and 2,000 photographs of life in early Maine. Its railroad collection includes one of the first Bangor & Aroostook diesels, a Canadian Pacific section shack, a Maine Central caboose, and a relocated station. It is open daily May until November.

LOCATION: 405 Perry Road, Bangor
PHONE: 207-990-3600
WEBSITE: colemuseum.org
E-MAIL: form on website

Oakfield Railroad Museum

Exhibits in the restored Oakfield station include hundreds of photographs dating to the beginning of the Bangor & Aroostook Railroad in 1891, vintage signs, signal lanterns, railroad maps, and telegraph equipment. A restored caboose, handcar, and motor car are also displayed. It is open summer Saturday and Sunday afternoons.

LOCATION: 40 Station Street, Oakfield
WEBSITE: facebook.com/Oafieldrailroadmuseum

Downeast Scenic Railroad

Downeast Scenic Railroad

The Downeast Scenic Railroad offers a 90-minute round-trip excursion that travels along the former Calais Branch of the Maine Central Railroad from Ellsworth to Ellsworth Falls, and then to Washington Junction and back. Along this stretch of the Calais Branch Line, you'll see Little Rocky Pond, Green Lake, marshes, and glacial deposits including massive boulders. You may even see ospreys, eagles, and deer.

CHOICES: The train is pulled by a vintage diesel locomotive. Seating options include restored passenger coaches from the 1910s, an open-air car made from a log car, and a caboose. You can reserve tickets, but specific seats are not assigned, so arrive early to pick out your seat. The open-air car has picnic tables for dining al fresco, and well-behaved dogs are allowed on this car.

WHEN TO GO: The railroad runs excursions on weekends starting Memorial Day weekend. That weekend, service begins with one trip each day. From the end of June to mid-October, two trips are offered. The Touch-A-Train event in June gives you a close-up look at the equipment.

GOOD TO KNOW: At Washington Junction Yard, the recently rehabilitated wye turns the train for the return trip to Ellsworth.

WORTH DOING: The coast is less than an hour away, where you can visit Mount Desert Island and Acadia National Park. Activities in the area include hiking, kayaking, and whale watching. Also, while in the area, be sure to indulge in fresh lobster and other seafood and homemade blueberry pie in many of the local restaurants.

DON'T MISS: At Washington Junction Yard, the staging area for the railroad, you'll be able to see vintage maintenance-of-way equipment and diesel locomotives.

GETTING THERE: Ellsworth is 24 miles east of Bangor. From there, take Highway 1A straight into Ellsworth. The boarding location is behind the Maine Community Foundation building at 245 Main Street, where you can park as well.

LOCATION: 245 Main Street, Ellsworth
PHONE: 866-449-7245
WEBSITE: downeastscenicrail.org
E-MAIL: form on website

Maine Narrow Gauge Railroad & Museum

Jeff Terry

The Maine Narrow Gauge Railroad runs along the Eastern Promenade fronting Casco Bay. Excursions offer spectacular views of ferries, sailboats, cruise ships, lobster boats, and freighters as well as the many islands that dot the bay. The museum helps preserve Maine's 2-foot-gauge railways.

CHOICES: The railroad operates diesel-powered trains with historic open-window coaches and open-sided excursion cars. Most of the railroad's equipment once operated on two of Maine's famed two-footers: the Sandy River & Rangeley Lakes and the Bridgton & Harrison. You can tour the museum and see several beautifully restored passenger coaches, including *Rangeley*, the only 2-foot-gauge parlor car ever built. Also on display is a railbus used on the Sandy River and Bridgton & Harrison Railroads.

WHEN TO GO: The museum is open daily May through October. Various special events, including a Polar Express train, take place throughout the year.

GOOD TO KNOW: The museum is continuing preparations for a move to Gray, 25 miles north of Portland. Currently, all trains are diesel powered until locomotive No. 7 returns to service.

WORTH DOING: The Portland waterfront is a busy area for tourists, and there are many other attractions in the area, including excellent seafood restaurants and shops constructed in Federal-style architecture.

DON'T MISS: Ride on the water side of the train for the best views. A walking and bike path follows the line for its entire length, which makes taking action photos easy.

GETTING THERE: Amtrak's *Downeaster* makes several daily trips between Boston and Portland. I-95 passes just west of the city.

LOCATION: 58 Fore Street, Portland
PHONE: 207-828-0814
WEBSITE: mainenarrowgauge.org
E-MAIL: info@mainenarrowgauge.org

Seashore Trolley Museum

Karl Zimmermann

Founded in 1939, the Seashore Trolley Museum is touted as the oldest, largest electric railway museum in the world. Its international collection includes more than 250 transit vehicles, mostly streetcars, and virtually every major United States city that operated trolleys is represented. Much of this equipment is under cover in three exhibit carbarns.

CHOICES: Included in the museum admission is a streetcar ride over the 2 miles of rebuilt trackage. This ride, a treat for all the senses, is the best way to relive the trolley and interurban experience. If just riding isn't enough, you can take advantage of the Be a Motorman program and actually operate a trolley. In the visitor center, you can view an exhibit chronicling the way trolleys changed life in Maine and their relevance to the contemporary world.

WHEN TO GO: The museum is open seven days a week from Memorial Day through Columbus Day, weekends in May, and for the balance of October. In early December, the museum opens for Kennebunkport's Christmas Prelude, with rides and refreshments. There are a number of additional special events, such as pumpkin patch trolleys in September.

GOOD TO KNOW: On Transit Weekend in October, the museum brings out rapid transit cars, buses, and trackless trolleys that do not usually operate.

WORTH DOING: Kennebunkport and adjacent Kennebunk are resort towns with Atlantic beaches and old-world New England charm. There are antique shops, galleries, restaurants (lobster a specialty), and opportunities for whale watching and other sea-related activities.

DON'T MISS: The restoration shop is open to the public. From elevated walkways, you can watch the painstaking work on the cars going forward.

GETTING THERE: The museum is located just a few miles from I-95 (the Maine Turnpike) off Exit 25. Amtrak's Boston-Rockland *Downeaster* stops in Saco, about 8 miles away, where taxis are available.

LOCATION: 195 Log Cabin Road, Kennebunkport
PHONE: 207-967-2800
WEBSITE: trolleymuseum.org
E-MAIL: form on website

Wiscasset, Waterville & Farmington Railway Museum

Wayne Laepple

Operating over a portion of the original WW&F Railway, which was abandoned in 1933, the WW&F is a faithful re-creation of a segment of the original Wiscasset, Waterville & Farmington, one of Maine's five 2-foot-gauge common carrier railroads.

CHOICES: Steam and diesel trains operate from Sheepscot station to Top of the Mountain, passing the flag stop station at Alna Center. A journey on the WW&F takes riders back to the early years of the last century, when the railroad carried the commerce and the people of the inland region to the seaport town of Wiscasset. Visitors are welcome to tour the railway's shops, where volunteers maintain and rebuild rolling stock, using traditional skills and techniques. A Model T Ford railcar also operates based on crew and equipment availability.

WHEN TO GO: The museum is open every Saturday year-round, and on Sundays from Memorial Day weekend through mid-October. Steam-hauled trains run from June through October, with diesel trains running in May through October.

GOOD TO KNOW: No. 9, a Portland Company engine built in 1891, was recently returned to service, having last run in 1933, and is the regular power on weekend trains during the summer months.

WORTH DOING: The mid-coast region of Maine features plenty of attractions, lodging choices, and restaurants. Nearby attractions include scenic Boothbay Harbor, Boothbay Railway Village, Owl's Head Transportation Museum, Maine Maritime Museum, and L.L. Bean.

DON'T MISS: The museum holds annual spring and fall work sessions, when members lay track, work on equipment, paint buildings, and build structures over long weekends. Visitors are welcome to join in.

GETTING THERE: Alna is located north of Wiscasset, approximately 50 miles northeast of Portland. The museum is on Cross Road, just off Route 218 about 4.5 miles from Wiscasset and Route 1.

LOCATION: 97 Cross Road, Alna
PHONE: 207-882-4193
WEBSITE: wwfry.org
E-MAIL: info@wwfry.org

MASSACHUSETTS

Chatham Railroad Museum

This restored country depot is situated on its original site. Museum exhibits feature hundreds of railroad artifacts from the Chatham Railroad Company and other railroads, including a restored 1910 New York Central caboose and telegraph instruments. It is open Tuesdays through Saturdays mid-June to mid-September.

LOCATION: 153 Depot Road, Chatham
PHONE: 508-945-5780
WEBSITE: chathamrailroadmuseum.com

Edaville USA

This is a family fun park with a 2-mile train ride through a 1,300-acre cranberry plantation. It operates both a steam engine and a diesel locomotive. There is a variety of amusement rides and an indoor play area. It is open daily in the summer, weekends in the spring and fall. Check the website for special events.

LOCATION: 5 Pine Street, Carver
PHONE: 508-866-8190
WEBSITE: edaville.com
E-MAIL: info@edaville.com

Lowell National Historical Park

The park includes a variety of structures related to industry, 5.6 miles of canals, and restored mill buildings. It displays a Boston & Maine 0-6-0 Manchester locomotive built in 1910, a combine car, and several open-air trolleys. Trolley tours as well as several boat tours are available, except in winter. You can also take in the National Streetcar Museum, which is across from the park's visitor center.

LOCATION: Visitor center, 246 Market Street; Parking, 304 Dutton Street, Lowell
PHONE: 978-970-5000
WEBSITE: nps.gov/lowe
E-MAIL: form on website

Shelburne Falls Trolley Museum

The museum features a 15-minute ride on restored trolley car No. 10, which was built in 1896. For an added fee, and with a little instruction, you can become an instant motorman and run No. 10 yourself. Pump car rides are also available. The museum displays railroad and trolley artifacts, a steam locomotive, and a caboose. It is open Saturdays, Sundays, and holidays late May through October.

LOCATION: 14 Depot Street, Shelburne Falls
PHONE: 413-625-9443
WEBSITE: sftm.org
E-MAIL: trolley@sftm.org

Berkshire Scenic Railway Museum

Berkshire Scenic: Dan Howard

The Berkshire Scenic Railway Museum operates its Hoosac Valley Train Ride between Adams and North Adams, a distance of approximately 5 miles, on the onetime New York Central North Adams Branch. BSRM's Lenox Station Museum and rolling stock collection are located in Lenox, approximately 25 miles south of Adams.

CHOICES: Berkshire Scenic operates on Saturday, Sundays, and federal holidays from Memorial Day through late October, with two to four trains a day, depending on the month. The hour-long ride is aboard a former Boston & Maine Budd Rail Diesel Car, and features narration of the various scenic and historic locales seen from the train. *Tinseliner* holiday trains run from late November through December, and other special event trains also are offered. BSRM's museum and the majority of its collection is in Lenox, open on Saturdays 10 a.m. to 2 p.m. from late May to early September. Exhibits include a train dispatcher's console, a replica block station, several vintage diesel locomotives, and a wooden baggage car.

WHEN TO GO: New England's famed fall foliage peaks in this region in early October. During this time, expect crowded roads and high lodging rates. It is less congested at other times.

GOOD TO KNOW: Lodging is available in the Adams/North Adams and Pittsfield/Lenox/Lee areas. The Berkshires feature many cultural and natural attractions. Fine dining as well as fast-food chains can be found throughout the region.

WORTH DOING: The museum's beautifully restored 1903 New Haven Railroad station at Lenox contains an impressive collection of railroad historical artifacts, and offers a short "Jitney" ride within the grounds.

DON'T MISS: The Western Gateway Heritage State Park in North Adams includes two museums: The North Adams Museum of History and Science and the Visitor's Center and Museum, which features exhibits on the nearby 4.75 mile Hoosac Tunnel.

GETTING THERE: Adams is located on Route 8 between North Adams and Pittsfield. Lenox is near U.S. Routes 7 and 20, south of Pittsfield. Amtrak's *Lake Shore Limited* Boston section stops daily at Pittsfield.

LOCATION: 10 Willow Creek Road, Lenox (museum);
3 Hoosac Street, Adams (train ride)
PHONE: 413-637-2210
WEBSITE: berkshirescenicrailroad.org and
hoosacvalleytrainride.com
E-MAIL: forms on websites

Cape Cod Central Railroad

Karl Zimmerman

The Cape Cod Central operates diesel-powered scenic excursions and meal trains, which include luncheon and Sunday brunch as well as dinner outings, on select dates from early May through mid October. Trains run from Hyannis over the former Old Colony Railroad, which became part of the New York, New Haven & Hartford. Along the way, they pass cranberry bogs, sand dunes, forests, and marshes until reaching the Cape Cod Canal.

CHOICES: Three-hour "Coastal Excursions" leave from Hyannis. Recently added are two-hour "Canal Excursions" from Buzzards Bay. Brunch trains, two hours in length, and two-and-a-half-hour, three-course luncheon trains all operate from Hyannis, while three-hour, five-course dinner trains depart alternately from Buzzards Bay and North Falmouth as well as Hyannis. The excursions offer three classes of service: basic coach, first (with table seating), and diamond (table seating in a full-length dome).

WHEN TO GO: Trains run from early May through mid October in various combinations and with varying frequencies, all listed on the website. Sea breezes mean that Hyannis typically remains temperate throughout the operating season, but visiting outside of summer may minimize crowds. Christmas trains operate in November and December from the Buzzards Bay depot.

GOOD TO KNOW: Hyannis is quintessential Cape Cod, with all the sun, sand, salt— and tourists. Whale watching, beaching, fishing, golfing, and biking are among the available outdoor activities. The John F. Kennedy Hyannis Museum is located in town.

WORTH DOING: An ideal accompaniment to the train ride is an hour-long boat tour of Hyannis harbor and the Kennedy compound offered by Hy-Line Cruises.

DON'T MISS: Dinner trains from all three locations cross the spectacular 1935 vertical-lift bridge over the Cape Cod Canal, as do the "Canal Excursions." This bridge features outstanding aesthetics, and is the highlight of the route.

GETTING THERE: Hyannis, the primary departure point, is on the Atlantic Ocean on the south side of Cape Cod, 70 miles from Boston. Hyannis and the Cape Cod Central depot are easily accessed from Highway 6 or Highway 28. Buzzards Bay is at the southwest end of the Cape Cod Canal and also reached from Highway 6.

LOCATION: 252 Main Street, Hyannis
PHONE: 888-797-7245
WEBSITE: capetrain.com
E-MAIL: form on website

NEW HAMPSHIRE

Ashland Railroad Station Museum

The museum was built by the Boston, Concord & Montreal Railroad as a station around 1869. It is one of the state's best preserved examples of a 19th century passenger station. The museum contains rail artifacts and photo displays. Occasionally, an excursion train stops at the museum. It is open Saturdays during July and August.

LOCATION: 69 Depot Street, Ashland
PHONE: 603-968-7716
WEBSITE: aannh.org/heritage/grafton/ashland.php

Café Lafayette Dinner Train

The Café Lafayette Dinner Train provides a top fine-dining experience while traveling through the lush forest and open fields of the Pemigewasset River Valley, which is surrounded by mountains that bear witness to New Hampshire's nickname—the Granite State. The 20-mile round trip follows an ex-Boston & Maine right-of-way that once ran into nearby Lincoln. Café Lafayette operates seasonally, mid-May through October. Runs occur on Saturdays and Sundays in May and June, then Thursdays through Sundays late June to late October.

LOCATION: 3 Crossing at River Place, Route 112, North Woodstock
PHONE: 603-745-3500
WEBSITE: cafelafayettedinnertrain.com
E-MAIL: form on website

Gorham Historical Society Museum

The 1907 former Grand Trunk Railroad station houses a museum that exhibits rail and local historical items. It displays a 1911 Baldwin steam locomotive, a 1949 F7 diesel locomotive, and several boxcars. Operated by the Gorham Historical Society, the museum is open Wednesdays through Saturdays late May into October.

LOCATION: 25 Railroad Street, Gorham
PHONE: 603-466-5338
WEBSITE: gorhamnewhampshire.com/Railroad_Museum
E-MAIL: gorhamhistoricalsociety@gmail.com

Potter Place Railroad Station

The Potter Place station, which was built in 1874, features striking Victorian Stick-style architectural elements. Listed on the National Register of Historic Places, the station includes a preserved station master's office and exhibits on local history. This historical site also includes a Central Vermont caboose and freight house, both from the early 1900s, as well as a general store and schoolhouse. It is open weekends late May to early October.

LOCATION: 105 Depot Street, Andover
WEBSITE: andoverhistory.org
E-MAIL: pres@andoverhistory.org

Sandown Depot Museum

Located in a former 1874 Worcester, Nashua & Portland Railroad depot, the museum displays two 1914 Maine Central Railroad flanger cars, an 1880s velocipede, a restored 1958 speeder, and various railroad exhibits. It is open Saturdays May through September.

LOCATION: 6 Depot Road, Sandown
WEBSITE: sandownnhdepot.org
E-MAIL: form on website

Silver Lake Railroad

Situated just south of North Conway, the Silver Lake Railway offers a 55-minute round trip through this scenic area. From the open-air cars, passengers can see a variety of scenery, from mountains to swamps, as well as an occasional moose. The railroad's museum displays a range of vintage equipment and buildings, including a restored 1941 diner, which you can use for picnics. It is open weekends July to September. Train rides are by donation.

LOCATION: 1381 Village Road, Madison
WEBSITE: silverlakerailroad.com
E-MAIL: silverlakerr@yahoo.com

Conway Scenic Railroad

Scott Hartley

Here is a New England excursion train ride bursting with great scenery and Yankee character. The setting is in the Mount Washington Valley in the charming village of North Conway. With three different trips to choose from, this railroad offers a bounty of great journeys.

CHOICES: Two Valley Train excursions are offered: a 55-minute, 11-mile round trip to Conway and a longer 21-mile round trip to Bartlett. Valley Train passengers have lunch and dinner options aboard the *Chocorua*. The Notch Train carries passengers from North Conway into the rugged Crawford Notch on a 5-hour round trip, as the first trains did more than 130 years ago. Passengers may choose from coach or first-class service, which includes lunch aboard the *Hattie Evans*. Vintage diesel locomotives pull most trains, but some midweek Valley Trains take place on a Budd Rail Diesel Car.

WHEN TO GO: Valley Trains operate excursions April through December, and the Notch Train runs mid-June through mid-October. Nothing is better than an autumn train ride in New England, but special trains operate throughout the year. For a change of scenery, try riding through snow-covered woods during December.

GOOD TO KNOW: Stick to the right side of the Notch Train as it ascends Crawford Notch and crosses the Frankenstein Trestle (named for artist Godfrey Frankenstein, not because it's a monster trestle) and Willey Brook Bridge for excellent views of bluffs, ravines, and streams. Also look for the Elephant's Head rock formation. The later in fall you travel, the fewer colors you'll see, but the better the vistas are from the train.

WORTH DOING: The surrounding Mount Washington Valley and White Mountain National Forest offer four seasons of recreational activities, attractions, and spectacular scenery.

DON'T MISS: Well, you can't miss the Victorian station in North Conway. Take some time to appreciate this structure that's been at work as a railroad depot since 1874.

GETTING THERE: The Conway Scenic Railroad is less than a 3-hour drive from Boston. From Boston, take 1-95 to Route 16, which runs to North Conway.

LOCATION: 38 Norcross Circle, North Conway
PHONE: 800-232-5251 or 603-356-5251
WEBSITE: conwayscenic.com
E-MAIL: info@conwayscenic.com

Hobo & Winnipesaukee Scenic Railroads

David Lustig

Boston & Maine's 72-mile White Mountain Branch from the state capital of Concord north to Lincoln long served paper mills and other forestry companies, but the railroad abandoned this route as those businesses shut down. Fortunately, the entire line has survived, and two tourist train operations on the northern 54 miles keep portions busy for visitors throughout the year.

CHOICES: The Hobo Railroad offers 15-mile round trips on the north end of the branch to the many tourists who visit the White Mountain region. Trains out of Lincoln follow the scenic Pemigewasset River south, crossing numerous trestles and passing such locations as Grandma's Crossing and Swimming Hole Bridge, before changing directions at the Jack O'Lantern Resort near Thornton. Farther south, on the shores of its namesake lake, the Winnipesaukee Scenic Railroad offers trains out of Meredith and Weirs Beach to and from Lakeport, always in view of New Hampshire's largest lake. Trains include open-window coaches, as well as cabooses on the Winnipesaukee. Two rare Alco 660-hp diesel switchers work with newer EMD locomotives to power the two railroads' trains.

WHEN TO GO: Both railroads operate weekends from May through mid-June, and daily through the summer. The daily operations continue through the fall foliage season on the Hobo, while the Winnipesaukee reverts to a weekend schedule. Santa Claus and Polar Express trains run during late November and December.

GOOD TO KNOW: Lake Winnipesaukee is a major summer vacation destination, and the White Mountains also attract large crowds in summer and early October for fall foliage.

WORTH DOING: To see more of Lake Winnipesaukee, daytime and dinner cruises are available from Weirs Beach and other towns. You can explore the quaint shops, antique stores, and historic buildings of Meredith. There is much to do in the White Mountains, from hiking and kayaking to viewing covered bridges, waterfalls, and wildlife.

DON'T MISS: Try a hobo picnic lunch, complete with a souvenir bindle stick.

GETTING THERE: For the Hobo, take I-93 to Exit 32. For the Winnipesaukee, take I-93 to Exit 23. The drive through the center of New Hampshire is beautiful year-round.

LOCATION: 64 Railroad Street, Lincoln (Hobo)
154 Main Street, Meredith (Winnipesaukee)
PHONE: 603-745-2135
WEBSITE: hoborr.com
E-MAIL: info@hoborr.com

Mount Washington Cog Railway

Karl Zimmermann

England may have invented the railroad, but the United States invented the mountain-climbing cog railroad. The first such successful cog—a standard railroad with flanged wheels but with the addition of a gear engaging a toothed "rack" rail in the center of the tracks—was the Mount Washington Cog Railway, which opened in 1869 and has been in operation ever since. The trip takes you to the top of 6,288-foot Mount Washington, infamous for its bad weather but famous for its vistas when the clouds part.

CHOICES: Sit back and enjoy the views during the trip to the summit and back. On a clear day, you can see four states, Canada, and the Atlantic Ocean. The trains operate on a steep track that resembles a ladder plunked down on the mountainside. The diesel-powered runs up the mountain allow visitors a full hour at the summit.

WHEN TO GO: Excursion trains operate daily from late April through November. Reservations are recommended. In fall, the White Mountains are always spectacular. During November, trains may run only part way to the summit if weather is inclement.

GOOD TO KNOW: Though most trips are powered by the railroad's biodiesel engines, from Memorial Day weekend through October the first trip of the day is typically operated with one of the railroad's coal-burning steam locomotives, and in season there may be an afternoon trip as well. In 2019 the railroad marks its 150th birthday with a number of special events.

WORTH DOING: Explore the mountains. Mount Washington State Park is at the summit and contains hiking trails, an observatory, a visitor center, and the stone Tip Top House—a hotel built in 1853 and restored as a museum. The surrounding White Mountain National Forest offers a variety of recreational activities.

DON'T MISS: View the railway's original cog engine, *Old Peppersass*, at Marshfield Base Station. The railway's museum there is both comprehensive and interactive.

GETTING THERE: The Cog Railway is a pleasant drive from Boston, Hartford, New York, or Montreal. It is 90 miles from Portland off Route 302. From Bretton Woods, follow Base Road for 6 miles to the railway.

LOCATION: 3168 Base Station Road, Marshfield Station
PHONE: 603-278-5404
WEBSITE: thecog.com
E-MAIL: info@thecog.com

White Mountain Central Railroad

Dave Crosby

The White Mountain Central Railroad is part of the popular family-owned Clark's Trading Post amusement park deep in New Hampshire's White Mountains. The railroad offers 30-minute excursions across the Pemigewasset River over a 1904 Howe truss railroad covered bridge that was moved from the Barre & Chelsea Railroad in Vermont.

CHOICES: Once a center for the logging and paper industries, the region now caters to tourists and skiers. The Clark family added a 1.25-mile railroad to their small amusement park six decades ago and acquired an impressive collection of geared steam locomotives. Admission to the still-growing park includes the train ride as well as other activities. During July and August, the train is usually powered by steam locomotive No. 6, a Climax geared engine built in 1920. At other times, a 1943 GE diesel switcher is used. The park includes a variety of rides, museums, and displays.

WHEN TO GO: Operations are daily from mid-June through the end of August and on weekends in late May, early June, September, and October. The best fall foliage usually occurs in early October, which is also the peak tourist season.

GOOD TO KNOW: Lodging, including motels and B&Bs, and restaurants can be found in Lincoln and the surrounding communities. Rates will be the highest during fall, so reservations should be made far in advance for this season.

WORTH DOING: The White Mountain National Forest is worth visiting any time of year for camping, hiking, history, and scenic drives.

DON'T MISS: The star attractions of the park's operating locomotive fleet are the Beebe River Lumber wood-burning, two-truck Climax, which was recently rebuilt. Also operational are a Baldwin 2-4-2T, a Porter 0-4-0T, and the only known Reo railbus. Other geared locomotives in the collection include an International Shoe two-truck Heisler and a Woodstock Lumber Shay.

GETTING THERE: From I-93, take Exit 33, and go south 1 mile on Route 3 (Daniel Webster Highway). In fall, driving along the Kangamangus Highway from Conway offers exceptional views and plentiful wildlife.

LOCATION: 110 Daniel Webster Highway, Lincoln
PHONE: 603-745-8913
WEBSITE: whitemountaincentralrr.com
E-MAIL: info@clarkstradingpost.com

NEW YORK

Brooks Alco Railroad Display

Located at the Chautauqua County Fairgrounds, this display features an Alco-Brooks 0-6-0 locomotive built in 1916, a Delaware & Hudson wood-sided boxcar, a wooden New York Central caboose, and other railroad artifacts.

LOCATION: 1089 Central Avenue, Dunkirk
PHONE: 716-366-3797
WEBSITE: dunkirkhistoricalmuseum.org
E-MAIL: contact@dunkirkhistoricalmuseum.org

Buffalo, Rochester & Pittsburgh Depot Museum

The brick station is being restored as it was in 1911 with separate men's and women's waiting rooms, a baggage room, and a station agent's desk. It is open Saturdays during the summer and hosts various events including an annual ice cream social.

LOCATION: 395 S. Lincoln Avenue, Orchard Park
PHONE: 716-662-7002
WEBSITE: wnyrhs.org

Central Square Station Museum

The museum has various pieces of rail equipment on outdoor display including two 0-4-0 steam locomotives, a 1929 Brill car, a circus car, a streetcar, and a GE diesel switcher. Indoor exhibits are housed in an early 20th century depot. It is open Sundays June through October.

LOCATION: 132 Railroad Street, Central Square
WEBSITE: cnynrhs.org/CentralSq.html
E-MAIL: contact@cnynrhs.org

Cooperstown & Charlotte Valley Railroad

Regular excursion and a variety of special trains travel between Milford Depot and Cooperstown Dreams Park. In the restored 1869 Milford depot, you can view an array of railroad displays. Regular excursions run on Thursdays during summer, and theme trains throughout the year. Railfan Day takes place in August.

LOCATION: 136 E. Main Street, Milford
PHONE: 607-432-2429
WEBSITE: lrhs.com
E-MAIL: wendy@lrhs.com

Empire State Railway Museum

Through photos, films, and artifacts, the museum highlights the history of railroads that served the Catskills. The museum, located in a refurbished 1899 Ulster & Delaware Railroad station, is also restoring several railway cars and a 1910 2-8-0 locomotive. It is open weekends and holidays from Memorial Day through October.

LOCATION: 70 Lower High Street, Phoenicia
PHONE: 845-688-7501
WEBSITE: esrm.com
E-MAIL: ovondrak@yahoo.com

Hyde Park Railroad Station

Built in 1914, the Hyde Park Railroad Station is listed on the National Register of Historic Places. You can tour the restored station, which was designed by the same architects who designed Grand Central Station, and view displays on the area's railroading history. It is open weekends and holidays during summer and on Monday evenings year-round.

LOCATION: 34 River Road, Hyde Park
PHONE: 845-229-2338
WEBSITE: hydeparkstation.com
E-MAIL: milotsukroff@netscape.net

Martisco Station Museum

This restored 1870 New York Central station contains two floors of local railroad artifacts. On the first floor of this Victorian-style brick structure, you'll enter a replica of a small-town railroad station. Items are displayed outside as well. It is open Sunday afternoons May until October.

LOCATION: 5085 Martisco Road, Marcellus
WEBSITE: cnynrhs.org/Martisco.html
E-MAIL: contact@cnynrhs.org

New York Museum of Transportation

The museum exhibits various trolley cars, a steam locomotive, a caboose, and rail artifacts, as well as highway and horse-drawn vehicles. Trolley rides from the museum take you to Midway station, where you can connect with a diesel train or track car that takes you to the nearby Rochester & Genesee Valley Railroad Museum. The NYMT is open Sundays year-round.

LOCATION: 6393 E. River Road, Rush
PHONE: 585-533-1113
WEBSITE: nymtmuseum.org
E-MAIL: info@nymtmuseum.org

New York Transit Museum

Located in a 1936 subway station, the New York Transit Museum features restored subway cars and other exhibits related to urban transit. Exhibits highlight elevated rail lines and the construction of New York City's first subway line. The museum also offers special subway tours and events during the year. It is closed Mondays.

LOCATION: Boerum Place at Schermerhorn Street, Brooklyn
PHONE: 718-694-1600
WEBSITE: nytransitmuseum.org

North Creek Railway Depot Museum

Step into the North Creek Depot Museum, and you'll relive a piece of presidential history. The depot is where Theodore Roosevelt learned he had become president upon the death of President McKinley. The museum features an exhibit on this event as well as displays on area history, the Adirondack Railroad, and other railroads. The museum complex includes a restored freight house, an engine house, and a working turntable. The Saratoga & North Creek Railway also boards from the depot's platform. It is open June into October.

LOCATION: 5 Railroad Place, North Creek
PHONE: 518-251-5842
WEBSITE: northcreekdepotmuseum.com
E-MAIL: director@northcreekdepotmuseum.com

Railroad Museum of Long Island

The Railroad Museum of Long Island has two locations: Greenport and Riverhead. Greenport, situated in a Victorian-style Long Island Rail Road freight station, exhibits photos and artifacts of Long Island rail history. It displays an 1898 snowplow and a 1927 wooden caboose. An operating tower and turntable are also on site. At Riverhead, the museum restores its rolling stock and displays several steam locomotives and various railcars. A miniature train ride also operates around the site. Both sites are open on weekends.

LOCATION: 440 Fourth Street, Greenport; 416 Griffing Avenue, Riverhead
PHONE: 631-477-0439 (Greenport) or 631-727-7920 (Riverhead)
WEBSITE: rmli.us
E-MAIL: info@rmli.us

Railroad Museum of the Niagara Frontier

Housed in a restored Erie Railroad freight depot, which was built in 1922, the museum contains a collection of artifacts that recognizes the region's railroading heritage. Also on display are several industrial locomotives, an Erie caboose, and a New York Central caboose. The museum is open Saturdays in June, July, and August.

LOCATION: 111 Oliver Street, North Tonawanda
PHONE: 716-694-9588
WEBSITE: nfcnrhs.com
E-MAIL: museum@nfcnrhs.com

Rochester & Genesee Valley Railroad Museum

The Rochester & Genesee Valley Railroad Museum is housed in a restored 1918 Erie Railroad depot. Inside, you'll see the original ticket agent's office, waiting room, and artifacts. You can also inspect various early diesel and steam locomotives, freight cars, and passenger cars. See the website for open days. Start your visit at nearby New York Museum of Transportation and take a train, trolley, or track-car ride over to the RGVRRM.

LOCATION: 282 Rush Scottsville Road, Rush
PHONE: 585-533-1431
WEBSITE: rgvrrm.org
E-MAIL: form on website

Salamanca Rail Museum

This Buffalo, Rochester & Pittsburgh depot has been fully restored right down to the telegraph key in the ticket office, and it includes a ladies retiring room and a baggage room. Artifacts and photos show the history of railroads in western New York and Pennsylvania. A boxcar, a crew camp car, and two cabooses are on display. See the Facebook page for open days.

LOCATION: 170 Main Street, Salamanca
PHONE: 716-265-2109
WEBSITE: facebook.com/salamanca-rail-museum-171739779583682

Trolley Museum of New York

The museum operates a trolley ride aboard No. 358, a restored 1925 trolley, from Kingston to the banks of the Hudson River, where you can enjoy a picnic lunch. With a stop at the museum, you can learn about trolleys and see them being restored. The museum's collection dates back to the early 1900s. The museum is open weekends and holidays May through October.

LOCATION: 89 E. Strand Street, Kingston
PHONE: 845-331-3399
WEBSITE: tmny.org
E-MAIL: admin@tmny.org

Adirondack Scenic Railroad

Karl Zimmermann

The Adirondack Scenic Railroad offers excursions behind classic diesel locomotives over 69 miles of the former New York Central's Adirondack Division from Utica to Big Moose.

CHOICES: The railroad offers day-long excursions, all the way from Utica to Big Moose, with a stop at Thendara, up to four times a week from mid-July through mid-October. Roughly half allow layover time in Thendara to visit the resort town of Old Forge (reached by a shuttle bus), where possibilities include a 2-hour cruise on the Fulton Chain of Lakes and a visit to the Goodsell Museum. Shorter round trips, either south to Otter Lake or north to Big Moose, run from Thendara from June through mid-October.

WHEN TO GO: The brilliant foliage of fall makes that season a fine time to ride.

GOOD TO KNOW: The railroad offers a smorgasbord of themed trains throughout the year. It's also possible to paddle down the Moose River and ride the Otter Lake train back from Whitewater to Thendara, with canoes or kayaks transported in the baggage car. The railroad now offers an "Adirondack Scenic Railbike Adventure," a 6-mile pedal in either direction between Thendara and Carter Station on four-person bikes, with train ride in the opposite direction.

WORTH DOING: Thendara and Big Moose are deep in the Adirondacks, replete with natural beauty. The region's history is beautifully presented at the Adirondack Museum in Blue Mountain Lake. Adirondack Park offers 2,000 miles of hiking trails and hundreds of miles of kayaking routes.

DON'T MISS: The Adirondack Scenic Railroad shares Utica's grand 1914 Union Station with Amtrak, making it among the few excursion railroads with national rail connections. Take time to look through this historic station.

GETTING THERE: Served by multiple Amtrak trains each day, Utica also has excellent highway access, being located right on the New York State Thruway (I-90).

LOCATION: 321 Main Street, Utica
PHONE: 800-819-2291
WEBSITE: adirondackrr.com
E-MAIL: form on website

Arcade & Attica Railroad

Arcade & Attica Railroad

Whether powered by steam locomotive No. 18 built in 1920 or vintage diesels dating to the 1940s, the Arcade & Attica Railroad is a true blast from the past. The railroad offers the only regularly scheduled steam excursion train in New York. The scenic ride passes through countryside that has changed little over the last two centuries.

CHOICES: On the 14-mile, 2.5-hour round trip, passengers may opt to ride in either 1915 era steel coaches built for the Delaware, Lackawanna & Western Railroad, or in a covered open-air car. Watch out for soot when the coal-fired steam locomotive leads the train!

WHEN TO GO: Regular steam excursions are scheduled once each day on weekends between May and September. Additional diesel-powered excursions are added on Wednesdays and Fridays during July and August. Extra departures are added during the fall foliage season and diesel trips are offered during the Christmas season.

GOOD TO KNOW: Snacks are available at the Arcade depot, on the train and at the Currier's depot, the halfway point where the engine runs around the train for the return trip to Arcade.

WORTH DOING: During the year, the railroad offers a variety of special events including a Civil War reenactment, Great Train Robbery, and a Murder Mystery Dinner Theater.

DON'T MISS: Be sure to check out a vintage freight train on display at the railroad's parking lot as well as artifacts, photographs and operating model railroads in the Arcade station.

GETTING THERE: Arcade is located about an hour's drive south of Buffalo. The museum is located 3 miles east of Route 16 on Main Street at Railroad Avenue.

LOCATION: 278 Main Street, Arcade
PHONE: 585-492-3100
WEBSITE: aarailroad.com
E-MAIL: aarailroadny@yahoo.com

Catskill Mountain Railroad

Karl Zimmermann

The Catskill Mountain Railroad operates a segment of the former Ulster & Delaware Railroad, which later became New York Central's Catskill Mountain Branch. The train runs from Kingston west toward Stony Hollow, in the foothills of the Catskill Mountains.

CHOICES: Themed excursions—music, train robbery, and the like—are powered by an Alco RS1 built in 1950 for Illinois Terminal. They board at the Westbrook Lane station on summer Saturdays and offer rides on open cars and ex-Long Island Rail Road coaches.

WHEN TO GO: In addition to the themed Saturday trains that run from Memorial Day through Labor Day, there are special-event excursions in spring and from October through December. CMRR also hosts a visiting steam engine at least once a year.

GOOD TO KNOW: For children, the CMRR runs an Easter train in the spring, *Pumpkin Patch Express* from late October into November, a night train called "Rails of Terror" in October, and the *Polar Express* in November and December.

WORTH DOING: Nearby uptown Kingston offers many stores and restaurants. Also in Kingston is the Trolley Museum of New York, which operates a restored streetcar along the banks of the Hudson River over another short stretch of the Ulster & Delaware.

DON'T MISS: A short drive west is the restored Phoenicia depot, opened in 1900 and now home to the Empire State Railway Museum. Farther west is the Delaware & Ulster Railroad, another piece of the old U&D, with excursions from Arkville.

GETTING THERE: The railroad is accessible from Exit 19 of the New York State Thruway (I-87). Follow I-587, then turn left on Albany Avenue. Make the first right on Clinton Avenue, then right on Westbrook Lane to the Kingston Plaza parking lot. The station is on the right.

LOCATION: 149 Aaron Court, Kingston
PHONE: 845-332-4854
WEBSITE: catskillmountainrailroad.com
EMAIL: form on website

Delaware & Ulster Railroad

Karl Zimmermann

The Delaware & Ulster Railroad's 24-mile round-trip excursions of roughly 2 hours run from Arkville north to Roxbury, with much of the ride along the East Branch of the Delaware River, across rolling fields, and through small towns in the heart of the Catskill Mountains.

CHOICES: In addition to the scenic excursions aboard open cars or ex-Pennsylvania Railroad coaches, the D&U also fields a luncheon train, the *Rip Van Winkle Flyer*. The *Flyer's* frequent days of operation are listed on the D&U website. Motive power for the excursion and luncheon trains is generally an Alco RS36 resplendent in its original Delaware & Hudson livery, though an ex-New York, Ontario & Western EMD NW2 switcher sometimes substitutes.

WHEN TO GO: The Delaware & Ulster operates on Saturdays and Sundays from Memorial Day through October, with trains added beyond those days and months. Check the website for information. There's no more spectacular time for a visit than during the fall foliage season.

GOOD TO KNOW: The *Rip Van Winkle Flyer* is a handsome, five-car Budd-built streamliner, featuring an ex-New York Central parlor-observation car and a dome diner that began life as a Missouri Pacific dome coach.

WORTH DOING: The Catskill Scenic Trail lies along 26 miles of the former Catskill Mountain Branch right-of-way. It passes through seven towns and connects with hundreds of miles of other trails. The four-season trail is used by hikers, bicyclists, cross country skiers, and horseback riders.

DON'T MISS: The depots at both Roxbury and Arkville offer displays of photographs and artifacts highlighting the history of the Ulster & Delaware.

GETTING THERE: Arkville is a 43-mile drive on Route 28 from Exit 19 on the New York State Thruway (I-87). Route 28 passes right by the depot.

LOCATION: 43510 Route 28, Arkville
PHONE: 800-225-4132 or 845-586-3877
WEBSITE: durr.org
E-MAIL: form on website

Medina Railroad Museum

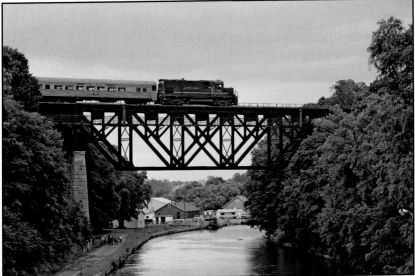

Jim Wrinn

The area east of Buffalo provides a pleasant distraction with small towns, farms, and a relaxed existence. Here, you'll find a museum located inside one of the largest surviving wooden freight houses around. You will also have the opportunity to ride a streamlined passenger train.

CHOICES: The old New York Central freight house is huge—301 feet long and 34 feet wide—and contains memorabilia, models, and artifacts. Enter the Union Station archway, and you'll see displays dedicated to the trains, such as the *Empire State Express* and *20th Century Limited*, and railroads, including the Pennsylvania Railroad, that helped develop the area. On a former New York Central main line, you can ride in 1947 Budd coaches pulled by a historic Alco Century diesel locomotive. The trains run on select days.

WHEN TO GO: The museum is open year-round Tuesday through Sunday. Specials that leave from the museum include fall foliage trips, Halloween trains, and Polar Express rides.

GOOD TO KNOW: Ask about the bridge at Lockport, which, according to legend, was built upside down so as to limit the size of barge traffic on the competing Erie Canal.

WORTH DOING: For a unique experience, take a one-of-a-kind ride in a mule-drawn packet boat on the Erie Canal.

DON'T MISS: In the museum, watch a large HO scale model railroad in action. The prototypical railroad layout measures 14 feet by 204 feet. Also, take a close look at the lobby, which is refinished as the freight depot office.

GETTING THERE: Medina is situated between Buffalo and Rochester, not far from Lake Ontario. From Buffalo, take I-90 east to Route 77. Continue north on Route 77/63 to downtown Medina. There, turn left onto North Avenue and then turn right onto West Avenue.

LOCATION: 530 West Avenue, Medina
PHONE: 585-798-6106
WEBSITE: medinarailroad.com
E-MAIL: mrrmuseum@yahoo.com

RHODE ISLAND

Newport & Narragansett Bay Railroad

Along scenic Narragansett Bay, the railroad operates several different train rides between May and December. On Saturdays, the Grand Bellevue provides dinner in elegantly restored 1940s Budd dining cars. Other offerings include a lunch train, ice cream train, and murder mysteries.

LOCATION: 19 America's Cup Avenue, Newport
PHONE: 401-295-1203
WEBSITE: trainsri.com
E-MAIL: info@trainsri.com

VERMONT

Shelburne Museum

Outside the museum, you'll see the 1890 Shelburne passenger station, locomotive No. 220, which pulled the trains of four presidents, and an 1890 private luxury car. Other historic buildings, a steamboat, and more than 200 horse-drawn vehicles are displayed at the museum. It is open daily May through December and Wednesday through Sunday January through April.

LOCATION: 6000 Shelburne Road, Shelburne
PHONE: 802-985-3346
WEBSITE: shelburnemuseum.org
E-MAIL: info@shelburnemuseum.org

Vermont Rail System

Scott Hartley

Vermont Rail System, through its Green Mountain Railroad, operates regular fall excursions and numerous special trains open to the public throughout the state.

CHOICES: The Green Mountain Railroad schedule begins in May, kicking off the season with the Burlington Kids Day train ride. The Champlain Valley Dinner Train departs every Friday and Saturday from Burlington, May to September, and on Saturday and Sunday from September to October on a three-hour fine dining journey to Middelbury. New in 2019 will be Lounge 91, where 18 passengers can ride along on a three-hour excursion with live music, cocktails and hors-d'ouevres, "speakeasy" style. Fall excursions make three round trips out of Chester operating during most days of the week and on the weekends in September and October. Green Mountain Railroad also runs special weekend excursions out of Burlington to celebrate Mother's Day, a Father's Day "rail and sail" event, and Murder Mystery dinner trains. The railroad operates chartered train rides throughout the state that benefit many organizations and charities, and many of these are open to the public. See the website for more options.

WHEN TO GO: Vermont is world-famous for its spectacular fall foliage, and VRS's fall foliage excursions are scheduled to offer the best views of that color.

GOOD TO KNOW: Train operations and special charters change from year to year, so be sure to check the website before planning your visit.

WORTH DOING: Chester has two districts in the National Register of Historic places to explore. Burlington is the state's largest city and home of the University of Vermont, and offers plenty to see and do.

DON'T MISS: Green Mountain Railroad's former Rutland Alco RS1 No. 405 has operated in Vermont since it was built in 1951, and sometimes appears on fall foliage trains.

GETTING THERE: Chester is located in south-central Vermont. Take Exit 6 from I-91 and drive 10 miles to Chester. Burlington's station is located downtown near the shore of Lake Champlain. Use Exit 14 from I-89 and go west on U.S. Route 2.

LOCATION: 563 Depot Street, Chester; 1 Main Street, Burlington
PHONE: 800-707-3530
WEBSITE: rails-vt.com
E-MAIL: passenger@vrs.us.com

REGION 2

DELAWARE
1 Wilmington & Western Railroad

DISTRICT OF COLUMBIA
2 Smithsonian National Museum of American History

KENTUCKY
3 Big South Fork Scenic Railway
4 Bluegrass Scenic Railroad
5 Historic Railpark & Train Museum
6 Kentucky Railway Museum
7 My Old Kentucky Dinner Train
8 Paducah Railroad Museum

17 National Capital Trolley Museum
18 Walkersville Southern Railroad
19 Western Maryland Scenic Railroad

NEW JERSEY
20 Black River & Western Railroad
21 Cape May Seashore Lines
22 Delaware River Railroad
23 Maywood Station Museum
24 New Jersey Museum of Transportation
25 Whippany Railway Museum

34 Greenville Railroad Park and Museum
35 Harris Tower Museum
36 Horseshoe Curve National Historic Landmark
37 Kiski Junction Railroad
38 Lake Shore Railway Museum
39 Lehigh Gorge Scenic Railway
40 Ligonier Valley Rail Road Museum
41 Ma & Pa Railroad Heritage Village
42 Middletown & Hummelstown Railroad
43 New Hope & Ivyland Railroad

Cincinnati

Louisville

Lexington

Huntington 72

75

64

4

Owensboro

65

7

6

KENTUCKY

75

Paducah 8

24

Mayfield

Hopkinsville

5

3

MARYLAND
9 B&O Railroad Museum
10 Baltimore Streetcar Museum
11 Bowie Railroad Museum
12 Chesapeake Beach Railway Museum
13 Ellicott City Station
14 Gaithersburg Community Museum
15 Hagerstown Roundhouse Museum
16 Irish Railroad Workers Museum

PENNSYLVANIA
26 Allegheny Portage Railroad
27 Allentown & Auburn Railroad
28 Bellefonte Historical Railroad Society
29 Colebrookdale Railroad
30 Electric City Trolley Museum
31 Everett Railroad
32 Franklin Institute Science Museum
33 Friends of the Stewartstown Railroad

44 Oil Creek & Titusville Railroad
45 Pennsylvania Trolley Museum
46 Pioneer Tunnel Coal Mine & Steam Train
47 Portage Station Museum
48 Railroad Museum of Pennsylvania
49 Railroaders Memorial Museum
50 Reading Railroad Heritage Museum
51 Rockhill Trolley Museum

PENNSYLVANIA

Erie

NEW JERSEY

Newark

Allentown

Pittsburgh

Philadelphia

York

Wilmington

MARYLAND

DELAWARE

Clarksburg

Baltimore

Washington D.C.

Fredericksburg

WEST VIRGINIA

Staunton

Charlottesville

VIRGINIA

Richmond

Roanoke

Pulaski

Hampton

Norfolk

Virginia Beach

---

52 The Stourbridge Line

53 Steam into History

54 Steamtown National Historic Site

55 Strasburg Rail Road

56 Tioga Central Railroad

57 Tunnels Park & Museum

58 Wanamaker, Kempton & Southern Railroad

59 West Chester Railroad

60 Williams Grove Railroad

VIRGINIA

61 C&O Railway Heritage Center

62 Crewe Railroad Museum

63 Eastern Shore Railway Museum

64 Fairfax Station Railroad Museum

65 O. Winston Link Museum

66 Rappahannock Railway Workers Museum

67 Richmond Railroad Museum

68 Suffolk Seaboard Station Railroad Museum

69 Virginia Museum of Transportation

WEST VIRGINIA

70 Cass Scenic Railroad State Park

71 Durbin & Greenbrier Valley Railroad

72 New River Train

73 Potomac Eagle Scenic Railroad

74 Princeton Railroad Museum

DELAWARE
Wilmington & Western Railroad

Dave Crosby

The Wilmington & Western is Delaware's only operating tourist railroad. Traversing the scenic Red Clay Valley, the line offers several excursion destinations and operates a variety of steam and diesel motive power.

CHOICES: Passengers have the choice of riding to the Mount Cuba picnic grove for a relaxing 90-minute ride or opting for the longer 2.5-hour trip to Hockessin, which is operated on select dates. Open window passenger coaches are usually pulled by one of several diesel locomotives or by coal-fired steam locomotive No. 58, which operates on special occasions. An interactive calendar on the railroad's website allows patrons to see when their choice of motive power is scheduled to pull trains.

WHEN TO GO: The railroad operates most weekends from April through December with weekday departures added during the summer months. Christmas and Easter trains are family favorites while late October and early November see vibrant fall foliage.

GOOD TO KNOW: Having celebrated its 50th anniversary in 2016, the Wilmington & Western is one of the country's longest-running excursion railroads. Floods nearly destroyed the railroad in 2007, but the company persevered and still maintains its original 10-mile route.

WORTH DOING: A number of historic sites are located in close proximity to the railroad. These include the nearby Greenbank Mill as well as Longwood Gardens and the Winterthur Estate.

DON'T MISS: On select dates—including the popular "Ride to Dine" dinner trains—the 1929 gas-electric motorcar *Paul Revere* from the Pennsylvania Railroad sees service.

GETTING THERE: Greenbank Station is about 4 miles southwest of downtown Wilmington on Route 41, close to I-95. Amtrak's Northeast Corridor trains provide service to downtown Wilmington.

LOCATION: 2201 Newport Gap Pike, Wilmington
PHONE: 302-998-1930
WEBSITE: wwrr.com
E-MAIL: form on website

DISTRICT OF COLUMBIA
Smithsonian National Museum of American History

National Museum of American History

The National Museum of American History features the landmark transportation exhibition "America on the Move." Eighteen multimedia dioramas, each re-creating a specific time and place using artifacts, images, and sound, demonstrate how road and rail transportation shaped America, from before 1876 to 2000.

CHOICES: Must-see exhibits include the massive Southern Railway No. 1401, a 280-ton passenger locomotive built in 1926; *Jupiter*, a Baldwin-built narrow gauge 4-4-0; and a 19th century streetcar. The museum also displays *John Bull*, one of the oldest surviving steam locomotives in North America. This 1831 English-made locomotive is displayed on a vintage iron truss bridge that once served the Philadelphia & Reading Railroad.

WHEN TO GO: The museum is open every day of the year except Christmas Day. Spring sees the renowned cherry trees in bloom at the nearby Tidal Basin. The Smithsonian Folklife Festival, a huge outdoor exposition of living cultural heritage, takes place each year around Independence Day on the National Mall.

GOOD TO KNOW: Much of the museum's west wing has been renovated, but third-floor work is expected to continue into 2020. The transportation displays are not affected.

WORTH DOING: Explore the National Mall, where you can visit the Washington Monument, Lincoln Memorial, Jefferson Memorial, and several war memorials.

DON'T MISS: Listen to the re-created conversation between the fireman and engineer of Southern No. 1401 as they discuss their upcoming run. Take a full-immersion multimedia journey around Chicago's famous loop as it was in 1959 aboard L car 6719.

GETTING THERE: Public transportation is the best option. The Metrorail subway offers convenient access to the museum from its Smithsonian and Federal Triangle stations. A DC Circulator bus loops around the museums.

LOCATION: 1300 Constitution Avenue NW, Washington, D.C.
PHONE: 202-633-1000
WEBSITE: americanhistory.si.edu
E-MAIL: info@si.edu

KENTUCKY

Historic Railpark & Train Museum

Bowling Green's restored Louisville & Nashville depot contains a rail museum featuring two floors of interactive exhibits. On guided tours, visitors can explore railcars including a post office car, diner, sleeper, business car, and E8 locomotive. The site is open year-round. Escape games are also available.

LOCATION: 401 Kentucky Street, Bowling Green
PHONE: 270-745-7317
WEBSITE: historicrailpark.com
E-MAIL: info@historicrailpark.com

Paducah Railroad Museum

Operated by the Paducah Chapter of the National Railway Historical Society, the museum displays equipment and memorabilia from railroads including the three that served Paducah. It operates a locomotive simulator, includes replicas of a waiting room and freight office, and has section cars, tools, and an operating signaling system. A steam engine, caboose, and baggage car are displayed a block away. It is open Wednesdays through Saturdays.

LOCATION: 200 Washington Street, Paducah
PHONE: 270-908-6451
WEBSITE: paducahrr.org

Big South Fork Scenic Railway

Big South Fork Scenic Railway

In the 20th century, short lines and branches brought forth coal for use nationwide, and one of the primary locations was Stearns, home of the Kentucky & Tennessee short line. The coal is gone now, but the K&T has been reborn as a scenic railroad.

CHOICES: The railway offers 3-hour trips through the Daniel Boone National Forest and Big South Fork National River and Recreation Area on the former Kentucky & Tennessee Railway. The train follows mountain streams, passes through a tunnel, and crosses a bridge as it descends 600 feet to the floor of the river valley. The ride includes a layover at the restored mining camp of Blue Heron.

WHEN TO GO: The railroad runs regular excursions on a varied schedule from April through October. During November, 2-hour excursions run to the Big South Fork gorge. The *Banjo Boogie Express*, *Moonshine Limited*, Halloween, Christmas, and other specials operate during the season. Spring is especially beautiful in this part of the Appalachians because of all of the blooming plants that inhabit the mountains.

GOOD TO KNOW: The bridge over Roaring Paunch Creek is unique. It was constructed in 1937 from a used railroad bridge. The bridge girders needed to be offset because the line crossed the creek at an angle. The bridge's girders were offset in the opposite direction, so it was placed upside down, and the ties and track then added.

WORTH DOING: The McCreary County Museum, which is housed in the Stearns Coal and Lumber Company headquarters that was built in 1907, exhibits many facets of Appalachian life including the coal and lumber industries.

DON'T MISS: Take the walking tour of the Blue Heron Mine at the end of the run. Built in 1937, this mine and coal tipple operated until abandoned in 1962. The mine was restored with ghost structures (representations of where the actual buildings stood) and oral history exhibits by the National Park Service as part of the Big South Fork River and Recreation Area. You can also camp, hike, fish, and raft the river.

GETTING THERE: Stearns is 70 miles from Knoxville, Tenn., and 120 miles from Lexington. From Knoxville, take I-75 north to Exit 141. Take Route 63 west to the junction with Route 27. Take Route 27 north to Stearns. Turn left on Route 92 and travel west 1 mile to the depot.

LOCATION: 100 Henderson Street, Stearns
PHONE: 800-462-5664
WEBSITE: bsfsry.com
E-MAIL: info.web@bsfsry.com

Bluegrass Scenic Railroad & Museum

Bluegrass Scenic Railroad

The railroad offers 90-minute, 11-mile round-trip excursions over former Southern Railway track through the heart of Kentucky's Bluegrass region.

CHOICES: The diesel-powered trains are made up of vintage coaches from the 1920s and 1930s. Accommodations include four commuter-style coaches with vinyl bench seating and two first-class coaches featuring plush reclining seats and air-conditioning. Many trips have a special theme, which include Civil War train robberies, Pumpkin Patch trains, and Santa specials. Locomotive cab rides are also available. You can view outdoor displays of railcars, equipment, and a rare watchman's shanty. Inside the museum, exhibits showcase artifacts from Kentucky's railroad history.

WHEN TO GO: The grounds of the museum are open every day, so you can inspect or photograph equipment when you like. The museum's indoor displays are open on Saturdays and Sundays from mid-May through October, with excursions also operating on those Saturdays and Sundays.

GOOD TO KNOW: While in Bluegrass Country, you can tour its noted horse farms and bourbon distilleries.

WORTH DOING: Minutes away from the museum are several other local attractions that include the Aviation Museum of Kentucky and the Wildside Winery and Vineyard. If you like smaller trains, visit the Nostalgia Station Toy Museum in downtown Versailles. It is housed in a restored 100-year-old Louisville & Nashville Railroad depot and contains numerous antique toy trains.

DON'T MISS: The museum has a large collection of locomotives and rolling stock in various stages of restoration. Interesting cars include U.S. Army boxcars, a Seaboard safety car, and a Louisville & Nashville bay window caboose.

GETTING THERE: From Versailles, proceed south and west on Highway 62 for approximately 1.5 miles. Turn right onto Beasley Road into Woodford County Park. The museum is on the left after you cross the tracks.

LOCATION: 175 Beasley Road, Versailles
PHONE: 800-755-2476 or 859-873-2476
WEBSITE: bluegrassrailroad.com
E-MAIL: form on website

Kentucky Railway Museum

Kentucky Railway Museum

Housed in a replica of the original New Haven station, the Kentucky Railway Museum has more than 50,000 items in its collection and more than 120 locomotives and pieces of rolling stock. The museum also operates excursions on 17 miles of former Louisville & Nashville track.

CHOICES: The museum's excursion trains take you on a 22-mile, 90-minute round trip through the scenic and historic Rolling Fork River Valley between New Haven and Boston. Diesel operating power includes ex-Monon BL2 No. 32 and ex-AT&SF CF7 No. 2546. You can ride in open-air or air-conditioned coaches.

WHEN TO GO: The museum is open year-round, and excursions take place April through December. Trains run on weekends throughout the season with Tuesday and Friday runs added during summer. Spring and fall scenery is nice, with temperatures in the 70s and low 80s.

GOOD TO KNOW: Steam engine No. 152 was built in 1905 and is listed on the National Register of Historic Places. It was designated the official steam locomotive of the Commonwealth of Kentucky, and is currently under restoration.

WORTH DOING: Abraham Lincoln was born nearby, and historical sites to visit include his birthplace, boyhood home, and the Lincoln Museum. Mammoth Cave National Park, Fort Knox, the General George Patton Museum, and My Old Kentucky Home State Park are also close by.

DON'T MISS: The museum offers special excursions that include dinner trains, murder mystery trains, locomotive cab rides, train holdups, Santa trains, and days out with Thomas the Tank Engine. A 1940s weekend also takes place.

GETTING THERE: The museum is about 45 miles from Louisville and 65 miles from Lexington. If driving from Louisville, take I-65 south to Exit 105, Route 61 to Boston, and then Route 52 to New Haven. From Lexington, take Highway 60 west to the Martha Layne Collins Parkway. Take the parkway to Exit 21 and then Route 31E to New Haven.

LOCATION: 136 S. Main Street, New Haven
PHONE: 800-272-0152 or 502-549-5470
WEBSITE: kyrail.org
E-MAIL: info@kyrail.org

My Old Kentucky Dinner Train

Jim Wrinn

My Old Kentucky Dinner Train operates in 1940s dining cars on 16 miles of former Louisville & Nashville track between Bardstown and Limestone Springs. The passenger waiting room is located in Bardstown's former limestone freight house, which dates from 1860 and is on the National Register of Historic Places.

CHOICES: The train offers both 2-hour lunch and dinner trips, as well as murder mystery, Valentine's Day, North Pole, and other special event trains. Trains are pulled by two ex-Southern FP7s. The Budd-built lightweight cars are of AT&SF, C&O, and PRR ancestry, including the former C&O No. 1921 that operated on President Dwight Eisenhower's funeral train. Two restored depots, Deatsville and Limestone Springs, can be seen on the line.

WHEN TO GO: The train operates year-round, and the scenery is especially nice in spring and fall, with temperatures in the 70s and low 80s.

GOOD TO KNOW: Founded in 1780, Bardstown is Kentucky's second-oldest city and features a mix of old and new inns, restaurants, and shops. Several local distilleries give tours, and the Kentucky Railway Museum is 15 minutes away.

WORTH DOING: The area is rich in history and includes Abraham Lincoln's birthplace and his boyhood home. The Civil War Museum at Old Bardstown Village is dedicated to the war's western theater. The village also contains 11 historic log cabins. The Women of the Civil War Museum and several other museums are also nearby.

DON'T MISS: The train passes through part of the Bernheim Forest, a private 14,000-acre nature preserve, a habitat for a variety of trees, vegetation, and wildlife. While in the forest, the train passes slowly over the 310-foot-long, 60-foot-high Jackson Hollow timber trestle built for predecessor Bardstown & Louisville Railroad in 1860.

GETTING THERE: Bardstown is about 40 miles south of Louisville and 55 miles southwest of Lexington. When driving from Louisville, take I-65 south to Exit 112 and then Route 245 east. From Lexington, take Route 60 west and then the Martha Layne Collins Parkway.

LOCATION: 602 N. Third Street, Bardstown
PHONE: 502-348-7300
WEBSITE: kydinnertrain.com
E-MAIL: info@rjcorman.com

MARYLAND

Bowie Railroad Museum

This museum consists of a renovated freight station, switch tower, waiting shed, and caboose. The station and tower contain photos and artifacts. The museum is open Tuesday through Sunday. The Old Town Bowie Welcome Center and Interactive Children's Museum is next to the railroad museum.

LOCATION: 8614 Chestnut Avenue, Bowie
PHONE: 301-809-3089
WEBSITE: cityofbowie.org
E-MAIL: pwilliams@cityofbowie.org

Chesapeake Beach Railway Museum

From 1900 until 1935, the Chesapeake Beach Railway carried passengers to the Chesapeake Beach resort in cars such as the *Dolores*, which is on display. Housed in the original station, the museum exhibits photographs and artifacts of the railroad and the resort. It is open daily April through October and on weekends in March and November. Special events also take place throughout the year.

LOCATION: 4155 Mears Avenue, Chesapeake Beach
PHONE: 410-257-3892
WEBSITE: cbrm.org
E-MAIL: cbrailway@co.cal.md.us

Ellicott City Station

Located on the B&O Railroad's historic Old Main Line, Ellicott City Station could be the oldest surviving railroad station in the country. The main depot building was completed in 1831, and the freight house was built in 1855. The museum displays a replica of the first horse-drawn passenger railcar, the *Pioneer*, and a 1927 caboose. The museum is now operated by the Howard County (Md.) Recreation and Parks department. It is open Wednesday through Sunday year-round.

LOCATION: 3711 Maryland Avenue, Ellicott City
PHONE: 410-313-1945
WEBSITE: www.howardcountymd.gov/Baltimore-Ohio-Station-at-Ellicott-City
E-MAIL: jfeirson@howardcountymd.gov

Gaithersburg Community Museum

The museum features permanent and rotating exhibits in a restored 1884 B&O freight house. Also on display are a B&O Budd Rail Diesel Car, a 1918 Buffalo Creek & Gauley steam locomotive, and a C&O bay window caboose. You can also visit the adjacent History Park and restored station, which is now a MARC station. The museum is open Tuesday through Saturday.

LOCATION: 9 S. Summit Avenue, Gaithersburg
PHONE: 301-258-6160
WEBSITE: gaithersburgmd.gov
E-MAIL: museum@gaithersburgmd.gov

Hagerstown Roundhouse Museum

Located near the roundhouse site in a historic building, the museum presents local rail history through artifacts, photos, and model train layouts. A Baldwin diesel, two Western Maryland cabooses, and a Hagerstown & Frederick trolley are on display. It is open Friday through Sunday year-round.

LOCATION: 296 S. Burhans Boulevard, Hagerstown
PHONE: 301-739-4665
WEBSITE: roundhouse.org
E-MAIL: info@roundhouse.org

Irish Railroad Workers Museum

Located a short walk from the B&O Railroad Museum, this preserved set of five 1840s rowhouses pays tribute to Irish immigrants who settled in Baltimore to help build the Baltimore & Ohio Railroad and work in its nearby shop complex, as well as the Irish-American cultural impact in Baltimore and Maryland history. Free tours highlight this and other historic locations in the neighborhood. Open Fridays, Saturdays, and Sundays, with special events monthly.

LOCATION: 918-920 Lemmon Street, Baltimore
PHONE: 410-347-4747 (during museum hours) or 410-669-8154 (after hours)
WEBSITE: irishshrine.org
E-MAIL: info@irishshrine.org

B&O Railroad Museum

Dave Crosby

With nearly 200 locomotives and railcars and thousands of smaller artifacts, the B&O Railroad Museum contains one of the largest and most diverse collections of railroad artifacts and history in a unique, 40-acre setting.

CHOICES: The museum occupies several vintage buildings, including a fully covered roundhouse and turntable built in 1884. The domed roundhouse is a distinctive feature of Baltimore's skyline. The museum houses the largest collection of 19th century locomotives in North America. Later steamers and diesels are well represented, and a wide selection of passenger cars and freight cars round out the collection.

WHEN TO GO: The museum is open year-round, with special events scheduled throughout the year. Train rides are offered Thursday through Sunday, April through December, weekends in January, and Wednesdays in April and May.

GOOD TO KNOW: Allow at least a half day for a full tour of the museum, and if your schedule allows, include a 20-minute train ride along the first commercial mile of railroad track laid in America. On selected dates, tours of the modern restoration facility, reached by a stop on the *First Mile Express*, are available for an additional charge.

WORTH DOING: The museum is in a residential neighborhood just west of downtown and the city's major sports stadiums. Baltimore has a host of other attractions, including the Irish Railroad Workers Museum two blocks away, the Baltimore Streetcar Museum, Civil War Museum (in the President Street Station, built 1850), the National Aquarium, Fort McHenry, and the nearby Edgar Allan Poe House.

DON'T MISS: Free tours are offered at the Irish Railroad Workers Museum, a set of 1840s rowhouses only two blocks away, on Fridays and weekends.

GETTING THERE: The museum is only a few minutes off I-95 by car. The Orange Route of the Charm City Circulator, a free bus service, connects the museum with downtown and the Inner Harbor, as do several MARC commuter trains connect Washington D.C. and Baltimore on weekends as well.

LOCATION: 901 W. Pratt Street, Baltimore
PHONE: 410-752-2490
WEBSITE: borail.org
E-MAIL: info@borail.org

Baltimore Streetcar Museum

Alexander Mitchell IV

Since 1968, the Baltimore Streetcar Museum has operated its distinctive and unique collection of streetcars and other transit equipment. In recent years, the collection's scope has expanded slightly to include cars from Philadelphia and New Jersey.

CHOICES: Take a 1-mile round trip up the former right-of-way of the Maryland & Pennsylvania RR in the Jones Falls Valley, passing the historic former Ma & Pa freight house and roundhouse before turning on a loop for return. The Visitors Center houses museum displays, a gift shop, auditorium, and a research library.

WHEN TO GO: The museum is open Sunday afternoons March through December and Saturday afternoons June through October; summers in Baltimore can be excessively hot and muggy. Holiday events run in December, and private and school charters occasionally run during the week.

GOOD TO KNOW: There is a family admission plan as well as individual admission; all include unlimited rides, car house tours, museum access, and a guide pamphlet.

WORTH DOING: Baltimore is a historic city full of things to see, from the B&O Railroad Museum and the Baltimore Civil War Museum (in a restored rail station headhouse) to the National Aquarium and the USS *Constellation*. The Mt. Vernon neighborhood, with the Walters Art Gallery, Meyerhoff Symphony Hall, the Peabody Institute, and shops and restaurants, is a short distance to the south.

DON'T MISS: Thirteen Baltimore streetcars, ranging from a horse car to the last PCC to run in Baltimore, plus three Philadelphia and Newark PCC cars, and snowsweepers as well as several buses and "trackless trolleys" are in the Museum's possession.

GETTING THERE: The museum is in the northern part of the central part of the city, two blocks west of the major north-south streets of Charles St. and Maryland Avenue. Amtrak's Penn Station is a couple minutes' walk to the east. The MTA Light Rail also serves Penn Station. The Purple Route of the city's free Charm City Circulator bus service connects downtown and Federal Hill with the aforementioned Penn Station.

LOCATION: 1901 Falls Road, Baltimore
PHONE: 410-547-0264
WEBSITE: baltimorestreetcar.org
E-MAIL: form on website

National Capital Trolley Museum

Ken Rucker/National Capital Trolley Museum

Inspired by streetcar buildings of the past, the National Capital Trolley Museum's visitor center provides an educational and entertaining look at the history of the region's streetcar systems, complete with an authentic trolley ride.

CHOICES: The museum is divided into three halls. In the Main Hall, you'll learn about the history of local streetcar systems, watch several silent films starring streetcars and actor Harold Lloyd, and see a model electric railway. Conduit Hall contains exhibits that explain how streetcars were powered. In Streetcar Hall, you get a close-up look at a variety of trolleys in the museum's collection. Unlimited trolley rides are included with admission.

WHEN TO GO: The museum is open weekends year-round as well as on select Thursdays and Fridays April through November. In summer, the museum offers special programs for children that include activities such as storytelling and crafts.

GOOD TO KNOW: Opportunities to ride a boat tram from Blackpool, England, occur on most Saturdays in warm, dry weather and during the Calvalcade of Street Cars each April and September. Recently restored Capitol Traction Company (CTCo) 522, built in 1898, and just restored CTCo 27, built in 1918, are exhibited in Street Car Hall.

WORTH DOING: Downtown Washington, with its wealth of cultural and historic attractions, is just 14 miles away.

DON'T MISS: In Streetcar Hall, look for CTCo 09, one of two remaining specialty cars that swept the snow from streetcar tracks in the nation's capital.

GETTING THERE: The museum is located in Northwest Branch Park, about a 20-minute drive from the Capital Beltway and adjacent to the Inter-County Connector toll highway. Bonifant Road is 5.5 miles north of I-495.

LOCATION: 1313 Bonifant Road, Colesville
PHONE: 301-384-6088
WEBSITE: dctrolley.org
E-MAIL: facebook.nctm@gmail.com

Walkersville Southern Railroad

Walkersville Southern, Randy Srba

The Walkersville Southern Railroad takes you on a pleasant 8-mile, 70-minute round trip through woods and farmland, past a restored century-old lime kiln, and across the scenic Monocacy River.

CHOICES: Trains depart from the original Pennsylvania Railroad depot pulled by one of the railroad's diverse collection of switchers, which includes a 1939 Davenport gas-mechanical, a rare 1942 EMD Model 40 four-wheel diesel, a GE side-rod 45-tonner, and two ex-PRR GE 44-tonners, used on this line in its last days in PRR service. Passengers may ride in former Long Island Rail Road coaches, a covered open-air car, or a caboose. Parks and picnic stands are located at both ends of the line.

WHEN TO GO: From May through October, there are two departures on Saturdays. In October, there are additional trips on Sundays. Dinner trains run on some major holidays and on two Saturdays every month May through November. Trains that combine a mystery adventure with dinner run on select dates in that period. Special events are scheduled throughout the year, including Wild West train robberies. For kids, there are Easter Bunny trains, teddy bear picnics, and superhero and Santa trains. Visiting steam locomotives also run on several weekends.

GOOD TO KNOW: The railroad also operates an additional 3 miles of track north of Walkersville, which is usually reserved for dinner trains or special runs.

WORTH DOING: For Civil War buffs, Gettysburg and Harpers Ferry are about an hour away; the railroad also conducts a Civil War reenactment weekend. Historic downtown Frederick, just down the road, is also a welcome respite.

DON'T MISS: The railroad's museum occupies a former ice plant and features rail artifacts from the line and a model railroad.

GETTING THERE: The railroad is 50 miles from Baltimore or Washington, D.C. From Baltimore, take I-70 west to Exit 53B near Frederick. Follow Route 15 north for 6 miles and then turn right onto Biggs Ford Road. Travel about 2 miles and look for a tall grain elevator, which is adjacent to the station.

LOCATION: 34 W. Pennsylvania Avenue, Walkersville
PHONE: 301-898-0899
WEBSITE: wsrr.org
E-MAIL: admin@wsrr.org

Western Maryland Scenic Railroad

Dave Crosby

Of all the Appalachian railroads, the Western Maryland was one of the most beloved because of its excellent steam power and beautiful mountain setting. Today, the trip out of Cumberland on the main line, with a short detour the last few miles onto a branch into Frostburg, is one of the best parts of the so-called "Wild Mary."

CHOICES: Traveling through the mountains of western Maryland, this 32-mile round trip takes you from Cumberland's restored Western Maryland Railway station to an 1891 Cumberland & Pennsylvania depot in Frostburg. You'll ride aboard restored coaches pulled by a 1949 Baldwin 2-6-6-2 steam locomotive or a vintage diesel engine. Regular excursions offer first-class seating, parlor car, dining car, premium coach, and standard coach. Dining car seating is available on Saturdays and most Fridays and Sundays. It includes reserved seating with a meal cooked on board. The railroad also offers murder mystery, wine tasting, Christmas, and other special trains.

WHEN TO GO: Trains run year round. The height of the fall color season is especially beautiful, and reservations are required for fall excursions.

GOOD TO KNOW: When the train arrives in Frostburg, you have a 45-minute layover. Be sure to find a good spot to watch the locomotive change directions on the turntable. You will also have time to walk down Main Street for shopping or quick dining.

WORTH DOING: The Western Maryland station houses the Chesapeake & Ohio Canal National Historical Park's Cumberland Visitor Center, where you can learn more about the C&O Canal.

DON'T MISS: Stick to the right side of the train. Leaving Cumberland, the train passes through the Narrows, a gap in the mountain that also allows the highway and parallel CSX (the former B&O) an escape to the west. Just beyond is famous Helmstetter's Curve, a classic horseshoe curve. From here on, views remain mostly on the right side as the train makes its way 1,300 feet higher into the mountains. Open vestibules are found throughout the train.

GETTING THERE: When driving, Cumberland is about 2.5 hours from Baltimore, Washington, or Pittsburgh. From either direction, the Western Maryland station is easily reached from Exit 43C off I-68 in downtown Cumberland.

LOCATION: 13 Canal Street, Cumberland
PHONE: 240-920-6273
WEBSITE: wmsr.com
E-MAIL: trainmaster@wmsr.com

NEW JERSEY

Cape May Seashore Lines

Ride the original equipment operated in south Jersey by the Pennsylvania-Reading Seashore Lines, the Reading Company, and the Pennsylvania Railroad on 30-mile round-trip excursions between Richland and Tuckahoe.

LOCATION: Reading Avenue and Mill Road, Tuckahoe
WEBSITE: capemayseashorelines.org
E-MAIL: conductor@capemayseashorelines.org

Maywood Station Museum

This station has been restored, inside and out, to preserve its Victorian style. The station museum features local history and railroad artifacts. Also on display are a restored caboose that contains additional exhibits and a New York, Susquehanna & Western Alco S2 diesel locomotive. It is open on a limited schedule April through December.

LOCATION: 269 Maywood Avenue, Maywood
WEBSITE: maywoodstation.com
E-MAIL: info@maywoodstation.com

Black River & Western Railroad

Dave Crosby

The Black River & Western, which also hauls freight, hosts 90-minute passenger excursions (operated by the nonprofit Black River Railroad Historical Trust) over a short segment of the former Pennsylvania Railroad's Flemington Branch between Flemington and Ringoes, and the shorter Browne Station local from Ringoes over 2.5 miles of recently reopened track.

CHOICES: In addition to standard excursions that operate on Saturdays and Sundays from Memorial Day through Labor Day, various family-friendly special trains are offered at other times of year. These include the *Easter Bunny Express*, *Pumpkin Train*, *Trick or Treat Express*, and the *North Pole Express*. Summer excursions board at both Ringoes and Flemington, while theme trains board at Flemington only. Most special-event trains and many summer excursions run with ex-Great Western Railway 2-8-0 No. 60, the balance with diesels.

WHEN TO GO: Each season on the BR&W has its own charm. For a special treat, catch the occasional mixed train behind No. 60 to Browne Station with photo stops.

GOOD TO KNOW: Flemington is a mixture of quaint and commercial. At Ringoes, a Jersey Central baggage car houses a display of railroad artifacts and a model railroad.

WORTH DOING: Northlandz, an extraordinary model railroad rich in spectacle, is located in Flemington. With 8 actual miles of track, dozens of trains moving at once, and 35-foot-tall model mountains, it's acres of whimsical fun.

DON'T MISS: Just across the Delaware River in Pennsylvania is the New Hope & Ivyland Railroad, which makes it easy to ride two excursion trains in the same day. Almost as close is the Delaware River Railroad in Phillipsburg, N.J.

GETTING THERE: Flemington is roughly 35 miles from Philadelphia and 50 miles from New York City. Ringoes is about 15 miles farther from each city. Both Ringoes and Flemington are located just off Route 202.

LOCATION: 80 Stangl Road, Flemington; 105 John Ringo Road, Ringoes
PHONE: 908-782-6622
WEBSITE: blackriverrailroad.com
E-MAIL: info@blackriverrailroad.com

Delaware River Railroad

Dave Crosby

Enjoy a 90-minute ride along the scenic Delaware River in western New Jersey from Phillipsburg to Riegelsville behind steam locomotive No. 142 or a vintage diesel.

CHOICES: Each excursion offers the opportunity for passengers to step off the train and take part in family-oriented activities. There is a gem mine offered May through October as well as seasonal events like the corn maze and pumpkin train. December sees the famous Polar Express operating on the line.

WHEN TO GO: Excursions operate May through October with special activities based on each season. Steam usually operates during the summer months with diesel power assigned to trains in December.

GOOD TO KNOW: The Delaware River Railroad is operated by the New York Susquehanna & Western Technical and Historical Society, a nonprofit volunteer organization that has spent years rebuilding the scenic right of way once operated by the Pennsylvania Railroad. Currently, the rehabilitated trackage allows for a 20-mile round trip.

WORTH DOING: Those seeking more adult fare may opt to purchase tickets on the Warren County Wine Train, which allows passengers to detrain and visit the Villa Milagro Vineyards for a tour and wine tasting.

DON'T MISS: Philipsburg is rich in railroad history and was once served by five different railroads. A few blocks away, the Phillipsburg Railroad Historians operate a small museum with artifacts and full-size railroad equipment on display.

GETTING THERE: Situated on the Delaware River, Phillipsburg is across the river from Easton, Pennsylvania. It is easily reached by automobile via Route 22 or I-78. The station is just off Main Street in Phillipsburg.

LOCATION: 99 Elizabeth Street, Phillipsburg
PHONE: 877-872-4674 or 908-454-4433
WEBSITE: nyswths.org
E-MAIL: ccotty@fastwww.com

New Jersey Museum of Transportation

New Jersey Museum of Transportation

The museum is home to many rare pieces of equipment, and it offers a short ride on a narrow gauge train on the grounds of Allaire State Park.

CHOICES: Besides looking at the equipment on display, you have the opportunity to tour the museum's shops and see the progress on various restoration projects. The train travels through the scenic state park, which is home to the Manasquan River.

WHEN TO GO: The vintage locomotives run weekends spring and fall, with daily operations during summer. During the Railroader's Weekend in mid-September, all the equipment in running shape operates. The *Christmas Express*, which started more than 30 years ago, begins running in late November and continues into December.

GOOD TO KNOW: Founded by one of the oldest all-volunteer railroad preservation groups, the museum began as the Pine Creek Railroad in 1952, using rail salvaged from sand pits.

WORTH DOING: In the park, you can explore Allaire Village, a historic 19th century ironmaking town. The park also contains hiking and biking trails.

DON'T MISS: Look for the Ely-Thomas Lumber Company Shay locomotive. While currently undergoing restoration, it is one of the smallest Shays left in existence.

GETTING THERE: The museum is located in Allaire State Park, not far from the ocean. It is easily accessible from the Garden State Parkway or I-195 off Exit 31B. Signs show the way to the park.

LOCATION: 4265 Atlantic Ave, Wall
PHONE: 732-938-5524
WEBSITE: njmt.org
E-MAIL: office@njmt.org

Whippany Railway Museum

Dave Crosby

The Whippany Railway Museum maintains a wide selection of locomotives and cars with ties to New Jersey railroading as well as exhibits and artifacts housed in a 1904 wooden freight house.

CHOICES: In addition to the buildings, grounds and equipment on display, several themed excursion trains depart from Whippany. Passengers my opt to ride in one of several cabooses or the restored club-car *Jersey Coast*. When trains are not operating there is still much to see in Whippany, including a Baldwin steam locomotive built in 1907, a fireless locomotive, and a 1910 railbus. Also on the grounds are an original water tower and fieldstone Morristown & Erie passenger station.

WHEN TO GO: Excursions operate on select dates throughout the year with Easter and Fall trips amongst the most popular. The museum grounds are open every Sunday from April through October.

GOOD TO KNOW: The museum's steam locomotive, No. 4035, built for the U.S. Army in 1942, is undergoing a long-term restoration to operational condition. The engine once powered excursion trains on the former Morris County Central Railroad, which was located in Whippany between 1965 and 1973.

WORTH DOING: Whippany is an outdoor-friendly community with several parks and trails, including the Patriots Path Hiking and Biking Trail.

DON'T MISS: The Whippanong Railroad, a large O scale model train display located inside the freight house, is a favorite of young and old alike.

GETTING THERE: Whippany is in northeast New Jersey, about 20 miles from Newark. It is easily reached via I-80, I-78, or I-287. The museum is located at the intersection of Routes 10 and 511 (Whippany Road) in Whippany.

LOCATION: 1 Railroad Plaza, Whippany
PHONE: 973-887-8177
WEBSITE: whippanyrailwaymuseum.net
E-MAIL: info@whippanyrailwaymuseum.net

PENNSYLVANIA

Allegheny Portage Railroad

This national historic site preserves the remains of the Allegheny Portage Railroad. You can explore the 900-foot Staple Bend Tunnel, the first railroad tunnel built in the United States, visit the engine house, or take a hike. The Staple Bend Tunnel is about 25 miles southwest from the site's main location. From that parking lot, it is a 2-mile hike or bike ride to the tunnel. The site conducts a large number of special events.

LOCATION: 110 Federal Park Road, Gallitzin
PHONE: 814-886-6150
WEBSITE: nps.gov/alpo
E-MAIL: form on website

Allentown & Auburn Railroad

Diesel-powered round trips to Topton over the 4-mile former Reading Company Kutztown Branch leave from the historic 1870 depot. Occasionally an ex-Pennsylvania Railroad "doodlebug" operates. Trains run about 40 times per season, with most departures scheduled around seasonal, or holiday events. The ride lasts roughly an hour.

LOCATION: 232 Railroad Street, Kutztown
PHONE: 570-778-7531
WEBSITE: allentownandauburnrr.com
E-MAIL: form on website

Bellefonte Historical Railroad Society

The society operates train rides in fall and winter. While destinations vary, all trains depart from the historic 1889 Bellefonte station. Fall foliage trains travel along Spring Creek and through the Bald Eagle Valley. Family-friendly Halloween and Santa Express rides also operate, using restored 1920s and 1940s passenger coaches.

LOCATION: 320 W. High Street, Bellefonte
PHONE: 814-355-1053
WEBSITE: bellefontetrain.org
E-MAIL: info@bellefontetrain.org

Franklin Institute Science Museum

The museum features the Train Factory, an interactive exhibit showcasing Baldwin's experimental locomotive No. 60000, which has been at the museum since 1933, and two other locomotives. You'll explore railroad technology as you journey through the exhibit and even take No. 60000 for a test run. The museum is open year-round.

LOCATION: 222 N. 20th Street, Philadelphia
PHONE: 215-448-1200
WEBSITE: fi.edu
E-MAIL: guestservices@fi.edu

Friends of the Stewartstown Railroad

This group works to preserve and promote the Stewartstown Railroad, a 7.4-mile bucolic rural country short line founded in 1885. Open houses, featuring track speeder rides, are held at the railroad's 1914 brick Stewartstown station.

LOCATION: 21 W. Pennsylvania Avenue, Stewartstown
PHONE: 717-654-7530
WEBSITE: stewartstownfriends.org
E-MAIL: friendsofstrt@hotmail.com

Greenville Railroad Park and Museum

This railroad museum displays Union Railroad 0-10-2 No. 604. Built in 1936, it is the largest steam switcher ever built. Several railcars are also on display. Museum exhibits highlight a CTC panel from Bessemer Railroad, Empire cars, and the invention of the parachute. It is open weekends during May, September, and October. During summer months, the museum is open Tuesday through Sunday.

LOCATION: 314 Main Street, Greenville
PHONE: 724-588-4009
WEBSITE: greenvilletrainmuseum.org
E-MAIL: greenvillerailroadpark@gmail.com

Harris Tower Museum

Visitors to the switch tower can operate an actual interlocking machine and model board that controls virtual trains from the 1940s. Throw any of the 113 levers on the interlocking machine, which controlled track switches and signals, and watch the model board light up to show what would happen. The tower is next to operating tracks, so railfans can watch Norfolk Southern and Amtrak trains go by. It is open Saturdays June through October.

LOCATION: 637 Walnut Street, Harrisburg
PHONE: 717-232-6221
WEBSITE: harristower.org
E-MAIL: NRHS.Harrisburg@gmail.com

Ligonier Valley Rail Road Museum

The Ligonier Valley Rail Road Museum is housed in the restored Darlington station, and its exhibits show the history of the Ligonier Valley Rail Road. It is open Saturdays. It displays a 1905 caboose and has 3,000 items in its collection.

LOCATION: 3032 Idlewild Hill Lane, Ligonier
PHONE: 724-238-7819
WEBSITE: lvrra.org
E-MAIL: info@lvrra.org

Ma & Pa Railroad Heritage Village

The village has been preserved as a rural commerce crossroads circa 1915, with a general store, post office, and mill. Several pieces of rolling stock are on site, and motor car rides are offered. The village is open on summer Sundays and for several additional special events. Fall foliage excursions take place in October, and the Christmas City Express runs in December.

LOCATION: 1258 Muddy Creek Forks Road, Airville
PHONE: 717-927-9565
WEBSITE: maandparailroad.com
E-MAIL: info@maandparailroad.com

Pioneer Tunnel Coal Mine & Steam Train

Take a scenic ride along Mahanoy Mountain as you hear stories about mining, bootlegging, and the Centralia Mine fire. A 1927 narrow gauge 0-4-0 steam locomotive takes you around the mountain. You can also tour a real anthracite coal mine in open mine cars. It is open April through October.

LOCATION: 19th Street and Oak Street, Ashland
PHONE: 570-875-3850
WEBSITE: pioneertunnel.com
E-MAIL: form on website

Portage Station Museum

The museum is located in a restored Pennsylvania Railroad train station, originally built in 1926. The first floor contains a stationmaster's office and items from the Pennsylvania Railroad, and on the second floor, there is a display of mining artifacts and a large model train that depicts railroading of the area. It is open Wednesday through Saturday.

LOCATION: 400 Lee Street, Portage
PHONE: 814-736-9223
WEBSITE: portagepa.us
E-MAIL: ihuschak@comcast.net

Reading Railroad Heritage Museum

You can't take a ride on the Reading Railroad, but you can discover its heritage in this museum. You can tour the museum's large outdoor collection of vintage Reading Company cars and locomotives. Inside, you can view a 1930s station agent's office, photographs, and artifacts. The museum is open weekends.

LOCATION: 500 S. Third Street, Hamburg
PHONE: 610-562-5513
WEBSITE: readingrailroad.org
E-MAIL: info@readingrailroad.org

The Stourbridge Line

The Stourbridge Line offers a scenic train ride that winds along 25 miles of historic railroad tracks in the Lackawaxen River Valley. Seasonal rides take place on weekends Memorial Day through fall, and special trains also operate.

LOCATION: 812 Main Street, Honesdale
PHONE: 570-470-2697
WEBSITE: thestourbridgeline.net
E-MAIL: info@thestourbridgeline.net

Tunnels Park & Museum

From the nearby Jackson Street Bridge, you get a great view of the twin tunnels, which are 3,605 feet long. The site also features a museum and a restored 1942 Pennsylvania Railroad caboose. The museum includes railroad artifacts and photos. It is open Monday through Friday May through October.

LOCATION: 411 Convent Street, Gallitzin
PHONE: 814-886-8871
WEBSITE: gallitzin.info
E-MAIL: info@gallitzin.info

Williams Grove Railroad

Operating as part of the Williams Grove Historical Steam Engine Association, the railroad operates steam or diesel train rides on select weekends May into October and during the annual fall steam show at the end of August. Steam power is provided by PRR No. 643. At times during the season, the Run-a-Locomotive program allows you to run one the association's engines.

LOCATION: 1 Steam Engine Hill, Mechanicsburg
PHONE: 717-766-4001
WEBSITE: wgrailroad.com or wghsea.org
E-MAIL: form on wghsea.org

Colebrookdale Railroad

Colebrookdale Railroad

The Colebrookdale Railroad, once a branch line of the Reading Company, winds through deep woods along the Manatawny and Ironstone creeks. The 8.6-mile route traveled on its 2-hour excursions features high trestles and deep rock cuts.

CHOICES: Both coach and first-class seating is available, and to take in the panoramic views, all passengers have access to the *Secret Valley Explorer* open observation car. Locomotive cab and caboose rides are also available. The railroad offers many themed rides, including autism friendly, Sunday brunch, wine tasting, and murder mystery trains.

WHEN TO GO: Excursions run Saturdays, Sundays, and select weekdays beginning in spring and running through December. Fall foliage can be enjoyed from the Hayride-on-Rails, and autumn evening mini-excursions include a bonfire with music, s'mores, and cider. Daytime Christmas trains include a stop at Santa's Secret Forest, where passengers can select Christmas trees.

GOOD TO KNOW: Fine china, silver service, and white jacketed-waiters highlight the Garden Café car, whose décor is inspired by the garden scene in *The Great Gatsby*. Try the Pennsylvania Dutch Pot Pie.

WORTH DOING: The Boyertown Museum of Historic Vehicles is adjacent to the railroad's station. Several rail museums and tourist railroads are within 45 minutes of the Colebrookdale. Also nearby are Valley Forge and Hopewell Furnace National Historic Sites.

DON'T MISS: Along Milepost 6, look for the Devil's Claw, one of the closest rock cuts on a railroad.

GETTING THERE: From Highway 100, head west on Route 73 into Boyertown, turn left onto Washington Street, and travel one block.

LOCATION: 64 S. Washington Street, Boyertown
PHONE: 866-289-4021 or 610-367-0200
WEBSITE: colebrookdalerailroad.com
E-MAIL: info@colebrookdalerailroad.com

Electric City Trolley Museum

Dave Crosby

The Electric City Trolley Museum is located on the grounds of Steamtown National Historic Site. The museum is in a former silk mill and offers 9-mile round-trip excursions along the former Lackawanna & Wyoming Valley Railroad interurban route.

CHOICES: Visitors may opt to visit the museum, ride the trolley or both. Inside the museum are several restored trolley cars, artifacts and photographs. There is also a theater and children's play room. Trolley excursions depart from a nearby platform also used by Steamtown excursions and operate to "The Trolley Works" restoration facility where visitors are given a short tour and can view restoration work in progress.

WHEN TO GO: The museum is open year-round with the exception of Thanksgiving, Christmas and New Year's Day. Excursions typically operate May through October with special holiday runs in November and December.

GOOD TO KNOW: Scranton has a rich industrial history. In addition to Steamtown, the nearby Lackawanna County Coal Mine Tour takes visitors into a genuine anthracite coal mine, while the adjacent Pennsylvania Anthracite Heritage Museum showcases the area's industrial heritage.

WORTH DOING: On select dates during the summer season, a combination ticket allows visitors to step off the trolley and enjoy a baseball game. The Scranton/Wilkes Barre Rail Riders AAA baseball stadium is located adjacent to the trolley restoration shop, and affords the unique opportunity for passengers to enjoy professional baseball and a vintage trolley ride.

DON'T MISS: Be sure to check out Scranton Transit No. 324—one of only two existing Scranton streetcars—in the final stages of a multi-year restoration effort inside the Trolley Works.

GETTING THERE: Take Exit 185 off I-81 to downtown Scranton and then follow the signs to the Steamtown grounds.

LOCATION: 300 Cliff Street, Scranton
PHONE: 570-963-6590
WEBSITE: ectma.org
E-MAIL: trolley@lackawannacounty.org

Everett Railroad

Everett Railroad

Located in south central Pennsylvania, the Everett Railroad provides a 1-hour (or longer) scenic train ride through green farmlands and along the banks of the Juniata River. You'll take it all in aboard open-window coaches pulled by a vintage steam locomotive for an authentic 1940s experience.

CHOICES: On this regional railroad, trains operate on many weekends during the year, from March through December. A variety of excursions and special events are offered including ice cream socials, holiday-themed rides, and even trips to a nearby annual agricultural parade. Steam locomotive No. 11, a 1920 Alco-Cooke 2-6-0, powers most trains. Excursions run to Brookes Mills, Roaring Spring, or Kladder.

WHEN TO GO: The fall foliage season from late September through October is a favorite time to ride the train, since the hills and mountains surrounding the railroad are prime areas for "leaf-peeping." The Pumpkin Patch and Santa trains have quickly become favorites of many area families.

GOOD TO KNOW: The Everett Railroad is also a freight hauler, serving a variety of area industries daily. Restored by Everett, No. 11 returned to service in 2015 for the first time since the 1970s. It was constructed in 1920 and put to work in 1923 by Rhode Island's Narragansett Pier Railroad.

WORTH DOING: From the Hollidaysburg station, which is a combination of architectural styles, you'll see Chimney Rocks, an interesting geological feature. Now developed into a park, the limestone pillars offer a scenic overlook of the area. The park includes picnic sites and makes for a relaxing place to visit.

DON'T MISS: Not far from the great railroad hub of Altoona, nearby attractions include the world-famous Horseshoe Curve and the Railroaders Memorial Museum, as well as the Allegheny Portage Railroad National Historic Site in Cresson.

GETTING THERE: Located about 10 miles south of Altoona, Hollidaysburg is a short distance from I-99. The station is on the south side of the town, where you can take Route 36 (Penn Street) to Loop Road and loop around the road to the station.

LOCATION: 244 Loop Road, Hollidaysburg
PHONE: 814-696-3877
WEBSITE: everettrailroad.com
E-MAIL: excursions@everettrailroad.com

Horseshoe Curve National Historic Landmark

Samuel Phillips

Horseshoe Curve is an engineering marvel completed in 1854 as part of the Pennsylvania Railroad's main line over the Allegheny Mountains. By curving the track across the face of a mountain, builders were able to gain elevation without making the grade too steep for trains to climb. Today, the curve is as vital as ever, serving as a key link in the Norfolk Southern system, with more than 50 trains passing over its three tracks each day.

CHOICES: Attractions at Horseshoe Curve consist of a visitor center at ground level and the trackside park, which is accessible by a 194-step walkway or by a funicular railway. First-timers will want to tour the visitor center, ride the funicular up to track level for some train-watching, and perhaps take the stairway back down. The best show at the curve is the passage of a heavy westbound train, laboring up the grade with helper engines on the front and/or rear. Try to stay long enough to catch this spectacle. Recent brush-clearing has greatly enhanced the view of the tracks from the park.

WHEN TO GO: The visitor center and funicular are open from early April through late November. In October, the fall colors can be brilliant. Freight traffic tends to build toward the end of each week, so there may be more trains to see on Thursday, Friday, and Saturday.

GOOD TO KNOW: The site is managed by the Altoona Railroaders Memorial Museum in downtown Altoona. Combined admission tickets are available.

WORTH DOING: Continue west on Kittanning Point Road to Gallitzin and visit the small park at the west portal of one of the tunnels the railroad uses to pierce the spine of the Alleghenies. Cresson, a little farther west is also a good place to watch trains, and the Station Inn railfan hostelry faces the tracks.

DON'T MISS: The longer you stay at Horseshoe Curve, the greater the chances of seeing two or even three trains rounding the curve simultaneously, a thrilling occurrence.

GETTING THERE: Horseshoe Curve is located 5 miles west of Altoona. Altoona is on I-99, 33 miles north of I-70/76. Amtrak's New York-Philadelphia-Pittsburgh *Pennsylvanian* stops at Altoona daily.

LOCATION: Veterans Memorial Highway, Altoona
PHONE: 888-425-8666 or 814-946-0834
WEBSITE: railroadcity.com
E-MAIL: info@railroadcity.com

Lake Shore Railway Museum

Lake Shore Railway Museum

On the grounds of a former New York Central passenger depot, you'll find a museum that maintains a collection focused on General Electric, Heisler, and Pullman equipment as well as on local railroads.

CHOICES: The restored New York Central passenger station houses numerous artifacts, and 24 pieces of rolling stock are displayed outdoors. A freight station built in 1869 by the Lake Shore & Michigan Southern also sits on the grounds. View fireless 0-6-0 No. 6, one of 29 such Heisler locomotives built between 1934 and 1941. Recent additions to the museum are a 1939 General Electric 23-ton diesel-electric boxcab, an 18-ton Plymouth model JHG locomotive, and Norfolk Southern GE Dash 8-32B, which is the first Dash-8 to be preserved in a museum.

WHEN TO GO: From Memorial Day through Labor Day, the museum is open Wednesdays through Sundays. It is open weekends in April, May, September, and October. January through March, it is open on Saturdays.

GOOD TO KNOW: Enjoy Christmas at the Station on weekends following Thanksgiving with caboose rides and other activities.

WORTH DOING: Time your visit with the cherry festival in July or the wine festival in September. There are more than five wineries in or near North East. You can also drive along Lake Erie and stop at one of the local beaches. Also, in December, look for the town's Sugar Plum Weekend.

DON'T MISS: CSX's Chicago-New York main line and Norfolk Southern's line to Buffalo run beside the museum. You can watch 60–80 trains each day from the platform, including Amtrak's *Lake Shore Limited* passenger train.

GETTING THERE: The museum is located about 15 miles east of Erie, Pa., near the New York state border. From Erie, take Route 20 to North East, where it becomes Main Street. Turn right on Clinton, right on Mill Street, and then left on Wall Street.

LOCATION: 31 Wall Street, North East
PHONE: 814-725-1911
WEBSITE: lakeshorerailway.com
E-MAIL: form on website

Pennsylvania
Lehigh Gorge Scenic Railway

Dave Crosby

This 16-mile round trip into the Lehigh Gorge is among the most beautiful in Pennsylvania, a state blessed with numerous great tourist railroads and museums. Trains run on the tracks of the Reading & Northern regional railroad, paralleling a bike path into an isolated, narrow chasm.

CHOICES: The 1-hour, narrated excursion follows the winding Lehigh River, curve after curve, and crosses it in several places, until it reaches Old Penn Haven. Leaving from the renovated, distinct Central Railroad of New Jersey depot, you can ride behind a diesel locomotive in a vintage 1920s coach or an open-air car.

WHEN TO GO: The railway operates on Saturdays and Sundays May through December. The mountains present a new look for each season, but fall offers beautiful foliage and an extended schedule in October. Santa trains run in December.

GOOD TO KNOW: In 1953, the towns of Mauch Chunk and East Mauch Chunk merged into one town with the name of Jim Thorpe when that famous athlete was buried there. Looking for a place that would help develop a memorial for her husband, who had no previous ties to the area, Thorpe's widow found assistance from the two towns.

WORTH DOING: Explore the town of Jim Thorpe, a charming village of shops, stores, and B&Bs, many featuring Victorian architecture. The town was once known as the Switzerland of America for its steep hillsides, narrow streets, and terraced gardens.

DON'T MISS: On the bike train to White Haven, you ride the train up Lehigh Gorge and pedal your bike back the 25 miles to Jim Thorpe along a scenic bike trail.

GETTING THERE: Located in the heart of the Poconos, Jim Thorpe is approximately 90 miles from Philadelphia. From there, take I-476 to Exit 74. Then take Route 209 south into Jim Thorpe, where it becomes Susquehanna Street, and follow it to the railway.

LOCATION: 1 Susquehanna Street, Jim Thorpe
PHONE: 610-562-2102
WEBSITE: lgsry.com
E-MAIL: form on website

Middletown & Hummelstown Railroad

Dave Crosby

If you're looking for a relaxing train ride in central Pennsylvania, here's your ride. The M&H provides a trip along the Swatara Creek that travels past the ruins of a canal and makes a dramatic bridge crossing of a creek on an 10-mile round trip.

CHOICES: The M&H offers plenty of different trips, from scenic outings to special event trains. Trains depart from the 1891 freight station in Middletown. Most trains are powered by a 65-ton GE diesel-electric center-cab locomotive. Aboard the train's Delaware, Lackawanna & Western coaches, you'll hear informative narration about the area.

WHEN TO GO: Excursions begin Memorial Day weekend and end in October. They run select Thursdays, Saturdays, and Sundays during summer and weekends during the remaining schedule. There are numerous special events during the year, including Easter Bunny, ice cream, murder mystery dinner, pumpkin patch, and Santa trains.

GOOD TO KNOW: Formerly part of the Reading Company, the M&H also provides freight service using Alco diesel switchers. At the Middletown yard, the railroad displays a collection of rolling stock that includes antique freight equipment, streetcars, and passenger cars.

WORTH DOING: Nothing finer than breakfast or lunch at Kuppy's Diner, a short walk from the boarding station. In Hershey, you can hop on more than 60 rides, including roller coasters and water rides, at Hersheypark amusement park.

DON'T MISS: Tour nearby Indian Echo Caves for an interesting underground outing.

GETTING THERE: Middletown is situated between Harrisburg and Hershey, both 10 miles away, and 100 miles from Philadelphia. Easily accessible from the PA Turnpike (Harrisburg East Exit), PA 283, and only 2 blocks from Amtrak's Keystone Middletown train station.

LOCATION: 136 Brown Street, Middletown
PHONE: 877-987-2469 or 717-944-4435
WEBSITE: mhrailroad.com
E-MAIL: form on website

New Hope & Ivyland Railroad

New Hope & Ivyland Railroad

The New Hope & Ivyland Railroad provides a scenic, 45-minute trip through the rolling hills and valleys of Bucks County, leaving from the quaint resort village of New Hope on the Delaware River.

CHOICES: In addition to the traditional excursion to Lahaska, New Hope also offers a 90-minute Buckingham Valley evening ride. The 1920s vintage passenger coaches are pulled by steam engine No. 40, a 1925 Baldwin type 2-8-0, or a diesel locomotive. Coach class, first-class, and open-air seating is available. Coach class provides standard seating and heating in winter, while first-class offers climate-control year-round and a full-service bar.

WHEN TO GO: The New Hope & Ivyland operates year-round. From January through March, excursions run on Saturdays and Sundays. In April, May, and November, Friday runs are added to the weekend schedule. And beginning Memorial Day weekend, excursions operate daily through the end of October. Special trains operate throughout the year, and December is filled with holiday trains.

GOOD TO KNOW: The restored Victorian station at New Hope has been in operation since 1891. An original "witch's hat" station, it once housed the railroad's telegraph operator.

WORTH DOING: While in New Hope, you can check out the many shops or stroll across the Delaware River bridge to Lambertville, N.J. Theater buffs can check out the Bucks County Playhouse, and history buffs can visit Washington Crossing Historic Park, which is about 15 minutes south of New Hope.

DON'T MISS: Try out open-air car No. 1525 and enjoy the breeze—and unobstructed views. The former Reading car was built in 1925.

GETTING THERE: New Hope is 45 miles northeast of Philadelphia. From Philadelphia, take the Pennsylvania Turnpike east to the Willow Grove exit. Then take Route 611 to Route 202. Turn north on Route 202 and go 10 miles to Route 179, which leads you into New Hope.

LOCATION: 32 W. Bridge Street, New Hope
PHONE: 215-862-2332
WEBSITE: newhoperailroad.com
E-MAIL: on website

Oil Creek & Titusville Railroad

Oil Creek & Titusville Railroad

The Oil Creek & Titusville Railroad follows Oil Creek through the nation's first oil patch, where oil was discovered by Colonel Edwin L. Drake in 1859. Along the way, the train passes a number of ghost towns that sprang up during the oil boom and just as quickly disappeared when the rush faded.

CHOICES: Much of the route along the 3-hour excursion runs through Oil Creek State Park, a popular venue for camping, fishing, and kayaking. Along the way, tour guides tell stories about Oil Country. One choice is to ride one way and then bike, hike canoe, or kayak back to your vehicle. For a more comfortable ride, try first-class seating in the *Wabash Cannonball*.

WHEN TO GO: The Oil Creek & Titusville operates weekends June through October, with select Wednesdays and Thursdays added in July and August, and October sees trains running Wednesday through Sunday. The fall foliage season is spectacular in the area and is a favored time to visit.

GOOD TO KNOW: At various times throughout the year, murder mystery dinner trains, Peter Cottontail trains, and Santa trains operate. A highlight is Speeder Day, when visitors have an opportunity to ride small railway maintenance cars along part of the line. A World War II reenactment also takes place.

WORTH DOING: Stopping at Drake Well Park gives you a chance to see a replica of the very first oil well in the United States, from which oil still flows today. The park also displays a large collection of machinery and equipment used to produce oil.

DON'T MISS: The OC&TR operates the only Railway Post Office in regular service in the United States. Postcards mailed on the train will receive the official "Oil Creek & Titusville R.P.O." cancellation.

GETTING THERE: Titusville is in the forested mountains of northwestern Pennsylvania. From I-80, take Exit 29 and then Route 8 north through Oil City to Titusville. From Erie and I-90, take Route 97 south to its junction with Route 8 and then follow Route 8 to Titusville.

LOCATION: 409 S. Perry Street, Titusville
PHONE: 814-676-1733
WEBSITE: octrr.org
E-MAIL: octrr@zoominternet.net

Pennsylvania Trolley Museum

Jeff terry

Starting operations in 1963, the Pennsylvania Trolley Museum is the oldest trolley museum in Pennsylvania. It offers a short trolley ride on which you can enjoy the clang of the gong and the rumble of steel wheels on the rails as the surge of electricity speeds a historic trolley along the line. Part of the 4-mile round trip is over track of the original interurban route to Pittsburgh.

CHOICES: The museum has an extensive collection (almost 50) of restored and operational trolleys, several of which are used on operating days. Your admission includes a short guided tour and unlimited trolley rides. On weekends, for an extra nominal fee, you can take an extended behind-the-scenes tour in the Trolley Display Building, where you can see many of the museum's restored trolleys.

WHEN TO GO: The museum is open daily in June, July, and August; however, with a few exceptions, there are no trolleys or tours on Mondays. It is also open weekends during April and May and then September through December. Special events, many aimed at children, take place throughout the year.

GOOD TO KNOW: One of the museum's restored structures is the Richfol shelter, where you can board the trolley. It was a stop in Canonsburg on the original Washington interurban trolley line. It was then moved to a farm, where it became a school bus stop, before being brought to the museum in 1982 and restored.

WORTH DOING: Washington is home to a craft distillery, the Washington Winery, and Meadows Racetrack and Casino, which conducts harness racing year-round. You can also take in a Washington Wild Things game at Wild Things Park, when the independent minor league baseball team is at home.

DON'T MISS: Be sure to view the 12-minute introductory video that presents an overview of the trolley era and the museum. The visitor center includes a pictorial exhibit about trolleys and interactive activities for kids including a small trolley to play on.

GETTING THERE: About 30 miles south of Pittsburgh, the museum is a short distance from I-79. You can reach it by taking either Exit 40 or Exit 41. From either exit, follow North Main Street to Museum Road, turn left and go a half-mile to the museum. It's very close to I-70 and Highway 19 as well.

LOCATION: 1 Museum Road, Washington
PHONE: 724-228-9256
WEBSITE: pa-trolley.org
E-MAIL: ptm@pa-trolley.org

Railroad Museum of Pennsylvania

Rob McGonigal

The Railroad Museum of Pennsylvania boasts one of the top rolling stock collections in the United States. A highlight is a dozen steam locomotives preserved by the Pennsylvania Railroad in the 1950s; few PRR engines exist elsewhere. The collection also includes about 100 other locomotives and cars from the PRR and from other railroads serving the state, many displayed in a 100,000-square-foot exhibition hall.

CHOICES: Go up, down and out: an elevated walkway gives a fine view of the Rolling Stock Hall, a pit between the rails allows inspection of the underside of one of the locomotives and tours of the rolling stock yard are sometimes available. Be sure to see recently restored PRR 4-4-2 No. 460, the engine that sped newsreel films to New York of Charles Lindbergh's arrival in Washington after his famous flight; PRR GG1 No. 4935, the best-preserved example of the most famous class of electric locomotives and PRR E7 No. 5901, the only surviving example of General Motors' top-selling passenger diesel.

WHEN TO GO: The museum is open daily year-round, except for few certain major holidays and most Mondays November through March. A variety of special events are scheduled throughout the year.

GOOD TO KNOW: Part of the exhibition hall is patterned after an early 20th century, glass-roofed train shed. The hall contains about 50 locomotives and railroad cars on five tracks.

WORTH DOING: Spend part of the day at the Museum and then take a ride on a steam train on the Strasburg Rail Road, located right across the road.

DON'T MISS: Take the controls of a diesel locomotive with the museum's cab simulator and feel the thrill of operating a locomotive on a trip from Lancaster to Harrisburg. Take advantage of a variety of hands-on and interactive exhibits and model railroad displays.

GETTING THERE: The museum is on PA Route 741 (300 Gap Road) 1 mile east of Strasburg, which is about 15 minutes from Lancaster, 1 hour from Harrisburg or Reading and 90 minutes from Philadelphia. Most folks take PA Route 30 to PA Route 896 south to PA Route 741.

LOCATION: 300 Gap Road, Strasburg
PHONE: 717-687-8628
WEBSITE: rrmuseumpa.org
E-MAIL: info@rrmuseumpa.org

Railroaders Memorial Museum

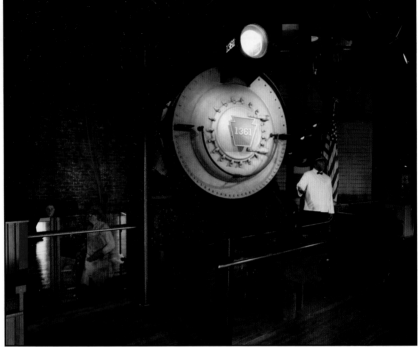

Jeff Terry

Known as the "Railroad City," more than 15,000 residents of Altoona were once employed by the Pennsylvania Railroad at various locations in the city. Today the Railroaders Memorial Museum celebrates that legacy with world class interactive exhibits, artifacts and full-size railroad equipment located in and around the former PRR master mechanics building, completed in 1882.

CHOICES: Visitors can take in the three floors of exhibits in the museum as well as explore the grounds outside that feature a re-created roundhouse, turntable and a collection of full-size railroad equipment.

WHEN TO GO: The museum is open daily May through October as well as select weekends in April and November.

GOOD TO KNOW: Pennsylvania Railroad steam locomotive No. 1361 is disassembled for overhaul in the museum's roundhouse. A member of the famous K-4 class of PRR steam locomotives, it has been dubbed "The Official State Steam Locomotive."

WORTH DOING: The Allegheny Portage Railroad National Historic Site, as well as the Everett Railroad, are less than 30 minutes by car from downtown Altoona.

DON'T MISS: For a change of pace, check out modern railroading at its finest as Norfolk Southern trains battle mountain grades on the world-famous Horseshoe Curve.

GETTING THERE: Altoona is about 95 miles east of Pittsburgh. From Pittsburgh, take Route 22 to I-99 north. Take Exit 33, 17th Street, and a right turn on Ninth Avenue takes you to the museum.

LOCATION: 1300 Ninth Avenue, Altoona
PHONE: 888-425-8666 or 814-946-0834
WEBSITE: railroadcity.com
E-MAIL: info@railroadcity.com

Rockhill Trolley Museum

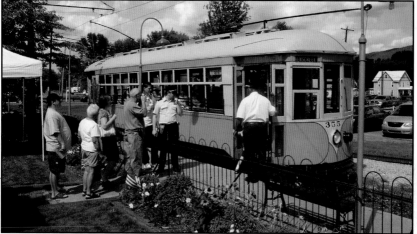

Rockhill Trolley, Joel Salomon

Established on the right of way of the former Shade Gap branch of the East Broad Top Railroad, the Rockhill Trolley Museum includes one of the nation's largest collections of historic trolleys, interurbans, and subway cars, ranging from wooden streetcars to one of the first modern "light rail" vehicles. Admission includes 3-mile round-trip rides from the museum's Meadow Street platform to Blacklog Narrows and return, with the option to stop off along the route for additional photos or rides, or to take a carbarn tour after your ride.

CHOICES: The Rockhill Trolley Museum includes one of the nation's most diverse collections of traction equipment, a total of 23 vehicles ranging from wooden trolleys to later high-speed interurbans and one of the first modern "light rail" vehicles.

WHEN TO GO: The museum is open Saturdays and Sundays Memorial Day weekend through October, with additional holiday events in November, December and at Easter. Special weekends for particular cars in the fleet are also scheduled through the year.

WORTH DOING: The annual Fall Spectacular occurs Columbus Day weekend, with extra runs and equipment on display and in operation. A food pavilion is available for private groups and catering.

DON'T MISS: Although the East Broad Top Railroad, immediately adjacent, is not currently operating, the historic narrow-gauge line is mostly visible (albeit overgrown), and can be explored from Mt. Union to Robertsdale and Wood over country roads. The Friends of the East Broad Top have a museum in Robertsdale, and do regular restoration and work sessions at Orbisonia.

GOOD TO KNOW: The Rockhill Furnace area is quite rural; the nearest concentrations of stores, restaurants, and lodging are in Huntingdon and Breezewood. Raystown Lake, a recreational lake and resort, is nearby. Football games at not-so-nearby State College can create tight demand for lodging and camping region-wide.

GETTING THERE: Rockhill Furnace/ Orbisonia is located on U.S. 522 between the Fort Littleton exit of the Pennsylvania Turnpike (toll road) and Mount Union (junction with U.S. 22).

LOCATION: 430 Meadow Street, Rockhill Furnace
PHONE: 610-428-7200 (weekdays) or 814-447-9576 (weekends)
WEBSITE: rockhilltrolley.org
E-MAIL: form on website

Pennsylvania
Steam Into History

Karl Zimmermann

With the mission of re-creating Civil War railroad history, Steam into History operates over 10 miles of the former Northern Central Railway, the line that Abraham Lincoln rode on the way to deliver his Gettysburg Address, and also the route of his funeral train two years later. This history is brought to life by a narrator, sometimes accompanied by re-enactors and musicians. Motive power is often 4-4-0 No. 17, an accurate replica of an 1869 Rodgers Locomotive Works engine. An ex-Pennsylvania Railroad GP10 shares duties.

CHOICES: Offerings include a 1-hour *Glen Rock Express* and a 2.5-hour *Hanover Junction Flyer*, both round-trips. The latter provides passengers a layover of 20 to 30 minutes to explore the original Hanover Junction station, which was completed in 1852.

WHEN TO GO: Trains operate on weekends from late March through December, and also certain weekdays as indicated on the website, which also shows the days of steam operation. The railroad offers a wide variety of themed rides, including Tannenbaum Christmas Tree Trains that allow passengers to harvest their own trees and Santa Sing-Along Caroling Trains. Other seasons feature such options as Wild West Express Train Robbery, and Sunday Brunch Excursions to a local inn.

GOOD TO KNOW: York County abounds in Civil War history, with Gettysburg and Gettysburg National Military Park only 35 miles from New Freedom.

WORTH DOING: Those wishing to explore more of the Northern Central, on foot or bicycle, can walk or ride the 21-mile Heritage Rail Trail, which extends from the Mason-Dixon Line (just south of New Freedom) north to York.

DON'T MISS: The fall is an especially busy time on the railroad and an attractive time to visit. There are multiple departures, including pumpkin rides and fall foliage trips.

GETTING THERE: New Freedom is 18 miles south of York. Steam Into History is 4 miles from the I-83 Shrewsbury exit. From there, take 851 west into Shrewsbury, turn left on Main Street, follow it for several miles, and turn right in New Freedom on Constitution Avenue. Then turn right on Main Street and go just past the tracks.

LOCATION: 2 W. Main Street, New Freedom
PHONE: 717-942-2370
WEBSITE: steamintohistory.com
E-MAIL: form on website

Steamtown National Historic Site

NPS

The former Delaware, Lackawanna & Western railroad shop complex is home to one of the East's most complete railroad history exhibits. Located on 66 acres, including the preserved Lackawanna roundhouse, Steamtown provides a shrine to steam-era railroading in the northeastern United States. It also offers both short and long train rides. The real treat is a walk through the active portion of the roundhouse, where steam locomotives are still maintained.

CHOICES: The site includes both a steam history museum as well as a technology museum. The orientation movie, archeology exhibit, and equipment displays offer hands-on experiences. For a brief visit, you can walk through the museums and take the *Scranton Limited*, a half-hour ride on vintage commuter coaches. If you have time, schedule your visit when you can spend a day with the exhibits and then ride a longer steam excursion train to Moscow, or other locations in the Pocono Mountain region.

WHEN TO GO: Steamtown is open daily year-round with the exception of Thanksgiving, Christmas, and New Year's Day. The *Scranton Limited* runs on select days mid-April through November. On some Sundays, the *Scranton Limited* transforms into the *Nay Aug Limited*, an expanded ride that travels to the Ice Age era Nay Aug Gorge Natural Landmark. Most Moscow excursions operate on weekends beginning in May.

GOOD TO KNOW: Monthly tour and *Scranton Limited* schedules are posted online about a week before the beginning of each month. The 45-minute shop tour, offered daily, provides a good behind-the-scenes look at heavy-duty restoration work underway on several locomotives.

WORTH DOING: Nearby, you can view the Scranton Iron Furnaces or tour a coal mine.

DON'T MISS: Union Pacific No. 4012 is one of the largest steam locomotives ever built. The Big Boy is the only one of its type on exhibit in the eastern United States.

GETTING THERE: From I-81, take Exit 185. At the first traffic light, turn left on Lackawanna Avenue. Pass the mall and turn left on Cliff Street. GPS: 350 Cliff St., Scranton, PA 18503

LOCATION: 350 Cliff Street, Scranton
PHONE: 888-693-9391 or 570-340-5200
WEBSITE: nps.gov/stea
E-MAIL: form on website

Strasburg Rail Road

Strasburg Rail Road

The 9-mile, 45-minute round trip from Strasburg to Paradise through Amish farmland, aboard authentic 19th century wooden coaches being pulled by a steam locomotive, recalls travel before automobiles. Narration provides an entertaining and educational ride.

CHOICES: Different types of service are available on regular excursions, and you can ride in a coach, open-air car, dining car, or first-class car. Get off the train at Groffs Grove for a picnic or to just watch the action. Lunch, dinner, wine and cheese, train robberies, and other special events and holiday trains are also offered. Tours of the shop and engine house are available.

WHEN TO GO: Steam trains are scheduled to run every day April through October and on weekends and for special events during February, March, November, and December. A rare, wooden self-propelled doodlebug from a long-abandoned Lancaster County short line runs several days in March and in November. Strasburg's Thomas the Tank Engine events draw big crowds three times a year.

GOOD TO KNOW: Locomotives pull trains tender-first on the outbound trips and engine-first on the return. Sit on the right-hand side of the train out of Strasburg for the best view of the locomotive changing ends at Paradise. For an interesting overnight experience, you can stay in one of 38 cabooses at the nearby Red Caboose Motel.

WORTH DOING: Take a drive through the heart of scenic Pennsylvania Dutch Country, one of the largest Amish communities in America. Buggy rides are offered by various enterprises.

DON'T MISS: View the Railroad Museum of Pennsylvania's world-class collection, which is right across the road, or take in the nearby Toy Train Museum.

GETTING THERE: The railroad is on Gap Road (Route 741) 1 mile east of Strasburg.

LOCATION: 301 Gap Road, Ronks
PHONE: 866-725-9666
WEBSITE: strasburgrailroad.com
E-MAIL: srrtrain@strasburgrailroad.com

Tioga Central Railroad

Sam Botts

Tioga Central operates over a right-of-way that in part dates to 1840. The ride takes you along Crooked Creek, through forests, and to Lake Hammond, a large reservoir. It's a good trip at a brisk pace behind rare Alco diesels.

CHOICES: The Tioga Central, in addition to operating its regular, 24-mile, 90-minute excursions, offers a dinner train. Ride the train's open-air car and keep a lookout for wildlife such as osprey, blue heron, deer, and even bald eagles.

WHEN TO GO: The railroad offers regular excursions Thursdays through Sundays from Memorial Day weekend into September. In fall, additional excursions operate to view the spectacular foliage.

GOOD TO KNOW: The railroad owes its good views of Lake Hammond, which it parallels for much of its journey, to a dam project that almost resulted in the railroad's abandonment. Fortunately, the railroad was relocated to the side of the reservoir.

WORTH DOING: Explore the nearby Pine Creek Gorge however you like. You can take a hike, ride a bike, or raft a river. Called the Grand Canyon of Pennsylvania, the 1,000-foot-deep gorge winds its way through acres of scenic landscape. Various parks provide breathtaking views of the canyon from hiking trails. You can also bike the Pine Creek Trail, a former rail line, through the canyon. Rafting is best in spring.

DON'T MISS: At the station, take a look at the railroad's oldest piece of rolling stock. Now an office, Car 54 was originally a double-ended, open-platform paymaster car built in 1894 for the Grand Trunk Western.

GETTING THERE: Wellsboro is in north-central Pennsylvania, 50 miles north of Williamsport. Trains leave from Wellsboro Junction, which is about 3 miles north of Wellsboro on Route 287.

LOCATION: 7 Muck Road, Wellsboro
PHONE: 570-724-0990
WEBSITE: tiogacentral.com

Wanamaker, Kempton & Southern Railroad

Jeff Terry

While it's short on mileage, the Wanamaker, Kempton & Southern, known as the Hawk Mountain Line, is long on atmosphere. For more than 50 years, this friendly little line has operated in the relaxed style of a country branch line railroad, with authentically painted and lettered equipment.

CHOICES: Diesel locomotives power trains on the 40-minute round trip, with hourly departures on operating days. In addition to scheduled trains, a variety of special events take place throughout the season, including Easter Bunny, Harvest Moon, Halloween and Santa specials, as well as murder mystery, wine and cheese, and fall foliage trains.

WHEN TO GO: WK&S operates trains on Sundays May through October. As it passes farms and orchards and crosses Ontelaunee Creek, the excursion takes riders through beautiful scenery at any time of year. The fall colors in late September and early October on the surrounding mountains are breathtaking.

GOOD TO KNOW: Every train includes an open-air car and a caboose as well as a standard, open-window coach.

WORTH DOING: A visit to WK&S can easily be combined with a trip to other rail attractions such as Steamtown National Historic Site and the Pioneer Tunnel Coal Mine. Also close by are the Mid-Atlantic Air Museum, Crystal Cave, Hawk Mountain Raptor Sanctuary, and Roadside America, where you can see 200 years of American life depicted in miniature.

DON'T MISS: Ride the left side of the train for the best views of Ontelaunee Creek and vistas of the nearby mountains, orchards, and farms. Be sure to leave the train during the layover at Wanamaker for a quick look at the original station and the old-fashioned general store just a few steps away.

GETTING THERE: WK&S is located in east-central Pennsylvania, 5 miles north of I-78, just off Route 737 in Kempton. Follow signs to the station, which is a short distance north of the village.

LOCATION: 42 Community Center Drive, Kempton
PHONE: 610-756-6469
WEBSITE: kemptontrain.com
E-MAIL: allaboard@kemptontrain.com

West Chester Railroad

West Chester Railroad, Derek Slifer

The West Chester Railroad operates 90-minute round-trip excursions over a historic route through the Chester Creek Valley on a former Pennsylvania Railroad branch line. The nostalgic train rides travel from West Chester to Glen Mills. Along the way, you'll see several historic railroad stations.

CHOICES: Ride through the scenic woods in comfortable and heated remodeled coaches that were built in 1931 and 1932 for the Reading Railroad. All trains stop for 20 minutes to allow passengers to explore the Glen Mills station. Pack a lunch and enjoy the picnic trains that run on summer Sundays. A history train provides a look at the area's history and what it was like to ride a train in past centuries.

WHEN TO GO: Trains operate most Sundays June through December. In addition to the regular trains, the schedule expands with Saturday rides for a number of special events including for Easter, Mother's Day, Father's Day, Memorial Day, Halloween, and Christmas. Fall foliage trains offer a look at the area's color.

GOOD TO KNOW: West Chester is the county seat of historic Chester County. The downtown district is listed on the National Register of Historic Places, and the town features more than 3,000 structures that date back to the colonial period.

WORTH DOING: Visit the nearby Brandywine River Museum, which features works of art by three generations of the Wyeth family. Also nearby is Longwood Gardens, a world-famous botanical garden and arboretum, the American Helicopter Museum, and the Brandywine Battlefield state historic site.

DON'T MISS: The West Chester's Christmas tree train allows passengers to ride the train to a Christmas tree farm and select their trees, which are then cut and loaded on the train for the return trip.

GETTING THERE: West Chester is in southeastern Pennsylvania, about 25 miles west of Philadelphia. Once in downtown West Chester, drive south on High Street and then east on Market Street. Parking is on the right, just past the bright yellow locomotive.

LOCATION: 230 E. Market Street, West Chester
PHONE: 610-430-2233
WEBSITE: westchesterrr.com
E-MAIL: info@westchesterrr.com

VIRGINIA

C&O Railway Heritage Center

A restored 1895 C&O freight depot exhibits the history of the Chesapeake & Ohio Railway. The center also displays a restored 1949 C&O caboose, dining car, and combination car. You can also climb into a replica signal tower and watch trains roll by. It is open Wednesday through Saturday, closed in January and February.

LOCATION: 312 E Ridgeway St, Clifton Forge
PHONE: 540-862-8653 or 540-862-2210
WEBSITE: candoheritage.org
E-MAIL: cohs@cohs.org

Crewe Railroad Museum

Housed in a rail station, the museum features memorabilia from the Norfolk & Western Railroad and a display of the Crewe roundhouse. The yard contains a steam locomotive, diesel engine, caboose, and several boxcars. The museum is open Friday through Sunday year-round.

LOCATION: 100 E. Virginia Avenue, Crewe
PHONE: 434-645-9868
WEBSITE: townofcrewe.com

Eastern Shore Railway Museum

The museum is housed in a restored 1906 Pennsylvania Railroad passenger station. On the siding are two cabooses, a baggage car, a Pullman sleeper, a Budd dining car, and a touring car. The museum also includes an 1890s maintenance-of-way tool shed, a crossing guard shanty, and various railroad artifacts. It is open Wednesday through Saturday March through October.

LOCATION: 18468 Dunne Avenue, Parksley
PHONE: 757-665-7245
WEBSITE: easternshorerailwaymuseum.com
E-MAIL: madm4jf@gmail.com

Fairfax Station Railroad Museum

At the Fairfax museum, visitors can learn about the Orange & Alexandria Railroad and Civil War history. Stations on the site played a role in several Civil War battles, and Clara Barton tended to wounded soldiers here. The current building is a restored 1903 station, and a Norfolk & Western caboose is also on display. The museum is open Sunday afternoons.

LOCATION: 11200 Fairfax Station Road, Fairfax
PHONE: 703-425-9225
WEBSITE: fairfax-station.org
E-MAIL: information@fairfax-station.org

Rappahannock Railway Workers Museum

Only at this museum can you ride the Little Yellow Train, a maintenance train composed of a speeder and various track cars, and learn more about working on the railroad. The museum contains dining car china, uniforms, lanterns, and other items. Also on display are several cabooses, a Pennsylvania baggage car, and a boxcar. It is open Saturdays mid-March through October.

LOCATION: 11700 Main Street, Fredericksburg
WEBSITE: rrmuseum.org
E-MAIL: form on website

Richmond Railroad Museum

With its exhibits, the museum highlights the railroads that served central Virginia. The restored Southern Railway passenger station includes a stationmaster's office and a freight room containing artifacts. Guided tours are available, and excursions are offered several times a year. On display outside are a steam saddle locomotive, baggage car, and caboose. It is open Saturdays and Sundays year-round.

LOCATION: 102 Hull Street, Richmond
PHONE: 804-231-4324
WEBSITE: richmondrailroadmuseum.org

Suffolk Seaboard Station Railroad Museum

The restored Victorian Seaboard Air Line passenger station features items from Seaboard, Virginian, Norfolk & Western, and Atlantic & Danville railroads. It is also home to a two-room HO scale model of Suffolk in 1907 and a caboose originally built for the Nickel Plate Line. It is open Wednesday through Sunday.

LOCATION: 326 N. Main Street, Suffolk
PHONE: 757-923-4750
WEBSITE: suffolktrainstation.org
E-MAIL: info@suffolktrainstation.org

O. Winston Link Museum

O. Winston Link Museum

Only two photographers in the United States have their own museums. One belongs to noted landscape photographer Ansel Adams. The other is O. Winston Link. A commercial photographer, Link was fascinated with steam locomotives and made a pilgrimage to record the last of these on the Norfolk & Western in the late 1950s.

CHOICES: The museum is housed in the former Norfolk & Western passenger station in downtown Roanoke. The station was the departure point for many of the trains Link photographed, making it an excellent departure point for a world of Link's photography. More than 300 of Link's photographs are on display. The museum includes interactive exhibits, Link's photography equipment, and his railroad sound recordings. Be sure to watch the documentary film on Link's life. It's an excellent look at the man and his work through his voice and those of many others.

WHEN TO GO: The museum is open Tuesdays through Saturdays. Fall and spring in the Blue Ridge Mountains are magnificent and wonderful times to explore the area.

GOOD TO KNOW: Famous for his nighttime scenes that record the passing railroad as well as slices of rural life, Link took many photos of the region in the late '50s and early '60s. For years, Link's work languished, but in the 1980s, his career rebounded as the art world discovered his genius of capturing steam at night in (mostly) black and white.

WORTH DOING: The museum offers guided tours to groups of all ages in which docents discuss the historic passenger station, the history of the N&W and Link's photography. Call ahead to book a tour.

DON'T MISS: The former station is a Virginia Historic Landmark and is listed on the National Register of Historic Places. It is one of several renovated railroad buildings in the area. Another is the Virginia Museum of Transportation, which is a short walk away. The two museums offer a combined admission.

GETTING THERE: Roanoke is about 190 miles west of Richmond and near West Virginia and North Carolina. To reach the museum from I-81, take I-581 south and exit at Williamson Road and turn right on Shenandoah Avenue.

LOCATION: 101 Shenandoah Avenue NE, Roanoke
PHONE: 540-982-5465
WEBSITE: linkmuseum.org
E-MAIL: info@vahistorymuseum.org

Virginia Museum of Transportation

Dave Crosby

Roanoke was once synonymous with the best steam locomotives in the land. The Norfolk & Western built many of them right here, just a few blocks away. While the museum's scope is the broad subject of transportation, with more than 50 pieces of rolling stock, its heart is and always will be railroading.

CHOICES: The museum is housed in a historic rail setting, the former N&W freight station. Through exhibits and rolling stock displays, you'll learn about how people got around in the Old Dominion State. It displays steam and diesel locomotives, antique automobiles, trucks, wagons, tractors, and even a post office bus.

WHEN TO GO: The museum is open daily throughout the year, except for some holidays and during inclement weather.

GOOD TO KNOW: Joint admissions are available with the O. Winston Link Museum. Discounts are available for members of several other rail-heritage organizations in western Virginia.

WORTH DOING: Stroll along the rail walk that connects the museum with the O. Winston Link Museum and Hotel Roanoke. The walk parallels the Norfolk Southern's mainline track and features displays and interactive exhibits along the way.

DON'T MISS: One of the museum's prize exhibits, Norfolk & Western 4-8-4 No. 611, has been restored and is in operation on mainline excursions. Known as the Spirit of Roanoke, it is the last of its kind, one of 13 Class J locomotives that pulled the N&W's named trains. Capable of sprinting faster than 100 mph or climbing the mountains of West Virginia, these locomotives were considered to be among the best and most powerful of their kind. Also note Norfolk & Western Y6a, No. 2156, on loan from the Museum of Transportation in St. Louis.

GETTING THERE: Roanoke is situated in Roanoke Valley in Virginia's Blue Ridge Mountains. The museum can be easily reached from I-81 via I-581/220 South. It is located downtown on Norfolk Avenue between Second and Fifth Streets. Look for the long building with the Jupiter rocket next to it.

LOCATION: 303 Norfolk Avenue SW, Roanoke
PHONE: 540-342-5670
WEBSITE: vmt.org
E-MAIL: info@vmt.org

WEST VIRGINIA

Princeton Railroad Museum

The museum is a replica of the Virginian Railway station that stood in Princeton for 70 years. It features exhibits devoted to the Virginian and Norfolk & Western Railways. It contains art, more than 100 lanterns, and other artifacts. A Virginian caboose is also on display. The museum is open Wednesday through Sunday May through September and Thursday through Sunday October through April.

LOCATION: 99 Mercer Street, Princeton
PHONE: 304-487-5060
WEBSITE: princetonrailroadmuseum.com
E-MAIL: princetonrailroadmuseum@aol.com

Cass Scenic Railroad

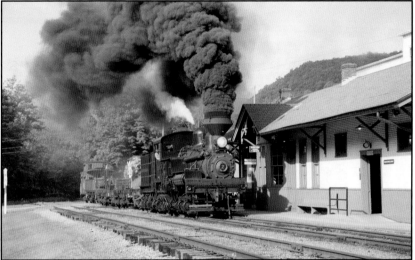

Jim Wrinn

The Cass Scenic Railroad is as close as you'll ever come to experiencing a mountain logging railroad—because it once was one. Leaving from the mill town of Cass along the beautiful Greenbrier River, trains climb steep grades out of the Leatherbark Creek area, negotiate two switchbacks, and hug hillsides to gain elevation.

CHOICES: For a shorter ride, you can take a 2-hour trip to Whitaker Station and back. For a longer ride, you can enjoy a half-day trip to Bald Knob and back. At Whittaker, trains pause for servicing, and there you can inspect a re-created railroad logging camp. Continuing on, trains powered by unusual geared steam locomotives work their way to Bald Knob, which is 4,880 feet high. The view is spectacular, and the trains climb an 11 percent grade. Other trips include a murder mystery train, and the Wild Heart of West Virginia package offers an excursion to Old Spruce with an option to transfer to a vintage, diesel-powered locomotive that continues to Elkins.

WHEN TO GO: The railroad runs late May through October, with heavy passenger counts during the colorful autumn. It schedules several special events during the season.

GOOD TO KNOW: The Cass Scenic Railroad regularly operates, in conjunction with preservation and railfan partners, special photo trips featuring Shay geared locomotives and authentic log and freight consists.

WORTH DOING: Near Cass, there are several state parks and forests, including Droop Mountain Battlefield State Park, the site of the state's last major battle during the Civil War. The Greenbrier River Trail is a biking and hiking trail that runs along the river for many of its 78 miles.

DON'T MISS: The state park features a logging museum, Cass Showcase diorama, logging camp tour, and shop tour (when available).

GETTING THERE: Cass Scenic Railroad is located in eastern West Virginia. Once off the Interstate, two-lane state and county roads are the rule. Route 66 becomes Main Street in Cass.

LOCATION: 242 Main Street, Cass (Cass Scenic Railroad State Park)
PHONE: 877-686-7245
WEBSITE: mountainrailwv.com

Durbin & Greenbrier Valley Railroad

Dave Crosby

The Durbin & Greenbrier Valley Railroad operates several separate and distinct trains in the Mountain State. The *Cheat Mountain Salamander* offers a ride into the high country of Cheat Mountain, the *Durbin Rocket* operates a 1910 Climax locomotive, and the *New Tygart Flyer* is a diesel-powered train that pulls coaches and first-class cars through the wilderness. It also now operates the Cass Scenic Railroad.

CHOICES: This railroad is all about choices. The *Cheat Mountain Salamander* offers an 8-hour round trip through remote high mountain country to Old Spruce where passengers can transfer to or from the Cass Scenic Railroad. The *Durbin Rocket* is a 2-hour ride aboard a caboose, coach, or open gondola behind a Climax or Heisler geared steam locomotive traveling along the unspoiled Greenbrier River. The *New Tygart Flyer* provides a dramatic 4-hour round trip through a curved tunnel, across a deep canyon, and over a rushing river to an impressive waterfall that puts an exclamation point on the journey. A *Mountain Explorer* dinner train also operates.

WHEN TO GO: Trains operate April through December. Murder mystery, Polar Express, Elf Unlimited, and other special trains are scheduled throughout the season.

GOOD TO KNOW: To get closer to nature, you can stay overnight along the Greenbrier River in a Castaway Caboose, a restored Wabash caboose, on the *Durbin Rocket*.

WORTH DOING: In the surrounding Monongahela National Forest, you can mountain bike, view waterfalls, and see trees that are more than 300 years old.

DON'T MISS: All Durbin & Greenbrier Valley railways are located close to each other, enabling multiple train excursions in one impressive mountain setting.

GETTING THERE: Route 250 connects Elkins and Durbin, which is 35 miles south. The Elkins station, where the *New Tygart Flyer* and the *Cheat Mountain Salamander* board, is downtown near the river. The *Durbin Rocket* takes off from the restored C&O Railway depot in Durbin. Cass is 19 miles south of Durbin via Routes 92 and 66.

LOCATION: 315 Railroad Avenue, Elkins; 4759 Staunton Parkersburg Turnpike, Durbin
PHONE: 877-686-7245
WEBSITE: mountainrailwv.com

New River Train

Chase Gunoe

The Collis P. Huntington Railroad Historical Society sponsors the New River Train, which runs all-day excursions during October to view autumn foliage. The society also maintains an outdoor museum and sponsors trips to other locations, such as New York City and Washington, D.C., during the year.

CHOICES: The New River Train travels over the former Chesapeake & Ohio main line from Huntington to Hinton. You'll go under the New River Gorge Bridge, the largest arch bridge in the country, and enjoy a spectacular view of it. Other sights along the way include Kanawha Falls, Hawks Nest Dam, and Stretcher Neck Tunnel. You'll also roll past ghost towns and old mining sites. Seating choices are coach, premium coach, and dome. You can board the Amtrak-powered train at Huntington or St. Albans. The outdoor museum, open Memorial Day to Labor Day, displays ex-C&O Class H-6 articulated No. 1308, a saddle-tank switcher, a B&O section house, and other items.

WHEN TO GO: The New River Train runs two October weekends during the peak fall foliage season. The museum is open Sundays Memorial Day to Labor Day.

GOOD TO KNOW: The town and society were named for Collis P. Huntington, who helped develop the transcontinental railroad and the Chesapeake & Ohio.

WORTH DOING: While in Huntington, stop by the Cabell-Huntington Convention & Visitors Bureau. The bureau is housed in a former B&O passenger station, where the former Elk River Coal & Lumber Co. locomotive No. 10 is displayed.

DON'T MISS: Huntington is 2 hours away from the New River Gorge National Park, which contains the bridge. You can plan a trip to the park by driving or by Amtrak's *Cardinal.* The third Saturday of October is Bridge Day, the only day you are allowed to walk across the bridge—or parachute from it.

GETTING THERE: To reach the outdoor museum, take I-64 to Exit 6. Follow Highway 52 north toward the Ohio River and get off at the first exit, Madison Avenue. Go east on Madison Avenue about 3 blocks to 14th Street West, turn right, and go south three more blocks and through the CSX underpass. The museum is on the right.

LOCATION: Memorial Boulevard and 14th Street West, Huntington (outdoor museum)
PHONE: 866-639-7487 or 304-523-0364
WEBSITE: newrivertrain.com
E-MAIL: info@newrivertrain.com

Potomac Eagle Scenic Railroad

Mark Perri

Here's a 3-hour train ride that goes in search of bald eagles down a remote stretch of the Potomac River just inside West Virginia.

CHOICES: Most trains depart from the Wappocomo station, just north of Romney. The 40-mile excursion travels along the South Branch of the Potomac River and through the 6-mile Trough, a narrow mountain valley where eagles are often seen. You can ride in open-air coaches or first-class cars. Historic narration adds extra insight into the journey. EMD F units in striking C&O and B&O heritage schemes provide power for most of the trains.

WHEN TO GO: Trains run Memorial Day weekend into November. Departures are on Saturdays with a few Sundays sprinkled in. Autumn makes an especially great time to visit this railroad, and it offers trips almost daily during October.

GOOD TO KNOW: The railroad says eagles are spotted on 90 percent of its trains. As it enters the most remote and steepest portion of the valley, the train pauses, so you can find a seat in the open gondola for the best views.

WORTH DOING: Explore Romney, which includes numerous historic homes and buildings. Possibly the oldest town in West Virginia, it is said to have changed hands 56 times during the Civil War.

DON'T MISS: The railroad runs all-day trips the length of the railroad on the last Saturday of each month, and on special occasions, runs short trips from Petersburg, at the south end of the railroad.

GETTING THERE: Romney is located on Route 50 in the northeast corner of the state. It is about 25 miles south of Cumberland, Md. Route 28 takes you to the station, which is 1.5 miles north of Romney on Eagle Drive.

LOCATION: 149 Eagle Drive, Romney
PHONE: 304-424-0736
WEBSITE: potomaceagle.info
E-MAIL: potomaceaglewv@gmail.com

REGION 3

Tweetsie Railroad, page 120

ALABAMA

1 Foley Railroad Museum
2 Fort Payne Depot Museum
3 Huntsville Depot & Museum
4 Leeds Historic Depot
5 Heart of Dixie Railroad Museum
6 North Alabama Railroad Museum
7 Stevenson Railroad Depot Museum
8 Tuscumbia Railway Museum

FLORIDA

9 Boca Express Train Museum
10 Central Florida Railroad Museum
11 Flagler Museum
12 Florida Railroad Museum
13 Gold Coast Railroad Museum
14 Henry B. Plant Museum
15 Naples Depot Museum
16 Orlando & Northwestern
17 Seminole Gulf Railway
18 Tampa Union Station
19 TECO Line Streetcar System
20 West Florida Railroad Museum

GEORGIA

21 Atlanta History Center
22 Blue Ridge Scenic Railway
23 Georgia Museum of Agriculture and Historic Village
24 Georgia State Railroad Museum
25 Okefenokee Heritage Center
26 St. Marys Railroad
27 SAM Shortline

28 Southeastern Railway Museum
29 Southern Museum of Civil War & Locomotive History
30 Stone Mountain Scenic Railroad
31 Thronateeska Heritage Center

MISSISSIPPI

32 Canton Train Museum
33 McComb Railroad Museum
34 Water Valley Casey Jones Railroad Museum

NORTH CAROLINA

35 Craggy Mountain Line
36 Great Smoky Mountains Railroad
37 New Hope Valley Railway
38 North Carolina Transportation Museum
39 Tweetsie Railroad
40 Wilmington Railroad Museum

SOUTH CAROLINA

41 Best Friend of Charleston Railway Museum
42 Railroad Historical Center
43 South Carolina Railroad Museum

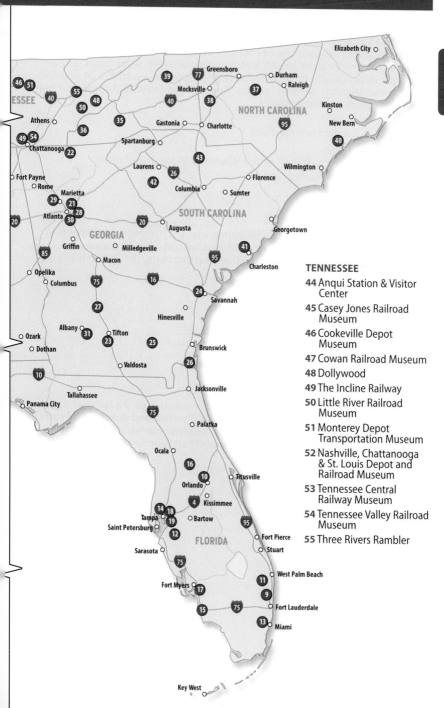

TENNESSEE

44 Anqui Station & Visitor Center

45 Casey Jones Railroad Museum

46 Cookeville Depot Museum

47 Cowan Railroad Museum

48 Dollywood

49 The Incline Railway

50 Little River Railroad Museum

51 Monterey Depot Transportation Museum

52 Nashville, Chattanooga & St. Louis Depot and Railroad Museum

53 Tennessee Central Railway Museum

54 Tennessee Valley Railroad Museum

55 Three Rivers Rambler

ALABAMA

Foley Railroad Museum

Housed in a former Louisville & Nashville depot, the museum contains photos and artifacts relating to railroads, the city of Foley, and Baldwin County history. A static equipment display includes an L&N switch engine, several boxcars, and a caboose. The museum is open Monday through Saturday. The model train exhibit, a 24 x 60-foot O-gauge train layout, is open on Tuesday, Thursday and Saturday. Admission is free to both the museum and model layout.

LOCATION: 125 E. Laurel Avenue, Foley
PHONE: 256-845-5714
WEBSITE: facebook.com/ Foley Railroad Museum & Model Train Exhibit
E-MAIL: foleymuseum@gulftel.com

Fort Payne Depot Museum

Located in northeast Alabama, the museum is a former passenger station built in the late 1800s of pink sandstone, and it displays railroad artifacts in a caboose. It also includes local historical, military, and Native American items. The museum is open Wednesday through Sunday.

LOCATION: 105 Fifth Street NE, Fort Payne
PHONE: 256-845-5714
WEBSITE: fortpaynedepotmuseum.com
E-MAIL: depotmuseum@bellsouth.net

Huntsville Depot & Museum

Built in 1860, the depot is the oldest in Alabama and is listed on the National Register of Historic Places. You can read graffiti left by Civil War soldiers and climb aboard several steam locomotives for an up-close look. The museum is open Wednesday through Saturday, March through December. The annual WhistleStop festival takes place in early May.

LOCATION: 320 Church Street NW, Huntsville
PHONE: 256-564-8100
WEBSITE: earlyworks.com
E-MAIL: form on website

Leeds Historic Depot

Built in 1884 for the Georgia & Pacific Railway, the Leeds depot was restored in 1984. It serves as headquarters for the Mid-South Chapter of the Railway & Locomotive Historical Society. The agent-operator's office has been authentically restored, and a former waiting room houses the Frank E. Ardrey Jr. Photographic Exhibit.

LOCATION: 933 Thornton Ave NE, Leeds
PHONE: 205-405-1623
WEBSITE: rlhs.org/Chapters/mid_south.shtml

Stevenson Railroad Depot Museum

Situated at an important Civil War railroad junction on the Tennessee River, the former Nashville, Chattanooga & St. Louis depot is listed in the National Register of Historic Places. It houses a collection of railroad, military, agricultural, and other local artifacts and memorabilia. Open Monday through Friday.

LOCATION: 207 W. Main Street, Stevenson
PHONE: 256-437-3012
WEBSITE: cityofstevensonalabama.com

Tuscumbia Railway Museum

The museum is in the restored Southern Railway depot built in 1888 by the Memphis & Charleston Railroad as a division headquarters. It houses an early carriage that belonged to Helen Keller's family. Anne Sullivan and Helen Keller traveled using this depot often in its early years. Open Tuesday through Friday. Groups call for appointment. The roundhouse is available for events.

LOCATION: 204 W. Fifth Street, Tuscumbia
PHONE: 256-389-1357
WEBSITE: facebook.com/tuscumbia-depot-and-roundhouse-175461209295798
E-MAIL: tuscumbiadepot@comcast.net

Heart of Dixie Railroad Museum

Heart of Dixie Railroad Museum, Alan Dismukes

The museum features exhibits housed in a restored depot from Wilton, Ala. It operates two trains and displays a variety of locomotives and rolling stock. The Heart of Dixie has been designated as the official railroad museum for the state of Alabama.

CHOICES: The museum's Calera & Shelby Railroad operates over 5.5 miles of the Louisville & Nashville's former Alabama Mineral branch line through the forested countryside. One-hour, diesel-powered excursions run every Saturday. The museum is open Tuesdays through Saturdays mid-March through mid-December. Admission to the depot museum and outdoor exhibits is free (donations are welcome). A pavilion is available for picnics.

WHEN TO GO: With comfortable temperatures and lower humidity, spring and autumn are ideal seasons for a visit, as well as the best times to enjoy the colorful foliage along the heavily wooded Calera & Shelby right-of-way. For family outings, the museum regularly operates a number of theme-related excursions including the Cottontail Express, Day Out with Thomas, Pumpkin Patch Express, Santa Special, and the ever-popular North Pole Express.

GOOD TO KNOW: The Ozan Winery offers wine tasting and a train ride on Saturday afternoons. Trains board at the winery, where tickets are available.

WORTH DOING: Located only a 15-minute drive from the museum, the American Village provides a delightful setting for a Revolutionary-era village, complete with special events and tours.

DON'T MISS: Housed in an early 20th century L&N freight house, the museum's Boone Library contains an extensive archive of books, periodicals, maps, and other local railroadiana. It is open on Saturdays.

GETTING THERE: The museum is located 30 miles south of Birmingham, just 1 mile off I-65 at Exit 228. Drive towards Calera and turn left onto Ninth Street to the museum.

LOCATION: 1919 Ninth Street, Calera
PHONE: 205-757-8383 or 205-668-3435
WEBSITE: hodrrm.org
E-MAIL: info@hodrrm.org

North Alabama Railroad Museum

Bryan Turner

Combining a nicely restored country depot with a surprising variety of early diesel motive power and vintage rolling stock, the North Alabama Railroad Museum is a hidden jewel tucked away in the scenic Tennessee Valley.

CHOICES: The museum's depot and collection of rolling stock with more than 30 pieces is open for self-guided tours Wednesdays and Saturdays April through October. The museum also runs a diesel-powered, 10-mile round-trip excursion over its Mercury & Chase Railroad. Trains are air-conditioned, and all seats are reserved.

WHEN TO GO: Excursions operate primarily on select Saturdays April through December. Many trips have a special theme, such as the Punkin' Pickin' run and Santa rides. Regular excursions last an hour, while other rides can last 35 or 45 minutes. North Alabama's Tennessee Valley is at its scenic best in the early spring and late fall when the weather is typically ideal for taking a train ride.

GOOD TO KNOW: The centerpiece of the museum is the Chase depot built by the Chase family in 1937 to serve its nursery business and the community that grew around it. The depot served the Southern Railway and the Nashville, Chattanooga & St. Louis.

WORTH DOING: No trip to the Huntsville area is complete without a visit to the U.S. Space & Rocket Center, a 10-minute drive from the museum. Other area attractions include the EarlyWorks Children's Museum, the Museum of Art, and Monte Sano State Park.

DON'T MISS: The historic Huntsville Depot is located downtown. Built in the 1860s by the Memphis & Charleston Railroad, this building is steeped in Civil War history. It features exhibits on Alabama railroads, with displays of rolling stock, locomotives, and Civil War artifacts.

GETTING THERE: The museum is located a few minutes east of Huntsville. Take Highway 72 to Moores Mill Road for about a mile and then turn left onto Chase Road for a half mile. The museum grounds are on the left.

LOCATION: 694 Chase Road, Huntsville
PHONE: 256-851-6276
WEBSITE: northalabamarailroadmuseum.com
E-MAIL: narm-mail@comcast.net

FLORIDA

Boca Express Train Museum

Guided tours take you through two restored 1947 Seaboard Air Line streamlined rail cars, both of which are listed on the National Register of Historic Places. The museum also includes a 1930 restored Florida East Coast depot, a 1940s Atlantic Coast Line caboose, and a Baldwin steam engine. It is open select Fridays January through April.

LOCATION: 747 S. Dixie Highway, Boca Raton
PHONE: 561-395-6766
WEBSITE: bocahistory.org
E-MAIL: tours@bocahistory.org

Central Florida Railroad Museum

Located in a former 1913 Tavares & Gulf Railroad station, the museum features a Clinchfield caboose and a 1938 Fairmont motor car. Exhibits focus on central Florida railroads. The museum is operated by the Winter Garden Heritage Foundation, which also operates the nearby Heritage Museum. That museum is housed in a 1918 Atlantic Coast Line depot and exhibits some railroad memorabilia, a Chessie caboose, and local historical items. Both museums are open daily.

LOCATION: 101 S. Boyd Street, Winter Garden
PHONE: 407-656-0559
WEBSITE: cfrhs.org
E-MAIL: info@cfrhs.org

Flagler Museum

The home of Henry Flagler, who developed the Florida East Coast Railway, is now a museum of the Gilded Age. Docent-led tours are offered, or you can tour the 55-room Whitehall on your own. The Flagler Kenan Pavilion, designed in the style of a 19th century Beaux Arts railway palace, houses Henry Flagler's private railcar. It is closed Mondays.

LOCATION: 1 Whitehall Way, Palm Beach
PHONE: 561-655-2833
WEBSITE: flaglermuseum.us
E-MAIL: form on website

Henry B. Plant Museum
You'll find the Henry B. Plant Museum on the University of Tampa campus in the Tampa Bay Hotel, a listed National Historic Landmark that features Moorish architecture. The building now contains exhibits on Plant and his network of Southeastern railroads. You can also view restored period rooms from America's Gilded Age. The museum is open Tuesdays through Sundays year-round. During the Plant's signature Victorian Christmas Stroll event, the museum is also open Sundays.

LOCATION: 401 W. Kennedy Boulevard, Tampa
PHONE: 813-254-1891
WEBSITE: plantmuseum.com
E-MAIL: forms on website

Naples Depot Museum
Recently renovated, the museum is housed in a former Seaboard Air Line passenger station and listed on the National Register of Historic Places. It features restored railcars, interactive exhibits, and a model railroad. Miniature train rides are also offered. It is open Monday through Saturday.

LOCATION: 1051 Fifth Avenue South, Naples
PHONE: 239-262-6525
WEBSITE: colliermuseums.com
E-MAIL: form on website

Tampa Union Station
Tampa Union Station was opened in 1912 by the Atlantic Coast Line, Seaboard Air Line, and Tampa Northern Railroads and is listed on the National Register of Historic Places. The Italian Renaissance Revival-style building was restored in 1998. Displays in the ornate waiting room of the station chronicle the history of the station and the story of railroading on the west coast of Florida.

LOCATION: 601 N. Nebraska Avenue, Tampa
PHONE: 813-445-3493, 800-872-7245 (Amtrak tickets and information)
WEBSITE: tampaunionstation.com
E-MAIL: friends@tampaunionstation.com

West Florida Railroad Museum
The museum is located in the 1909 L&N depot and exhibits a variety of memorabilia from the L&N, Frisco, and other railroads. On display are various railcars including an L&N dining car, boxcar, flatcar, and caboose. You can also see a bridge tender's house from the Escambia Bay trestle and a section shed with a motor car. The museum is open Fridays and Saturdays.

LOCATION: 5003 Henry Street, Milton
PHONE: 850-623-3645
WEBSITE: wfrm.org
E-MAIL: conductor@wfrm.org

Florida Railroad Museum

Jackson McQuigg

The Florida Railroad Museum operates diesel-powered trains on a 13-mile round trip in southwest Florida. Leisurely rides in air-conditioned and open-air coaches through farmland, piney woods, and palmetto flats give riders a glimpse of Florida before Disney and interstate highways.

CHOICES: In recent years, the Florida Railroad Museum has worked to obtain additional equipment with Florida heritage. Rolling stock from the Atlantic Coast Line and the Seaboard Air Line are now among the railroads represented on the museum's trains, and choices include a variety of air-conditioned coaches, an open-air coach and even an old gondola turned open-air coach. Special events are numerous and include a popular World War II reenactment called Von Kessinger's Express, train robberies, and trains with holiday themes depending on the time of year.

WHEN TO GO: The Florida Railroad Museum is open Wednesdays through Sundays year-round, with train rides operating weekends year-round. Mid-December through Easter is Florida's high season. The Florida Railroad Museum is busiest then, but this season also boasts Florida's mildest weather, making it the perfect time to combine a ride on the railroad with a canoe trip or a picnic at nearby Little Manatee River State Park.

GOOD TO KNOW: The Florida Railroad Museum's locomotive rental program allows you to learn the operation of a locomotive and then take the controls for an hour.

WORTH DOING: Other area attractions include Manatee Village Historical Park, which displays a variety of historic buildings and a steam locomotive, the South Florida Museum that also includes an aquarium and planetarium, and the Gamble Plantation Historic State Park.

DON'T MISS: The museum's static exhibits at Parrish are worth taking in. Included among them is the *Bradenton* sleeping car built in 1949 for service on New York-Florida streamliners and named for the Florida city located near the museum.

GETTING THERE: Amtrak serves Tampa by train and Sarasota and Bradenton by dedicated connecting motor coach. By car, take I-75 for speed or Highway 301 to see more of the real Florida.

LOCATION: 12210 83rd Street East, Parrish
PHONE: 941-776-0906
WEBSITE: frrm.org
E-MAIL: form on website

Gold Coast Railroad Museum

Jim Wrinn

With its impressive collection of rolling stock and locomotives—featuring the *Ferdinand Magellan*, a Pullman office car used by Presidents Roosevelt, Truman, Eisenhower, and Reagan—and its historic location on the site of a World War II airship base, the Gold Coast Railroad Museum is a fascinating place to visit.

CHOICES: On most weekends, an on-site train ride operates, powered by a diesel locomotive. Seating is in coaches from the Florida East Coast Railway and cabooses. Thoughtful static equipment displays include both a streamlined passenger train (complete with cars from the famed *California Zephyr*, including a dome-observation rounded-end lounge car) and a heavyweight passenger train, both arranged as complete sets. Other preserved passenger and freight equipment is also on display.

WHEN TO GO: The Gold Coast Railroad Museum is open daily year-round, except for some holidays. The museum offers special events throughout the year, including a Polar Express train ride.

GOOD TO KNOW: Currently, restoration of the *Ferdinand Magellan's* interior is taking place. The museum is home to Florida East Coast caboose No. 715, which is also being restored. Florida East Coast Railway 4-6-2 steam locomotive No. 153, like the *Ferdinand Magellan*, is a National Historic Landmark. Used on "the railroad that died at sea," No. 153 pulled a rescue train that delivered evacuees safely to Miami just before a hurricane destroyed the Key West line in 1935.

WORTH DOING: Consider combining your trip to the Gold Coast with a visit to Zoo Miami, which is located next to the railroad museum.

DON'T MISS: The Gold Coast offers a unique Train Crew Member for a Day program in which visitors can assist with either conductor duties or engineer duties for a day of railroading. Time at the throttle of a diesel is also available. Make sure, however, you make reservations ahead of time.

GETTING THERE: The museum is located between Miami and Homestead, just off the Florida Turnpike. Use the Zoo Miami's main entrance to enter the museum.

LOCATION: 12450 SW 152nd Street, Miami
PHONE: 305-253-0063
WEBSITE: goldcoastrailroadmuseum.org
E-MAIL: webmaster@gcrm.org

Orlando & Northwestern

Jim Wrinn

Orlando & Northwestern Railway's Royal Palm Railway Experience offers a variety of services on two branch lines.

CHOICES: Less than an hour northwest of Orlando's busy tourist destinations are several older, smaller towns located along picturesque lakes. The Royal Palm Railway Experience runs trains on two branches of freight carrier Florida Central Railroad. The tourist operator is based in Tavares, which bills itself as "The seaplane capital of the world." Diesel-hauled 1940s-era climate-controlled streamlined passenger cars make regular Thursday-Sunday "Golden Triangle Route" runs on branches to Mount Dora and Eustis. It is possible to ride both on a single day. Several other options include the Royal Pizza Express, the BBQ Limited, Rails and Ales Brew Train, the Royal Wine Limited, the Rum Runner Train, and a Japanese food Sumo Express. The railroad operates a busy Polar Express schedule through November and December. Schedules change, so check the website before your visit.

WHEN TO GO: Florida's pleasant winter weather make this the most popular time for Northerners to visit, but the region is popular year-round.

GOOD TO KNOW: Hotels and B&Bs can be found throughout the railroad's service area. It also is possible to make a day trip from greater Orlando.

WORTH DOING: The railroad partners with local enterprises to offer visitors seaplane flights and lake boat tours.

GOOD TO KNOW: Both branches were once part of the Atlantic Coast Line Railroad. The Orlando & Northwestern uses historic diesel locomotives, including an Electro-Motive Division road-switcher painted in the purple and silver colors that ACL used through the 1950s.

GETTING THERE: Tavares is approximately a 60 minute drive from Orlando. Use I-4 or Florida's Turnpike to access state and local roads to reach Tavares.

LOCATION: 503 East Ruby Street, Tavares
PHONE: 352-742-7200
WEBSITE: thefloridatrain.com
E-MAIL: tickets@thefloridatrain.com

Seminole Gulf Railway

Scott Hartley

Seminole Gulf is a regional railroad with about 118 miles of track that operates a murder mystery dinner train, as well as providing freight service to Gulf communities in the Fort Myers and Sarasota areas.

CHOICES: Throughout the year, the railroad offers a variety of themed murder mysteries aboard a dinner train. Along the 3.5-hour entertaining journey, the train takes you across the Caloosahatchee River over a railroad drawbridge. The views from this and other numerous bridges you cross are especially scenic, not that you'll be able to watch the scenery. You will be busy enjoying a five-course meal cooked on board and trying to solve a mystery. If you do, you may even win a prize.

WHEN TO GO: The mystery dinner train operates Wednesday through Sunday evenings year-round, but of course, Florida is always best enjoyed in winter! Several specials take place around various holidays. People who want to see scenery in daylight may wish to ride during the spring and summer periods with their later sunsets.

GOOD TO KNOW: The railroad operates on the tracks of the former Atlantic Coast Line and Seaboard Air Line, which joined in 1967 to become Seaboard Coast Line.

WORTH DOING: Southwest Florida is home to some of the world's best beaches and golf courses, and Lee County is home to both the Boston Red Sox and the Minnesota Twins spring training centers. For the adventurer, the region boasts miles of rivers and estuaries for canoeing and kayaking, and Everglades National Park is about a 2-hour drive from Fort Myers.

DON'T MISS: Several Christmastime rail-boat events combine a longer train trip to Punta Gorda with dinner and a boat ride through Punta Gorda Isles' lighted holiday festivities.

GETTING THERE: The railway is located in Fort Myers, which is on the southwestern Florida coast 40 miles north of Naples. The depot is located 1.5 miles from Route 41 and 3 miles from I-75.

LOCATION: 2805 Colonial Boulevard, Fort Myers
PHONE: 800-736-4853 or 239-275-8487
WEBSITE: semgulf.com

TECO Line Streetcar System

Scott Hartley

Replica streetcars take passengers along a 2.7-mile route that connects downtown Tampa, Channelside, and the Ybor City entertainment district.

CHOICES: You can ride a streetcar to Whiting Station in downtown Tampa, or board at any of the line's other 10 stops. Get off, enjoy the neighborhood, and catch a later car. Five stops are located in Tampa's Channelside District, four are in the historic Ybor City section, and another is downtown at Dick Greco Plaza. The TECO fleet includes a restored original Birney streetcar, replicas of Birney safety streetcars, and an open-air streetcar. Fares are charged per person per trip, but one-day unlimited, three-day, and family cards also are available. The streetcar system also offers guided group tours.

WHEN TO GO: Cars operate daily, starting at noon, on 20- to 30-minute intervals. Evening hours are extended on Fridays and Saturdays, and on nights of music and sporting events at the Amalie Arena.

GOOD TO KNOW: Tampa's streetcar system dates back to 1892, when it carried local residents to and from work, and families to weekend recreational destinations. At its peak, it operated 11 lines totaling 53 miles. The last streetcar lines were shut down in 1946. The revived system began operation in 2002.

WORTH DOING: The Florida Aquarium, Amalie Arena, the Tampa Convention Center, the Tampa History Center, the Ybor City Museum, and cruise ship terminals are accessible from the TECO line.

DON'T MISS: Public art at some stations reflects historical and contemporary designs. In Ybor City, bronze chair sculptures replicate the lectern chairs used in area cigar factories at the beginning of the 20th century.

GETTING THERE: From I-4, follow signs to Ybor City on the east side of Tampa. The TECO line connects with buses, including service to and from Tampa International Airport, at Greco Plaza. Amtrak's *Silver Star* serves Tampa Union Station, near Ybor City.

LOCATION: E. 8th Ave. at N. 19th St., Ybor City
PHONE: 813-254-4278
WEBSITE: tecolinestreetcar.org
E-MAIL: customerservice@gohart.org

GEORGIA

Georgia Museum of Agriculture & Historic Village

On the 95-acre site, you can tour 35 buildings from the state's past including a railroad depot, sawmill, and steam-powered woodworking shop. Costumed interpreters explain the lifestyle found in the late 19th century. On Saturdays and during special events, you can ride aboard a narrow gauge steam train that takes you around the site. The Agriculture Center contains exhibits related to Georgia's farming history. The site is open Tuesday through Saturday year-round.

LOCATION: 1392 Whiddon Mill Road, Tifton
PHONE: 229-391-5205
WEBSITE: abac.edu/museum
E-MAIL: abacinfo@abac.edu

Okefenokee Heritage Center

This regional art and history museum displays Old Nine, a restored 1912 Baldwin 2-8-2 steam locomotive. The rail exhibit also includes a baggage car, REA Express car, passenger coach, caboose, and an early Waycross depot that describes regional rail history. Music fans may be interested in the exhibit of Waycross native Gram Parsons. It is open Tuesday through Saturday year-round but closed major holidays.

LOCATION: 1460 N. Augusta Avenue, Waycross
PHONE: 912-285-4260
WEBSITE: okefenokeeheritagecenter.org
E-MAIL: okeheritage@gmail.com

St. Marys Railroad

St. Marys Express is powered by a 1952 diesel locomotive, or sometimes a steam engine, as it travels through the surrounding woods and marshes and across picturesque Borrell Creek. Along the way, narrators give you a glimpse into the past, and you may encounter live scarecrows, superheroes, cowboys, zombies, or Santa, depending on the excursion. See the website for dates.

LOCATION: 1000 Osborne Street, St. Marys
PHONE: 912-200-5235
WEBSITE: stmarysrailroad.com
E-MAIL: form on website

Stone Mountain Scenic Railroad

A 1940s locomotive with open-air cars takes you on a 5-mile, 30-minute excursion around Stone Mountain. Narration offers a look at rail history and provides interesting facts about the mountain. The train can be boarded from the marketplace depot in the Crossroads area. The park has plenty of other fun events and attractions including a mini golf course themed around the Great Locomotive Chase. In December, the train ride becomes a Christmas sing-along.

LOCATION: 1000 Robert E. Lee Boulevard, Stone Mountain
PHONE: 800-401-2407
WEBSITE: stonemountainpark.com
E-MAIL: form on website

Thronateeska Heritage Center

The Thronateeska Heritage Center contains several historic railroad structures including an original 1857 freight depot and Railway Express Agency building, and its history museum is located in the 1912 Union Depot. Its transportation annex displays a variety of railcars and Georgia Northern Railway steam locomotive No. 107. The complex also includes a planetarium and science center. It is open Thursday through Saturday.

LOCATION: 100 W. Roosevelt Avenue, Albany
PHONE: 229-432-6955
WEBSITE: heritagecenter.org
E-MAIL: ayoung@heritagecenter.org

Atlanta History Center

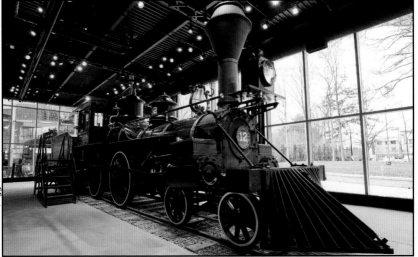

Jackson McQuigg

The Western & Atlantic Railroad locomotive *Texas*, restored to its period appearance circa 1886, anchors the Atlanta History Center's railroads exhibit.

CHOICES: The Atlanta History Center's railroad exhibit occupies a prominent, but relatively small, portion of its main building, the Atlanta History Museum. Admission covers the cost of all of the History Center's exhibits (signature exhibitions include Civil War, Atlanta history and folklife), as well as three historic houses and 33 acres of gardens on the site. Plan to spend at least 2 hours here.

WHEN TO GO: The Atlanta History Center is open year-round except major holidays such as Thanksgiving, Christmas Eve, and Christmas Day.

GOOD TO KNOW: The locomotive *Texas* is one of two remaining participants in an often-retold Civil War episode that's come to be known as the Great Locomotive Chase. The History Center includes a brief retelling of this story in its exhibit, but mainly emphasizes the broader history of railroads in the city and their local and regional impact.

WORTH DOING: For over 100 years, the *Texas* has been displayed with the "Battle of Atlanta," a large panoramic Cyclorama painting completed in 1886. An epic retelling of the July 1864 Civil War battle on the scale of a modern Imax theatre, the painting was moved to the Atlanta History Center from the Grant Park neighborhood of Atlanta in 2017. Newly restored, the painting and an accompanying film opened to the public in February 2019.

DON'T MISS: The Southern Museum of Civil War and Locomotive History in Kennesaw, 22 miles north of Atlanta via I-75, houses the locomotive *General*, the other remaining participant in the Great Locomotive Chase.

GETTING THERE: The Atlanta History Center is in the Buckhead neighborhood, between I-75 and Peachtree Road. It is about 45 minutes from Atlanta's airport by car. A MARTA bus stop is a short walk away. Amtrak's *Crescent* serves the city daily.

LOCATION: 130 West Paces Ferry Road NW, Atlanta
PHONE: 404-814-4000
WEBSITE: atlantahistorycenter.com
E-MAIL: information@atlantahistorycenter.com

Blue Ridge Scenic Railway

Blue Ridge Scenic Railway, Tim Griffin

The Louisville & Nashville's original route from Knoxville to Atlanta covered some rugged territory, and today it makes for a scenic ride into the wilderness. Following the unspoiled Toccoa River, this 26-mile round trip takes riders between the depot at Blue Ridge and McCaysville on the Tennessee border.

CHOICES: Trains depart downtown Blue Ridge from the depot, which was constructed in 1906 and is listed on the National Register of Historical Places. You can ride in either a closed-window car or an open-air car. As the diesel-powered train climbs through the north Georgia mountains, commentary is piped into the cars, and a conductor may add his own perspective to the trip. Premier class gives you first-class service.

WHEN TO GO: Trains run mid-March through December, and spring and fall are great seasons for travel in the Southeast. The region's lush vegetation has a tendency to create a tunnel effect. During spring and fall, you have the chance to see into the forest as well as take in the scenery. Santa trains offer family fun.

GOOD TO KNOW: This railroad started out as a narrow gauge line in the late 1880s with the tracks being 3 feet wide. Later investors changed it to standard gauge. The railway is the only mainline railroad excursion service based in Georgia.

WORTH DOING: For a wet and wild adventure, you can raft the nearby Oconee River or tube down the Toccoa River.

DON'T MISS: On the 2-hour layover in McCaysville, you can actually explore two towns in one. It is split by the state line with Tennessee, where it is called Copperhill. You will have time to eat lunch, poke around craft stores and antique shops, and walk across an old bridge to view the river.

GETTING THERE: Blue Ridge is about 90 miles north of Atlanta and about 80 miles from Chattanooga, Tenn. From Atlanta, take I-75 north to I-575, which turns into Highway 515, and continue on Highway 515 to Blue Ridge. The depot is on the left side of Depot Street.

LOCATION: 241 Depot Street, Blue Ridge
PHONE: 877-413-8724
WEBSITE: brscenic.com
E-MAIL: info@brscenic.com

Georgia State Railroad Museum

Dave Crosby

Part of the multi-site Coastal Heritage Society museum complex, Georgia State Railroad Museum is a destination for those interested in early American railroading technology. Located on the edge of Savannah's renowned historic district, the museum encompasses 13 structures from the original Central of Georgia shops site, several of which date back to the early 1850s.

CHOICES: The 1926 roundhouse contains a collection of Georgia steam locomotives, passenger cars, and freight cars, including the 1886 0-6-0 shop switcher No. 8 and a rare 1878 wooden business car. A self-guided tour provides information about the history and technology of the site. The operating turntable in the roundhouse is a must-see. Every month, the museum offers train rides powered by a diesel or steam locomotive. April through July offers the most opportunities with rides offered five days a week.

WHEN TO GO: The museum is open year-round. Savannah's near-tropical climate offers a welcome relief from northern cold throughout the winter months.

GOOD TO KNOW: Georgia State Railroad Museum is built on the site of the Battle of Savannah, which was fought in 1779. It is the largest pre-Civil War era railroad complex of it's size still operating.

WORTH DOING: The Savannah Historic District, a National Historic Landmark, is one of America's premier urban historic neighborhoods. You'll find fine examples of buildings in Georgian, Greek Revival, and Gothic styles.

DON'T MISS: Expand your tour with a visit to the other sites in the complex. The Savannah History Museum is housed in the 1850s Central of Georgia passenger station and train shed one block north of the roundhouse. Old Fort Jackson, a brick fort built before the War of 1812, presents cannon-firing demonstrations. Battlefield Park commemorates a Revolutionary War battle fought in Savannah.

GETTING THERE: Amtrak's station is 3 miles away. By car, Highways 16 and 17 lead to Martin Luther King Jr. Boulevard, which takes you to the museum.

LOCATION: 655 Louisville Road, Savannah
PHONE: 912-651-6823
WEBSITE: chsgeorgia.org
E-MAIL: info@chsgeorgia.org

Georgia

SAM Shortline

SAM Shortline

The SAM Shortline offers a relaxing trip through the small towns of southwest Georgia. The train leaves from Cordele, and along the way, you travel through the towns of Leslie, Americus, Archery, and Plains, the home of President Jimmy Carter.

CHOICES: There are several different excursion trains, and each one stops for a layover in a different town along the route. Trains leave from either the depot in Cordele or from Georgia Veterans State Park. You can also board at several depots along the route. SAM offers coach, premium, and VIP lounge seating. Coach class provides bench seating. Premium seating is in the *Americus* car and features tables and chairs. Lounge seating is in the *Samuel H. Hawkins* car, and it offers lounges, booths, tables, and an observation area. All the cars are climate-controlled.

WHEN TO GO: Most trains run on Saturdays as well as on many Fridays February through December. Candy cane and other Christmas specials operate in December.

GOOD TO KNOW: Why SAM? The original railroad was the Savannah, Americus & Montgomery Railroad built during the 1880s and headed by Colonel Samuel Hugh Hawkins of Americus.

WORTH DOING: In Americus, you can visit Habitat for Humanity's Global Village, and if you want to make a longer trip, the Andersonville National Historic Site and National POW Museum is 11 miles northeast.

DON'T MISS: The *Peanut Express* stops in Plains, and the *Presidential Flyer* goes to Archery, where you can visit Jimmy Carter's childhood farm. In Plains, the Seaboard Coast Line depot was his campaign headquarters during the 1976 election.

GETTING THERE: Cordele is about 140 miles south of Atlanta. To reach the Cordele depot, from I-75, take Exit 101 and go west on Highway 280 for 1 mile. Turn right and head north on Highway 41 for another mile and turn right after the first set of railroad tracks. Georgia Veterans State Park is west on Highway 280 about 8 miles past Cordele.

LOCATION: 105 E. Ninth Avenue or 2459 Highway 280 West, Cordele
PHONE: 229-276-0755
WEBSITE: samshortline.com
E-MAIL: form on website

112

Southeastern Railway Museum

Jeff Terry

This museum showcases railroading in Georgia and the Southeast with exhibits and more than 90 pieces of rolling stock. Among the highlights are a business car used to help convince leaders to bring the 1996 Olympics to Atlanta, a private car once used by President Warren G. Harding, and one of the famous green and gold *Southern Crescent* passenger diesels. It also offers short train rides.

CHOICES: The 35-acre museum features a variety of buildings and displays. Building 1, the main exhibit hall, contains excursion queen Savannah & Atlanta No. 750 and the 1911 Pullman private car *Superb*, which was used by President Harding and is on the National Register of Historic Places. The museum's collection includes passenger coaches, private cars, baggage cars, freight cars, cabooses, and maintenance-of-way equipment. In Building 2, you'll find a collection of stainless steel passenger equipment as well as a MARTA historic diesel bus collection. A diesel-powered train ride takes you around the museum's site aboard vintage cabooses, including the recently restored N&W 500837.

WHEN TO GO: The museum is open Wednesday through Saturday, March through December. In June and July, it is also open on Tuesdays. During January and February it is open Thursday through Saturday. Train rides are offered in season, and special days take place during the year including with Santa. Second Thursdays at the museum are geared toward preschool children and feature a different program each month.

GOOD TO KNOW: The museum also operates a miniature train ride on the grounds.

WORTH DOING: From professional sports to botanical gardens and the zoo, take a few days and see all that the Atlanta area has to offer.

DON'T MISS: View famous excursion engines Savannah & Atlanta Pacific type No. 750, known for appearing in the film *Biloxi Blues*. Also look for *General II*, which was rebuilt to resemble the *General* of Civil War fame.

GETTING THERE: The museum is located in Duluth, a northeast suburb of Atlanta. It is just south of downtown Duluth. From Atlanta, take I-85 to Exit 104 and take Pleasant Hill Road to Buford Highway. Turn right on Buford Highway and then left onto Peachtree Road to the museum.

LOCATION: 3595 Buford Highway, Duluth
PHONE: 770-476-2013
WEBSITE: train-museum.org
E-MAIL: form on website

Southern Museum of Civil War & Locomotive History

A museum of high-caliber exhibits and static displays, the Southern Museum of Civil War & Locomotive History displays the famed steam locomotive *General*. The *General*, a Western & Atlantic Railroad 4-4-0 built in 1855, was the star in one of the Civil War's greatest acts of intrigue—the Great Locomotive Chase.

CHOICES: While the story of the Andrews Raid and the *General* is still the biggest offering at the museum, additional railroading and Civil War displays are featured. It also chronicles the story of Georgia locomotive manufacturer Glover Machine Works, which manufactured steam locomotives, locomotive parts, and other industrial products from 1902 until the 1930s. Patterns from the casting shop are artfully displayed, and extensive exhibits cover the story of the locomotive manufacturer.

WHEN TO GO: The museum is open daily year-round, except for major holidays, and the weather is generally mild. The Atlanta area has lots of modern railroad action and Kennesaw, where the Southern Museum is located, is a good place to watch modern CSX trains on its busy Atlanta-Chattanooga main line.

GOOD TO KNOW: The story of the Andrews Raid was thrilling enough to attract the attention of the Walt Disney Co., which released the *The Great Locomotive Chase* in 1956.

WORTH DOING: Take a walking tour of historic Kennesaw (once known as Big Shanty) after exiting the front door of the museum and view a 1908 Western & Atlantic Railroad depot, numerous 19th century residences, and an 1887 grocery store.

DON'T MISS: The Atlanta History Center, in Buckhead, houses the *Texas*, the Western & Atlantic Railroad locomotive used by Confederates to hunt down the Andrews Raiders.

GETTING THERE: Kennesaw is between I-75 and Highway 41, about 30 miles from Atlanta. From I-75, take Exit 273 and go west on Wade Green Road, which becomes Cherokee Street. The museum is on the right.

LOCATION: 2829 Cherokee Street, Kennesaw
PHONE: 770-427-2117
WEBSITE: southernmuseum.org
E-MAIL: events@southernmuseum.org

MISSISSIPPI

Canton Train Museum

Canton's depot served Illinois Central freight and passenger trains such as the *Green Diamond, Panama Limited,* and *City of New Orleans*. Built in 1890, the depot has been restored as a museum that showcases the rail history of Canton and the surrounding area. While in town, you can also visit several movie museums, which are dedicated to films such as *O Brother, Where Art Thou* that were filmed in Canton.

LOCATION: 108 Depot Drive, Canton
PHONE: 601-859-4733
WEBSITE: facebook.com/Canton-Train-Museum-138674146545431/
E-MAIL: trains@canton-mississippi.com

McComb City Railroad Depot Museum

Housed in an Illinois Central passenger terminal, the museum contains almost 1,500 artifacts related to railroading in southwest Mississippi. Outside, you can view a restored Illinois Central steam locomotive, aluminum refrigerator car, and caboose. The museum is open Mondays through Saturdays.

LOCATION: 108 N. Railroad Boulevard, McComb
PHONE: 601-684-2291
WEBSITE: mcrrmuseum.com
E-MAIL: trainmaster@mcrrmuseum.com

Water Valley Casey Jones Railroad Museum

The restored Water Valley depot contains Illinois Central and local railroad items, photographs, and documents. It also displays an Illinois Central caboose and a banana car. It is open Thurday through Saturday.

LOCATION: 105 Railroad Avenue, Water Valley
PHONE: 662-473-1154
WEBSITE: caseyjonesmuseum.com
E-MAIL: jackgurner@yahoo.com

NORTH CAROLINA

Craggy Mountain Line

This operation offers a trolley ride over 3 miles of historic track from Asheville to Craggy Branch. Its collection of equipment includes several restored Southern Railway cabooses, an original 1925 Asheville trolley car, and a Tweetsie gas-powered motor car.

LOCATION: 111 N. Woodfin Avenue, Asheville
PHONE: 828-808-4877
WEBSITE: craggymountainline.com
E-MAIL: rocky@craggymountainline.com

Wilmington Railroad Museum

The museum is housed in an 1880s railroad freight warehouse, where you can view Atlantic Coast Line artifacts and a re-creation of a country station. Outside, you can inspect a 1910 Baldwin steam locomotive, a hobo display in a boxcar, and an Atlantic Coast Line caboose. The museum is open daily year-round, except for Sundays mid-October through mid-April.

LOCATION: 505 Nutt Street, Wilmington
PHONE: 910-763-2634
WEBSITE: wrrm.org
E-MAIL: form on website

Great Smoky Mountains Railroad

Dave Crosby

Few mountain railroads in the southeastern United States traverse such splendid scenery as this line does. Created from a portion of Southern Railway's Murphy Branch, the GSMR hugs the rushing Tuckasegee and Nantahala rivers and rolls out over a 700-foot-long trestle at Fontana Lake.

CHOICES: GSMR offers a variety of accommodations on two different train rides. The train features open-air cars, traditional sealed-window coaches, and air-conditioned lounge cars. A 4.5-hour excursion travels to Nantahala Gorge and back and includes a layover at the Nantahala Outdoor Center. The other ride is a 32-mile round trip along the Tuckasegee River to Dillsboro. Seating options include coach class, crown class, open-air, and first class. First-class service includes lunch options.

WHEN TO GO: The railroad runs year-round. Beginning in April, there is a train running five days a week and then every day during summer and fall. Spring and fall offer mild weather best suited to open cars and the chance to see beyond the trees and into the forest. Summer can be humid, and the tremendous foliage of the Southeast can restrict the views. The autumn color show in the Smokies is long and gorgeous.

GOOD TO KNOW: The railroad offers several special events throughout the year, including some that are ideal for kids (Pumpkin Patch Express and the Polar Express).

WORTH DOING: Steam locomotive No. 1702, a Consolidation built for the U.S. Army in World War II, has returned to service and pulls select excursions.

DON'T MISS: Try an adventurous combination package in which you ride the train from Bryson City into the Nantahala Gorge and then raft the river for 3 hours. There are also packages that include ziplining and Jeep tours to the Appalachian Trail.

GETTING THERE: The railroad is about 3 hours north of Atlanta and 1 hour west of Asheville. Major highways to the area include I-40, Route 19/23, and Route 441. The station in Bryson City is downtown.

LOCATION: 45 Mitchell Street, Bryson City
PHONE: 800-872-4681
WEBSITE: gsmr.com
E-MAIL: form on website

New Hope Valley Railway

New Hope Valley Railway

Operating from the North Carolina Railway Museum, the New Hope Valley Railway provides an hour-long trip through the scenic pine forests situated south of Raleigh and Durham in central North Carolina.

CHOICES: The railway offers 60-minute round trips between Bonsal and New Hill in covered, open-air railcars. The museum features an outdoor exhibit of railroad equipment as well as displays of local rail artifacts. It includes a variety of industrial and shortline diesel locomotives.

WHEN TO GO: Trains operate from April to December. Typically, weekend rides take place the second Sunday and last Saturday of each month. Weekday rides for tour groups and others are held the second Wednesday and fourth Friday. Monthly events include a strawberry festival, ice cream social, Brew 'n' Choo, and beach party and luau days.

GOOD TO KNOW: In 2017, the railway moved the 1884 Goldston Train Depot 25 miles from Goldston to its site for renovation and display.

WORTH DOING: Built over part of an old rail line that carried tobacco, the American Tobacco Trail runs near the railway. You can hike, bike, and ride horses along the trail.

DON'T MISS: Kids will especially enjoy the G scale garden railroad that operates on the grounds. It features more than 1,000 feet of track, tunnels, bridges, trees, houses, and its own engine house.

GETTING THERE: Located between Bonsal and New Hill, the railroad is a 30-minute drive from Raleigh along Route 1. Take Exit 89, turn right on New Hill Holleman Road, and then turn left onto old Route 1 for 2.5 miles. The museum is on the right on Daisey Street, and parking for the train rides is on the left on Bonsal Road.

LOCATION: 3900 Bonsal Road, New Hill
PHONE: 919-396-5833
WEBSITE: triangletrain.com
E-MAIL: info@triangletrain.com

North Carolina Transportation Museum

Dave Crosby

The state's transportation museum is housed in buildings from Southern Railway's largest steam locomotive repair shop that date from before 1900 to 1924. But this is no static museum. Trains run on 2.5 miles of track, giving visitors the chance to experience a 25-minute train ride that covers most of the 60-acre site.

CHOICES: Among the giant structures you'll see are the nation's largest preserved roundhouse, the 37-stall Bob Julian Roundhouse, which houses railroad displays, a restoration shop, active locomotives, and rolling stock. You will also see the Back Shop, a 600-foot-long, 80-foot-tall building once used to overhaul steam locomotives. The narrated train rides take place daily during summer, Saturdays during January and February, and Thursday through Sunday the rest of the year. You can ride in the locomotive cab for an extra fare. You'll get a unique view and a personalized tour. You might even get to blow the horn.

WHEN TO GO: The museum is open Wednesday through Sunday in winter (November through February) and Tuesday through Sunday March through October. Any time of the year is enjoyable for a visit. An annual railfan event typically takes place in summer. Summer can be sweltering, but fall is long and mild.

GOOD TO KNOW: The museum offers guided tours of the roundhouse Friday through Sunday for no extra charge, as well as other seasonal tours, like Legends by Lantern, or restoration tours.

WORTH DOING: There are plenty of pork barbecue places in the region if you want to sample real local food, and a diner is right across the street.

DON'T MISS: Take a 5-minute ride on the museum's turntable. The 100-foot-long lazy Susan is used to turn locomotives at the roundhouse, and it helps define the term *in the round*.

GETTING THERE: About an hour's drive from Charlotte or Winston-Salem, the museum is a few minutes off I-85. Take Exit 79 and then follow the signs to the museum in Spencer.

LOCATION: 411 S. Salisbury Avenue, Spencer
PHONE: 704-636-2889
WEBSITE: nctrans.org
E-MAIL: form on website

Tweetsie Railroad

Dave Crosby

One of the original Wild West theme parks of the 1950s, when TV cowboys were popular, Tweetsie has roots in one of the most famous Southeastern narrow gauge railroads, the East Tennessee & Western North Carolina. The 3-mile train ride gives the historic, coal-fired engines a chance to work and show that they are still the real thing.

CHOICES: The train is pulled by original ET&WNC steam locomotive No. 12 or No. 190, *Yukon Queen*, which came from Alaska's White Pass & Yukon Railway. No. 12 is listed on the National Register of Historic Places. Ride in a coach close to the engine, so you can hear it work up grade and listen to the whistle echo about the mountains.

WHEN TO GO: The park is open April through October. From Memorial Day weekend through mid-August, it is open daily. Otherwise, it is open Friday through Sunday. A rail heritage weekend is held in August, and a ghost train runs in fall.

GOOD TO KNOW: The East Tennessee & Western North Carolina ran from Johnson City, Tenn., to Boone, N.C., for many years. Its whistle sounded a "tweet," and from that, locals nicknamed the railroad *Tweetsie*.

WORTH DOING: Visit the Blowing Rock and learn its legend. Hike or drive through the scenic Blue Ridge Mountains. At Grandfather Mountain, you can cross the Mile High Swinging Bridge, a 228-foot long suspension bridge that spans an 80-foot chasm.

DON'T MISS: Bring the entire family along—there's lots to see and do for kids in the park. Admission to the railroad includes amusement rides, live shows, and other attractions.

GETTING THERE: The railroad is west of Winston-Salem in the Blue Ridge Mountains near the Tennessee border. It is located off Route 321 between Boone and Blowing Rock.

LOCATION: 300 Tweetsie Railroad Lane, Blowing Rock
PHONE: 800-526-5740 or 828-264-9061
WEBSITE: tweetsie.com
E-MAIL: info@tweetsie.com

SOUTH CAROLINA

Best Friend of Charleston Railway Museum

Built in 1830, the *Best Friend of Charleston* was an early steam locomotive used for passenger service. A full-size replica of the engine was built, and is now on display in the museum along with Southern Railway artifacts. The museum is open daily.

LOCATION: 23 Ann Street, Charleston
WEBSITE: bestfriendofcharleston.org
E-MAIL: bfoc1830@gmail.com

Hub City Railroad Museum

Located in a former Southern Railway depot, the museum highlights the history of Spartanburg's railroads, including the Southern Railway, Clinchfield, and Piedmont & Northern, as well as two major industries of the area, textiles and peaches. A Southern Railway caboose is on display. It is open Wednesdays and Saturdays.

LOCATION: 298 Magnolia Street, Spartanburg
WEBSITE: hubcityrrmuseum.org
E-MAIL: form on website

Railroad Historical Center

A walk-through display of rolling stock includes a 1906 2-8-2 steam engine, Pullman cars, and Piedmont & Northern cars. It is operated in partnership with The Museum in Greenwood, located four blocks north, which features a wide range of historical exhibits and educational programs. The Railroad Historical Center is open Fridays and Saturdays May through September.

LOCATION: 908 S. Main Street, Greenwood
PHONE: 864-229-7093
WEBSITE: emeraldtriangle.us
E-MAIL: greenwoodmuseumoffice@gmail.com

South Carolina Railroad Museum

South Carolina Railroad Museum, Vince LiBrizzi

The South Carolina Railroad Museum's Rockton, Rion & Western Railroad offers visitors a slice of Southeastern shortline history. A former granite-hauling freight line, the RR&W brings the experience of a casual Southeastern short line to life on a scenic 10-mile, 1-hour round trip excursion. It is the only tourist railroad in the state.

CHOICES: The railroad runs past antebellum plantation remains and through pine forests and a hand-hewn rock cut on the way to Rion. On most excursions, passengers have the choice of riding in a historic Southern Railway dining car, coach, open-air car, or caboose. The museum's collection showcases South Carolina's railroad heritage through track tools, artifacts, and photographs. Rolling stock includes passenger cars, freight cars, cabooses, and other equipment from the Lancaster & Chester, Southern, Seaboard, and other railroads.

WHEN TO GO: The museum is open Wednesdays through Saturdays, June through December, with most train rides scheduled on Saturdays. It also hosts a variety of special events throughout the year, including Easter, barbecue, twilight, and Santa trains.

GOOD TO KNOW: The railroad is more than 100 years old and is listed on the National Register of Historic Places. Its two 100-ton SW8 diesels saw action for the U.S. Army during the Korean War.

WORTH DOING: Wet a fishing line in one of the state's top fishing lakes. Lake Wateree has more than 13,700 acres and contains bream, catfish, crappie, and bass. Lake Wateree State Recreation Area also features a nature trail for a short hike.

DON'T MISS: Take a look at steam locomotive 4-6-0 No. 44 from the Hampton & Branchville. It is one of the few steam locomotives on display in South Carolina. The gallery and display train contain bells, whistles, and other railroad artifacts.

GETTING THERE: About 70 minutes from Charlotte, N.C., Winnsboro is between Columbia and Rock Hill, just off I-77. Take Exit 34 and follow Route 34 about 5 miles and turn left before the museum sign and railroad crossing. The entrance and parking lot is on the right.

LOCATION: 110 Industrial Park Road, Winnsboro
PHONE: 803-635-9893
WEBSITE: scrm.org
E-MAIL: info@scrm.org

TENNESSEE

Amqui Station & Visitor Center

A former Louisville & Nashville Railroad combination depot and tower once owned by singer Johnny Cash is now restored, serving as a historic museum and a part of the Madison Visitors Center. This unique structure contains railroad memorabilia and exhibits related to country music. Museum tours available by request only.

LOCATION: 303 Madison Street, Madison
PHONE: 615-891-1154
WEBSITE: amquistation.org
E-MAIL: execdirector@amquistation.org

Casey Jones Railroad Museum

At Casey Jones Village, you can learn about the life and legend of this famous engineer by touring his family home and a replica of No. 382, Casey's engine. The museum contains related displays and artifacts as well as those of Jackson's railroad history. It is open daily. Be sure to walk through the *Judge Milton Brown* Pullman railcar.

LOCATION: 30 Casey Jones Lane, Jackson
PHONE: 731-668-1222
WEBSITE: caseyjones.com
E-MAIL: caseyjonesmuseum@gmail.com

Cookeville Depot Museum

The railroad museum is housed in a 1909 Tennessee Central Railway depot. It contains changing displays of railway artifacts and photos highlighting local railroad history. A renovated L&N caboose contains additional exhibits, and a Tennessee Central locomotive, tender, and caboose are on display. It is open year-round Tuesday through Saturday.

LOCATION: 116 W. Broad Street, Cookeville
PHONE: 931-528-8570
WEBSITE: cookevilledepot.com
E-MAIL: depot@cookeville-tn.org

Cowan Railroad Museum

Featured in this century-old depot are displays, photographs, and artifacts relating to Cowan and the railroads around the city. Led by a 1920 Porter locomotive, a complete train is displayed next to the museum. Also on display are a GE diesel switcher and several motor cars. It is open Thursday through Sunday, May through October.

LOCATION: 108 Front Street, Cowan
PHONE: 931-967-3078
WEBSITE: cowanrailroadmuseum.org
E-MAIL: secretary@cowanrailroadmuseum.org

Dollywood

A family tradition for decades, the Dollywood amusement park is in the heart of the Smoky Mountains near the entrance to the Great Smoky Mountains National Park. Two 3-foot-gauge, coal-burning steam locomotives from the White Pass & Yukon Railway take turns leading the *Dollywood Express* train of open-air cars on a winding 3-mile trip through the surrounding mountains. The train is scheduled to operate each day the park is open, between May and December.

LOCATION: 2700 Dollywood Parks Boulevard, Pigeon Forge
PHONE: 800-365-5996
WEBSITE: dollywood.com
E-MAIL: form on website

Little River Railroad Museum

The museum holds a number of tools, artifacts, and photographs dedicated to the Little River Railroad and the lumber company it served. It displays a restored 1909 Shay locomotive, several pieces of rolling stock, logging equipment, and a water tower. It is open daily June through August and in October; weekends in April, May, September, and November; and by appointment December through March.

LOCATION: 7747 E. Lamar Alexander Parkway, Townsend
PHONE: 865-661-0170
WEBSITE: littleriverrailroad.org
E-MAIL: littleriverrailroadmuseum@gmail.com

Monterey Depot Museum

The museum, a replica of the town's earlier Tennessee Central depot, preserves transportation-related items, which include artifacts from the Tennessee Central and other railroads that operated in the area, and features other exhibits. The museum is open daily.

LOCATION: 1 E. Depot Street, Monterey
PHONE: 931-839-2111
WEBSITE: montereytn.com
E-MAIL: depotadm@montereydepot.net

Nashville, Chattanooga & St. Louis Depot and Railroad Museum

The museum houses a collection of artifacts, photographs, and memorabilia associated with railroad and local history. The grounds feature a dining car and two cabooses. Built in 1907, the depot is listed on the National Register of Historic Places. It is open year-round, Monday through Saturday.

LOCATION: 582 S. Royal Street, Jackson
PHONE: 731-425-8223
WEBSITE: jacksonrecandparks.com
E-MAIL: thedepot@cityofjackson.net

The Incline Railway

Incline Railway

This is not a trip for the faint of heart. Lasting only 15 minutes, the 1-mile journey from the base of Lookout Mountain to the top is one of the steepest rides around, with grades of up to 72.7 percent.

CHOICES: A trolley-style railcar takes you slowly up and back down the mountain. You'll pass the houses of many people living on the side of the mountain. The best place to ride is at the end of the car—you can't beat the view from there. From the observation decks at the top of the mountain, you can watch the cars ascend and descend, as well as view the Tennessee Valley.

WHEN TO GO: You can ride the railway any day of the year except Thanksgiving and Christmas.

GOOD TO KNOW: Designated as both a National Historic Site and a National Historic Mechanical Engineering Landmark, the Incline Railway has been carrying people up the mountain since 1895. Heavy-duty cables handle the duties today, but when the railroad was originally in service, steam locomotives were the power. They were replaced in 1911.

WORTH DOING: Combo tickets are available that allow you to see Rock City Gardens and Ruby Falls, as well as ride the Incline Railway. Rock City Gardens is a walking trail that showcases rock formations, caves, and gardens. At Ruby Falls, you can take a guided cave tour to see a 145-foot underground waterfall.

DON'T MISS: At the top of the mountain, you can walk to Point Park Battlefield, which is a unit of Chickamauga and Chattanooga National Military Park. The visitor center contains a mural and videos about the battle of Chattanooga.

GETTING THERE: Many highways can take you to the St. Elmo base station including I-24, Highway 17, and Highway 58.

LOCATION: 3917 St. Elmo Avenue, Chattanooga
PHONE: 423-821-4224
WEBSITE: ridetheincline.com
E-MAIL: pettman2001@yahoo.com

Tennessee Central Railway Museum

Ralcon Wagner

The museum, operating excursions for over 25 years, offers day trips on a streamlined passenger train through scenic middle Tennessee over the tracks of the Nashville & Eastern Railroad to various locations. Duration of excursions vary from 2 to 12 hours, depending on the destination.

CHOICES: Excursions run throughout the year to Watertown, Baxter, Lebanon, Cookeville, Monterey, and other destinations. Dome seating is limited and sells out early on most trips. All excursion seats are reserved and offer large windows with great views. Trains are air-conditioned, and refreshments and snacks are available. All trains have a special theme: from on-board train robberies, murder mysteries and winery trains to seasonal Easter Bunny or North Pole trips during the holidays. During each September, TCRM offers rides behind Thomas the Tank Engine.

WHEN TO GO: Excursions run on select Saturdays throughout the year. The longer trips to Cookeville or Monterey take place in the fall when the foliage is most brilliant. Tours of the museum grounds and equipment are available on select days.

GOOD TO KNOW: The museum is housed in the former Tennessee Central Railway's master mechanic's office, and it includes a large collection of Tennessee Central artifacts and memorabilia.

WORTH DOING: Only minutes away are numerous downtown attractions that will appeal to the entire family. These include the Country Music Hall of Fame and Museum, Music City Center, Ascend Amphitheater, Frist Center for the Visual Arts, Tennessee State Capitol building, and Riverfront Park.

DON'T MISS: Tour Nashville's historic 117-year-old restored Union Station, which is now a hotel. Ride Nashville's *Music City Star* commuter train from downtown's Riverfront Station. Both are a short drive from the museum.

GETTING THERE: The museum is located a mile east of downtown Nashville. From I-40, take Exit 212 and turn left. Go a block to Hermitage Avenue (Highway 70) and turn left. Turn right at Fairfield Avenue which becomes Willow Street. Follow signs to the museum, which is located at bottom of the hill on the left.

LOCATION: 220 Willow Street, Nashville
PHONE: 615-244-9001
WEBSITE: tcry.org

Tennessee Valley Railroad Museum

Jimm Wrinn

If you were to take a major steam railroad from the 1920s, shrink it, and preserve it, you'd have the Tennessee Valley Railroad. It offers a variety of steam- or diesel-powered excursions that depart from its magnificent Chattanooga station or from its satellite operation in Etowah.

CHOICES: The *Missionary Ridge Local* takes you on a 6-mile, 60-minute round trip between Grand Junction and East Chattanooga. It crosses a high trestle and other bridges and passes through a pre-Civil War horseshoe tunnel. The *Chickamauga Turn*, a 6-hour ride, takes you to Chickamauga and back. It includes a 90-minute layover in Chickamauga and a shorter layover at Wilder Tower in Chickamauga & Chattanooga National Military Park on the return trip. Departing out of Etowah, the railroad offers trips through Cherokee National Forest, along the scenic Hiwassee River, and through the secluded Hiwassee River Gorge. At the Great Hiwassee Loop, you pass over a bridge 62 feet above the tracks you just rode on.

WHEN TO GO: Excursions run every month, and except for some weekdays, there is a train running almost every day March through October. Dinner trains and other specials are scheduled throughout the year. In fall, the Summerville Steam Special takes you on an all-day trip to Summerville, Ga., for a look at the area's foliage.

GOOD TO KNOW: Railfest takes place in September and features various train rides, live music, family activities, special displays, and food.

WORTH DOING: In Chattanooga, activities include visiting the Tennessee Aquarium and taking a riverboat cruise on the Tennessee River. History buffs can explore both the Lookout Mountain and Chickamauga battlefields.

DON'T MISS: At East Chattanooga, a guided tour of the shop and turntable is included with the *Missionary Ridge Local*.

GETTING THERE: The railroad is in the northeast section of Chattanooga. To get there, take Route 153 to Exit 3. At the end of the exit ramp, turn left over Route 153 and turn right onto Cromwell Road.

LOCATION: 4119 Cromwell Road, Chattanooga
PHONE: 423-894-8028
WEBSITE: tvrail.com

Three Rivers Rambler

Dave Crosby

There are few perfect chances to ride a steam train in a beautiful part of the Appalachians, leaving from one of the more pleasant areas of a small city like Knoxville. But the Three Rivers Rambler offers just such an outing. From its departure point on the Tennessee River, it makes its way into the country to its namesake point: the confluence of the Holston and French Broad Rivers that creates the mighty Tennessee. The train bridges this point on a magnificent trestle that puts an exclamation point on the trip.

CHOICES: On the 90-minute round trip, you'll ride in a coach or an open-air car. A steam engine and various diesel locomotives provide the power. The premier locomotive is No. 154, an 1890 steam engine.

WHEN TO GO: Excursions operate around holidays and special events during the year, with an extended schedule for Christmas trains. Since the Rambler hauls freight Monday through Friday, most passenger trains run on Saturdays and Sundays.

GOOD TO KNOW: Before its return to the rails, former Southern Railway steam engine No. 154, a 2-8-0 Consolidation built by Schenectady Locomotive Works, had been on display since 1953 in Knoxville's Chilhowee Park. It is the oldest Southern Railway locomotive in operation.

WORTH DOING: The departure point is near the University of Tennessee in an area with several good restaurants within walking distance. Sports fans could try and catch a Volunteers football or basketball game, or visit the Women's Basketball Hall of Fame.

DON'T MISS: Along the way, feel free to ask the conductor or volunteer staff questions about the train or local history.

GETTING THERE: From I-40, take Exit 386B to U.S. 129 (Alcoa Highway). Drive a half mile to the off-ramp for Kingston Pike. Keeping to the outer lane, turn left onto Kingston Pike. In less than a quarter of a mile, turn right into the University Commons Plaza. The depot and parking lot are located on the left. Cross the tracks to reach the parking lot.

LOCATION: 2560 University Commons Way, Knoxville
PHONE: 865-524-9411
WEBSITE: threeriversrambler.com
E-MAIL: form on website

REGION 4

East Troy Electric Railroad, page 165

REGION 4

130

ILLINOIS

Amboy Depot Museum

Built in 1876, this former Illinois Central division headquarters building has been restored inside and out. It is now a museum that presents the history of Amboy and features artifacts of the Illinois Central Railroad. The museum also contains a freight house with additional artifacts, a Baldwin 0-8-0 steam engine, a wooden caboose, and a schoolhouse. It is open Thursday through Sunday, April through October. The Depot Days festival takes place in August.

LOCATION: 99 E. Main Street, Amboy
PHONE: 815-857-4700
WEBSITE: amboydepotmuseum.org
E-MAIL: information@amboydepotmuseum.org

Chicago Great Western Railway Depot Museum

This depot museum displays artifacts of the Chicago Great Western Railway. The depot serviced the nearby Winston Tunnel, the longest railroad tunnel in Illinois. The museum features a Milwaukee Road caboose, a working telegraph, and operating model railroads. It is open weekends May through October.

LOCATION: 111 E. Myrtle Street, Elizabeth
PHONE: 815-858-2343
WEBSITE: elizabethhistoricalsociety.com
E-MAIL: elizabethhistoricalsociety@gmail.com

Chicago History Museum

This museum traces the development of railroads in Chicago through exhibits that include the first L car, the *Pioneer* locomotive, and the history of the Union Stock Yard. You can explore other elements of the city's history in additional galleries. The museum is open daily.

LOCATION: 1601 N. Clark Street, Chicago
PHONE: 312-642-4600
WEBSITE: chicagohistory.org
E-MAIL: form on website

Galesburg Railroad Museum

The Galesburg Railroad Museum displays a Chicago, Burlington & Quincy Hudson steam locomotive, a Railway Post Office car, a 1930 caboose, a Pullman parlor car, and various pieces of rail equipment and artifacts. The museum is open April through September, and Railroad Days take place in June. It is closed Mondays.

LOCATION: 211 S. Seminary Street, Galesburg
PHONE: 309-342-9400
WEBSITE: galesburgrailroadmuseum.org
E-MAIL: form on website

Greenup Depot

The historic Greenup depot is a museum that displays artifacts of railroad and telegraph history. The preserved 1870 Vandalia Line depot also maintains a collection of audio, visual, and written materials related to these subjects. It is open Saturday and Sunday year-round. Just west of the town is a 200-foot reconstructed covered bridge; Abraham Lincoln helped construct the original bridge.

LOCATION: 216 W. Cumberland Street, Greenup
PHONE: 217-923-9306
WEBSITE: cumberlandcountyhistory.org
E-MAIL: historic1895@gmail.com

Historic Pullman Foundation

Now a National Monument, the Pullman Visitor Center features artifacts, photos, and a video that informs visitors about George Pullman, the Pullman Company, and Pullman's 1880s model industrial town. You can take a self-guided tour of the historic area or a guided walking tour, which are offered the first Sunday of the month from May through October. The visitor center is closed Mondays.

LOCATION: 11141 S. Cottage Grove Avenue, Chicago
PHONE: 773-785-8901
WEBSITE: pullmanil.org
E-MAIL: foundation@pullmanil.org

Kankakee Railroad Museum

Kankakee's restored train depot displays railroad memorabilia and a model train layout of Kankakee in the 1950s. Also on display are a 1947 Pullman coach, a caboose, and a trolley that ran in Kankakee from 1916 until 1932. The museum is open Friday through Sunday.

LOCATION: 197 S. East Avenue, Kankakee
PHONE: 815-929-9320
WEBSITE: kankakeerrmuseum.com

Trolley Car 36

Departing from downtown's Riverview Park, a 45-minute trolley ride transports you along Rockford's historic riverfront, with a 10-minute stopover at Sinnissippi Rose Garden and Eclipse Lagoon. Excursions on the trolley take place Fridays and Saturdays during the summer. Riverboat cruises are also available.

LOCATION: 324 N. Madison Street, Rockford
PHONE: 815-987-8894
WEBSITE: rockfordparkdistrict.org
E-MAIL: rpdmail@rockfordparkdistrict.org

Union Depot Railroad Museum

The railroad museum is housed in an 1888 depot building. It contains displays related to the Chicago, Burlington & Quincy; Illinois Central; and Milwaukee Road. You can tour a 1923 Mikado type 2-8-2 steam locomotive, a Milwaukee Road combine car, and a 1911 caboose. You can also ride on the Gandy Dancer Express, a motorized inspection car. It is open Saturdays and Sundays March through mid-December.

LOCATION: 783 Main Street, Mendota
PHONE: 815-539-3373
WEBSITE: mendotamuseums.org
E-MAIL: mmhsmuseum@yahoo.com

Wheels O' Time Museum

Started by two guys looking for a place to store some collector cars, the museum now includes planes, trains, tractors, trucks, and smaller artifacts. Displayed outdoors are a Rock Island steam locomotive, Milwaukee Road combine car, Plymouth switch engine, and caboose. The museum is open Wednesday through Sunday, May through October.

LOCATION: 1710 W. Woodside Drive, Dunlap
PHONE: 309-243-9020
WEBSITE: wheelsotime.org
E-MAIL: wotmuseum@aol.com

Fox River Trolley Museum

Fox River Trolley Museum

Tucked away in the western suburbs of Chicago is the Fox River Trolley Museum, where young and old can take a nostalgic trolley ride along the scenic Fox River.

CHOICES: The museum operates a 4-mile round trip over the last remaining section of the original Aurora, Elgin & Fox River electric line that once linked Carpentersville, Elgin, Aurora, and Yorkville. The trolley ride travels from South Elgin to the Jon J. Duerr Forest Preserve just north of St. Charles. A variety of trolleys run, including Car 20, which could be the oldest operating interurban car in the country. It entered service in 1902. Also look for Car 304, which is one of the last cars to operate on the Aurora, Elgin & Fox River electric line back in 1935. The trolleys board at the Castlemuir depot. A caboose and occasionally some of the museum's other cars are on display. And when the carbarn doors are open, you can sneak a peek at the cars inside.

WHEN TO GO: The museum is open on weekends and summer holidays as well as for several special events. It is open on Sundays from Mother's Day through October and on summer Saturdays through Labor Day weekend. Trolleys depart every 30 minutes. On October weekends, families can enjoy the Pumpkin Trolley or Halloween ghost trains.

GOOD TO KNOW: Picnic tables are available around the depot, and in the Jon J. Duerr Forest Preserve, there are covered shelters with grills that can be reserved.

WORTH DOING: For a unique look at the trolleys in action, hike or bike along the Fox River Bike Trail, which parallels the trolley line and crosses the Fox River on a bridge built on old railway piers and abutments.

DON'T MISS: The Village of South Elgin celebrates Riverfest in August with live entertainment, carnival rides, food, fireworks, a craft show, and a car show. In conjunction, the museum runs Trolleyfest with trolley rides and railcar displays.

GETTING THERE: The museum is 40 miles west of Chicago. From Chicago, take I-90 or Highway 20 west to Elgin. Exit on Highway 31 (State Street which becomes LaFox Street) and go south 2 miles to the museum.

LOCATION: 365 S. LaFox Street, South Elgin
PHONE: 847-697-4676
WEBSITE: foxtrolley.org
E-MAIL: info@foxtrolley.org

Illinois Railway Museum

Jim Wrinn

Just 90 minutes northwest from downtown Chicago, and about half an hour from Union Pacific's Geneva Subdivision, lies the Illinois Railway Museum. It operates both diesel and steam trains. The museum also pays homage to its beginnings as an electric railway museum by operating streetcars and interurban cars.

CHOICES: As an operating museum, there are a variety of trains to ride. You can even ride a trolley or electric bus from one equipment barn to another. When you're not riding trains, explore the 80 acres filled with 400 pieces of equipment, including almost 90 freight cars, plus signals, tools, signage, and other artifacts. Six barns contain rail equipment, and another has bus equipment. Admission includes unlimited rides.

WHEN TO GO: The museum is open daily Memorial Day through Labor Day and weekends in April, September, and October. If visiting in July or August, remember that not all the cars and none of the barns are air-conditioned. The museum operates numerous special events including Happy Holiday Railway, Vintage Transport Extravaganza, and two Day Out with Thomas weekends.

GOOD TO KNOW: IRM's signature piece, the Chicago, Burlington & Quincy *Nebraska Zephyr*, runs on Diesel Days, Museum Showcase Weekend, and several other days.

WORTH DOING: Union is centrally located between Rockford and suburban Chicago. It also offers tourists Donley's Wild West Town with gunslinger shows, pony rides, and gold panning.

DON'T MISS: Diesel Days in July and Museum Showcase Weekend in September are great times to see a lot of equipment running. Typically, a variety of vintage locomotives are put to work pulling freight and commuter trains on Diesel Days. On Museum Showcase Weekend, the staff operates less-frequently run equipment.

GETTING THERE: If driving from Chicago, take I-90 to Highway 20, the Marengo exit. Drive northwest about 4.5 miles to Union Road and then take Union Road to Coral Road. Turn right on Coral Road and then left on Olson Road.

LOCATION: 7000 Olson Road, Union
PHONE: 800-244-7245 or 815-923-4000
WEBSITE: irm.org

Monticello Railway Museum

Dave Crosby

Ride behind an oil burning steam locomotive, Southern 401, a 2-8-0 Consolidation restored over a 15-year period by an all-volunteer Monticello Railway Museum workforce.

CHOICES: Although the museum runs an operable steam engine, it has one of the Midwest's premier diesel locomotive collections. The collection includes a Milwaukee Road NW2, a Wabash F7A, a Canadian National FPA-4, as well as more than 80 pieces of rolling stock. You board the 8-mile round trip over former Illinois Central and Illinois Terminal trackage from the museum grounds. Open air coaches, an open-air car and caboose are the standard equipment on the train, subject to availability and maintenance schedule.

WHEN TO GO: Monticello Railway Museum's operating season runs from May 1st through the end of October. Steam weekends are once a month, the yearly Railroad Days event is held in September, where most of the museum's operating motive power will operate subject to availability. The Polar Express is a popular yearly event.

GOOD TO KNOW: Docent volunteers will describe your nearly 7-mile round-trip train ride over former Illinois Central and Illinois Terminal trackage.

WORTH DOING: Just a short drive away, on Allerton Road, is one of the Seven Wonders of Illinois. The Allerton Park and Retreat Center was once a private mansion. And you can walk through its 14 miles of wooded trails and gardens, with 100 sculptures.

DON'T MISS: Southern Railway steam engine 401 runs are once a month. The beautifully restored 2-8-0 Consolidation stops outside the former Wabash depot, built in 1899, which now sits along the former Illinois Central in downtown Monticello.

GETTING THERE: The museum is located between Champaign and Decatur, just off I-72. At Exit 166, take Market Street to Iron Horse Place and follow the frontage road to the end. The town of Monticello is 2 miles away via Highway 105.

LOCATION: 992 Iron Horse Place, Monticello
PHONE: 877-762-9011 or 217-762-9011
WEBSITE: mrym.org
E-MAIL: info@mrym.org

Museum of Science and Industry

Museum of Science and Industry, J. B. Spector

One of the Windy City's premier attractions, the Museum of Science and Industry provides an enjoyable, interactive, and educational experience for everyone. You can "ride" the famous *Pioneer Zephyr*, take a coal mine adventure, and view a railroad journey from Chicago to Seattle in miniature.

CHOICES: The museum has many railroad-themed exhibits, highlighted by the *Pioneer Zephyr*, which completed a record-setting 13-hour run from Denver to Chicago in 1934. You can tour the locomotive cab, and a tour guide takes you through an observation car, a baggage car, and several other cars. You'll also want to take the coal mine tour, where you can see coal loaded onto a train, and then board a work train.

WHEN TO GO: The museum is open daily with extended hours on select days. Special exhibits, including the coal mine and submarine, cost extra.

GOOD TO KNOW: There's a lot to see, so it's best to plan your day around the coal mine tour and the *Pioneer Zephyr* experience. You can bring your lunch or grab sandwiches at the museum's Brain Food Court. (The museum is not within walking distance of restaurants.) When exiting the food court, watch the Swiss Jolly Ball, where a metal ball rides a locomotive while navigating around a pinball-type contraption.

WORTH DOING: The museum is home to the only German submarine in the United States, which is a popular tour. Also, there are many other interesting permanent and changing exhibits to take in.

DON'T MISS: The Great Train Story runs on 1,425 feet of track with 30 trains making their way through Midwest farm fields, around mountains, and over 28 bridges.

GETTING THERE: Take a train. Chicago's Metra Electric Line and Indiana's South Shore Line trains stop two blocks from the museum's north entrance (the 57th Street Station).

LOCATION: 5700 S. Lake Shore Drive, Chicago
PHONE: 773-684-1414
WEBSITE: msichicago.org
E-MAIL: form on website

Silver Creek & Stephenson Railroad

Dave Crosby

This railroad offers a 4-mile ride behind a 1912 geared Heisler steam engine. Trains leave from a reproduction of the original Illinois Central depot in Elroy, and the building houses a large collection of railroad memorabilia.

CHOICES: A Heisler steam locomotive pulls several cabooses and an open-air car through farmlands and across Yellow Creek on a 30-foot-high cement and stone pier bridge. The Silver Creek depot houses the ticket office and railroad displays.

WHEN TO GO: The train ride operates on various weekends and holidays between Memorial Day and the end of October. The Train of Terror operates in October.

GOOD TO KNOW: Volunteers created this railroad on the abandoned right-of-way of the Chicago, Milwaukee, St. Paul & Pacific Railroad. Because rails and ties were removed prior to purchase, members had to haul rail in from as far away as Minnesota, and ties were salvaged from across Illinois.

WORTH DOING: While in Freeport, visit the Silver Creek Museum. It contains 28 rooms of historical displays. It is open the same days as the railroad.

DON'T MISS: Give the 36-ton Heisler a close inspection. Unlike most steam locomotives, it is driven with a V-2 arrangement of the cylinders on either side of the boiler; they run a crankshaft that moves a gearbox and wheels. Fewer than 1,200 of these locomotives were built, and only a handful remain in operation today.

GETTING THERE: Freeport is about 20 miles west of Rockford on Highway 20, and the museum is on the corner of Walnut and Lamm Roads.

LOCATION: 2954 S. Walnut Road, Freeport
PHONE: 815-232-2306 or 815-235-2198
WEBSITE: thefreeportshow.com
E-MAIL: thefreeportshow@thefreeportshow.com

INDIANA

The Depot

A replica of Salem's former Monon depot, this museum was built by high school students. It features a Monon caboose, various artifacts, and a model railroad. The museum is open Tuesdays through Saturdays April through December and Saturdays only the rest of the year. The depot is part of the John Hay Center museum complex, which also contains a pioneer village and the Stevens Memorial Museum.

LOCATION: 206 S. College Avenue, Salem
PHONE: 812-883-1884
WEBSITE: salemdepot.com
E-MAIL: info@johnhaycenter.org

Hoosier Valley Railroad Museum

The museum sits in an area rich in railroad history. HVRM brings the past back to life with historic equipment that served not only North Judson, but northern Indiana, Illinois, and Michigan. Open Saturdays year-round, the museum has more than 30 pieces of rolling stock. It also offers 45-minute train rides every Saturday May through October and for special events.

LOCATION: 507 Mulberry Street, North Judson
PHONE: 574-896-3950
WEBSITE: hoosiervalley.org
E-MAIL: questions@hoosiervalley.org

Linden Depot Museum

The Linden Depot Museum contains memorabilia from the two railroads it served, the Nickel Plate Road and the Monon Railroad. It displays a caboose from the NKP, several railcars, and other pieces of equipment. Built in 1907, it is listed on the National Register of Historic Places. It is open Fridays through Sundays April through October with special hours for winter holidays.

LOCATION: 520 N. Main Street, Linden
PHONE: 765-427-3630
WEBSITE: lindendepotmuseum.org
E-MAIL: lindendepotmuseum@gmail.com

Madison Railroad Station

This restored 1895 Pennsylvania Railroad station is known for its unique octagon waiting room with stained glass windows. Exhibits describe the railroad station and Madison's railroad incline. You can visit an agent's office, try the functional telegraph key, and examine a restored, wooden caboose. It is open March and April, and November through Mid-December, Tuesday through Friday; May through October, Monday through Saturday; closed mid-December through February.

LOCATION: 615 W. First Street, Madison
PHONE: 812-265-2335
WEBSITE: jchshc.net
E-MAIL: info@jchshc.org

Monon Connection Museum

The museum features a completely furnished, full-size replica of an Illinois Central depot and outdoor displays. Exhibits include a large collection of dining car china, hundreds of hand-held lanterns, and restored brass steam locomotive bells and whistles. It is open Tuesday through Sunday. The Whistle Stop restaurant adjoins the museum.

LOCATION: 10012 N. Highway 421, Monon
PHONE: 219-253-4101
WEBSITE: mononconnection.com
E-MAIL: form on website

National New York Central Railroad Museum

You begin your journey through the history of the New York Central by entering through a 1915 passenger coach. In the main gallery, which is a 100-year-old freight house, hands-on exhibits let you construct track and operate a steam locomotive. Outside, the museum's collection of locomotives and rolling stock includes a New York Central Mohawk 4-8-2 and a Pennsylvania Railroad GG1. The museum is closed Mondays and major holidays.

LOCATION: 721 S. Main Street, Elkhart
PHONE: 574-294-3001
WEBSITE: nycrrmuseum.org
E-MAIL: info@nycrrmuseum.org

Nickel Plate Express

Unveiled in 2018, the Nickel Plate Express runs on 12 miles of track between Atlanta and Noblesville. The trains run Saturday and Sunday with special themed trains at various times of the year. Equipment includes ex-Santa Fe Hi-Level passenger cars built for the El Capitan luxury train.

LOCATION: 105 E. Main St., Atlanta
PHONE: 317-285-0682
WEBSITE: nickelplateexpress.com
E-MAIL: info@nickelplateexpress.net

Indiana

Princeton Train Depot

The Princeton depot features artifacts of the railroads that served the area and displays a caboose. The restored Chicago & Eastern Illinois passenger depot was built in 1875. The Gibson County Visitors Bureau is also housed in the depot. It is open Monday through Friday.

LOCATION: 702 W. Broadway Street, Princeton
PHONE: 812-385-0999
WEBSITE: gibsoncountyin.org
E-MAIL: info@gibsoncountyin.org

Spirit of Jasper

Owned by the city, the Spirit of Jasper operates an excursion to French Lick as well as a dinner train. The excursion allows you to explore the Indiana Railway Museum, French Lick Springs Resort & Casino, and the West Baden Springs Hotel. Aboard the dinner train, you can partake in a meal provided by a local German restaurant. Fall foliage, Strassenfest, and other dinner excursions also run.

LOCATION: 201 Mill Street, Jasper
PHONE: 812-482-5959 or 812-482-9229
WEBSITE: spiritofjasper.com
E-MAIL: form on website

Wabash Valley Railroaders Museum

The museum features two interlocking towers with operating machines, a depot, a Pennsylvania Railroad caboose, and a viewing platform adjacent to CSX Transportation main lines. Haley Tower was one of the last manned interlocking towers in the Midwest, and the 1910 Spring Hill Tower was the last lever interlocking machine on the Canadian Pacific. It is open weekends May through October.

LOCATION: 1316 Plum Street, Terre Haute
PHONE: 812-238-9958
WEBSITE: wvrrm.org
E-MAIL: wvrrminfo@gmail.com

Fort Wayne Railroad Historical Society

Samuel Phillips

The Fort Wayne Railroad Historical Society operates one of the nation's largest operational, mainline steam locomotives, Nickel Plate Road 2-8-4 No. 765, which runs on excursions in the Northeast, Midwest, and Chicago areas.

CHOICES: On weekends when the locomotive is not on tour, you can tour the shop and check out the 400-ton No. 765 and other pieces of historic rail equipment. Make sure to talk with volunteers who restore everything from baggage carts to locomotives.

WHEN TO GO: During the society's annual open house, you can view No. 765 and ride aboard a vintage caboose. Santa trains run in December. The locomotive typically visits the Cuyahoga Valley Scenic Railroad between Cleveland, Ohio, and Akron, Ohio, each September. Check the website for current details.

GOOD TO KNOW: No. 765, a 1944 Berkshire type and a product of the Lima (Ohio) Locomotive Works, is one of the most modern and powerful steam locomotives still capable of operation. It was restored to operation in 1979 after years of work and, before that, display in Fort Wayne.

WORTH DOING: Excursions typically offer coach, lounge, and first-class seating. A ride in a dome car is an exceptional experience that provides a unique vantage point.

DON'T MISS: You can track No. 765 using a GPS app available from the society's website.

GETTING THERE: The restoration shop is just east of Fort Wayne in the village of New Haven. From Fort Wayne, take I-469 to Exit 21. Turn right on Harper Road, then right on Ryan Road, and left on Edgerton Road.

LOCATION: 15808 Edgerton Road, New Haven
PHONE: 260-493-0765
WEBSITE: fortwaynerailroad.org
E-MAIL: contact@fwrhs.org

French Lick Scenic Railway

Steve Patterson

For many years, the Southern Railway and the Monon Railroad brought scores of vacationers to the mineral spring baths in the southern Indiana hill country. Today, the museum offers an 18-mile diesel-powered round trip that leaves from the historic 1907 depot that served both railroads and travels through beautiful forested country and the 2,200-foot Burton tunnel.

CHOICES: Located in a historic passenger depot, the Indiana Railway Museum operates the French Lick Scenic Railway. Two-hour excursions through the Hoosier National Forest travel along lakes and limestone cuts. The museum also features an impressive collection of equipment that includes more that 65 pieces of rolling stock, including steam and diesel locomotives.

WHEN TO GO: The museum is open year-round. Trains begin operating in March with special trains running throughout the year including train robberies and the popular Polar Express in November and December. Trips in October feature beautiful fall colors of the scenic Hoosier National Forest.

GOOD TO KNOW: French Lick is on Eastern Standard Time, which is good to remember when visiting from the Central time zone. You are still able to soak in the sulfur-rich spring water with 25-minute baths at the spas of the French Lick Springs Hotel and the West Baden Springs Hotel.

WORTH DOING: Southern Indiana is home to a variety of caves ready for exploring, such as Squire Boone Caverns, Wyandotte Caves, and Marengo Cave.

DON'T MISS: Be sure to check out the former Louisville, New Albany & Corydon Railroad boxcar No. 14023 repainted as a Pluto water car that shipped Pluto mineral water, which was bottled by the French Lick Springs Hotel.

GETTING THERE: French Lick is in southern Indiana, easily accessible from Bloomington (60 miles), Columbus (90 miles), and Indianapolis (110 miles). From Indianapolis or Bloomington, take Highway 37 to Highway 56. Take Highway 56 west to French Lick and the museum. From Columbus, take I-65 to Highway 56.

LOCATION: 8594 W. State Road 56, French Lick
PHONE: 800-748-7246
WEBSITE: frenchlickscenicrailway.org
E-MAIL: info@frenchlickrr.org

Hesston Steam Museum

Dave Crosby

This museum runs steam trains of two narrow gauges, 2-foot and 3-foot, in a parklike setting. It also offers miniature live steam operations and other steam-powered attractions including a sawmill and a steam crane.

CHOICES: Ride a steam locomotive, in your choice of gauges, through the museum's 155-acre site. Each train travels over a different route. Wander through a unique collection of steam equipment. Be sure to look for a 1929 Shay logging locomotive and a Czech 0-4-0 built in 1940. On special days, watch the 92-ton, steam-powered log crane feed logs to the steam-powered lumber mill.

WHEN TO GO: Trains run weekends and holidays Memorial Day through Labor Day and then on several Sundays in October. On Memorial Day weekend and over the July 4th holiday, additional steam equipment runs, the sawmill operates, and other activities take place. In fall, ride the ghost train if you dare, and in December, try the Candy Cane Express. Several other special days take place during the season.

GOOD TO KNOW: Keep an eye out for a Kiddieland train ride. The museum operates two of the locomotives from the former suburban Chicago amusement park. The locomotives are coal-powered steam engines.

WORTH DOING: You can visit the La Porte County Historical Society Museum, which contains 80,000 artifacts. Among them are more than 800 antique firearms and weapons.

DON'T MISS: At the steam museum, Doc's 1930's vintage soda fountain serves up ice cream treats in a historic setting. The annual Hesston Steam & Power Show takes place over Labor Day weekend. In addition to train rides, the event features the operation of antique farm equipment, tractors, and other machinery.

GETTING THERE: The museum is in northern Indiana near the Michigan border and is about a 90-minute drive from Chicago. It is easily accessible from either I-94 (Exit 1) or the Indiana toll road (Exit 49) on County Road 1000.

LOCATION: 1201 E. County Road 1000 North, La Porte
PHONE: 219-778-2783 or 219-872-5055
WEBSITE: hesston.org
E-MAIL: ted.rita@hesston.org

Whitewater Valley Railroad

WVRR Collection/Thomas Bookout

This surprising 19-mile line travels from Connersville to Metamora with much of the trip near the Whitewater Canal. The scenic route features excellent views of area forests and farms.

CHOICES: The railroad offers standard, open-window coaches as well as caboose rides on its 32-mile, 5-hour round trip. A 2-hour layover gives you a chance to tour Metamora, a restored canal town.

WHEN TO GO: Regular excursion trains operate on Saturdays and Sundays from May through October. During the year, watch for special event trains, such as the Metamora Canal Days Limited, the Wild West Train, a dinner train, and fall foliage trains. Other events are themed around holidays and children's activities.

GOOD TO KNOW: Look for New York Central transfer caboose No. 18278 and try to ride aboard this unique railcar.

WORTH DOING: Metamora is a popular getaway spot with plenty of art galleries, shops, and restaurants. Take time to explore the city's historic buildings. You can also watch its water-powered grist mill in action and take a boat ride along the canal. Enjoy Canal Days in early October with a train ride, shopping, food, and arts and crafts.

DON'T MISS: Inspect the operating diesel built by the Lima-Hamilton Locomotive Works. Believed to be the last of its kind in operation today, locomotive No. 25 was one of only 174 diesels built by this company. The museum also owns three others from this builder, making this the largest collection of Lima-built diesel locomotives in existence.

GETTING THERE: Connersville is about 65 miles southeast of Indianapolis and is accessible from all directions. If coming from the north, take Highway 1 off I-70 into Connersville. The depot is on your left between Fourth and Fifth Streets.

LOCATION: 455 Market Street, Connersville
PHONE: 765-825-2054
WEBSITE: whitewatervalleyrr.org
E-MAIL: form on website

MICHIGAN

Clinton Northern Railway Museum

Housed in a historic Grand Trunk depot, the museum's artifacts include tools, signs, and station agent items. A 1902 Barney & Smith sleeper car, a 1903 post office-baggage car, a 1926 Ann Arbor maintenance-of-way crew car, and a 1927 wooden caboose are also on display. It is open Sundays May through October.

LOCATION: 107 E. Railroad Street, St. Johns
PHONE: 989-224-6134
WEBSITE: clintonnorthernrailway.org
E-MAIL: mccampbell60@gmail.com

Coopersville & Marne Railway

Powered by an EMD SW9 diesel locomotive, this railway's 14-mile, 90-minute round-trip excursion travels through farmland and over an open-deck girder bridge. At Marne, you can watch the engine uncouple, run along a passing siding, and couple to the other end. Excursions run Wednesdays and Saturdays May through September with special theme trains in other months. Look for a new station at 306 E. Main Street.

LOCATION: 311 Danforth Street, Coopersville
PHONE: 616-997-7000
WEBSITE: coopersvilleandmarne.org
E-MAIL: info@mitrain.net

Durand Union Station

This 100-year-old depot museum was the second busiest depot in Michigan, and its lower level has been restored to its former glory with terrazzo floors and oak trim. Still functioning as an Amtrak depot, the building also houses the Michigan Railroad History Museum. Open Tuesday through Sunday year-round, closed Sundays in February, the museum contains changing exhibits on state and local railroading.

LOCATION: 200 Railroad Street, Durand
PHONE: 989-288-3561
WEBSITE: durandstation.org
E-MAIL: form on website

Michigan

Flushing Area Museum

The museum's collection includes permanent displays of railroad artifacts as well as local historical exhibits. It is housed in the Flushing depot, which was built in 1888 and provided passenger service until 1971. The building was restored to its former appearance by the Flushing Area Historical Society. It is open Sundays, April to December.

LOCATION: 431 W. Main Street, Flushing
PHONE: 810-487-0814
WEBSITE: flushinghistorical.org
E-MAIL: fahs@att.net

148

Houghton County Historical Museum

The museum includes the restored Mineral Range depot, which contains a collection of Copper County railroad artifacts, and other historic buildings. The museum operates the Lake Linden & Torch Lake Railroad. A narrow gauge 0-4-0 Porter steam locomotive or a diesel engine takes you on a half-mile ride. The museum is open June through September. Trains run on Saturdays and Sundays.

LOCATION: 53102 Highway M-26, Lake Linden
PHONE: 906-296-4121
WEBSITE: houghtonhistory.org
E-MAIL: info@houghtonhistory.org

Michigan Transit Museum

The Michigan Transit Museum is housed in a depot restored to its 1900 appearance and includes railroading exhibits from that time. The transit museum displays several locomotives and railcars. It also offers a 30-minute, round-trip train ride that departs from Joy Park. Located near the Selfridge Military Air Museum, the transit museum is open weekends year-round, and trains run Sundays, June through October.

LOCATION: 200 Grand Avenue, Mount Clemens
PHONE: 586-463-1863
WEBSITE: michigantransitmuseum.org
E-MAIL: Riley.allendorf@michigantransitmuseum.org

New Buffalo Railroad Museum

The museum is housed in a replica of a Pere Marquette depot that stood nearby. It features artifacts from the Pere Marquette, Chesapeake & Ohio, and CSX. Pullman Company memorabilia is also on display. You can walk through a restored Chessie boxcar and a Pullman troop sleeper, which contains World War II artifacts. It is open Saturday and Sunday April through October.

LOCATION: 530 S. Whittaker Street, New Buffalo
PHONE: 269-469-8010
WEBSITE: new-buffalo-railroad-museum.org
E-MAIL: ask@new-buffalo-railroad-museum.org

Old Road Dinner Train

Aboard dining cars from the 1930s, the train provides dining and entertainment from two locations, Blissfield and Charlotte. The murder mystery dinner trains provide a five-course dinner as you participate in a comical, interactive mystery show. Other excursions, both themed and non-themed, are available.

LOCATION: 301 E. Adrian Street, Blissfield
PHONE: 888-467-2451
WEBSITE: murdermysterydinnertrain.com
E-MAIL: form on website

Saginaw Railway Museum

Located in a restored 1907 Pere Marquette depot, this museum displays an RS1 locomotive, several cabooses, a combine coach, and various boxcars. It includes an 1898 armstrong interlocking tower as well as a variety of smaller artifacts. It is open the first and third Saturdays May through November.

LOCATION: 900 Maple Street, Saginaw
PHONE: 989-790-7994
WEBSITE: facebook.com/saginawrailwaymuseum
E-MAIL: info@saginawrailwaymuseum.org

Southern Michigan Railroad

The railroad offers passenger excursions between Clinton and Tecumseh. Along the 2-hour round trip, the train crosses River Raisin and the Red Mill Pond on a trestle. The railroad also operates a museum. Rides begin in May and go into December with Santa specials. In fall, you can see the colors or travel to the Clinton Fall Festival and Appleumpkin Festival. Some rides leave from Tecumseh.

LOCATION: 320 S. Division Street, Clinton
PHONE: 517-456-7677
WEBSITE: southernmichiganrailroad.com
E-MAIL: ridesmr@gmail.com

SS City of Milwaukee

The SS *City of Milwaukee*, a national historic landmark, is the last surviving traditional Great Lakes railroad car ferry. Built in 1931, the *City of Milwaukee* served the Grand Trunk Western and Ann Arbor Railroads. The car deck houses five Ann Arbor boxcars that serve as exhibit spaces and a theater. The Coast Guard cutter *Acacia* is docked on site, and tours of both ships are offered. In summer, the car ferry provides bed & breakfast service, and in fall, it becomes a ghost ship. Tours are offered May through September.

LOCATION: 99 Arthur Street, Manistee
PHONE: 231-723-3587
WEBSITE: carferry.com

Tri-Cities Historical Museum

The Tri-Cities Historical Museum operates out of two buildings including a former Grand Trunk Western depot that was built in 1870. Located on the banks of the Grand River, the Depot Museum of Transportation contains exhibits related to railroad, maritime, and other forms of transportation. On display is a Pere Marquette Railway steam locomotive. The Depot Museum of Transportation closes during winter.

LOCATION: 200 Washington Ave., Grand Haven
PHONE: 616-842-0700
WEBSITE: tri-citiesmuseum.org
E-MAIL: form on site

Wheels of History

This history museum is housed in a pre-1905 wooden railroad passenger car and a caboose. Exhibits include photographs and artifacts of area railroads, logging, Lake Superior fishing boats, and everyday life in early Brimley. It is open weekends mid-May to mid-October, with an expanded schedule (Wednesday through Sunday) during summer.

LOCATION: Depot Street and M-221, Brimley
PHONE: 906-248-3665
WEBSITE: baymillsbrimleyhistory.org
E-MAIL: euprussell@yahoo.com

Greenfield Village at The Henry Ford

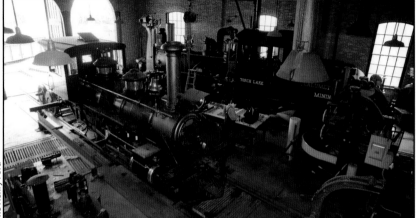

The Henry Ford

The Henry Ford claims to be America's greatest history attraction, and even though it's in the capital of—and shrine to—the automobile, railroads are well represented here. The centerpiece for this is the Detroit, Toledo & Milwaukee roundhouse, a reconstruction of the original in Marshall, Mich., believed to be one of only seven 19th century roundhouses remaining. A steam railroad encircles the historic 90-acre village.

CHOICES: You can ride the train around the village in open-air cars on a 30-minute narrated trip. Departing from the 1859 Smiths Creek depot, the train also makes stops at strategic locations throughout the village. The roundhouse includes hands-on railroading displays and a 1902 Atlantic engine. A mezzanine provides an excellent vantage point from where you can see work going on. Also, be sure to go inside the Henry Ford museum to view railroad cars and locomotives, including a Chesapeake & Ohio 2-6-6-6 Allegheny type, one of the largest steam locomotives ever built.

WHEN TO GO: Greenfield Village is open daily mid-April until early November. In mid-November, it is open Friday through Sunday, and in December, it is open select evenings for Holiday Nights. It is closed the remainder of the year.

GOOD TO KNOW: Railroad Junction, where the roundhouse and depot are located, is one of seven different historic districts in Greenfield Village. In Henry Ford's Model T District, you can tour a replica of Ford's first factory and ride in a Model T.

WORTH DOING: On December nights, celebrate the holidays in Greenfield Village. The Holiday Nights event features entertainment, carriage and Model T rides, Santa and his reindeer, ice skating, and fireworks.

DON'T MISS: Get to the roundhouse early in the day to help the crew turn the steam engine on the turntable. It's so well balanced that two people can do it, but it's more fun when you get to push a giant engine around.

GETTING THERE: Just west of Detroit, the Henry Ford is located in Dearborn on the corner of Village Road and Oakwood Boulevard, just west of the Southfield Freeway and south of Michigan Avenue (Highway 12). There is easy access from I-94 or I-75.

LOCATION: 20900 Oakwood Boulevard, Dearborn
PHONE: 800-835-5237 or 313-982-6001
WEBSITE: thehenryford.org
E-MAIL: form on website

Huckleberry Railroad

Huckleberry Railroad

The Huckelberry Railroad is a narrow-gauge steam railroad operated by Genesee County Parks as part of Crossroads Village in Flint, Mich.

CHOICES: Visitors may opt to ride the steam train only or enjoy other attractions at the historical site, such as the *Genesee Belle*, a paddle-wheel riverboat.

WHEN TO GO: The Huckelberry Railroad operates Memorial Day through Labor Day weekend and then reopens in October for Halloween trains and again in late November and December for Christmas Holiday Magic weekends. Of special interest to history buffs is the annual Railfan Weekend held each August when special tours and photo trains are operated. Thomas the Tank Engine visits the Huckelberry Railroad for several dates during the summer as well.

GOOD TO KNOW: The Huckelberry Railroad is built on a former Pere Marquette right of way. Excursions typically take 40 minutes and cover 8 miles round trip.

WORTH DOING: Be sure to allow extra time for your visit to Crossroads Village with more than 30 historic buildings in the 51-acre park. Costumed interpreters are often on hand to guide you through some of the restored homes, businesses and shops.

DON'T MISS: The railroad has just completed a multi-year overhaul of locomotive No. 152, a 1920 Baldwin 4-6-0 once employed by the U.S. War Department. Also on the roster is No. 464, a 1903 2-8-2 locomotive from the Denver & Rio Grande Western Railroad.

GETTING THERE: The railroad is located just north of Flint, about an hour from Detroit. From Detroit, take I-75 to I-475. Follow I-475 north to Saginaw Street (Exit 13). Take Saginaw Street north to Stanley Road, turn east on Stanley Road, and then turn south on Bray Road to the village and railroad.

LOCATION: 6140 Bray Road, Flint
PHONE: 800-648-7275 or 810-736-7100
WEBSITE: geneseecountyparks.org
E-MAIL: parkswebteam@gcparks.org

Little River Railroad

Dave Crosby

The Little River Railroad is named for its star attraction, locomotive No. 110, which was built in 1911 for a railroad with the same name in eastern Tennessee. Excursions depart from Coldwater, Mich., and operate to nearby Quincy.

CHOICES: Passengers may choose to ride in an observation car, coaches, open-air cars or a caboose. For an additional charge, guests 18 years or older can ride in the steam locomotive cab.

WHEN TO GO: Regular excursions operate weekends only from Memorial Day through September with fall color runs in October and Christmas trains in December.

GOOD TO KNOW: Locomotive No. 110 is the smallest standard gauge 4-6-2 Pacific type locomotive ever constructed, weighing in at just under 58 tons. When No. 110 isn't running, No. 1, an 0-4-0T tank engine takes its turn leading excursions.

WORTH DOING: The Capri Drive-In Theater, one of the last of its kind, is located nearby as are several restored buildings and shops.

DON'T MISS: Be sure to see the exhibits located in the railroads Coldwater Depot, built in 1883 for the Lake Shore & Michigan Southern Railroad.

GETTING THERE: Coldwater is in south-central Michigan. Take I-69 to Exit 13 for Coldwater. Follow Highway 12 west, turn left onto Division Street, and then turn right onto Park Avenue to the depot.

LOCATION: 29 W. Park Avenue, Coldwater
PHONE: 574-215-0751
WEBSITE: littleriverrailroad.com
E-MAIL: customerservice@
littleriverrailroad.com

Steam Railroading Institute

Jim Wrinn

The Steam Railroading Institute is all about preserving steam locomotives, and there is always restoration work going on. The institute displays equipment and offers some all-day train rides.

CHOICES: Both steam- and diesel-powered excursions are offered. Steam power is provided by Pere Marquette 2-8-4 No. 1225. The 7-acre site includes a roundhouse, a turntable, and a variety of railcars. Look around the museum, which is housed in a renovated freight warehouse that was also a creamery. It now contains exhibits, artifacts, and a model train layout.

WHEN TO GO: The museum is open Wednesday through Sunday, Memorial Day to Labor Day, and special events are scheduled as well. It closes in January and February and then reopens Fridays to Sundays. In November and December, the North Pole Express is the big event as a diesel locomotive takes visitors on a 24-mile round trip to the North Pole, where kids can enjoy hot cocoa, activities, and visiting Santa. Reserve early, as this event sells out fast.

GOOD TO KNOW: No. 1225 was the model and sound effects source for the steam train in the popular movie, *The Polar Express*.

WORTH DOING: If you like to watch things go fast, the Owosso Speedway offers short track racing on Saturday, Saturday, Saturday.

DON'T MISS: The Michigan Railroad History Museum is housed in historic Durand Union Station, 20 minutes away in Durand.

GETTING THERE: Owosso is about 30 miles northeast of Lansing and 30 miles west of Flint. From Flint, take Highway 21 west to Owosso. From Lansing, take I-69 to Highway 52 north to Owosso. In Owosso, the Steam Railroading Institute is on south Washington Street.

LOCATION: 405 S. Washington Street, Owosso
PHONE: 989-725-9464
WEBSITE: michigansteamtrain.com
E-MAIL: info@mstrp.com

OHIO

Bradford Railroad Museum

Located in a former bank building, the museum contains photos and displays that allow you to journey through Bradford's railroad history. The museum has also restored Bradford's former PRR interlocking tower. It is open Saturdays, April through October.

LOCATION: 200 N. Miami Avenue, Bradford
PHONE: 937-552-2196
WEBSITE: bradfordrrmuseum.org
E-MAIL: bradfordohiorrmuseum@gmail.com

Carillon Historical Park

Resembling a train station, as well as a roundhouse, the park's transportation center houses the 1835 B&O *John Quincy Adams* (the oldest existing American-built locomotive), a Barney & Smith parlor car, and other rail and transportation exhibits. It is open daily.

LOCATION: 1000 Carillon Boulevard, Dayton
PHONE: 937-293-2841
WEBSITE: daytonhistory.org
E-MAIL: info@daytonhistory.org

Cedar Point

Located within the world-famous Cedar Point amusement park, the Cedar Point & Lake Erie Railroad is a throwback to the railroads of a century ago with several coal-fired steam locomotives and link-and-pin couplers. During the busier times, two trains will operate over the 1.5-mile loop of track that winds through "The Roller Coaster Capitol of the World." The train operates whenever the park is open, typically May through October.

LOCATION: 1 Cedar Point Drive, Sandusky
PHONE: 419-627-2350
WEBSITE: cedarpoint.com
E-MAIL: form on website

Cincinnati Dinner Train

Operating every Saturday throughout the year except during January and February, the dinner train travels east from Madisonville to downtown Cincinnati, along the riverfront, and back. You'll enjoy the scenery and a four-course meal during a leisurely 3-hour excursion aboard two restored 1940s dining cars or the *Silver Sword*, which was originally a Chicago, Burlington & Quincy coach.

LOCATION: 2172 Seymour Ave., Cincinnati
PHONE: 513-791-7245
WEBSITE: cincinnatirailway.com/dinnertrain
E-MAIL: form on website

Conneaut Railroad Museum

Located in a Lake Shore & Michigan Southern depot, which was built in 1900, this museum displays railroad memorabilia, photos, and artifacts such as lanterns and timetables. Be sure to climb aboard and inspect the cab of Nickel Plate Berkshire No. 755 displayed outside. It is open Memorial Day weekend through Labor Day.

LOCATION: 363 Depot Street, Conneaut
PHONE: 440-599-7878
WEBSITE: facebook.com/chrrm

EnterTrainment Junction

In addition to a world class model railroad display that traces the history of railroading in the United States, EnterTrainment Junction features a 5,000 square foot railroad museum with interactive kiosks and full-sized railroad equipment. A narrow-gauge kids train and kid-powered locomotives are offered seasonally. EnterTrainment Junction is open daily except some holidays.

LOCATION: 7379 Squire Court, West Chester
PHONE: 513-898-8000, 877-898-4656
WEBSITE: entertrainmentjunction.com
E-MAIL: Form on website

Jefferson Depot Village

The Jefferson Depot is more than a depot. It is a small village. In addition to the restored 1872 Lake Shore & Michigan Southern Railroad station, the site features a 1918 caboose and several 19th century buildings including a one-room schoolhouse, a post office, and a church. It is open Saturdays, Sundays, Mondays, and Thursdays, June through mid-October.

LOCATION: 147 E. Jefferson Street, Jefferson
PHONE: 614-507-5246 or 440-576-0496
WEBSITE: jeffersondepotvillage.org
E-MAIL: duttonjg@hotmail.com

Marion Union Station

The station contains a museum, and a fully restored Erie Railroad tower is also on site. Located between two diamond crossings, the station is also a great place to watch trains from. More than 100 go by daily. The museum is open Tuesdays and Thursdays.

LOCATION: 532 W. Center Street, Marion
PHONE: 740-383-3768
WEBSITE: facebook.com/MarionUnionStationAssociation/
E-MAIL: link on Facebook page

Northern Ohio Railway Museum

Numbering more than 40, the museum's collection of streetcars, interurbans, and other railcars continues to grow. It features streetcars and equipment that operated in Cleveland, Shaker Heights, and other cities. You can stop in and take a guided walking tour on Saturdays mid-May through October. Rides are offered the second Saturday of the month.

LOCATION: 5515 Buffham Road, Seville
PHONE: 330-769-5501
WEBSITE: northernohiorailwaymuseum.org
E-MAIL: wstoner001@neo.rr.com

Ohio Railway Museum

This museum displays more than 30 pieces of equipment, including locomotives, passenger cars, and streetcars, with a focus on the Ohio Railway. It offers 2-mile streetcar rides as well as some rides in its diesel-pulled passenger car. The museum is open Sunday afternoons, May through December.

LOCATION: 990 Proprietors Road, Worthington
PHONE: 614-885-7345
WEBSITE: ohiorailwaymuseum.org
E-MAIL: info@ohiorailwaymuseum.net

Orrville Railroad Heritage Society

Railroad Days in August and other special events take place at the restored Orrville depot. During events, the society's collections can be viewed in the depot. A former Pennsylvania Railroad caboose and interlocking tower are also on the site.

LOCATION: 145 Depot Street, Orrville
PHONE: 330-683-2426
WEBSITE: orrvillerailroad.com
E-MAIL: form on website

Cuyahoga Valley Scenic Railroad

Jim Wrinn

The Cuyahoga Valley Scenic Railroad regularly operates 25 miles of track through northeastern Ohio, from Independence (near Cleveland) through Peninsula to downtown Akron. Much of the railroad is in the picturesque Cuyahoga Valley National Park, along the Cuyahoga River and the route of the abandoned Ohio & Erie Canal.

CHOICES: The CVSR runs an extensive schedule of regular trains, beginning in late January, from various boarding stations. In addition, special events run February through November. They include a variety of wine trains, educational trains, and a premier Polar Express train. There are several seating options including those in an elevated dome section that offer a panoramic view of the park. In 2018, the railroad added four cars from the famous *California Zephyr* train, including two dome cars.

WHEN TO GO: The summer months offer the most extensive schedule of regular trains. Mid-October offers extra trains for viewing the beautiful fall foliage. Trains are less crowded yet still offer spectacular scenery in April and September.

GOOD TO KNOW: The Cuyahoga Valley National Park features the Towpath Trail, which was built along much of the Ohio and Erie Canal Towpath. It is excellent for hiking and biking, and the railroad has an extensive schedule of heavily discounted Bike Aboard fares that cater to bicyclists.

WORTH DOING: Explore many of the restored historical buildings in the national park, including the Canal Visitor Center (accessible by train) that details the canal's history and includes an operating canal lock.

DON'T MISS: The east side of the train generally includes the best views of the Cuyahoga River, which parallels the railroad, especially on the north end from Peninsula up to Independence. Many photo opportunities abound, and the park has re-created the feel of the early 1900s by building many of the railroad's depots and shelters in a style modeled after the railroad's original structures.

GETTING THERE: The Ohio Turnpike crosses the CVSR near Peninsula, and I-77 generally parallels the railroad from Cleveland to Canton.

LOCATION: 1630 W. Mill Street, Peninsula
PHONE: 800-468-4070 or 330-439-5708
WEBSITE: cvsr.com
E-MAIL: customerservice@cvsr.com

Dennison Railroad Depot Museum

Mark Perri

This meticulously restored ex-Pennsylvania Railroad depot, built in 1873, houses a comprehensive collection of exhibits highlighting the depot's significance as a World War II serviceman's canteen. It was awarded National Historic Landmark status.

CHOICES: Dennison Railroad Depot Museum offers both guided and self-guided tours. The museum's Chesapeake & Ohio 2-8-4 Berkshire steam locomotive, No. 2700, recently completed a cosmetic restoration. A variety of interactive exhibits, many designed for children, allows visitors to climb in a caboose, sleep in a Pullman bunk, and send a message by telegraph. The museum also contains local history exhibits, houses a research library, and features a collection of railcars.

WHEN TO GO: The museum is open year-round but is closed on Mondays. It hosts numerous special events including an annual three-day Soldiers Homecoming Festival, complete with reenactors that celebrates the museum's wartime heritage.

GOOD TO KNOW: If you are hungry, a diner-style restaurant, the Over the Rails Diner, is located in the depot and offers excellent meals. Across the street, Dennison Yard, a local bar and grill, features a wonderful home-cooked Italian menu. There is also a picnic area on the museum's platform.

WORTH DOING: Dennison is close to Ohio's Amish Country in the east-central part of the state. The Pro Football Hall of Fame is 45 minutes north in Canton. The museum offers a Golden Triple Ticket, which provides discounted admission to its nearby affiliated museum partners, the Uhrichsville Clay Museum and Historic Schoenbrunn Village.

DON'T MISS: If you would like to see a hand-carved wooden locomotive, Warther Carvings Museum, 15 minutes away near Dover, features an extensive collection of carved railroad pieces in walnut, ebony, and ivory.

GETTING THERE: By car, Dennison is easily reached from I-77 via Route 250 (from the north) or Route 36 (from the south). Once in Dennison, take Second Street past the tracks and then turn left on Center Street.

LOCATION: 400 Center Street, Dennison
PHONE: 740-922-6776
WEBSITE: dennisondepot.org
E-MAIL: director@dennisondepot.org

Hocking Valley Scenic Railway

Hocking Valley, Scenic Railway, T.L. Warren

The Hocking Valley Scenic Railway offers diesel-powered excursions with vintage open-window coaches between Nelsonville and East Logan, over part of the original Hocking Valley Railway's Athens branch. The train takes you through Wayne National Forest, in the foothills of the Appalachians, and along the Hocking River.

CHOICES: The railroad's basic excursions are a 14-mile trip to Haydenville and a 22-mile trip to East Logan. The trips are narrated, and you can ride in a 1920s coach, a 1930s heavyweight passenger car, or an open-air car. Along the way, besides enjoying the scenery, you'll see a canal lock, take in historical landmarks, and stop at Robbins Crossing, an 1850s-era log village. The railroad has returned 1920 Baldwin 0-6-0 No. 3 to service for steam power.

WHEN TO GO: Regular excursions begin Memorial Day weekend and end in October. To view the stunning fall foliage, Friday trains are added in October. Various holiday and theme trips are offered throughout the year, and include Easter, Halloween, Christmas and train robbery excursions.

GOOD TO KNOW: Once a year, the HVR runs a special caboose train that railfans and photographers will especially enjoy.

WORTH DOING: There is something to do for everyone in Wayne National Forest. It has more than 300 miles of trails for hiking and riding bikes, horses, and ATVs. In Nelsonville, you can explore the Public Square, which contains Stuart's Opera House, the Dew House, and other historic buildings.

DON'T MISS: On your visit to Robbins Crossing, you'll see a group of original log cabins arranged into a historical village. They include a schoolhouse, blacksmith shop, general store, and several homes. Costumed guides offer commentary and demonstrate crafts.

GETTING THERE: Nelsonville is approximately 56 miles from Columbus and about 200 miles from Cleveland. From Columbus, take Route 33 to Nelsonville. In downtown Nelsonville, take Hocking Parkway south to the depot.

LOCATION: 33 W. Canal Street, Nelsonville
PHONE: 740-249-1452
WEBSITE: hvsry.org

Lebanon Mason Monroe Railroad

Lebanon Mason Monroe Railroad

The Lebanon Mason Monroe Railroad offers a relaxed, 10-mile round-trip through Warren County and features a choice between air-conditioned or vintage open-window coaches.

CHOICES: The railroad's 1-hour 15-minute excursions offer seating in either open-window coaches or in air-conditioned deluxe seats. On the trip, conductors provide narration that describes the railroad's history and operation. In addition to their basic Turtle Creek Valley Flyer excursions, the LM&M offers many seasonal and theme trains, such as a pizza trains, wine trains, and trains featuring PBS Kids characters.

WHEN TO GO: Trains operate February through December. The regular season begins in May with trains running at least 2-3 days a week. The season concludes in December with North Pole Express trains. Check the LM&M's website for specific operating dates and departure times.

GOOD TO KNOW: The LM&M partners with the Ohio Rail Experience, which operates rare-mileage excursion trains elsewhere in Ohio. Ohio Rail Experience schedules are posted on the LM&M website's calendar.

WORTH DOING: Kings Island, one of Ohio's premier roller-coaster amusement parks, is about 20 minutes away, and provides family entertainment and many dining and hotel options.

DON'T MISS: Plan on spending time in historic downtown Lebanon, with its classic small town charm. Shopping, arts, antique stores, and restaurants are all within walking distance of the station.

GETTING THERE: Lebanon is north of Cincinnati and south of Dayton between I-71 and I-75.

LOCATION: 127 S. Mechanic Street, Lebanon
PHONE: 513-933-8022
WEBSITE: lebanonrr.com
EMAIL: info@lebanonrr.com

Mad River & NKP Railroad Museum

Mad River & NKP Railroad Museum, Brandon Townley

The Mad River & NKP Railroad Museum opened on our nation's bicentennial in 1976 as a lasting tribute to the transportation industry. The museum has a widely varied collection of railroad locomotives, coaches, freight cars, equipment, and structures.

CHOICES: While the museum focuses on the Nickel Plate Road and its successors, and includes a substantial collection of diesel locomotives, many unique pieces of equipment, such as CB&Q Silver Dome No. 4714 (the first dome car built in the United States) are present. Static exhibits comprise the museum collection. However, many pieces, especially the passenger equipment, have interiors that are open for inspection. In addition, some cars are outfitted with museum displays.

WHEN TO GO: The museum is open afternoons daily Memorial Day through Labor Day. In addition, the museum is open weekends in May, September, and October.

GOOD TO KNOW: Bellevue is a thriving, quaint rural Ohio town, with ample amenities for food and lodging, and many other options for tourists such as antique shops and flea markets. In 2018, the museum was working to return NKP Berkshire No. 757 to Ohio.

WORTH DOING: Bellevue is a 30-minute drive from Sandusky and the Cedar Point amusement park, which is known for its roller coasters and its steam-powered, narrow gauge railroad.

DON'T MISS: Many opportunities exist for watching and photographing trains from public property around town. Mainline tracks bisect the museum, where you can see Norfolk Southern Heritage units or regional Wheeling & Lake Erie Railway trains. The new Kemper Railroad Park pavilion, located a short walk from the museum, provides a safe vantage point for railfans.

GETTING THERE: Bellevue is 20 minutes from the Ohio Turnpike. From the east, take Exit 110, Route 4 south to Route 113, and west to Route 20. From the west, use Exit 91, Route 53 south, and Route 20 east to Bellevue.

LOCATION: 253 Southwest Street, Bellevue
PHONE: 419-483-2222
WEBSITE: madrivermuseum.org
E-MAIL: madriver@onebellevue.com

WISCONSIN

Brodhead Historical Society Depot Museum

This restored Chicago, Milwaukee & St. Paul depot, built in 1881, houses a permanent railroad display with rotating historical displays. Milwaukee Road Fairbanks-Morse switch engine No. 781 and caboose No. 01900 stand alongside the depot. It is open on Wednesdays, Saturdays, and Sundays, May through September.

LOCATION: 1108 First Center Avenue, Brodhead
PHONE: 608-897-4150
WEBSITE: brodheadhistory.org
E-MAIL: info@brodheadhistory.org

Colfax Railroad Museum

This museum includes a large collection of railroad memorabilia and an outdoor display of locomotives and rolling stock that features a Porter steam locomotive, Soo Line GP30 diesel engine, a wooden Soo caboose, a heavyweight coach, and other pieces of rolling stock. It is open Wednesday through Sunday May through October.

LOCATION: 500 E. Railroad Avenue, Colfax
PHONE: 715-962-2076
WEBSITE: colfaxrrmuseum.org
E-MAIL: form on website

Frederic Historical Society Museum

This museum is housed in a restored 1901 Soo Line depot. It features railroad memorabilia as well as displays of the area's history. Also on display is Soo Line wide-vision caboose no. 137. The museum is open weekends Memorial Day into fall.

LOCATION: 210 W. Oak Street, Frederic
PHONE: 715-327-4158 or 715-327-4892
WEBSITE: fredericwi.com

Historical Village

The village features a restored C&NW depot and several other historical structures, including an octagon house. Built in 1923, the depot is authentically furnished and contains railroad artifacts. It also displays a 1941 diesel locomotive, a Soo caboose, and a C&NW caboose. The museum is open the first and third Sundays during summer and Heritage Days & Rail Fest in August.

LOCATION: 900 Montgomery Street, New London
PHONE: 920-982-8557 or 920-982-5186
WEBSITE: historicalvillage.org

Mineral Point Railroad Museum

The museum is housed in a stone Milwaukee Road depot, which is the oldest depot building in the state. It contains exhibits on the two Mineral Point railroads as well as others. An interactive diorama of the area around 1920 is a popular attraction. The museum is open Thursdays through Sundays May through October.

LOCATION: 11 Commerce Street, Mineral Point
PHONE: 608-987-2695
WEBSITE: mineralpointrailroads.com
E-MAIL: form on website

Railroad Memories Museum

This museum contains 12 rooms filled with railroad memories. Artifacts include lanterns, track equipment, photos, and other items. Housed in a former C&NW depot, it is located next to the Wisconsin Great Northern Railroad. The museum is open Memorial Day weekend through Labor Day.

LOCATION: 424 N. Front Street, Spooner
PHONE: 715-635-3325
WEBSITE: facebook.com/railroadmemoriesmuseumspooner
www.spoonerrrmuseum.net/
E-MAIL: rrmuseumspoonx@gmail.com

East Troy Electric Railroad

East Troy Electric Railroad, Larry Pearlman

Interurban railroads once plied much of the Midwest, moving passengers easily from farm to city and vice versa. Today, a sprig of that heritage remains at the East Troy Electric Railroad, where electric trains run through the scenic countryside.

CHOICES: On a 14-mile round trip, the railroad offers a variety of cars to ride that includes trolleys, streetcars from Milwaukee and the Twin Cities, and electrically powered traditional coaches from the famous South Shore Line. Trains depart from both East Troy and Mukwonago. The railroad also offers picnic trains and dinner trains that run to Phantom Lake and back. After viewing the exhibits in the depot, you can walk two blocks to the shops and look at the equipment being refurbished.

WHEN TO GO: Regular weekend excursions run May through October. From late May through September, trains also operate on Fridays. There are several special events during the year including a Christmas Express that runs in November and December.

GOOD TO KNOW: Sheboygan car No. 26 is a 1908 interurban built by the Cincinnati Car Company for Sheboygan Light, Power and Railway. No. 26 later became a summer cottage until it was restored.

WORTH DOING: Regular excursions operate from East Troy to the Indianhead Park in Mukwonago, with stops at the Elegant Farmer. What's an Elegant Farmer? It makes a great destination as the Farmer provides a deli, greenhouse, and market all in one. Be sure and try the award-winning apple pie baked in a bag.

DON'T MISS: You can explore the substation in East Troy, which is the heart of the operating gear for the electric railroad.

GETTING THERE: East Troy is located in southeastern Wisconsin, about 35 miles from Milwaukee and 15 miles from Lake Geneva. From Milwaukee, take I-43 south to Exit 38. Take Highway 20 to Main Street. Follow Main Street to Church Street and turn right to the museum.

LOCATION: 1992 Church Street, East Troy
PHONE: 262-642-3263
WEBSITE: easttroyrr.org
E-MAIL: form on website

Lumberjack Steam Train—Camp Five

Jeff Terry

Camp Five offers a steam train powered by a vintage 2-6-2 type logging locomotive. It takes you to the site of a timber company's 1914 farm camp, where you can tour a logging museum and other buildings.

CHOICES: Camp Five offers a unique experience to visitors. After boarding the Laona & Northern Railway's Lumberjack Steam Train at an 1880s-vintage Soo Line depot, you are transported through the unspoiled Wisconsin Northwoods and across the Rat River on a timber trestle before arriving at the Camp Five Museum, a reconstructed early 20th century logging farm camp.

WHEN TO GO: Mid-June through mid-August, Thursday-Monday (closed Tuesday and Wednesday). Additionally, there are special fall runs in September.

GOOD TO KNOW: If you plan on spending all day at Camp Five, bring a picnic lunch or dine at the Choo Choo Café, which offers a variety of food options. Candies, fudge, and souvenirs are available at the Cracker Barrel Store & Gift Shop.

WORTH DOING: Laona is in the heart of Forest County, home to the Nicolet National Forest, an area renowned for its hunting and fishing. The Otter Springs Recreational Area, with several well-maintained hiking trails, is located in nearby Crandon.

DON'T MISS: Camp Five is filled with artifacts from Wisconsin's pioneer logging days. The Green Treasure Forest Tours takes you on a 30-minute journey through an industrial forest. For railroad enthusiasts, there is a Wisconsin Central SW1 locomotive on display along with a wooden snow plow.

GETTING THERE: Camp Five is located off Highway 8 west of Laona, about 2 hours north of Green Bay. From Green Bay, take Highway 141 north to Highway 64. Follow Highway 64 west to Highway 32. Continue on Highway 32 and turn left on Highway 8.

LOCATION: 5064 Highway 8, Laona
PHONE: 715-674-3414
WEBSITE: camp5museum.org
E-MAIL: info@lumberjacksteamtrain.com

Mid-Continent Railway Museum

Jim Wrinn

One of the best museums for the preservation of wooden railroad cars, Mid-Continent features numerous exhibits and a large collection of rolling stock, much of it kept indoors. The museum also offers a diesel train ride. It's all aimed at re-creating the experience of a branch line or short line between 1885 and 1915.

CHOICES: Leaving from a restored 1894 C&NW depot, the 7-mile, 55-minute ride takes you through the rolling countryside. You can ride the restored 1915 steel coaches, but you can also get a ticket for a caboose.

WHEN TO GO: The railway operates from May into October and also includes a variety of special events. From June until Labor Day, it is open daily; otherwise, on weekends only. Fall color, pumpkin, and Santa specials operate, as does a snow train and a variety of food and dinner trains.

GOOD TO KNOW: More than 100 pieces of equipment are on display. One is an office car of Great Northern Railway founder James J. Hill's son that included space for hauling an automobile. Structures include a water tower, a crossing shanty, a section shed, a crossing tower, and a freight house.

WORTH DOING: Explore Devil's Lake State Park near Baraboo. This large park features 500-foot cliffs, hiking trails, and kayaking.

DON'T MISS: Make sure you go into the coach shed to see some of the finest wood craftsmanship around when it comes to railroad cars. On one September weekend, you can view the cars' interiors on a guided tour.

GETTING THERE: The scenic route from Madison is along Highway 12 going north. Turn left on Highway 36 and then left again on Highway PF to North Freedom. In North Freedom, follow Walnut Street west to the museum.

LOCATION: E8948 Museum Road, North Freedom
PHONE: 800-930-1385 or 608-522-4261
WEBSITE: midcontinent.org
E-MAIL: inquiries@midcontinent.org

National Railroad Museum

National Railroad Museum

Begun in 1956 by a group wishing to preserve a steam locomotive, the only congressionally designated national railroad museum has grown to encompass more than 70 pieces of rolling stock, 100,000 objects, a seasonal train ride, and an unmatched collection of drumheads—the illuminated signs seen on the rear of many passenger trains.

CHOICES: Explore the museum on your own and then take a train ride. During the 25-minute train ride, the conductor provides information about railroad history and museum exhibits. Highlights include a Union Pacific Big Boy, a 1950s Aerotrain, and a Pennsylvania Railroad GG1 electric locomotive. The command train for General Dwight D. Eisenhower is also located at the museum. Guided group tours are available.

WHEN TO GO: The museum is open daily year-round, except for Mondays January through March and several holidays. Train rides operate May through October, and numerous special events are scheduled during the year.

GOOD TO KNOW: The museum features exhibits on Pullman porters and rotating exhibits. In the museum's theater, you can view *Last of the Giants*, a 25-minute documentary chronicling the Union Pacific's Big Boys.

WORTH DOING: Take the kids to Bay Beach Amusement Park for some old-fashioned fun on classic midway rides. Football fans can visit the Green Bay Packers Hall of Fame and tour historic Lambeau Field.

DON'T MISS: Climb to the top of the 85-foot-tall observation tower for a bird's-eye view of the museum and its extensive rolling stock collection.

GETTING THERE: Green Bay is 2 hours north of Milwaukee. From Milwaukee, take I-43 to Exit 180. Take Highway 172 west and exit at Ashland Avenue. Bear right on Pilgrim Way and then turn left on Broadway Street.

LOCATION: 2285 S. Broadway Street, Green Bay
PHONE: 920-437-7623
WEBSITE: nationalrrmuseum.org
E-MAIL: form on website

Osceola & St. Croix Valley Railway

Steve Glischinski

The Minnesota Transportation Museum's Osceola & St. Croix Valley offers rides through the scenic St. Croix River Valley on former Soo Line tracks now owned by Canadian National.

CHOICES: The Osceola & St. Croix Valley offers both open and closed window coaches. If riding in the open cars during early spring or fall, be prepared to dress for cool weather. Two routes can be ridden from Osceola. One heads west 10 miles to Marine on St. Croix, Minn., while the other heads east 5 miles to Dresser, Wis., a former Soo Line junction town that still sports its original wooden Soo Line depot. We'd recommend the Marine trip, since it follows the beautiful St. Croix Valley for its entire length.

WHEN TO GO: For the best views of the St. Croix River, May is the time to ride before the leaves have a chance to obstruct views of the river. The first or second week of October offer the chance to view the autumn colors before the long northern winter begins. There's nothing like a crisp, blue sky autumn day in the open window coaches rolling through the St. Croix Valley.

GOOD TO KNOW: Osceola is a small town of slightly over 2,000. There are several good local hotels, restaurants and bed and breakfasts, but those who desire all the amenities may wish to drive south to the larger communities of Stillwater, Minn., or Hudson, Wis.

WORTH DOING: Take the train to Marine to ride over the Cedar Bend swing bridge across the St. Croix River from Wisconsin into Minnesota. While the bridge doesn't swing open any more, it's a classic steel structure complete with "tell tales" on each end to warn brakemen of close clearances.

DON'T MISS: The museum occasionally picks up mail on the fly with ex-Northern Pacific Railway Post Office car No. 1102 from a mail crane at Osceola's restored passenger depot.

GETTING THERE: Osceola is about an hour's drive from Minneapolis. For a scenic drive, follow Highway 95 along the east bank of the St. Croix from Stillwater north to Osceola. Once in Osceola, you'll come to Highway 35. Turn right and proceed under the railroad bridge and immediately turn right again onto Depot Road.

LOCATION: 114 Depot Road, Osceola
PHONE: 715-755-3570 or 651-228-0263
WEBSITE: transportationmuseum.org
E-MAIL: contact@mtmuseum.org

Wisconsin Great Northern Railroad

The Wisconsin Great Northern Railroad operates excursion and dinner trains on approximately 9 miles of former Chicago & North Western track between Trego and Veazie Springs, Wis.

CHOICES: Wisconsin Great Northern offers several choices for riders: 90-minute "sightseeing" train rides that operate from May to October primarily on Fridays, Saturdays and Sundays; afternoon and evening Family Pizza Trains; Sunday Brunch trains; and a dinner train. In November and December, WGN operates a Thanksgiving Buffet Train and a Santa's Pizza Party train. The railroad bills itself as the only railroad in the United States with a moving bed & breakfast train. Passengers check in between 4 and 5:30 p.m. and board a sleeping car, which is coupled to the dinner train.

WHEN TO GO: Summer and early fall are the best. Summers in Wisconsin are usually not as hot as other parts of the U.S., and September in Wisconsin is usually one of the best periods for weather anywhere in the country.

GOOD TO KNOW: In 2013 the railroad opened a new depot and tourist information center just north of Spooner. The facility features a large, regionally focused gift shop, a children's play area, and picnic grounds.

WORTH DOING: Take a drive 30 miles to Hayward, Wis. The town is the site of many festivals and events, including the annual Lumberjack World Championships and Chequamegon Fat Tire Festival, the largest mass start mountain bike race in the United States.

DON'T MISS: In Spooner, you'll find the Railroad Memories Museum. Housed in the former Chicago & North Western Spooner depot, the museum contains lanterns, track equipment, photos, and other railroad memorabilia.

GETTING THERE: The Wisconsin Great Northern is about 90 minutes from Eau Claire and 2 hours from Minneapolis and St. Paul. To get to the depot, from Spooner take Highway 63 north, which joins with Highway 53. After about 5 miles from Spooner, turn on Dilly Lake Road and continue to the depot.

LOCATION: N6639 Dilly Lake Road, Trego
PHONE: 715-635-3200
WEBSITE: spoonertrainride.com
E-MAIL: info@spoonertrainride.com

Boone & Scenic Valley Railroad, page 176

REGION 5

IOWA

1 Boone & Scenic Valley Railroad
2 Hub City Railroad Museum
3 Marquette Depot Museum
4 Minneapolis & St. Louis No. 457
5 Midwest Central Railroad
6 RailsWest Railroad Museum
7 Sioux City Railroad Museum
8 Union Pacific Railroad Museum

MINNESOTA

9 Depot Museum
10 End-O-Line Railroad Park & Museum
11 Jackson Street Roundhouse
12 Kandiyohi County Historical Museum
13 Lake Superior & Mississippi Railroad
14 Lake Superior Railroad Museum
15 Milwaukee Road 261
16 Minnehaha Depot
17 Minnesota Discovery Center
18 Minnesota Museum of Mining
19 Minnesota Streetcar Museum
20 North Shore Scenic
21 Western Minnesota Steam Threshers Reunion

NEBRASKA

22 Cody Park Railroad Museum
23 Durham Museum
24 Golden Spike Tower
25 Lauritzen Gardens
26 Rock Island Depot Railroad Museum
27 Stuhr Museum of the Prairie Pioneer
28 Trails & Rails Museum

NORTH DAKOTA

29 Bonanzaville USA
30 Fort Lincoln Trolley
31 Midland Continental Depot Transportation Museum
32 North Dakota State Railroad Museum
33 Old Soo Depot Transportation Museum
34 Railroad Museum of Minot

SOUTH DAKOTA

35 Black Hills Central Railroad
36 Prairie Village
37 South Dakota State Railroad Museum

IOWA

Hub City Railway Museum

This museum consists of a former Railway Express Agency building, a Chicago Great Western yard office, and a tower, with a display of locomotives, railcars, and artifacts. It is open Sundays, May through September. During Oelwein's annual Heritage Days weekend, you can ride on one of the museum's handcars.

LOCATION: 26 Second Avenue SW, Oelwein
PHONE: 319-283-1939
WEBSITE: cgwoelwein.org
E-MAIL: info@cgwoelwein.org

Marquette Depot Museum

Housed in a renovated Milwaukee Road depot, the museum contains Milwaukee Road exhibits and general railroad artifacts. A restored caboose is on display. The museum is open daily May through October, and the depot also contains a travel information center. Railroad Days take place in September.

LOCATION: 216 Edgar Street, Marquette
PHONE: 563-873-1200
WEBSITE: marquetteiowa.city/marquette-depot-museum--information-center.html
E-MAIL: marquettedepotmuseum@alpinecom.net

Minneapolis & St. Louis No. 457

Get an up-close look at M&StL No. 457, a Consolidation type steam locomotive built in 1912, which has been in East Park since 1959. Fog machines provide smoke and steam, and a sound system provides an engine's whistle. It is open to the public on weekend afternoons mid-May through October.

LOCATION: East Park, Mason City
WEBSITE: friendsofthe457.org
E-MAIL: form on website

RailsWest Railroad Museum

This former Chicago, Rock Island & Pacific passenger depot was built in 1899. The museum displays a Lincoln, Neb.-built Chicago, Burlington & Quincy 4-6-0 locomotive, Union Pacific 4-8-4 (Northern) locomotive, Plymouth locomotive, and Rock Island caboose. A large HO scale model railroad is also part of the museum and worth seeing. Check the museum website for days and hours.

LOCATION: 16th Avenue and South Main Street, Council Bluffs
PHONE: 712-323-2509
WEBSITE: thehistoricalsociety.org
E-MAIL: form on website

Sioux City Railroad Museum

The 30-acre Sioux City Railroad Museum is in a former Milwaukee Road roundhouse and shop complex. In addition to static displays, the museum offers rides on its grand scale 15-inch gauge railroad as well as 2-hour sessions at the throttle of a 1943 General Electric center cab locomotive. The roundhouse is also home to Great Northern steam locomotive No. 1355, which has been cosmetically restored.

LOCATION: 3400 Sioux River Road, Sioux City
PHONE: 712-233-6996
WEBSITE: siouxcityrailroadmuseum.org
E-MAIL: contact@milwaukeerailroadshops.org

Boone & Scenic Valley Railroad

Steve Smedley

The Boone & Scenic Valley operates over an 11-mile section of former Fort Dodge, Des Moines and Southern Railroad, between Boone and Wolf, Iowa, a former junction with the Minneapolis & St. Louis Railway. The scenic highlight of the trip is the Bass Point Creek High Bridge, a 156-foot-tall steel bridge spanning Bass Point creek. For a shorter trip visitors can ride on the East End Electric Traction Company, an overhead-wire-fed trolley to downtown Boone, and return.

CHOICES: Several classes of tickets are available, Classic Coach Class, bench seating in a coach with operating windows; ride an open-air former CNW transfer caboose, the *Valley View*; Climate Controlled Coach, a former Chicago & North Western bi-level commuter car; or ride aboard a caboose.

WHEN TO GO: Boone & Scenic Valley Railroad operating season runs daily from Memorial Day through the end of October.

GOOD TO KNOW: The train departs from a replica depot dedicated in 1985 and rolls along the former electric right of way of the Fort Dodge, Des Moines & Southern Railroad. The FDDMS system was purchased by the Chicago & North Western RR in 1968, which shortly afterward began abandoning portions of the line. A former C&NW transfer caboose, the *Valley View*, is the best way to enjoy an open-air ride over the line.

WORTH DOING: Iowa Arboretum, Snus Hill Winery, both in nearby Madrid, Iowa

DON'T MISS: A Chinese built steam locomotive, No. 8419, is currently undergoing a 15-year overhaul with hopes to be ready for the 2019 operating season. A former Lake Superior & Ishpeming Alco RS1 has been repainted in classic Minneapolis & St. Louis Railway colors. The Charles City and Western Railway trolley car X50 operates from the depot east powered by an overhead wire to downtown Boone, a 20-minute round trip.

GETTING THERE: The railroad is in central Iowa, an hour's drive northwest of Des Moines. Take I-35 to Ames and travel west on Highway 30 to Boone. Go north on Story Street through the business district to 10th Street and then go west 6 blocks to the depot.

LOCATION: 225 10th Street, Boone
PHONE: 800-626-0319 or 515-432-4249
WEBSITE: bsvrr.com/wp
E-MAIL: info@bsvrr.com

Midwest Central Railroad

Steve Glischinski

The Midwest Central Railroad was established when volunteers built a 1.25-mile loop of track around the Midwest Old Threshers Reunion site and acquired several steam locomotives and cars. Later, to bring visitors and exhibitors into the grounds, a counterclockwise trolley loop line was built, dubbed the Midwest Electric Railway.

CHOICES: The Midwest Electric Railway runs its trolleys Wednesday through Labor Day of the Reunion. Trolleys load on the main grounds and travel through the campgrounds with five different stops. The Midwest Electric Railway is also available for charter throughout the year for special occasions such as birthdays, weddings, and picnics. Both the railway and the electric line operate "Ghost" trains and trolleys each October, and the railroad also runs a "North Pole Express" in December.

WHEN TO GO: Both the Midwest Central Railway and the Midwest Electric Railway are in full operation during the Old Threshers Reunion, which runs for five days ending on Labor Day. During the Reunion trains run from about 8:30 a.m. to 10 p.m. In addition to rides, during the Reunion the railroad offers numerous seminars explaining how steam engines, airbrakes, track signals and other railroad systems function.

GOOD TO KNOW: During the Old Threshers Reunion, the trains haul approximately 35,000 to 40,000 passengers on its 1¼ mile circle track.

WORTH DOING: If you're a camper, stay at the Old Threshers campground and take the trolley into the grounds and then ride the train. You can take in the whole show without the hassle of parking and enjoy the sights and sounds of steam as you camp.

DON'T MISS: On the grounds, two museums operate during the year. Open year-round, the Heritage Museum focuses on agriculture, and in summer, you can visit the Theatre Museum, which preserves artifacts from early repertoire theater, and even take in a live performance.

GETTING THERE: Probably the best way to visit Mount Pleasant is by driving. Located in southeastern Iowa, Mount Pleasant is south of Iowa City on Highway 218. The city is also served daily by Amtrak trains 5 and 6, the *California Zephyr*.

LOCATION: 405 E. Threshers Road, Mount Pleasant
PHONE: 319-385-2912 or 319-385-8937
WEBSITE: oldthreshers.org or mcrr.org
E-MAIL: info@oldthreshers.org

Union Pacific Railroad Museum

Jim Wrinn

Few railroads have gone to the great lengths of the Union Pacific to preserve and document their past. The Union Pacific Railroad Museum houses one of the oldest corporation collections of any kind in the country. Visitors will not find lines of steam locomotives, diesels, or rolling stock. Rather, they will be inundated with a tasteful display of artifacts, photographs, and documents that trace the development of the UP and the role it played in the American West.

CHOICES: The museum can be taken in whole or digested by specific eras depending on your interests. The Union Pacific's history is a history of the American West. The collection dates from the mid-1800s and features materials highlighting the building of the transcontinental railroad. Surveying equipment, early rail equipment, firearms, and other artifacts fill the building.

WHEN TO GO: With the exception of a raging snowstorm, even winter is a good time to visit the museum. It is open Thursdays through Saturdays. Exhibits are changed and special events occur periodically during the year.

GOOD TO KNOW: One of the museum's permanent exhibits is devoted to passenger service. It features a cutaway coach, lounge, and dining cars as well as multimedia exhibits and thousands of artifacts.

WORTH DOING: Take time to tour both Council Bluffs and Omaha. Both are culturally rich cities with much to offer visitors. Council Bluffs has several casinos and is Iowa's leading gaming spot. The Henry Doorly Zoo in Omaha is a world-class zoo that appeals to adults and children alike.

DON'T MISS: The museum has a combination of static and interactive displays. The working locomotive simulator is educational as well as a lot of fun.

GETTING THERE: Located on the east side of Council Bluffs, the museum is easily accessible for motorists from I-80 or I-29. It is near Bayliss Park with its lighted water fountain, monuments, and sculptures.

LOCATION: 200 Pearl Street, Council Bluffs
PHONE: 712-329-8307
WEBSITE: uprrmuseum.org
E-MAIL: form on website

MINNESOTA

Depot Museum

Located in the 1907 headquarters of the Duluth & Iron Range Railroad, this museum highlights the timber industry, iron mining, and the railroad. It displays a Mallet steam locomotive and a Baldwin 3-Spot. The Lake County Historical Society operates this museum and two others including an 1892 lighthouse. They are open daily Memorial Day weekend into October, and the Depot Museum is open Saturdays in winter.

LOCATION: 520 South Avenue, Two Harbors
PHONE: 218-834-4898
WEBSITE: lakecountyhistoricalsociety.org
E-MAIL: lakehist@lakeconnections.net

End-O-Line Railroad Park & Museum

End-O-Line Railroad Park includes a 1901 manually operated turntable, a rebuilt engine house, an original four-room depot, a water tower, an 1899 section foreman's house, a Grand Trunk Western caboose, and two steam locomotives. Open Wednesdays through Sundays Memorial Day weekend to Labor Day weekend, the site also includes other buildings of local historical interest.

LOCATION: 440 N. Mill Street, Currie
PHONE: 507-763-3708
WEBSITE: endoline.com
E-MAIL: endoline@co.murray.mn.us

Kandiyohi County Historical Museum

The museum complex consists of several buildings including a one-room schoolhouse and the former Kandiyohi railroad station depot, which is the entrance to the main museum. Great Northern No. 2523, a Baldwin P-2 class steam locomotive, is also on display. It is open daily Memorial Day through Labor Day.

LOCATION: 610 NE Highway 71, Willmar
PHONE: 320-235-1881
WEBSITE: kandiyohicountyhistory.com
E-MAIL: kandhist@msn.com

Minnehaha Depot

Located in Minnehaha Park, the tiny depot's architecture features delicate gingerbread details. Built in 1875, the building replaced an earlier Milwaukee Road depot on the first line into the Twin Cities from Chicago. Managed by the Minnesota Transportation Museum, the depot is open Sundays Memorial Day weekend through Labor Day.

LOCATION: Highway 55 and Minnehaha Parkway, Minneapolis
PHONE: 651-228-0263
WEBSITE: transportationmuseum.org
E-MAIL: form on website

Minnesota Discovery Center

The center offers a 2.5-mile trolley ride to a re-created mining community. The 40-minute trip, aboard a 1928 Melbourne trolley, offers views of the Pillsbury mine. Preserving Iron Range history, the center includes a museum, hall of geology, and mini golf course. It is open year-round, but closed Mondays all year and Sundays during winter. Trolleys operate late May to October.

LOCATION: 1005 Discovery Drive, Chisholm
PHONE: 218-254-7959
WEBSITE: mndiscoverycenter.com
E-MAIL: info@mndiscoverycenter.com

Minnesota Museum of Mining

The museum tells the story of iron ore mining in the state. Along with mining equipment and vehicles, a 1907 Alco steam locomotive is on display with ore cars and a caboose. Inside, you'll find a re-created mining town, a building-filling train layout by landscape artist Francis Lee Jacques, and a simulated underground mine. It is open Memorial Day to Labor Day, and picnicking is encouraged.

LOCATION: 701 West Lake Street, Chisholm
PHONE: 218-254-5543
WEBSITE: mnmuseumofmining.org
E-MAIL: info@mnmuseumofmining.org

Minnesota Streetcar Museum

This museum operates two different streetcar lines from May into fall, with a variety of special events. Located southwest of downtown Minneapolis, the Como-Harriet Line runs between Lake Harriet and Bde Mka Ska (former Lake Calhoun). The Excelsior Line is about 15 miles west of downtown Minneapolis. The museum exhibits electric streetcars.

LOCATION: 2330 W. 42nd Street, Minneapolis; 400 George St., Excelsior
PHONE: 952-922-1096
WEBSITE: trolleyride.org
E-MAIL: info@trolleyride.org

Western Minnesota Steam Threshers Reunion

This event has been a Labor Day tradition since 1954. The grounds cover 210 acres filled with steam-powered equipment, historic buildings, tractor pulls, and a steam-powered earth mover, among other items. The star of the show is 1920-built Alco 0-6-0 No. 353, an ex-Soo Line steam locomotive that pulls passengers in modified (and cleaned!) stockcars around a 2-mile loop of track.

LOCATION: 27488 102nd Avenue South, Hawley
PHONE: 701-212-2034
WEBSITE: rollag.com
E-MAIL: secretary@rollag.com

Jackson Street Roundhouse

Jeff Terry

The Minnesota Transportation Museum's former Great Northern Jackson Street Roundhouse was built by GN in 1907 to service passenger locomotives. Closed in 1959, the roundhouse was converted to non-railroad use and the tracks removed. In 1985 it was purchased by the Minnesota Transportation Museum and renovations began. One of the highlights was reinstalling the turntable and installing new roundhouse doors built to the 1906 blueprints. The roundhouse is open on Wednesdays, Saturdays and Sundays year-round. Included in the collection are three Northern Pacific steam locomotives. A variety of freight and passenger cars are displayed outside.

CHOICES: Visitors can roam the roundhouse and the outdoor grounds, take a short caboose ride pulled by a switch engine on Saturdays, and participate in interactive exhibits. Visitors can also ride one of the classic buses. No train or bus rides are offered Wednesdays or Sundays.

WHEN TO GO: The museum is open year-round, but it can be chilly inside the roundhouse in the winter and downright cold outside. Summer or early fall are the best times to visit.

GOOD TO KNOW: St. Paul and Minneapolis have a wide diversity of restaurants and hotels for any taste and budget. After taking in the roundhouse, if you have a desire to learn more about the Great Northern Railway, visit the St. Paul home of James J. Hill at 240 Summit Avenue. The famous "Empire Builder" founded the Great Northern.

WORTH DOING: Make sure to inquire about seeing the Northern Pacific steam locomotives undergoing restoration in the roundhouse. The area is not open to the public, but museum personnel offer guided tours to see the two Pacifics.

DON'T MISS: Walk inside the cab of Dan Patch Lines No. 100, built in 1913 by General Electric, and you've walked into history. It is one of the first locomotives that used an internal combustion engine and is the "granddaddy" of today's diesel locomotives.

GETTING THERE: The roundhouse is located north of the Minnesota State Capitol. Take the Pennsylvania Avenue exit off I-35E and drive west 2 blocks to the roundhouse.

LOCATION: 193 E. Pennsylvania Avenue, St. Paul
PHONE: 651-228-0263
WEBSITE: transportationmuseum.org
E-MAIL: form on website

Lake Superior & Mississippi Railroad

Jeff Terry

Situated south of downtown Duluth across from the Duluth Zoo, the Lake Superior & Mississippi takes riders on a scenic excursion along the St. Louis River. The railroad travels over a portion of original LS&M, the first railroad to be built between Minneapolis and Duluth.

CHOICES: Passengers ride in vintage coaches once used on the Duluth, Missabe & Iron Range Railway, or aboard the unique "Safari Car," a converted flatcar that provides excellent views of the surrounding area. The locomotive that powers the train is a 1946 industrial switch engine that once served Northwest Paper in nearby Cloquet.

WHEN TO GO: Saturdays and Sundays, from mid-June through mid-October. The train makes two 90-minute trips to New Duluth and return.

GOOD TO KNOW: The railroad had its start in the 1980s, and is operated by volunteers from the Lake Superior Transportation Club.

WORTH DOING: Across St. Louis Bay in Superior, Wisconsin, don't miss the SS *Meteor*, the last surviving "whaleback"-type steamship in existence. Built in 1896, it spent much of its career hauling iron ore and other freight on the Great Lakes.

DON'T MISS: Spotting wildlife in the incredible scenery that forms the St. Louis River Estuary is a fun part of the trip; deer and native birds are regularly seen from the train.

GETTING THERE: Duluth is on Lake Superior, about 150 miles from the Twin Cities. In Duluth, go south on I-35, take Exit 251B onto Grand Avenue. The boarding location is across from the Lake Superior Zoo.

LOCATION: 7100 Grand Avenue, Duluth
PHONE: 218-624-7549
WEBSITE: lsmrr.org
E-MAIL: lsmrr46@hotmail.com

Lake Superior Railroad Museum

Jeff Terry

183

This is a combination of a great railroad museum and a great train ride. The Lake Superior Railroad Museum is located in a historic depot in downtown Duluth. Its extensive rolling stock collection rests in the train shed, and just outside, excursion trains ply the route to Two Harbors, with outstanding views along the way.

CHOICES: The Lake Superior Railroad Museum has a large collection of steam, diesel, and electric locomotives as well as passenger coaches, freight cars, and cabooses. Much of the equipment was used on Minnesota railroads, including the first locomotive operated in the state. The museum also operates the North Shore Scenic Railroad, which conducts two regular excursions. A 6-hour round trip takes you through the countryside into Two Harbors. A shorter (90-minute) excursion runs along the shores of Lake Superior to Lester River. Also operating are a pizza train and a variety of specials.

WHEN TO GO: The museum is open daily year-round, with extended summer hours. Regular excursions are offered late May through mid-October.

GOOD TO KNOW: Take a close look at the *William Crooks*, the first locomotive operated in Minnesota. Built in 1861, it is one of a handful of engines remaining from the Civil War era. Duluth & Northeastern 2-8-0 No. 28 pulls steam excursions.

WORTH DOING: The Duluth depot (St. Louis County Heritage and Arts Center) is also home to the Duluth Art Institute, St. Louis County Historical Society museum, and several arts groups.

DON'T MISS: Watch the massive Duluth, Missabe & Iron Range Railroad Yellowstone type locomotive come to life. Clever museum folks have set it up so that every 30 minutes an electric motor sets the drivers in motion, rotating the running gear, and lights and sounds operate.

GETTING THERE: Situated on Lake Superior, Duluth is 150 miles from the Twin Cities. To reach the museum, take Exit 256 off I-35 and follow Michigan Street to the depot.

LOCATION: 506 W. Michigan Street, Duluth
PHONE: 218-727-8025 (museum) or
218-722-1273 (train)
WEBSITE: lsrm.org or northshorescenicrailroad.org
E-MAIL: forms on websites

Milwaukee Road 261

Dave Crosby

Railroading Heritage of Midwest America and its operating arm, The Friends of the 261, operate excursion trips pulled by Milwaukee Road steam locomotive No. 261, a 4-8-4 built by American Locomotive Company in 1944. In 2008 work began on an extensive five-year overhaul of the locomotive and it returned to excursion service in May 2013. The Friends also operate historic passenger cars on Amtrak trains, most frequently on the *Empire Builder* between the Twin Cities and Chicago. These trips are usually open to the public.

CHOICES: The Friends of the 261 offer several options for passengers. All trips include coach, first class and premium class services. Premium class includes hors d'oeuvres and gourmet meals prepared on board and a ride in one of two former Milwaukee Road *Hiawatha* cars: Skytop lounge observation *Cedar Rapids* and full-length Super Dome No. 53. First class includes an upscale meal plan with hors d'oeuvres and a ride in parlor or lounge cars, including two recently purchased Budd and ACF-built dome cars. Both first and premium class include complimentary beverages.

WHEN TO GO: Generally, the Friends operate trips beginning in May and running as late as October.

GOOD TO KNOW: Downtown Minneapolis is near the 261 shop and has a variety of hotels and restaurants. For a complete Milwaukee Road experience, stay in one of the two hotels at the former Milwaukee Road Minneapolis passenger depot, built in 1898 and beautifully restored.

WORTH DOING: Trains usually leave from the 261 facility in northeast Minneapolis. Head down to the shop in Minneapolis the evening before a trip just to take in the sights and sounds of a large steam engine at night. Usually the crew has a donation box out and for a small price you can have a look in the cab.

DON'T MISS: Get a look at Skytop lounge observation car *Cedar Rapids*. Built by the Milwaukee Road in 1948, with their large glass area the Skytops were unlike any other rail passenger car. The *Cedar Rapids* is the only Skytop still in operation.

GETTING THERE: A short walk from the Metro Transit bus stop at Central Avenue and Broadway will get you to the shop, or you can take a taxi. Ample parking is available at the shop on excursion days.

LOCATION: 401 Harrison Street NE, Minneapolis
WEBSITE: 261.com
E-MAIL: form on website

North Shore Scenic Railroad

Steve Glischinski

The North Shore Scenic Railroad offers rides along the scenic North Shore of Lake Superior between downtown Duluth and Two Harbors, Minn., a 27-mile trip on former Duluth, Missabe & Iron Range Railway trackage.

CHOICES: The most popular train is the *Duluth Zephyr* that operates daily in the summer and offers a 1½ hour trip through downtown, along the shoreline of Lake Superior, and up the shore to the Lester River. Music and pizza trains run from Duluth to Palmers, about halfway to Two Harbors. The *Two Harbors Turn* is a six-hour trip up the North Shore with a layover-stop for lunch, touring and shopping in Two Harbors. First class service is offered in ex-Burlington dome car *Silver Club*. Trains run from May to late October, with Thomas the Tank Engine specials operated each August. In December, holiday specials using a Budd RDC car operate from the Fitgers complex in Duluth's east end to the Lake Superior Railroad Museum.

WHEN TO GO: Summer in Duluth is short and tourists flock to the city for its "air conditioning" provided by Lake Superior. It's less hectic in early September, after the summer season is over but before the fall leaf viewing season starts.

GOOD TO KNOW: Book your train rides and especially hotel rooms early. Getting rooms on summer weekends can be difficult. Consider airbnb or VRBO if you are planning to be in the area for an extended period.

WORTH DOING: Take the North Shore Scenic trip to Two Harbors that connects two museums located in former railroad depots: the Lake Superior Railroad Museum in the Duluth Union Depot, and the Lake County Historical Society Museum in the Duluth & Iron Range Depot in Two Harbors. Both museums offer the chance to view DM&IR 2-8-8-4 "Yellowstone" steam locomotives: No. 227 in Duluth and No. 229 in Two Harbors.

DON'T MISS: The run along Duluth's Lake Walk just after departure from the Duluth depot offers great views of Lake Superior and the famous Aerial Lift Bridge.

GETTING THERE: Duluth is about 150 miles north of the Twin Cities of Minneapolis and St. Paul, and has airline and bus service. If driving, instead of Interstate 35 follow old Highway 61 north to see the small towns along the former Northern Pacific line to Duluth, which parallels the highway.

LOCATION: 506 West Michigan Street, Duluth
PHONE: 218-722-1273, 800-423-1273
WEBSITE: northshorescenicrailroad.org

NEBRASKA

Cody Park Railroad Museum

The Cody Park Railroad Museum displays one of the two remaining Union Pacific Challenger class locomotives. Also displayed are a UP Centennial diesel engine, baggage car, mail car, and caboose. The restored Hershey depot contains Union Pacific items, telegraph equipment, and other exhibits. It is open daily May through September.

LOCATION: 1400 N. Jeffers Street, North Platte
PHONE: 308-532-4729
WEBSITE: visitnorthplatte.com
E-MAIL: info@visitnorthplatte.com

Durham Museum

Built in 1931, Omaha's Union Station is a beautiful example of Art Deco style. This historic railroad station now houses both permanent and temporary historical exhibits. Rail displays include a Union Pacific 4-6-0 No. 1243 steam locomotive, which was built in the 1890s, a streetcar, caboose 25559, and several passenger cars. Be sure to have a malt, ice cream soda, or phosphate at the restored soda fountain as travelers did in 1931. Railroad Days take place during the summer. Open Tuesday through Sunday year-round, plus Mondays in summer. Closed major holidays.

LOCATION: 801 S. 10th Street, Omaha
PHONE: 402-444-5071
WEBSITE: durhammuseum.org
E-MAIL: info@durhammuseum.org

Golden Spike Tower

Golden Spike Tower is an observation tower that overlooks the world's largest railroad yard. The visitor center includes artifacts of the Union Pacific. The lobby features equipment exhibits and a model train. The enclosed 8th floor includes informational kiosks with children's activities. The tower is open daily.

LOCATION: 1249 N. Homestead Road, North Platte
PHONE: 308-532-9920
WEBSITE: goldenspiketower.com
E-MAIL: info@goldenspiketower.com

Lauritzen Gardens

What does a botanical garden have to do with railroad history? Plenty, since it exhibits two of the largest locomotives ever built, Union Pacific DDA40X diesel locomotive No. 6900 and Big Boy steam locomotive No. 4023. Viewing platforms allow a peek inside the cabs of both locomotives. The gardens are open daily, with extended evening hours on Mondays and Tuesday mid-May through mid-September.

LOCATION: 100 Bancroft Street, Omaha
PHONE: 402-346-4002
WEBSITE: lauritzengardens.org
E-MAIL: form on website

Rock Island Depot Railroad Museum

The museum is located in one of the state's two remaining brick Rock Island depots. Built in 1914, the brick building also housed the railroad's Western Division Headquarters. The collection features Rock Island artifacts and a restored baggage room, lobby, and ticket office. The site also includes restored gardens. Rock Island Rail Days take place in June. It is open Friday through Sunday.

LOCATION: 910 Second Street, Fairbury
PHONE: 402-729-5131
WEBSITE: fairbury.com facebook.com/RockIslandMuseum/
E-MAIL: fairburyridepot@windstream.net directorjchs@gmail.com

Stuhr Museum of the Prairie Pioneer

This interactive museum takes you back to an 1890s railroad town with more than 60 restored buildings. During the summer, townspeople dressed in period clothing demonstrate daily life on the Plains. A 1901 steam locomotive, a 1912 caboose, an 1871 coach, and other railcars are on display. It is open daily except for Mondays in January, February, and March.

LOCATION: 3133 W. Highway 34, Grand Island
PHONE: 308-385-5316
WEBSITE: stuhrmuseum.org
E-MAIL: info@sturhmuseum.org

Trails & Rails Museum

The Rails portion of the museum includes an 1898 Union Pacific depot. The depot houses transportation exhibits, and its waiting room and ticket office have been restored. On display are a 2-8-0 Baldwin steam engine, a UP flatcar, a caboose, and other equipment. The museum contains other historic buildings including the distinctive Freighters Hotel. It is open year-round, except for weekends September through May.

LOCATION: 710 W. 11th Street, Kearney
PHONE: 308-234-3041
WEBSITE: bchs.us
E-MAIL: bchs.us@hotmail.com

NORTH DAKOTA

Bonanzaville USA

The museum features more than 40 historic buildings and 400,000 artifacts that depict life when bonanza homes dotted the Plains. Rail structures include a vintage Northern Pacific train depot, a water tower, and a train shed. The train shed displays an 1883 Northern Pacific 4-4-0 steam locomotive, a caboose, and a 1930s Pullman car. It is open May through September.

LOCATION: 1351 W. Main Avenue, West Fargo
PHONE: 701-282-2822
WEBSITE: bonanzaville.org
E-MAIL: form on website

Fort Lincoln Trolley

The trolley car takes you on a 9-mile excursion along the Heart River from Mandan to Fort Abraham Lincoln State Park and back. The park features several reconstructed buildings that would have been found in the original fort.

LOCATION: 2000 Third Street SE, Mandan
PHONE: 701-663-9018
WEBSITE: ndtourism.com/mandan/forts/fort-lincoln-trolley

Midland Continental Depot Transportation Museum

The restored depot is the only surviving Midland Continental station and is on the National Register of Historic Places. The first floor houses railroad exhibits and the upper floor, once the agent's living quarters, has exhibits honoring singer Peggy Lee, who lived in the depot when her father was the agent. It is open from Memorial Day to Labor Day.

LOCATION: 401 Railway Street, Wimbledon
PHONE: 701-320-1020 or 701-435-2875
WEBSITE: midlandcontinentaldepot.com
E-MAIL: midlandcontinentaldepot@gmail.com

North Dakota State Railroad Museum

New exhibits to the 5-acre museum include an 1890 depot moved from Steele and a 1953 diesel switcher. The main museum building, a former Burlington Northern yard office, houses artifacts from several railroads. Rolling stock includes cabooses, boxcars, and a tank car. It is open daily Memorial Day through Labor Day, with special events, such as Watermelon Days, scheduled during the summer.

LOCATION: 3102 37th Street NW, Mandan
PHONE: 701-663-9322
WEBSITE: ndsrm.org
E-MAIL: ndstaterrmuseum@gmail.com

Old Soo Depot Transportation Museum

This museum focuses on the transportation history of the American West and includes materials on trains, planes, and automobiles. Located in a completely restored 1912 Soo Line depot, it also offers an excellent location for train-watching. The museum is open Monday through Friday.

LOCATION: 15 N. Main Street, Minot
PHONE: 701-852-2234
WEBSITE: visitminot.org
E-MAIL: soodepot@srt.com

Railroad Museum of Minot

The Railroad Museum of Minot contains artifacts relating to the Great Northern Railway and other railroads of the area. A Great Northern Railway caboose and a snowplow car are also on display. The museum is open 10-2 on Saturdays.

LOCATION: 19 First Street NE, Minot
PHONE: 701-852-7091
WEBSITE: facebook.com/pages/RailRoad-Museum-of-Minot/276975999071833
E-MAIL: railroadmuseum@srt.com

SOUTH DAKOTA

Prairie Village

Prairie Village is a collection of restored buildings, rail equipment, and farm machinery that preserves the past. Rail structures include several historic depots, a roundhouse, and an operating turntable. The museum is open daily mid-May until Labor Day. On Saturdays, you can take a 2-mile train ride around the village. Steam and diesel locomotives are featured as well as Chapel Car Emmanuel, one of the only chapel cars remaining in existence. Major events featuring the railroad include Railroad Days in early July, Steam Threshing Jamboree in late August, and a pumpkin train in early October.

LOCATION: 45205 Highway 34, Madison
PHONE: 800-693-3644 or 605-256-3644
WEBSITE: prairievillage.org
E-MAIL: info@prairievillage.org

South Dakota State Railroad Museum

The museum contains artifacts and rolling stock related to the railroads that have served South Dakota since 1872. It also features additional displays and seasonal activities including the annual Trees and Trains exhibit. The museum is located next to the Black Hills Central Railroad. It is open daily May into October.

LOCATION: 222 Railroad Avenue, Hill City
PHONE: 605-574-9000
WEBSITE: sdsrm.org
E-MAIL: sdsrrm@gmail.com

Black Hills Central Railroad

Dave Crosby

This railroad gives you a chance to ride on a real mountain railroad with its steep grades, mines, and scenic hills. Situated close to Mount Rushmore, the Black Hills Central, also known as the 1880s Train, carries riders between Keystone and Hill City.

CHOICES: The 2-hour, 20-mile round trip is a beautiful journey through the historic, rugged landscape of the Black Hills. Both steam and diesel locomotives power the train, with steam engines being more prevalent. You can ride in a coach or climb into the drover's car, believed to be one of only two left from the Chicago & North Western Railroad and the only one in use. Cattlemen lived in these cars while following their herds to market. Fitting for the area, Wild West shootouts take place several times during the season. Other special events also take place.

WHEN TO GO: With a few exceptions, trains operate daily between mid-May and mid-October, departing from both Keystone and Hill City. Trains make several trips a day on most days. Some last-train departures from Keystone are one-way trips only. Holiday trains run in November and December.

GOOD TO KNOW: Keystone is rich in tourist offerings including restaurants, shows, and shops. Hill City has amenities but without the tourist hubbub.

WORTH DOING: The Black Hills area is filled with must-see activities, including a trip to Mount Rushmore. You can experience the rugged beauty of the Badlands, see bison in Custer State Park, and visit the Wild West town of Deadwood. The South Dakota State Railroad Museum is right next to the Black Hills Central's depot in Hill City.

DON'T MISS: Try to ride behind steam locomotive No. 110, one of only three operating Mallet locomotives. The locomotive is impressive as it tackles grades as steep as 5 percent for almost a mile but never breaks a sweat.

GETTING THERE: Whether traveling east or west, I-90 gets you to the train. To reach Keystone from Rapid City, take Highway 16 to Highway 244. To reach Hill City from Deadwood, take Highway 385.

LOCATION: 222 Railroad Avenue, Hill City
PHONE: 605-574-2222
WEBSITE: 1880train.com
E-MAIL: form on website

REGION 6

ARKANSAS

1 Arkansas & Missouri Railroad
2 Arkansas Railroad Museum
3 Eureka Springs & North Arkansas Railway
4 Fort Smith Trolley Museum
5 Frisco Depot Museum
6 METRO Streetcar

KANSAS

7 Abilene & Smoky Valley Railroad
8 Atchison Rail Museum
9 The Great Overland Station
10 Great Plains Transportation Museum
11 Heart of the Heartlands
12 Kansas Belle Dinner Train
13 Midland Railway

LOUISIANA

14 DeQuincy Railroad Museum
15 New Orleans Streetcars
16 Southern Forest Heritage Museum

MISSOURI

17 Belton, Grandview & Kansas City Railroad
18 Branson Scenic Railway
19 Chicago & Alton Railroad Depot
20 KC Rail Experience
21 Museum of Transportation
22 Railroad Historical Museum
23 St. Louis Iron Mountain & Southern Railway

OKLAHOMA

24 Frisco Depot Museum
25 Heritage Express Trolley
26 Oklahoma Railway Museum
27 Railroad Museum of Oklahoma
28 Route 66 Historical Village
29 Santa Fe Depot Museum
30 Waynoka Air-Rail Museum

TEXAS

31 Austin Steam Train
32 B-RI Railroad Museum
33 Eagle Lake DepotMuseum
34 Ennis Railroad and Cultural Heritage Museum
35 Galveston Railroad Museum
36 Grapevine Vintage Railroad
37 History Center
38 Interurban Railway Museum
39 Lehnis Railroad Museum
40 McKinney Avenue Trolley
41 Museum of the American Railroad
42 New Braunfels Railroad Museum
43 Railroad & Heritage Museum
44 Railway Museum of San Angelo
45 Rosenberg Railroad Museum
46 Texas & Pacific Railway Museum
47 Texas State Railroad
48 Texas Transportation Museum
49 Wichita Falls Railroad Museum

KANSAS

- 70 Hays
- Garden City
- Dodge City
- Liberal
- Manhattan
- 7
- Salina
- Topeka
- 11
- 12
- Olathe
- Saint Joseph
- 8
- Kansas City
- 19
- 18
- 16
- 29
- 35
- Trenton
- Macon
- 70
- Saint Louis
- 20
- MISSOURI
- 44
- Emporia
- Hutchinson
- 9
- Wichita
- El Dorado
- Winfield
- 10
- Carthage
- Springfield
- 21
- 22
- 55
- 29
- Woodward
- Enid
- 26
- 35
- 27
- Tulsa
- Bartlesville
- 17
- 3
- Fayetteville
- 1
- 5
- Jonesboro
- OKLAHOMA
- 24
- 25
- Oklahoma City
- 40
- Norman
- Shawnee
- Muskogee
- 4
- ARKANSAS
- 40
- Altus
- Lawton
- 28
- Ada
- Mcalester
- Little Rock
- 6
- 40
- Vernon
- Wichita Falls
- 48
- Atoka
- Durant
- 23
- Pine Bluff
- 2
- 30
- Sherman
- Paris
- Bastrop
- Monroe
- Sweetwater
- Abilene
- 20
- Fort Worth
- 35
- 40
- 37
- 39
- 33
- Dallas
- Waxahachie
- 45
- Shreveport
- 49
- LOUISIANA
- 38
- Waco
- 31
- 46
- Nacogdoches
- San Angelo
- 43
- TEXAS
- 42
- 45
- Lufkin
- 15
- 10
- Bryan
- Huntsville
- 36
- 13
- 10
- Baton Rouge
- 14
- Austin
- 30
- Beaumont
- Port Arthur
- Houma
- New Orleans
- Kerrville
- 41
- 32
- 44
- Houston
- 34
- Galveston
- Del Rio
- San Antonio
- 47
- Victoria
- Bay City
- 35
- Beeville
- Port Lavaca
- Laredo
- Corpus Christi
- Kingsville
- Edinburg
- Harlingen

ARKANSAS

Fort Smith Trolley Museum

Visit this museum and you can see its collection of railroad, streetcar, and transportation exhibits, including Frisco steam locomotive 4003. Board No. 224, a restored Fort Smith streetcar at the Fort Smith Museum of History on Rogers Avenue for an enjoyable trolley ride. The museum is open Saturdays year-round, and trolleys run daily May through October and Friday through Sunday the rest of the year.

LOCATION: 100 S. Fourth Street, Fort Smith
PHONE: 479-783-0205
WEBSITE: fstm.org
E-MAIL: info@fstm.org

Frisco Depot Museum

This restored Victorian depot was built in 1886 and operated by the Frisco Railroad. Take a self-guided tour and hear the stories of 14 figures representing passengers, station workers, and a train crew. You can also examine a Frisco caboose. Located in Mammoth Spring State Park, the depot is closed on Mondays.

LOCATION: Highway 9 and Highway 63, Mammoth Spring
PHONE: 870-625-7364
WEBSITE: arkansasstateparks.com/mammothspring
E-MAIL: mammothspring@arkansas.com

METRO Streetcar

METRO Streetcar is a heritage trolley line operated by the Rock Region METRO between Little Rock and North Little Rock using replica vintage electric cars. The 3.4-mile route connects historical districts and tourist attractions in both cities.. All cars are climate-controlled and handicap accessible. The streetcars operate year-round except on major holidays.

LOCATION: Scott and Markham streets (Main Street Bridge), Little Rock
PHONE: 501-375-6717
WEBSITE: rrmetro.org/services/streetcar
E-MAIL: info@rrmetro.org

Arkansas & Missouri Railroad

David Hoge

From the highest point to down in the hollers, the Arkansas & Missouri operates excursion trains powered by its all-Alco roster of diesels. Rebuilt air-conditioned coaches transport riders through some of the most rugged terrain between the Appalachians and the Rockies. The A&M operates 139 miles of former St. Louis-San Francisco trackage from Monett, Mo., to Fort Smith, Ark., through the Boston Mountains of northwest Arkansas.

CHOICES: The longest ride is a 134-mile round trip from Springdale to Van Buren with a 3-hour stop in Van Buren, where passengers can shop or dine near the 1901 Frisco depot. Another ride is a 70-mile round trip from Van Buren to Winslow with a ride over 100-foot trestles and through the 1,700-foot-long Winslow tunnel. A winter excursion takes you from Fort Smith over the Arkansas River to Winslow.

WHEN TO GO: With its schedule of special events, trains run all year. Fall offers the best scenery, and fall trips sell out quickly, but spring is also popular because everything is blooming.

GOOD TO KNOW: Three classes—first class, club, and coach—are offered on all trips, with lunch or snacks provided for first class and club class. Fares increase for trips during the fall foliage season.

WORTH DOING: The A&M excursion fits in nicely with a trip to Branson or to the William J. Clinton Presidential Library in Little Rock. Eureka Springs offers shopping, and the nearby Buffalo and Mulberry Rivers provide camping, canoeing, and hiking opportunities. Two Civil War battlefields are nearby.

DON'T MISS: For an old-time railroading experience, you can purchase a ticket for the restored B&O cupola caboose, which holds about a dozen passengers.

GETTING THERE: Traveling over I-540, I-49, and I-40 gives the area quick access, making the A&M easily accessible for a day of fun.

LOCATION: 306 E. Emma Avenue, Springdale
PHONE: 800-687-8600 or 479-751-8600
WEBSITE: amrailroad.com
E-MAIL: brenda@amrailroad.com

Arkansas Railroad Museum

David Hoge

The Arkansas Railroad Museum is the state's largest railroad museum. The museum is located in the machine shop built in the later part of the 19th century for the St. Louis Southwestern Railway, or Cotton Belt. The machine shop was part of a large complex of buildings and shops once located at Pine Bluff.

CHOICES: The museum's most famous tenant is the last steam locomotive built for the St. Louis Southwestern. No. 819 was assembled in the building that now houses the museum and was placed in service in early 1943. Along with No. 819, SSW No. 336 is also housed at the museum. Several diesel Alcos are also on display along with some passenger cars, a complete SSW work train, cabooses, and a Jordan snowplow. The museum features a large collection of memorabilia from the Cotton Belt and other Arkansas and east Texas railroads.

WHEN TO GO: The museum is open Monday through Saturday. Most exhibits are located inside, but much of the museum is not climate-controlled and therefore subject to the heat and cold. Operating hours can be affected by extreme temperatures.

GOOD TO KNOW: Engines 819 and 336 are the only surviving Cotton Belt steam locomotives, and both are on the National Register of Historic Places.

WORTH DOING: While in Pine Bluff, you can take in the historical museum, which is located in a restored union station that is also listed on the National Register of Historic Places.

DON'T MISS: The museum holds an annual railroadiana show in April.

GETTING THERE: The museum is easily accessible from Little Rock, which has a daily Amtrak stop. The museum lies just a short distance off I-530, which connects Little Rock and Pine Bluff.

LOCATION: 1700 Port Road, Pine Bluff
PHONE: 870-535-8819
WEBSITE: arkansasrailroadmuseum.org
E-MAIL: info@arkansasrailroadmuseum.org

Eureka Springs & North Arkansas Railway

Patrick Hiatte

Spend a pleasant hour on one of the last remnants of the original Missouri & North Arkansas Railroad from Eureka Springs north to Junction, where the train pauses then makes the return trip to Eureka Springs. Enjoy the natural beauty of the Leatherwood Valley.

CHOICES: Ride an ex-Rock Island commuter coach (complete with straps for standees) or choose lunch or dinner aboard the Eurekan dining cars. There are multiple daily departures from May through October, Tuesday through Saturday, and the train also operates on Saturdays in April.

WHEN TO GO: Eureka Springs is a year-round resort, but most visitors arrive during the summer months and autumn, when the thickly wooded surrounding hills are ablaze with fall color. The tourist tide ebbs briefly in mid- and late August.

GOOD TO KNOW: The dining cars are climate-controlled, but the coach is not, except for the pot-bellied stove and ceiling fans. Coach windows can be opened to catch the Ozarks breeze in the summer and on warm days in spring and fall. The train is powered by a 1942-vintage SW1 diesel locomotive. Dining cars and excursion cars may be combined into one train with the locomotive in the middle.

WORTH DOING: Rubber-tired-tram tours and walking tours offer insights into the history of "Little Switzerland." Wander the steep, winding streets of Eureka Springs and browse the art galleries and boutiques. Visit the many springs and the classic Victorian hotels, including The Crescent (built with railroad backing) and the Basin Park, which has ground-level access to each of its eight stories (the hillside on which it's built is that steep). Attend a performance of *The Great Passion Play*, just 4 minutes from the depot.

DON'T MISS: The Eureka Springs depot, built in 1913, and the rail equipment displayed outside. Gems include steam locomotive No. 201, built for service in Panama, and a station wagon equipped to run on rails as an inspection car, as well as a turntable and water tank.

GETTING THERE: Eureka Springs is about an hour northeast of Fayetteville along Highway 62 or an hour southwest of Branson, Mo., via Highways 65, 86, and 23.

LOCATION: 299 N. Main Street, Eureka Springs
PHONE: 479-253-9623, or 479-253-9677
WEBSITE: esnarailway.com
E-MAIL: depot@esnarailway.com

KANSAS

Atchison Rail Museum

The Atchison Rail Museum features an outdoor collection of railcars. On summer weekends, the cars are open for viewing and a miniature railroad operates. It is adjacent to a restored 1880 Santa Fe depot that now houses the county's historical society museum. In summer, trolleys leave from the depot on 45-minute, narrated historical tours.

LOCATION: 200 S. 10th Street, Atchison
PHONE: 913-367-2427
WEBSITE: visitatchison.com/

The Great Overland Station

The museum is housed in the former Union Pacific Topeka station. Opened in 1927, the last passenger train stopped in Topeka on May 2, 1971. Housing Union Pacific and Santa Fe artifacts and photographs, the museum also has exhibits on local history and Kansas trains back to 1932. A display on Harvey Houses and the Harvey Girls can be brought to life for groups of 25 to 200 with costumed servers and authentic Harvey House menus. The station is open year-round Tuesday through Saturday except holidays.

LOCATION: 701 N Kansas Avenue, Topeka
PHONE: 785-232-5533
WEBSITE: greatoverlandstation.com
E-MAIL: form on website

Great Plains Transportation Museum

The museum features an outdoor display of locomotives, cabooses, and cars, including Santa Fe steam locomotive No. 3768 and Santa Fe FP45 diesel No. 93. Indoor exhibits feature railroad signs, lanterns, tools, and other artifacts. It is open year-round on Saturdays and also on Sundays from April to October. On the museum's website, you can view historical railroad documents such as timetables, train orders, and waybills.

LOCATION: 700 E. Douglas Avenue, Wichita
PHONE: 316-263-0944
WEBSITE: gptm.us
E-MAIL: info@gptm.us

Heart of the Heartlands Museum

The museum complex includes a building of rail exhibits, two Missouri Pacific depots, and a collection of locomotives, including the restored Kansas City Southern no. 1023, and railcars. The museum offers several short train excursions and motor car rides. The buildings are open the first and third weekends June through August.

LOCATION: 6769 NW 20th Street, Scammon
PHONE: 620-396-8594
WEBSITE: heartlandstrainclub.org
E-MAIL: heartlands@cox.net

Kansas Belle Dinner Train

The Kansas Belle Dinner Train operates 3-hour Saturday evening runs using 1940s-themed cars, more formal and romantic, with an optional murder mystery play, WWII USO show, or melodrama. Sunday afternoon dinner trips offer a more casual setting, better suited for families, with a slightly shorter run time. The trips operate over Midland Railway track between Baldwin City and Ottawa using Midland's locomotives.

LOCATION: 1515 High Street, Baldwin City
PHONE: 785-594-8505
WEBSITE: kansasbelle.com
E-MAIL: form on website

Abilene & Smoky Valley Railroad

Patrick Hiatte

Ride behind an ex-Santa Fe Pacific or an Alco S-1 on an 11-mile, 90-minute round trip over an ex-Rock Island line from the restored Rock Island depot in Abilene to Enterprise and return. Cross the Smoky Hill River on an early steel truss bridge.

200

CHOICES: A restored coach, open-air (but shaded) gondola cars and an ex-Union Pacific caboose are the regular consist; extra fare will get you on board the caboose or in the cab of the steam or diesel locomotive. On the second Saturday of each month ASV offers a historic home and barn tour. On the fourth Saturday, you can extend your trip on the Silver Flyer railbus, which meets the train in Enterprise and runs on rail to the German/Swedish community of Woodbine.

WHEN TO GO: Trains run Wednesday through Sunday from Memorial Day through Labor Day, and on weekends in May, September and October. The steam engine typically runs on the Memorial Day, Independence Day and Labor Day weekends, the National Day of the Cowboy the fourth weekend in July, and Heritage Day the first weekend in October. ASV also operates for school field trips and dinner trains on selected Saturday evenings.

GOOD TO KNOW: The Dwight D. Eisenhower Presidential Library and Museum complex, including Ike's boyhood home, is just across the tracks from the ASV depot.

WORTH DOING: Wander Abilene Old Town just south of the depot and enjoy a fried-chicken dinner. Visit the Dickinson County Heritage Center a block northeast of the depot to ride the carousel and view the Museum of Independent Telephony. See the Greyhound Hall of Fame a block northwest of the depot.

DON'T MISS: In addition to the ASV's Rock Island depot, the Santa Fe (now BNSF) combination depot and the Union Pacific depot and freight house are still standing. The UP depot is open to the public and houses the Abilene Visitors Center, where you can take home a copy of Mamie Eisenhower's sugar cookie recipe.

GETTING THERE: Abilene is on I-70 about 150 miles west of Kansas City and about 90 miles north of Wichita. The ASV depot is about 2 miles south of I-70 off Highway 15 (Buckeye Avenue), just south of the Eisenhower complex.

LOCATION: 200 SE Fifth Street, Abilene
PHONE: 888-426-6687 or 785-263-1077
WEBSITE: asvrr.org
E-MAIL: asvrail@gmail.com

Midland Railway

Ralcon Wagner

The Midland Railway offers 20-mile round trips in the pleasant Kansas countryside between Baldwin City and Ottawa. The museum has a roster of first-generation diesels that includes an ex-Missouri-Kansas-Texas Alco RS-3 and a former Chicago, Burlington & Quincy EMD NW2. The Midland uses passenger coaches, cabooses, and a transfer caboose on its excursions.

CHOICES: Regular service includes 1-hour excursions from Baldwin City to Norwood that cross two 200-foot trestles and 2-hour trips to the end of the line at Ottawa Junction, where the line meets BNSF's Transcon. Midland also offers Thomas the Tank Engine, Halloween Night Trains of Terror, Santa trains, an Ice Cream Express, and other special excursions.

WHEN TO GO: The Midland operates primarily on weekends from June to October, with Thursday trains added for summer. The Midland also participates in various community festivals including the Maple Leaf Festival, which takes place the third weekend in October.

GOOD TO KNOW: The Kansas Belle Dinner Train operates over the Midland Railway's route from Baldwin City to Ottawa on many weekends.

WORTH DOING: Journey south to Ottawa and visit the Old Depot Museum, housed in an old 1888 Santa Fe depot or stroll down the Prairie Spirit Trail (the trailhead is behind the Old Depot Museum), a converted rail trail.

DON'T MISS: Look through the Midland's 1906 Baldwin City depot, which is listed on the National Register of Historic Places.

GETTING THERE: Baldwin City is 45 miles southwest of Kansas City on Highway 56. The Midland depot is on High Street, just west of the town square.

LOCATION: 1515 W. High Street, Baldwin City
PHONE: 913-721-1211 or 785-594-6982 (depot)
WEBSITE: midlandrailway.org
E-MAIL: form on website

LOUISIANA

DeQuincy Railroad Museum

Home to the DeQuincy Railroad Museum, the former Kansas City Southern depot is an outstanding example of Mission Revival architecture and is on the National Register of Historic Places. It displays a 1913 Alco steam locomotive, a caboose, and a passenger coach as well as artifacts and memorabilia. It is open Tuesdays through Saturdays. The annual Louisiana Railroad Days Festival is held here in April.

LOCATION: 400 Lake Charles Avenue, DeQuincy
PHONE: 337-786-2823
WEBSITE: dequincyrailroadmuseum.com
E-MAIL: dequincyrailroadmuseum@centurylink.net

Southern Forest Heritage Museum

At this museum, a guided tour takes you around a 57-acre historic sawmill complex, where you'll see a roundhouse and other industrial structures, three early logging locomotives, two McGiffert loaders, a Clyde skidder, and other steam equipment. Railbus rides on original Red River & Gulf Railroad track are available. An exhibit also highlights the history of the railroad. It is open Tuesdays through Sundays but closes during winter.

LOCATION: 77 Long Leaf Road, Long Leaf
PHONE: 318-748-8404
WEBSITE: forestheritagemuseum.org
E-MAIL: sfhmwebadmin@cox.net

New Orleans Streetcars

Elrond Lawrence

Streetcars are a great way to see New Orleans, and if you have the desire, you can ride several different streetcar lines, operated today by the city's transit agency. While all of them make it simple to get around the Big Easy, each has its own character and charm that truly offers a fascinating view of this diverse city.

CHOICES: The St. Charles Line features the oldest continuously operating street railway system in the world. Named as a National Historic Landmark, it passes antebellum mansions, historic monuments, universities, and other sights. The Canal Street Line, which has two branches, takes passengers from the French Market through the central business district to City Park Avenue or to an area of historic cemeteries. The Riverfront Line travels the downtown area along the Mississippi River. The Rampart-St. Claude Streetcar Line runs down Loyola from New Orleans Union Passenger Terminal to Elysian Fields.

WHEN TO GO: All lines run every day of the year. As with most coastal cities, expect humidity and high temperatures in summer; this is especially noticeable on the St. Charles Line as its historic Perley Thomas cars lack air-conditioning.

GOOD TO KNOW: Despite fewer amenities, fans of history and interurbans alike will enjoy the trip along St. Charles Avenue. The line was built in 1835, and since it's on the National Register of Historic Places, the cars must remain as they were back in 1923.

WORTH DOING: It's hard to think of New Orleans and not associate Mardi Gras with it. The parties and parades actually begin the weekend before, and as the city's population explodes during this time, consider that when making travel plans.

DON'T MISS: Sure, there's the French Quarter, but outside this half-square-mile box, you'll find a Mississippi River cruise aboard an authentic steamboat, the National World War II Museum, the Audubon Nature Institute, plus music festivals and restaurants featuring notable indigenous cuisine.

GETTING THERE: Thanks to the line's sprawling routes, there are many places to catch a New Orleans streetcar. One of the best is via the Canal Street Line connection at the New Orleans Union Passenger Terminal.

LOCATION: Carrolton Avenue, Claiborne Avenue, Canal Street, New Orleans
PHONE: 504-248-3900
WEBSITE: norta.com
E-MAIL: comments@norta.com

MISSOURI

Belton, Grandview & Kansas City Railroad

At this laid-back railroad, you can walk around the yard, look at displayed equipment, and talk to the crew before boarding a 5-mile excursion. The 45-minute round trip runs south from Belton. Rides in the locomotive with the engineer are also available. Trains run May through October with additional Santa trains.

LOCATION: 502 E. Walnut Street, Belton
PHONE: 816-331-0630
WEBSITE: beltonrailroad.org
E-MAIL: info@beltonrailroad.org

Chicago & Alton Railroad Depot

Built in 1879, the two-story Chicago & Alton depot features a restored four-room stationmaster's residence on the second floor. The first floor contains a waiting room, baggage room, and stationmaster's room. The depot contains hundreds of C&A artifacts. It is open daily except Tuesdays, April through October.

LOCATION: 318 W. Pacific Avenue, Independence
PHONE: 816-325-7955
WEBSITE: chicagoaltondepot1879.org/
E-MAIL: chicagoaltondepot@gmail.com

KC Rail Experience

Located in historic Union Station, the KC Rail Experience features a vintage railcar, a diesel engine, artifacts, and a locomotive simulator. Admission is included with a ticket to Science City, an interactive science center. You can also view trains of all sizes, from a model railroad exhibit to actual operating trains that you can see from a footbridge over the tracks.

LOCATION: 30 W. Pershing Road, Kansas City
PHONE: 816-460-2020
WEBSITE: unionstation.org
E-MAIL: visitor@unionstation.org

Railroad Historical Museum

Located in Grant Beach Park, this train museum is an actual train. A locomotive, baggage car, commuter car, and caboose contain artifacts from the St. Louis-San Francisco and other railroads. After touring the museum, you can enjoy the park's pool, playground, and picnic area. It is open Saturdays, May through October.

LOCATION: 1353 N. Douglas Avenue, Springfield
PHONE: 417-833-0994
WEBSITE: rrhistoricalmuseum.zoomshare.com
E-MAIL: railroadhistoricalmuseum@yahoo.com

St. Louis Iron Mountain & Southern Railway

From April through December, this railway offers a large variety of trips including sightseeing excursions, murder mysteries, train robberies, and holiday-themed rides. Trains are pulled by Pennsylvania Railroad No. 5898, a 1950 E unit.

LOCATION: 252 E. Jackson Boulevard, Jackson
PHONE: 573-243-1688
WEBSITE: slimrr.com
E-MAIL: slimrr1@gmail.com

Branson Scenic Railway

Patrick Hiatte

Enjoy a 40-mile round trip through the Ozarks on the former Missouri Pacific Railroad White River Line, built more than a century ago. View historic towns and pass through tunnels and over high bridges along the banks of the White River and its tributaries.

CHOICES: There's open seating in the dome cars, 60-seat deluxe coach and concession/lounge cars that comprise the regular train. A dinner train operates on Saturday evenings from April through October. Polar Express trains operate on Fridays, Saturdays and Sundays in November and December and most weekdays in December.

WHEN TO GO: The Ozarks are scenic any time of the year. Spring brings wildflowers, and white dogwoods and redbuds color the green hills. In fall oaks and other hardwoods turn red, yellow and orange. Branson Scenic operates three trains a day during the two weeks in October when the colors are usually at their height, as well as during Branson's peak summer season in June and July. At least two or three trains a day operate from mid-March through mid-December. Trains also operate on Sunday on holiday weekends.

GOOD TO KNOW: Seating is open and boarding is by group based on ticket number; the sooner you buy your ticket, the more likely you are to get a seat in one of the three domes. Free parking for BSR is across Main Street from the depot. The train usually runs south from Branson, but may run north depending on freight traffic and track work on the host Missouri & Northern Arkansas Railroad.

WORTH DOING: Branson offers more than 100 shows, from tribute bands to illusionists and comedians to dozens of country music shows. Other attractions run the gamut from exhibits of *Titanic* artifacts to cruises on Table Rock Lake to Silver Dollar City, a theme park emphasizing Ozarks heritage and crafts.

DON'T MISS: At Silver Dollar City, ride the Frisco Silver Dollar Line, named for the Frisco Railway, which had its operating headquarters just up the road in Springfield.

GETTING THERE: Branson is in southwest Missouri about 45 miles south of Springfield on Highway 65. The depot is downtown on Main Street (Highway 76).

LOCATION: 206 E. Main Street, Branson
PHONE: 800-287-2462 or 417-334-6110
WEBSITE: bransontrain.com
E-MAIL: reservations@bransontrain.com

Museum of Transportation

Jeff Terry

If you want to be surrounded by trains, this is the place. A visit here brings you in touch with more than 70 locomotives of steam, diesel, and electric power. You'll see scores of railcars and even one of the first railroad tunnels west of the Mississippi. The 150-acre site also houses airplanes, cars, and riverboats.

CHOICES: The museum features a visitor center, 10 other buildings, and almost 200 pieces of rail equipment. Its collection has more than 30 steam locomotives, and stairs let you climb into the cabs of many of them. Many rare and unusual items grace the site, including an Aerotrain, and even a cast-iron turntable.

WHEN TO GO: The museum is open year-round with variable hours. It is open daily during its summer schedule and open Thursday through Sunday during January and February. Trolley rides are offered April through October.

GOOD TO KNOW: At the visitor center, you can board the miniature train that runs through the site. The Creation Station is a hands-on learning center for children 5 and under. It is open weekday mornings and first and third Sundays. It has an extra fee.

WORTH DOING: Of course, if you haven't already done so, enjoy the view from the top of Gateway Arch. You can also take a riverboat cruise, play some ragtime at Scott Joplin's home, enjoy the Missouri Botanical Garden, or view the mosaics at Cathedral Basilica.

DON'T MISS: The only surviving Bi-Polar Electric, Milwaukee Road EP-2 is also on display. In addition, several unusual freight car types are on display, including, GATX 96500, nicknamed the "Rail Whale", a 98-foot-long, 60,000-gallon tank car built in 1965, one of only two.

GETTING THERE: The museum is about 12 miles west of downtown St. Louis. When driving from I-270, either north or south, exit at Dougherty Ferry Road (Exit 8), go west about 1 mile to Barrett Station Road, and turn left. The museum is on the right.

LOCATION: 3015 Barrett Station Road, St. Louis
PHONE: 314-965-6212
WEBSITE: transportmuseumassociation.org
E-MAIL: museum@transportmuseumassociation.org

OKLAHOMA

Frisco Depot Museum

Once a main hub for the Frisco, the depot in Hugo is now a museum. Listed on the National Register of Historic Places, the museum features preserved Harvey Girl rooms, railroad artifacts, and displays on local history. It also includes a restored and operational Harvey House restaurant. Outside the museum, the depot park contains a narrow gauge steam locomotive and picnic areas. It is open Tuesday through Saturday.

LOCATION: 307 N. B Street, Hugo
PHONE: 580-326-6630
WEBSITE: friscodepot.org
E-MAIL: friscodepot@live.com

Heritage Express Trolley

This 25-minute trolley ride is the only rail-based trolley in operation in Oklahoma. It runs from Heritage Park to downtown El Reno. Heritage Park is also home of the Canadian County Museum, which is based in a historical Rock Island train depot. A Rock Island caboose, coal car, and various historic buildings are located on the museum grounds. The trolley runs and the museum is open Wednesdays through Sundays.

LOCATION: 300 S. Grand Avenue, El Reno
PHONE: 405-262-5121
WEBSITE: elrenotourism.org

Railroad Museum of Oklahoma

Located in a former Santa Fe freight house, this museum houses a large collection of railroad artifacts and memorabilia including a replica Pullman car interior. In the yard, you can climb aboard a 1925 Baldwin 4-8-2 steam locomotive, wander through cabooses from nine different railroads, and view an assortment of freight cars. It is open Tuesdays through Saturdays year-round.

LOCATION: 702 N. Washington Street, Enid
PHONE: 580-233-3051
WEBSITE: railroadmuseumofoklahoma.com
E-MAIL: railroad_museum@att.net

Route 66 Historical Village

The new visitors center is a re-creation of a 1920s-1930s Phillips 66 service station, with a new train depot to begin construction in 2019 or 2020 .In the village, you'll see the restored Frisco 4500 *Meteor* steam engine along with a passenger coach, tank car, caboose, and trolley car. A 154-foot oil derrick stands next to the railcars. It also features indoor historical exhibits related to Route 66 from Chicago to Los Angeles.

LOCATION: 3770 Southwest Boulevard, Tulsa
PHONE: 918-857-3782
WEBSITE: facebook.com/route66village

Santa Fe Depot Museum

This 1905 Santa Fe depot has been restored and now contains a collection of railroad photos and other local historical artifacts. On display are 1907 Baldwin steam locomotive Santa Fe No. 1951, a coal tender, and a caboose. The museum is open Tuesday through Saturday, and it features a convenient picnic area. A toy and action figure museum is also located in Pauls Valley.

LOCATION: 204 S. Santa Fe Street, Pauls Valley
PHONE: 405-238-2244
WEBSITE:

Waynoka Air-Rail Museum

The Waynoka Station complex includes a restored 1910 Santa Fe depot and Harvey House, 1918 section foreman's house, water tower, and diesel locomotive. The museum contains displays on Fred Harvey, the Santa Fe Railroad, Waynoka transportation history, and other subjects. The museum is open Tuesday through Saturday.

LOCATION: 1386 S. Cleveland Street, Waynoka
PHONE: 580-824-1886
WEBSITE: waynoka.org
E-MAIL: waynokahs@hotmail.com

Oklahoma Railway Museum

Jeff Terry

The Oklahoma Railway Museum boasts an impressive collection of vintage railroad equipment with ties to the Sooner State. The museum is best known for its collection of working first-generation diesel locomotives, which includes a former Rock Island Alco RS-1, a Santa Fe CF7, and an EMD F7A painted in Frisco colors. On the spacious grounds are more than a dozen freight cars, cabooses, and passenger cars from Oklahoma railroads. Work equipment on exhibit includes a 1954 rail crane and a unique inspection car that was home-built by the Missouri-Kansas-Texas in 1973.

210

CHOICES: On the first and third Saturday of each month, from April through August, museum visitors are offered a 40-minute train ride over an original MKT line. Passengers may choose to ride in an open-air excursion car or aboard one of three 1940s-era streamlined cars that were used on Santa Fe trains such as the *Texas Chief* and *El Capitan*. The train is often pulled by an 1952 SW8 diesel locomotive that's been painted in MKT's classic green and yellow livery.

WHEN TO GO: Besides the regular Saturday excursions, special train rides are scheduled throughout the year, including an Easter Bunny Express, Halloween and Christmas trains, and Day Out with Thomas events.

GOOD TO KNOW: Start your visit at the Oakwood depot, a traditional small-town station built in 1905 to serve the Kansas City, Mexico & Orient Railway. Unused after 1958, the wooden depot was moved to its present location in 2000 and restored.

WORTH DOING: Two miles north of the museum is Oklahoma City's Adventure District, which is home to many of the city's most visited attractions. These include the Oklahoma City Zoo and Botanical Garden, which features 1,900 animals, and Science Museum Oklahoma, where visitors can inspect a full-size replica of NASA's Apollo lunar lander. And lovers of western history, art, and culture will enjoy the National Cowboy & Western Heritage Museum.

DON'T MISS: Santa Fe 2-8-0 steam locomotive No. 643 is one of the oldest AT&SF steam locomotives in existence, having been constructed as an American-type in 1879 and rebuilt into its present configuration in 1897.

GETTING THERE: The museum is located a half-mile west of I-35 off Exit 131 (NE 36th Street) on historic Grand Boulevard.

LOCATION: 3400 NE Grand Boulevard, Oklahoma City
PHONE: 405-424-8222
WEBSITE: oklahomarailwaymuseum.org
E-MAIL: form on website

TEXAS

B-RI Railroad Museum

This two-story 1906 depot served as a Burlington Route & Rock Island transportation hub to the surrounding farming communities until becoming a museum showcasing the local area in 1970. Numerous vintage rail artifacts and photos are displayed on the first floor are while upstairs local history is presented. Outside are lumber hauler W. T. Carter Bros.' No. 1, a 2-8-2 steam locomotive, and a BN caboose. Open on weekends, closed major holidays. Weekday openings can be made for special groups by calling in advance.

LOCATION: 208 S. Third Avenue, Teague
PHONE: 254-739-2153 or 254-359-4100 (evenings)
WEBSITE: therailroadmuseum.com
E-MAIL: adladyginny@gmail.com

Eagle Lake Depot Museum

The Eagle Lake Depot Museum presents a varied and wonderful collection of artifacts from the numerous past railroads of the area presented in a historically accurate setting. Inside the 1911 Santa Fe depot, the agent's office displays authentic furnishings and equipment of a working depot including an operating telegraph. In the west waiting room, an O scale model layout of the Eagle Lake area greets visitors. New exhibits showcase the depot's role in the World War I and USRA eras. Open on the second and fourth Saturdays of the month or by appointment.

LOCATION: 322 E. Main Street, Eagle Lake
WEBSITE: eaglelakedepot.org
E-MAIL: facebook.com/Eagle-Lake-Depot-Inc-156299711091792/

Ennis Railroad and Cultural Heritage Museum

Housed in a 1915 building, the museum contains railroad memorabilia, dioramas, depot replicas, and china, as well as a variety of cultural exhibits. It is open daily, and an MKT caboose is displayed outside. Nearby, the city's visitor center is located in a former Wells Fargo freight office. It is open Tuesdays through Sundays.

LOCATION: 105 NE Main Street, Ennis
PHONE: 972-875-1901 or 972-878-4748
WEBSITE: visitennis.org

History Center

The History Center features indoor and outdoor interpretive exhibits. Permanent displays include a 1920 Baldwin 4-6-0 from Texas Southeastern Railroad—on which you can ring its bell and blow its whistle—a log car, and a caboose. The center contains many photos on east Texas railroading and logging operations. It is closed Sundays.

LOCATION: 102 N. Temple Drive, Diboll
PHONE: 936-829-3543
WEBSITE: thehistorycenteronline.com
E-MAIL: info@thehistorycenteronline.com

Interurban Railway Museum

Located in downtown Plano, the Interurban Railway Museum is housed in a building that served as a primary stop on the Texas Electric Railway that ran from Denison to Dallas beginning in 1908. The museum contains artifacts associated with the interurban line and the history of Plano. Open Monday through Saturday, it also offers guided tours through restored trolley car 360.

LOCATION: 901 E. 15th Street, Plano
PHONE: 972-941-2117
WEBSITE: interurbanrailwaymuseum.org
E-MAIL: info@interurbanrailwaymuseum.org

Lehnis Railroad Museum

This railroad museum displays an AT&SF steam locomotive, a business car, and a caboose. It includes a collection of railroad china, lanterns, equipment, and photos. From the train-watching platform, you can look for passing BNSF trains. Located next to a Harvey House and Santa Fe depot, the museum is open Tuesdays through Saturdays.

LOCATION: 700 E. Adams Street, Brownwood
PHONE: 325-643-6376
WEBSITE: brownwoodtexas.gov
E-MAIL: cstanley@brownwoodtexas.gov

McKinney Avenue Trolley

Vintage electric trolley cars take riders back in time during a leisurely 4.6-mile ride down McKinney Avenue and other streets in Dallas' historic Uptown neighborhood. To board a trolley, just locate an M-Line street sign and wait for a trolley car. Trolleys operate year-round and run every 15 to 25 minutes from morning through evening with extended hours on Fridays and Saturdays.

LOCATION: McKinney Avenue, Dallas
PHONE: 214-855-0006
WEBSITE: mata.org
E-MAIL: form on website

New Braunfels Railroad Museum

Housed in the restored 1907 International & Great Northern depot, the museum displays an 0-6-0T Porter oil-fired steam locomotive, a Missouri Pacific caboose, and numerous railroad artifacts. It is open daily Memorial Day through Labor Day; Thursday through Monday, Labor Day through Memorial Day.

LOCATION: 302 W. San Antonio Street, New Braunfels
PHONE: 830-627-2447
WEBSITE: newbraunfelsrailroadmuseum.org
E-MAIL: info@newbraunfelsrailroadmuseum.org

Railway Museum of San Angelo

Located in a historic Kansas City, Mexico & Orient depot, which was completed in 1910, the museum highlights local railroad history. It features a large collection of railroad photos by Allen Johnson. Static displays include two diesel locomotives and a Santa Fe boxcar and caboose. It is open on Saturdays. For a unique special event for kids, try Hobo Day in August and try to fry an egg on the track.

LOCATION: 703 S. Chadbourne Street, San Angelo
PHONE: 325-486-2140
WEBSITE: railwaymuseumsanangelo.homestead.com
E-MAIL: form on website

213

Rosenberg Railroad Museum

The museum features Tower 17, the last manned interlocking tower in Texas. Inside the fully restored tower, you can work the interlocking machine. Also on display are the *Quebec*, an 1879 business car, diesel switcher No. 2350, and a Missouri Pacific caboose. The museum building, modeled after the city's original depot, contains signaling, station agent, and telegraph artifacts. It is open Wednesdays through Sundays.

LOCATION: 1921 Avenue F, Rosenberg
PHONE: 281-633-2846
WEBSITE: rosenbergrrmuseum.org
E-MAIL: info@rosenbergrrmuseum.org

Temple Railroad and Heritage Museum

Housed in a 1910 Santa Fe depot, the museum features exhibits related to the Santa Fe Railway and the city of Temple including those on Harvey Houses, the Santa Fe Hospital, and railroad lanterns. Outdoor displays feature a variety of cars, including a troop sleeper, a 1921 Pacific type Baldwin steam locomotive, and a 1937 diesel engine. The museum is open Tuesday through Saturday.

LOCATION: 315 W. Avenue B, Temple
PHONE: 254-298-5172
WEBSITE: templerrhm.org
E-MAIL: rrhm@templex.gov

Texas & Pacific Railway Museum

Located in the Ginocchio National Historic District, the restored 1912 depot still operates as a passenger station, now for Amtrak. The T&P museum is on the second floor, and T&P 2-8-2 Mikado No. 400 and a Union Pacific caboose are displayed on the grounds. It is open Tuesday through Saturday.

LOCATION: 800 N. Washington Avenue, Marshall
PHONE: 903-938-9495
WEBSITE: facebook.com/marshall.depot

Texas Transportation Museum

The museum displays automobiles, fire trucks, and carriages, as well as a variety of railroad structures and equipment, including two steam locomotives, two diesel engines, and rolling stock. It features a Southern Pacific depot built in 1913 that was moved from Converse. The two-room building contains memorabilia from the railroads that served San Antonio. The museum operates a short train ride on weekends. It is open Friday through Sunday.

LOCATION: 11731 Wetmore Road, San Antonio
PHONE: 210-490-3554
WEBSITE: txtransportationmuseum.org
E-MAIL: form on website

Wichita Falls Railroad Museum

The museum's collection includes a Fort Worth & Denver steam locomotive, a Missouri-Kansas-Texas switch engine, a 1913 Pullman all-steel sleeper, troop sleepers, cabooses, and other cars. Artifacts center on the railroads that served Wichita Falls. The museum is open Saturdays year-round.

LOCATION: 500 Ninth Street, Wichita Falls
PHONE: 940-386-1626
WEBSITE: wfrrm.com
E-MAIL: susieacain@sbcglobal.net

Austin Steam Train

Mike Harbour

This tourist line was formed in 1989 to provide weekend service over a portion of a 167-mile route purchased from Southern Pacific. The train operates out of Cedar Park and rolls through the scenic Texas hill country.

CHOICES: The railroad offers two regular excursions. The *Hill Country Flyer* makes a 66-mile, 6-hour round trip between Cedar Park and Burnet. The trip includes a leisurely layover, allowing you to enjoy lunch, explore the town, and watch a Wild West gunfight. On the 44-mile round trip aboard the *Bertram Flyer*, you'll leave Cedar Park, cross the South San Gabriel River, and arrive in Bertram. Rolling stock consists of vintage coach and lounge cars. You have a choice of riding excursion coach or first class (coach or lounge). The cars are climate-controlled.

WHEN TO GO: Excursions run weekends all year. Many visitors choose to ride during the spring and fall and bypass the summer heat. Some midweek and evening trains run. A variety of specials operate including Day Out with Thomas, murder mysteries, and the North Pole Flyer.

GOOD TO KNOW: Trains are pulled by an Alco RSD15, a unit originally built for Santa Fe, that's been repainted in an SP-inspired "black widow" scheme. Namesake motive power No. 786, an ex-SP Mikado, is undergoing restoration.

WORTH DOING: Both Cedar Park and Burnet have numerous lodging and dining options for visitors, while Austin is famous for its museums, entertainment, scenic drives, and area lakes.

DON'T MISS: Special events for adults usually take place in the *Nambe* or the *Rippling Stream*, a 1949 Budd car that served on the New York Central.

GETTING THERE: Cedar Park is 20 miles north of Austin. You can reach the station by exiting I-35 at Exit 256. Follow RM 1431, which turns into Whitestone Boulevard, for 8 miles. The station is in the Cedar Park Shopping Center.

LOCATION: 401 E. Whitestone Boulevard, Cedar Park
PHONE: 512-477-8468
WEBSITE: austinsteamtrain.org
E-MAIL: info@austinsteamtrain.org

Galveston Railroad Museum

Galveston Railroad Museum

Housed in the former Gulf, Colorado & Santa Fe headquarters on Galveston Island's east end, the museum features a 5 acre yard full of fascinating rolling stock, including a pair of EMD F7s painted in AT&SF's classic warbonnet scheme.

CHOICES: After a tour of the static displays, take a trip on the Harborside Express, a 15-minute excursion aboard an ex-Missouri Pacific caboose that runs from 11 a.m. to 1:45 p.m. most Saturdays. The museum features one of the largest collections of railroad china and dinnerware in the United States. In the station's waiting room, you'll see Ghosts of Travelers Past, full-sized plaster figures of people congregating there as it appeared in 1932. With the touch of a button, you can operate a large model train layout.

WHEN TO GO: The museum is open daily year-round, but summers on the Texas Gulf Coast tend to be hot and humid. The other three seasons are usually more pleasant when spending time outdoors.

GOOD TO KNOW: In spring, the museum hosts a train show weekend, complete with model railroads on display, caboose rides, and other activities.

WORTH DOING: Like in New Orleans to the east, Mardi Gras is a big deal on the island. The center of all the activity takes place near the museum on The Strand, Galveston's historic downtown district. The Lone Star Rally, held the first weekend in November, ends at the museum's 25th Street entrance.

DON'T MISS: No trip to the island would be complete without a visit to a beach. Galveston has 32 miles of beaches, most operated by the city. If you want to avoid crowds but still enjoy the surf, head to Galveston Island State Park, 2,000-plus-acres that offer camping, bird-watching, hiking, mountain biking, fishing, and swimming.

GETTING THERE: From Houston, take I-45 south to Exit 1C. Turn left onto Harborside Drive, then turn right on 25th Street/Rosenberg Street, turn right on Santa Fe, and then right again to the museum.

LOCATION: 2602 Santa Fe Place, Galveston
PHONE: 409-765-5700
WEBSITE: galvestonrrmuseum.com
E-MAIL: form on website

Grapevine Vintage Railroad

Grapevine operates the only 19th century steam locomotive in Texas. Based at the restored 1888 Cotton Belt depot in downtown Grapevine, the railroad runs over 21 miles of former Cotton Belt track into the famous Fort Worth Stockyards Station. It also includes a 6-mile branch line running south from the mall across the Trinity River.

217

CHOICES: A 90-minute ride takes you from Grapevine to the Stockyards, and the 1.5-hour layover allows ample time for exploring the Stockyard's many offerings. The Trinity River 1-hour excursion passes through Trinity Park and the Fort Worth Zoo along a segment of the famous Chisholm Trail. Vinny, a former AT&SF Electro-Motive GP7, provides the motive power for the train. Trains carry four 1925-era day coaches featuring 19th century décor, plus a pair of open-air excursion coaches.

WHEN TO GO: Regular excursions run March through December. From Memorial Day weekend through Labor Day weekend, they operate Friday through Sunday. Frequency is reduced to two days (Saturday and Sunday) during the rest of the season. One-hour fun trains operate on Saturdays. The line offers numerous special events including train robberies and wine tastings, as well as holiday trains.

GOOD TO KNOW: The Grapevine to the stockyards round-trip excursion has assigned seating. Puffy, an 1896 Cooke 4-6-0 steam locomotive, shares train-hauling duties with Vinny, the GP7 diesel, depending on availability.

WORTH DOING: True to its name, Grapevine is home to numerous wineries with regular tours and a special Grapefest celebration in September.

DON'T MISS: During the Trinity River trip, the train crosses both channels of the river, goes through Trinity Park, and stops in a switchyard before returning to the Stockyards. During the trip, a narrative of the history of Fort Worth and the railroad is provided.

GETTING THERE: The city of Grapevine is adjacent to the northwest corner of DFW Airport. Three highways (114, 121, and 360) intersect at Grapevine, with I-30 being a few miles south of the airport and I-35E a few miles east.

LOCATION: 705 S. Main Street, Grapevine
PHONE: 817-410-3185
WEBSITE: grapevinetexasusa.com
E-MAIL: form on website

Museum of the American Railroad

Jim Wrinn

One of the most comprehensive railroad museums in Texas, the Museum of the American Railroad features more than 50 pieces of equipment. In 2012 the museum relocated about 15 miles north of Dallas in the city of Frisco. The MARR built 12 tracks on its new grounds to permit display of its collection, and plans a replica roundhouse and a shop complex. The museum offices and a small collection of photos and railroad memorabilia are located nearby in the Frisco Heritage Center.

CHOICES: The museum hosts guided tours of the locomotives and rolling stock during the summer months. Check the museum's website for current tour offerings, as staff frequently adjusts tour times according to demand and weather conditions.

WHEN TO GO: The Frisco Heritage Center is open Wednesday to Saturday.

GOOD TO KNOW: Highlights of the museum's collection include Union Pacific Big Boy No. 4018, Frisco 4-8-4 No. 4501, and Santa Fe No. 51, one of only two surviving Alco PAs in the United States. Other displays include a Santa Fe interlocking tower. The museum features one of the nation's largest collections of heavyweight pre-World War II passenger cars and a variety of lightweight freight cars and cabooses.

WORTH DOING: Frisco has many activities and attractions, such as the Texas Sculpture Garden, the Sci-Tech discovery Center, the National Videogame Museum, and athletic activities at Dr. Pepper Ballpark and Toyota Stadium.

DON'T MISS: For a ride on a vintage train, take State Highway 121 to the Grapevine Vintage Railroad 30 miles southwest of Frisco.

GETTING THERE: The easiest route to Frisco from Dallas is on the Dallas North Tollway. Although when traffic is bad, the 30-mile drive may take an hour.

LOCATION: 6455 Page Street (Heritage Museum), Frisco
PHONE: 214-428-0101
WEBSITE: museumoftheamericanrailroad.org
E-MAIL: form on website

Texas State Railroad

Tom Kline

Built using prison inmate labor in 1896 and operating excursions since 1976, the Texas State Railroad offers a relaxing ride through the piney woods region of east Texas between the towns of Rusk and Palestine. Various steam and diesel locomotives with regional history pull trains at a leisurely pace through tall stands of timber in the I.D. Fairchild national forest, giving riders a glimpse into the railroad's long history of hauling agricultural and timber products in the early 20th century.

CHOICES: Operations begin at the end of May running through September on Thursdays, Fridays and Saturdays. Holiday trips are offered from October through December at various times. Round-trip excursions depart from Palestine in late May and run until the end of July, while Rusk departures operate between August and September.

WHEN TO GO: Texas summers are hot, so book early for air-conditioned seating options and wear cool clothing. Spring and autumn are generally mild, making Coach and Open-Air Class seating enjoyable. However, east Texas weather can change rapidly, so have a jacket or coat handy if you chose to ride in an open-air coach during these months.

GOOD TO KNOW: Excursions are pulled by both diesel and steam so check the website to see what type of locomotive will be pulling the train on your visit. Of the two towns Palestine is the largest and offers the most variety in accommodations and services. Rusk is headquarters for the railroad and offers several hotels and bed and breakfasts.

WORTH DOING: For the more adventurous, individuals over 18 can upgrade to a one-way or round trip cab ride in the engine at additional cost.

DON'T MISS: Each station has historical exhibits with pictures and displays including a section highlighting the role the railroad has played in numerous movie, TV and commercial productions.

GETTING THERE: From Dallas or Houston, it is a leisurely 3-hour drive to either east Texas town. Both depots are located off Highway 84, about 30 miles apart.

LOCATION: 535 Park Road 76, Rusk;
789 Park Road 70, Palestine
PHONE: 877-726-7245
WEBSITE: texasstaterr.com
E-MAIL: customerservice@premierrails.com

IDAHO

1 Nampa Train Depot Museum

2 Northern Pacific Depot Railroad Museum

3 Silverwood Central Railroad

4 Washington, Idaho & Montana Railway Depot

MONTANA

5 Alder Gulch Short Line

6 Charlie Russell Chew-Choo Dinner Train

7 Heritage Museum

8 Historical Museum at Fort Missoula

9 Livingston Depot Center

10 Old prison Museum

11 Upper Musselshell Museum

OREGON

12 Canby Depot Museum

13 Eagle Cap Excursion Train

14 Mount Hood Railroad

15 Oregon Coast Scenic Railroad

16 Oregon Electric Railway Museum

17 Oregon Rail Heritage Center

18 Sumpter Valley Railroad

19 Wilamette Shore Trolley

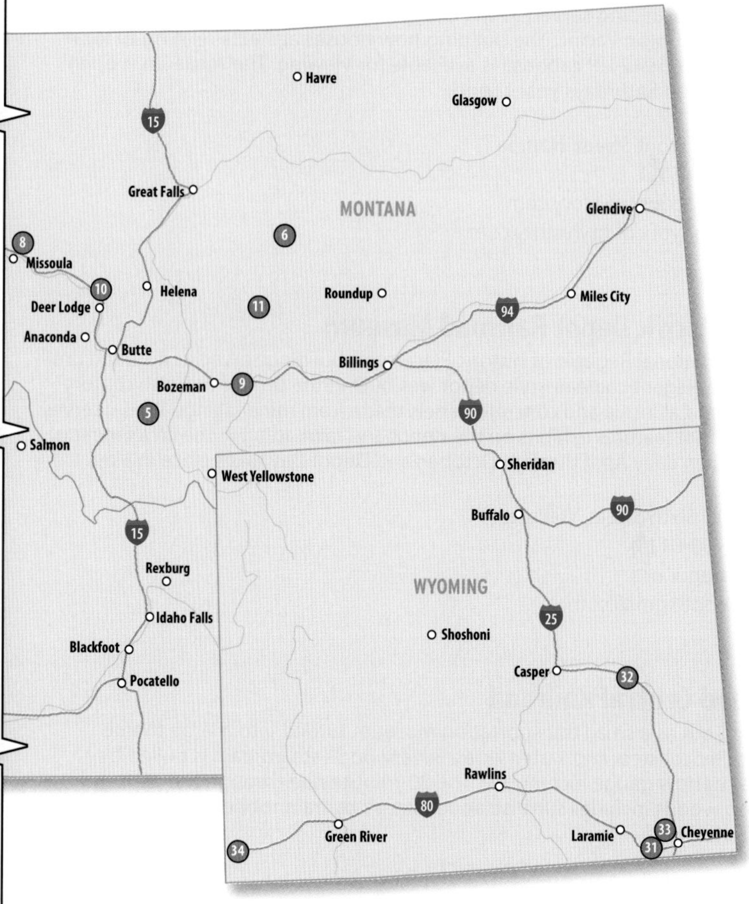

MONTANA

Havre ○
Glasgow ○
15
Great Falls ○
Glendive ○
8
Missoula ○
6
10
Helena ○
Roundup ○
Miles City ○
Deer Lodge ○
11
94
Anaconda ○
Butte ○
Billings ○
Bozeman ○
9
5
90
Salmon ○

WYOMING

West Yellowstone ○
Sheridan ○
Buffalo ○
90
15
WYOMING
Rexburg ○
Idaho Falls ○
25
Shoshoni ○
Blackfoot ○
Casper ○
Pocatello ○
32
Rawlins ○
80
Green River ○
Laramie ○
33 Cheyenne
34
31

WASHINGTON

20 Cashmere Museum & Pioneer Village

21 Chehalis-Centralia Railroad

22 Chelatchie Prairie Railroad

23 Dayton Historic Depot

24 Issaquah Depot Museum and Trolley

25 Lake Whatcom Railway

26 Mt. Rainier Scenic Railroad & Museum

27 Northern Pacific Railway Museum

28 Northwest Railway Museum

29 Ritzville Railroad Depot History Museum

30 Yakima Valley Trolleys

WYOMING

31 Cheyenne Depot Museum

32 Douglas Railroad Interpretive Center

33 Union Pacific Railroad

34 Union Pacific Roundhouse and Turntable

IDAHO

Nampa Train Depot Museum
Built in 1903, the building served as the Oregon Short Line depot and was then used as offices for the Union Pacific. The building now houses artifacts relating to local history. Outside, a 1942 UP caboose is available for viewing. The museum is open Thursdays through Saturdays year-round.

LOCATION: 1200 Front Street, Nampa
PHONE: 208-467-7611
WEBSITE: canyoncountyhistory.com
E-MAIL: info@canyoncountyhistory.com

Northern Pacific Depot Railroad Museum
Listed on the National Register of Historic Places, this building served as a station until the 1980s. The elegant chateau-style depot was built at the turn of the 20th century from brick from California and concrete panels made from mine tailings. It now serves as a museum that features exhibits on the depot and railroading in the area's mining district. It is open daily April through October, and Depot Day takes place in May.

LOCATION: 219 Sixth Street, Wallace
PHONE: 208-752-0111
WEBSITE: npdepot.org
E-MAIL: npdepot@gmail.com

Silverwood Central Railroad
What started out as a small transportation museum turned into a large theme park with roller coasters and water slides. Silverwood's steam train is pulled by a 1915 Porter narrow gauge locomotive. The 30-minute ride through the park and surrounding woods includes surprise appearances by train robbers. The train runs May through September.

LOCATION: 27843 N. Highway 95, Athol
PHONE: 208-683-3400
WEBSITE: silverwoodthemepark.com
E-MAIL: info@silverwoodthemepark.com

Washington, Idaho & Montana Railway Depot
Built in 1906, the restored depot now houses exhibits on the WI&M, logging, and Potlatch area history. It hosts an annual history day and speeder rides in July and other events throughout the year. It is open Wednesdays through Saturdays.

LOCATION: 185 Sixth Street, Potlach
PHONE: 208-875-1357
WEBSITE: wimryhpg.com

MONTANA

Alder Gulch Short Line

This narrow gauge railroad connects the former gold-mining towns of Virginia City and Nevada City. The line winds along Alder Creek, where you can view the remains of gold-mining operations, dredge tailings, and a variety of wildlife. Be sure to explore the historic buildings and displays in Nevada City. The railroad's 1910 Baldwin locomotive is stored in the Nevada City train barn, while a gas-powered engine pulls the train. It runs daily between Memorial Day and Labor Day.

LOCATION: Wallace Street, Virginia City
PHONE: 406-843-5247
WEBSITE: virginiacitymt.com
E-MAIL: form on website

Charlie Russell Chew-Choo Dinner Train

This dinner train takes you on a 3.5-hour excursion over the old Chicago, Milwaukee, St. Paul & Pacific Railroad line. The ride crosses three historic trestles, passes through a 2,000-foot tunnel, and travels through the land that inspired artist Charles Russell. Along the way, you'll enjoy a catered prime rib dinner. Just keep your eyes open for masked bandits! North Pole runs take place in November and December. The train boards about a 15-minute drive from downtown Lewistown. It operates on select Saturdays, and a few other days, June into October.

LOCATION: 7188 Hanover Road, Lewistown
PHONE: 866-912-3980 or 406-535-5436
WEBSITE: montanadinnertrain.com
E-MAIL: lewchamb@midrivers.com

Heritage Museum

On display is a Shay locomotive that worked for local logging companies in the early 1900s. Other exhibits are devoted to logging and early railroads as well as mining, wildlife, and life in Libby. The museum is open daily June through August and Tuesday, Friday, and Saturday during September.

LOCATION: 34067 Highway 2, Libby
PHONE: 406-293-7521
WEBSITE: libbyheritagemuseum.org
E-MAIL: heritagemuseum@frontier.com

Montana

Historical Museum at Fort Missoula

Located in Fort Missoula, the Historical Museum includes a variety of structures that depict the area's history. One is the Drummond depot, which was constructed by the Chicago, Milwaukee, St. Paul & Pacific Railroad in 1910. When the trolley barn is open, be sure to visit historic streetcar No. 50, a 100-year-old streetcar that was the last streetcar to run in Missoula. It is open daily except Mondays, October through May.

LOCATION: 3400 Captain Rawn Way, Missoula
PHONE: 406-728-3476
WEBSITE: fortmissoulamuseum.org
E-MAIL: fortmissoula@missoulacounty.us

Livingston Depot Center

The historic, Italianate-style Livingston depot was built in 1902 as the Northern Pacific's original access to Yellowstone National Park. Restored in the 1980s, the depot contains a museum that highlights local and railroading history. The building also hosts concerts, art festivals, and other events. The museum is open daily late May through mid-September.

LOCATION: 200 W. Park Street, Livingston
PHONE: 406-222-2300
WEBSITE: livingstondepot.org
E-MAIL: livingstondepot@gmail.com

Old Prison Museum

On display outside the museum complex is Milwaukee Road Little Joe No. E70, E9 locomotive No. 36A, and a caboose containing exhibits about the railroad. In addition to the prison, you'll find an auto museum, a firearms museum, and a collection of historic buildings. The museums are open daily.

LOCATION: 1106 Main Street, Deer Lodge
PHONE: 406-846-3111
WEBSITE: pcmaf.org
E-MAIL: info@pcmaf.org

Upper Musselshell Museum

This museum is located in two historic buildings. The Marshall Building contains a large collection of models related to the Milwaukee Road and other railroads. The Times Building contains 13 heritage rooms that are decorated by families who settled in the area. Also in town is a restored depot, Milwaukee Road ES-3 boxcab electric locomotive No. E57B, and several other pieces of equipment. It is open Mondays through Saturdays, Memorial Day through Labor Day.

LOCATION: 11 and 36 S. Central Avenue, Harlowton
PHONE: 406-632-5519
WEBSITE: harlowtonmuseum.org
E-MAIL: museum@mtintouch.net

OREGON

Canby Depot Museum

The Canby Depot Museum is housed in what could be the oldest railroad station in Oregon, which has been around since at least 1873. The museum's displays provide a look at 19th century life of this historic community and include a Union Pacific caboose and other rail items. It is open Thursday through Sunday, March through December.

LOCATION: 888 NE Fourth Avenue, Canby
PHONE: 503-266-6712
WEBSITE: canbyhistoricalsociety.org
E-MAIL: depotmusuem@canby.com

Oregon Electric Railway Museum

The museum's collection features a variety of trolleys and traction equipment from around the world. The museum offers trolley rides and carbarn tours. The museum is open weekends Memorial Day thru Labor Day, other times by appointment.

LOCATION: 3995 Brooklake Road, Brooks
PHONE: 503-393-2424, 971-701-6327
WEBSITE: museum.oregontrolley.com
E-MAIL: museum@oerhs.org

Oregon Rail Heritage Center

The Oregon Rail Heritage Center houses three historical steam locomotives: Oregon Railroad & Navigation 197, Southern Pacific 4449, and Spokane, Portland & Seattle 700. On summer Saturdays, you can ride an Oregon Pacific passenger train from the Oregon Rail Heritage Center and back via the Oaks Bottom Wildlife Refuge along the Willamette River. The center is open Thursday through Sunday.

LOCATION: 2250 SE Water Avenue, Portland
PHONE: 503-233-1156
WEBSITE: orhf.org
E-MAIL: form on website

Willamette Shore Trolley

Willamette Shore Trolley offers round-trip vintage trolley rides from Lake Oswego to the Southwest Portland Waterfront. The trolley also takes you through the 1,400-foot Elk Rock Tunnel. WST operates on weekends Memorial Day through October.

LOCATION: 311 N. State Street, Lake Oswego
PHONE: 503-697-7436
WEBSITE: wst.oregontrolley.com
E-MAIL: wst@oerhs.org

Eagle Cap Excursion Train

Ed Spaulding, La Grande, Oregon

The Eagle Cap Excursion Train offers 40-mile round trips along a portion of the Joseph Branch in northeastern Oregon that was first constructed in 1908. The excursion line passes through spectacular rugged and remote areas, most inaccessible to cars, following the Grande Ronde River downstream and then up the wild and scenic Wallowa River.

CHOICES: The railroad provides diesel-powered excursion trains with comfortably restored and recently painted coaches. The cars are climate-controlled and have restrooms. Certain excursions feature train robberies. Most trips include lunch.

WHEN TO GO: Excursions are available select Saturdays, May through October. Fall foliage trips in the heavily wooded forests are offered in October.

GOOD TO KNOW: In the remote areas, there is no cell phone coverage, so you'll have to stow away electronic devices and just enjoy the ride. It's all about being close to nature.

WORTH DOING: The towns of Elgin, Enterprise, and Joseph all contain historic buildings and quaint shops worth visiting during a trip to northeastern Oregon. Just off the Oregon Trail, the area is also known for outdoor recreation and scenery along the Hells Canyon Scenic Byway.

DON'T MISS: Along the ride, you may see bears, eagles, deer, and elk. In 1912, Rocky Mountain elk were transported from Wyoming to Wallowa County via the railroad to reestablish the area's depleted elk herds. These animals are responsible for many of the elk seen during your excursion. Open year-round, the depot contains historical exhibits and area information.

GETTING THERE: Exit I-84 at LaGrande and follow Highway 82 to Elgin. In the center of Elgin, continue past the opera house and city hall to the depot.

LOCATION: 300 N. Eighth Street, Elgin
PHONE: 800-323-7330 or 541-963-9000
WEBSITE: eaglecaptrainrides.com
E-MAIL: train@alegretravel.com

Mount Hood Railroad

Mount Hood Railroad

The Columbia River Gorge is filled with magnificent scenery, and the area around Mount Hood especially so because of its abundant orchards and vineyards. The Mount Hood Railroad offers a 44-mile round trip to Parkdale that features spectacular views of its namesake mountain.

CHOICES: The 4-hour excursion departs in the morning and follows the valley between the Columbia River and Mount Hood, providing views of Mount Adams as well. In addition, the railroad schedules a western train robbery excursion on select dates. You can choose standard class, first class, or diamond class levels of service.

WHEN TO GO: Trains run May through October, operating Thursday through Sunday during summer and Friday through Sunday in the fall.

GOOD TO KNOW: The railroad still carries a limited amount of freight, so don't be surprised if you see a boxcar somewhere along the line. Not far out of the Mount Hood depot, the train traverses a switchback, where it zigzags up the side of the mountain to gain elevation quickly. The rear of the train becomes the front for the rest of the trip into Parkdale.

WORTH DOING: There is much to do in the area. Sample apples and pears from orchards, visit a local winery or brewery, or watch wind surfers try to master the winds from the Columbia River Gorge. You can also take a drive on the Mount Hood Loop, which gives you a view of many scenic waterfalls.

DON'T MISS: Try first-class seating in the upper level of the dome car and get the same view as the engineer. Premium seating is available in the lower level of the dome car, and regular coach seating is found in other cars.

GETTING THERE: The Mount Hood Railroad is located 60 miles east of Portland off I-84. In Hood River, take Exit 63 to reach the depot. If driving from the south, Highway 35 also goes to Hood River.

LOCATION: 110 Railroad Street, Hood River
PHONE: 800-872-4661
WEBSITE: mthoodrr.com
E-MAIL: form on website

Oregon Coast Scenic Railroad

Dave Crosby

Experience the Pacific Ocean on a 10-mile, 90-minute excursion along the shores of Tillamook Bay. The train is pulled by a 1910 Heisler or a 1925 Baldwin 2-6-2 and runs between Garibaldi and Rockaway Beach.

CHOICES: On your trip along the coast, you can ride in a flatcar, in the restored Southern Pacific 1924 Wilson River coach, or for an extra fee, in the steam locomotive's cab. Wherever you sit, find a seat on the left side of the train. It's on the ocean side, and the views are spectacular. A special fireworks train runs in July, the Candy Cane Express runs in December, and other specials also operate, some departing from Wheeler.

WHEN TO GO: Regular excursions operate on weekends from mid-May through September. Daily service begins in June and runs into September.

GOOD TO KNOW: Dinner trains operate throughout the year and offer two seating options. Pulled by a diesel locomotive, these trains travel from Garibaldi to Wheeler and back along the coast.

WORTH DOING: Oregon's dairy industry is based in Tillamook, and it produces some of the best cheese and ice cream in North America. Be sure to stop at the Tillamook Cheese factory in nearby Tillamook. In addition, the area features an aviation museum housed in a World War II airship hanger. You can also view numerous lighthouses along the Pacific shore.

DON'T MISS: There is a layover between each run that provides the opportunity to explore Garibaldi or Rockaway Beach, get a bite to eat, or just enjoy the oceanside.

GETTING THERE: Garibaldi is located 10 miles north of Tillamook, just off Highway 101. At Tillamook, take Highway 101 north to Garibaldi. In Garibaldi, turn left on Third Street to Lumberman's Park, where the train boards.

LOCATION: 204 American Way, Garibaldi
PHONE: 503-842-7972
WEBSITE: oregoncoastscenic.org
E-MAIL: info@oregoncoastscenic.org

Sumpter Valley Railroad

Dave Crosby

A 5-mile portion of one of the most charming narrow gauge lines of the Pacific Northwest has been re-created amid forests and the spoils of a former gold-mining dredge operation. It is a good approximation of a remote steam line in eastern Oregon, where snowcaps rise in the distance even in June.

CHOICES: The railway runs between McEwen and Sumpter. Both round-trip and one-way excursions are available at either station. Locomotives currently operating are a wood-burning W. H. Eccles Lumber Co. two-truck Heisler and oil-burning Sumpter Valley Railway 2-8-2 No. 19. Train robberies and special events take place throughout the season.

WHEN TO GO: The railway is open on most weekends and holidays, starting with Memorial Day and running through September. A special fall foliage train runs in October, and Christmas trains run in December.

GOOD TO KNOW: The Sumpter depot is a replica of the original depot. Located on the Elkhorn Scenic Byway, Sumpter is surrounded by the Elkhorn Mountains. The area is filled with history, and nearby Baker City boasts at least 60 restored buildings.

WORTH DOING: Near the Sumpter station, in the Sumpter Valley Dredge State Heritage Area, visit the historic gold dredge that churned up all the rocks the railroad runs through—it's as big as a house and a monster of a machine well worth touring.

DON'T MISS: Cab rides aboard the steam locomotive are available.

GETTING THERE: The railway is about 330 miles from Portland in northeast Oregon. The McEwen depot is located 23 miles southwest of Baker City on Highway 7. The Sumpter depot is located at the entrance to Dredge State Heritage Area on Austin Street.

LOCATION: 211 Austin Street, Sumpter;
12259 Huckleberry Loop, Baker City (McEwen)
PHONE: 541-894-2268
WEBSITE: sumptervalleyrailroad.org
E-MAIL: info@sumptervalleyrailroad.org

WASHINGTON

Cashmere Museum & Pioneer Village

The pioneer village features 20 historical structures, dating back to the late 1800s. Railroad displays include a Great Northern section house, a ticket office, a caboose, equipment, and artifacts. The museum also includes exhibits regarding pioneer and Native American history. It is open daily April through October.

LOCATION: 600 Cotlets Way, Cashmere
PHONE: 509-782-3230
WEBSITE: cashmeremuseum.org
E-MAIL: info@cashmeremuseum.org

Dayton Historic Depot

Built in 1881, this is the oldest surviving railroad station in Washington. The stylish Stick/Eastlake building is now a museum of local history. It includes artifacts from the Union Pacific and the Oregon Railroad & Navigation Company, and a UP caboose is also on display. It is open Wednesday through Saturday year-round.

LOCATION: 222 E. Commercial Street, Dayton
PHONE: 509-382-2026
WEBSITE: daytonhistoricdepot.org
E-MAIL: info@daytonhistoricdepot.org

Issaquah Depot Museum and Trolley

The museum's display of railcars includes a World War II kitchen car with logging, mining, and railroad artifacts. The depot features a station agent's office with railroad and local history displays. Built in 1925 and powered by a generator car, the Issaquah Valley Trolley runs 1.2 miles to Gilman Boulevard. The museum is open Friday through Sunday with trolley rides on Saturday and Sunday.

LOCATION: 78 First Avenue NE, Issaquah
PHONE: 425-392-3500
WEBSITE: issaquahhistory.org
E-MAIL: info@issaquahhistory.org

Lake Whatcom Railway

This train ride takes you from the shores of Lake Whatcom into the wooded countryside and back. The vintage coaches and diesel locomotive were all used on the Northern Pacific. Speeder rides are also offered. A 100-year-old steam engine and wooden Great Northern freight cars are also on site. For a good workout, you can try your hand at riding a handcar. Excursions run during summer and for special events.

LOCATION: Highway 9 and NP Road, Wickersham
PHONE: 360-441-0719
WEBSITE: lakewhatcomrailway.com
E-MAIL: info@lakewhatcomrailway.com

Northern Pacific Railway Museum

The 1911 Northern Pacific Railway depot in Toppenish serves as a museum to that railroad. The site's freight house has been converted to an engine house, where several steam locomotives are being restored. The museum offers caboose rides during special events throughout the year. It is open Tuesday through Sunday, May through mid-October.

LOCATION: 10 S. Asotin Avenue, Toppenish
PHONE: 509-865-1911
WEBSITE: nprymuseum.org

Ritzville Railroad Depot Museum

The brick mission-style depot was built in 1910 and retains many of its original features, including floor scales that you can try out. The museum contains railroad memorabilia, a telegraph machine, and local historical items. Outside the depot, a cupula caboose painted in a yellow and green Northern Pacific scheme is on display. The museum is open Tuesdays through Saturdays, Memorial Day through Labor Day.

231

LOCATION: 201 W. Railroad Avenue, Ritzville
PHONE: 509-659-1656
WEBSITE: museums.goritzville.com
E-MAIL: museums@goritzville.com

Yakima Valley Trolleys

Yakima Valley trolleys have been operating for more than 100 years. You can ride along the historic line weekends and holidays from Memorial Day through September. Railcars used on the line date between 1910 and 1930. Trolleys leave from the carbarn and museum, which contains various pieces of rolling stock.

LOCATION: South Third Avenue at West Pine Street, Yakima
PHONE: 509-249-5962
WEBSITE: yakimavalleytrolleys.org
E-MAIL: info@yakimavalleytrolleys.org

Chehalis-Centralia Railroad

Dave Crosby

In the shadow of Mount St. Helens, this relaxing train ride takes you into the forests of western Washington. You'll ride behind a steam locomotive that saw many years of service logging these very forests.

CHOICES: The railroad offers two different excursions. The 12-mile Milburn run takes you through forests and countryside. A longer 18-mile round-trip to Ruth extends the ride by following the Chehalis River. The railroad's dinner trains follow the Ruth route and serve meals in a refurbished 1920s dining car.

WHEN TO GO: Train service begins in late May, and operates on Saturdays and Sunday until September. Sunday trains to Milburn conclude at the end of August. The Chehalis-Centralia also operates numerous dinner trains throughout the summer and early fall and hosts Polar Express in the winter.

GOOD TO KNOW: For an extra fee, you can experience what it is like to ride in the cab of a working steam locomotive with a cab ride in No. 15, a 2-8-2 Mikado type steam engine that was built in 1916.

WORTH DOING: Take time to visit Mount St. Helens National Volcanic Monument and view the dramatic changes the area has undergone since the 1980 eruption. The 110,000-acre site contains hiking trails, several visitor centers, and an observatory.

DON'T MISS: On clear days, at various spots along the line, you can view Mount Rainier and Mount St. Helens. When you cross the Newaukum River Bridge, you are crossing one of the few laminated wood-beam railroad bridges still in use in the United States.

GETTING THERE: The railroad is about a 90-minute drive from either Portland or Seattle. From I-5, take Exit 77 (Main Street) into Chehalis. Turn left on Riverside Drive and then left again on Sylvenus Street. Nearby Centralia is served by Amtrak.

LOCATION: 1101 SW Sylvenus Street, Chehalis
PHONE: 360-748-9593
WEBSITE: steamtrainride.com
E-MAIL: info@steamtrainride.com

Chelatchie Prairie Railroad

Chelatchie Prairie Railroad

Steam and diesel-powered trains operate on a bucolic railroad line completed in 1903. Now owned by Clark County and operated by volunteers, the 8-mile-long route features breathtaking scenery, a high trestle over the Lewis River and a 330-foot tunnel hand carved from solid rock.

CHOICES: Passengers may choose to ride in a caboose, open cars or heavyweight coach. Trains are powered by a 1929 Alco steam locomotive or a vintage Alco diesel from the 1940s. Patrons are encouraged to view the railroad's online schedule which indicates whether steam or diesel power is scheduled to operate.

WHEN TO GO: Excursions typically operate every other weekend between May and December. Many of the excursions are themed events, such as train robberies and wine tastings, as well as Halloween and Christmas runs.

GOOD TO KNOW: Although trains only operate as far as Lucia, volunteers are working to someday extend the route several additional miles to Battle Ground. The current excursion allows passengers a 30-minute layover at Moulton Falls Park, where passengers may view waterfalls and a tall arch bridge.

WORTH DOING: The railroad operates a unique Christmas Train and Tree experience in November and December. Once the train arrives at Moulton, families may visit with Santa and select a locally grown Christmas tree, which will then be carried on the same train back to the station at Yacolt.

DON'T MISS: Passengers may want to visit Moulton Falls Park on their own and spend more time than the 30-minute layover allows. The park features a hiking trail and connects to the nearby Lucia Falls Park and the Bells Mountain Trail.

GETTING THERE: The railroad is located an hour's drive from Vancouver, Wash., or Portland, Ore. From I-5, take Exit 11 to SR 502, travel to SR 503, turn right on Rock Creek Road for 11 miles to Yacolt. The station is on Railroad Avenue at Yacolt Road.

LOCATION: 207 N. Railroad Avenue, Yacolt
PHONE: 360-686-3559
WEBSITE: bycx.com
E-MAIL: admin@bycx.com

233

Mt. Rainier Scenic Railroad & Museum

Dave Crosby

The Mount Rainier Railroad operates steam- and diesel-powered excursion trains between Elbe and Mineral, where passengers may tour the railroad's repair shop and a re-created logging camp.

CHOICES: Passengers may ride in streamlined coaches from the 1950s or upgrade to First Class cars with complimentary snack and beverage service. Special events include beer and wine tasting excursions as well as the popular Mother's Day Brunch and Father's Day BBQ trains.

WHEN TO GO: Excursions typically operate Friday through Sunday during summer months. October sees "The Peanuts Great Pumpkin Patch Express" each weekend with the famous Polar Express hitting the rails in November and December.

GOOD TO KNOW: While most excursions operate with one of two conventional "rod" locomotives, several geared logging engines—including a rare Portland-built Willamette type—are kept in reserve at the railroad's repair shop and logging camp at Mineral.

WORTH DOING: The Nisqually Entrance to Mount Rainier National Park is less than 20 minutes by car from the railroad's depot in Elbe. Most roads around the 14,410-foot active volcano remain open during the railroad's summer and fall seasons.

DON'T MISS: The Mount Rainier Railroad's repair and restoration shops, as well as a re-created logging camp, are located at Mineral, the turnaround point for most excursions. The museum and grounds are only accessible to excursion passengers, so be sure to take advantage of the one-hour layover there.

GETTING THERE: The railroad is located in western Washington near Mount Rainier National Park, approximately 75 miles south of Seattle. To reach Elbe from the Seattle area, take I-5 to Highway 512 and then exit on Highway 7, which is also Mountain Highway. Mineral is 7 miles south of Elbe along Highway 7 and Mineral Road.

LOCATION: 54124 Mountain Highway East, Elbe; 349 Mineral Creek Road, Mineral
PHONE: 888-783-2611 or 360-569-7959
WEBSITE: mtrainierrailroad.com
E-MAIL: info@mtrainierrailroad.com

Northwest Railway Museum

Dave Crosby

The museum at Snoqualmie is home to the largest collection of Pacific Northwest railroad locomotives and rolling stock with more than 70 pieces on hand. Seasonal diesel-powered train rides are operated to North Bend and Snoqualmie Falls.

CHOICES: Visitors can opt to ride the train of vintage heavyweight passenger cars, visit the museum and exhibit buildings, or do both. Guided and self-guided tours are available.

WHEN TO GO: The museum itself is open year-round with the exception of Thanksgiving, Christmas and New Year's days. Excursions are operated on most weekends April through October. Santa Trains are operated on weekends late November through mid-December, while Thomas the Tank Engine pays a visit on selected summer weekends.

GOOD TO KNOW: The museum's Queen Anne style depot in Snoqualmie was completed in 1890. Now fully restored, the building is listed on the National Register of Historic Places.

WORTH DOING: Snoqualmie Falls, a 270-foot-high waterfall, is a short 5-minute drive and features a free observation area that is open dawn-till-dusk.

DON'T MISS: The museum is home to several significant pieces of rolling stock including a rare chapel car *The Messenger of Peace*, a 24-foot long caboose made of recycled materials during World War II, and a 1926 articulated 2-6-6-2 steam locomotive.

GETTING THERE: The museum is 30 miles east of Seattle on I-90. From I-90 east, take Exit 25. Heading north, follow Snoqualmie Ridge Parkway for approximately 4 miles to Highway 202. Turn right on Highway 202 and proceed a half mile to the Snoqualmie depot on your right. To get to the North Bend depot, take Exit 31 off I-90. Follow Bendigo Street into North Bend and turn right on North Bend Way.

LOCATION: 38625 SE King Street, Snoqualmie
PHONE: 425-888-3030
WEBSITE: trainmuseum.org
E-MAIL: info@trainumseum.org

WYOMING

Cheyenne Depot Museum

Cheyenne's architectural jewel is a major landmark in the city. Built in 1886, the Union Pacific depot houses a museum that details the history of the building, the operation of the railroad, and founding of the city. It is open daily year-round, and Depot Days take place in May.

LOCATION: 121 W. 15th Street, Cheyenne
PHONE: 307-632-3905
WEBSITE: cheyennedepotmuseum.org
E-MAIL: info@cheyennedepotmuseum.org

Douglas Railroad Interpretive Center

The Douglas Railroad Interpretive Center is housed in a restored 1886 passenger depot belonging to the Fremont, Elkhorn & Missouri Valley Railroad. It displays a 1940 Chicago, Burlington & Quincy steam locomotive and seven railcars, and recently added an over-60-year-old model train set. The building is listed on the National Register of Historic Places, and it is open daily.

LOCATION: 121 Brownfield Road, Douglas
PHONE: 307-358-2950
WEBSITE: facebook.com/douglasvisitorinfocenter

Union Pacific Roundhouse and Turntable

One section of the 28-bay roundhouse and the machine shop have been restored. (Check with the city for tour information.) In front, the large turntable is still operational. Nearby Railroad Park holds a 1915 steam engine and two boxcars. The Joss House Museum tells the story of the area's Chinese immigrants.

LOCATION: 1440 Main Street, Evanston
PHONE: 307-783-6320
WEBSITE: evanstonwy.org/374/roundhouse
E-MAIL: form on website

Union Pacific Railroad

Jim Wrinn

This Class I mainline railroad maintains the only steam locomotive never retired, No. 844, a 4-8-4 built in 1944. Rebuilt in 2016, it is used on an annual excursion out of Denver, and on display tours across the Union Pacific system. Big Boy No. 4014 is at the Cheyenne shop undergoing restoration with the aim of having it in steam by 2019. At that time, it will be the world's largest operating steam locomotive.

CHOICES: Visit the Cheyenne Depot Museum in the restored UP depot. The museum sponsors occasional tours of the steam shop, including in May during its annual festival. Two historic UP engines are displayed in Cheyenne parks: Big Boy No. 4004 in Holliday Park and the state's oldest steam locomotive, No. 1242, an 1890 4-6-0, in Lions Park.

WHEN TO GO: Schedules and routes vary from year to year. The Cheyenne Frontier Days excursion train from Denver to Cheyenne runs the third Saturday of each July, during Cheyenne's 10-day festival featuring rodeo action and Western entertainment.

GOOD TO KNOW: UP provides a GPS trace system for its steam train at up.com/aboutup/special_trains/steam/trace.cfm. The railroad also sends out updates on Twitter as the locomotive moves.

WORTH DOING: Follow I-80 West to Sherman Hill to watch UP freight trains. Then find your way to the site of the pyramid-like Ames Monument, celebrating the railroad's 1860s financiers. There, you can trace the original transcontinental railroad grade.

DON'T MISS: Stroll North Greeley Highway bridge for an overhead view of the shop.

GETTING THERE: Cheyenne is in southeast Wyoming, about 90 minutes from Denver.

LOCATION: UP Steam Shop, Cheyenne
PHONE: 307-778-3214
WEBSITE: up.com/aboutup

REGION 8

ARIZONA
1 Arizona Railway Museum
2 Grand Canyon Railway
3 Kingman Railroad Museum
4 Phoenix Trolley Museum
5 Scottsdale Railroad Museum
6 Southern Arizona Transportation Museum
7 Tucson Modern Streetcars
8 Verde Canyon Railroad

COLORADO
9 Boardwalk Park Museum
10 Castle Rock Museum
11 Colorado Railroad Museum
12 Cripple Creek & Victor Narrow Gauge Railroad
13 Cumbres & Toltec Scenic Railroad
14 Denver Trolley
15 Durango & Silverton Narrow Gauge Railroad
16 Forney Museum of Transportation
17 Fort Collins Municipal Railway
18 Georgetown Loop Railroad
19 Leadville, Colorado & Southern Railroad
20 Limon Heritage Museum
21 Moffat Railway Car
22 Pueblo Railway Museum
23 Ridgway Railroad Museum
24 Rio Grande Scenic Railroad
25 Rio Grande Southern Railroad Museum
26 Royal Gorge Route Railroad

NEW MEXICO
27 Belen Harvey House Museum
28 Las Cruces Railroad Museum

UTAH
29 Golden Spike National Historic Site
30 Heber Valley Railroad
31 Ogden Union Station
32 Tooele Valley Railroad Museum
33 Western Mining and Railroad Museum

238

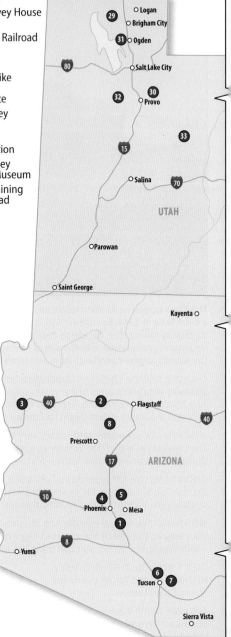

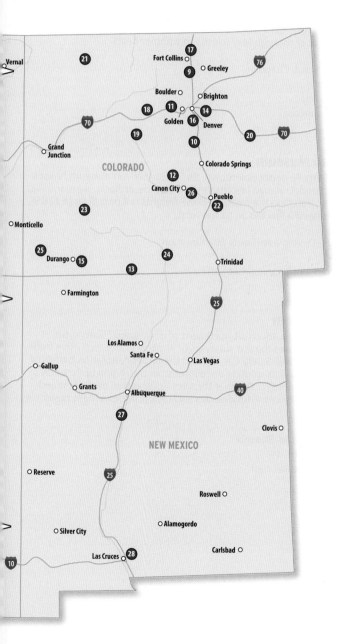

ARIZONA

Arizona Railway Museum

Located near Tumbleweed Park in Chandler, the Arizona Railway Museum houses a substantial and significant collection of rolling stock and artifacts in an open yard, including Santa Fe business and dome cars, coaches, freight cars, cabooses, industrial locomotives, a Baldwin diesel road switcher, and 1906 Southern Pacific 2-8-0 No. 2562. Open weekends September through May (closed in summer heat).

LOCATION: 330 E. Ryan Road, Chandler
PHONE: 480-821-1108
WEBSITE: azrymuseum.org
E-MAIL: info@azrymuseum.org

Kingman Railroad Museum

Located in the 1907 Santa Fe depot downtown, this volunteer-run museum houses a collection of several model railroad layouts, historic photos, artifacts, memorabilia, and a large window for watching the frequent BNSF freights roll past. A large AT&SF 4-8-4, No. 3759, is displayed a few blocks to the west.

LOCATION: 401 E. Andy Devine Ave (Route 66), Kingman
PHONE: 928-718-1440
WEBSITE: facebook.com_KingmanRailroadMuseum

Phoenix Trolley Museum

Recently relocated to a new location just northwest of downtown Phoenix, the Phoenix Trolley Museum houses the last survivors of Phoenix's once-extensive trolley system. Restored 1928-built Brill Safety Car 116 and the under-restoration bodies of two other Phoenix cars, as well as exhibits on rail transit in the region up to today's Light Rail are there. Open Saturdays October through April, as well as the first and third Fridays, and by appointment. A fundraising and capital improvement project is under way.

LOCATION: 1117 Grand Avenue, Phoenix
WEBSITE: phoenixtrolley.com
E-MAIL: phoenixtrolley@hotmail.com

Scottsdale Railroad Museum

The museum, which features the former Santa Fe Peoria depot, a Magma Arizona 2-6-0 steam locomotive, a private Pullman car used by former presidents, and numerous other railroad artifacts and memorabilia, is part of the McCormick-Stillman Railroad Park. The 30-acre campus in the heart of Scottsdale includes riding miniature railroads, model exhibits, and a vintage carousel. Though the park and rides are open year-round, the railroad museum is only open October through May and closes during summer heat.

LOCATION: 7301 E. Indian Bend Road, Scottsdale
PHONE: 480-312-2312
WEBSITE: therailroadpark.com
E-MAIL: therailroadpark@scottsdaleaz.gov

Southern Arizona Transportation Museum

You can tour the former Southern Pacific Railroad depot Tuesday through Sunday, and take in an exhibit that features oral history accounts of railroaders. The centerpiece of the museum is steam locomotive No. 1673, which was built in 1900. The museum is open daily except Mondays.

LOCATION: 414 N. Toole Avenue, Tucson
PHONE: 520-623-2223
WEBSITE: tucsonhistoricdepot.org
E-MAIL: satm1673@outlook.com

Tucson Modern Streetcars

Tuscon's streetcar system connects the downtown area with Mercado, the Fourth Avenue Business District, Main Gate Square, and the University of Arizona. The all-electric streetcars operate daily, with expanded schedules Thursday through Saturday.

LOCATION: Convento to Helen Street, Tucson
PHONE: 520-792-9222
WEBSITE: sunlinkstreetcar.com
E-MAIL: sunlinkstreetcarcomments@tucsonaz.gov

Grand Canyon Railway

Alexander D. Mitchell IV

This train doesn't take passengers into the canyon itself or even along the rim (except for a short distance near the end of the journey), but it offers a unique way to reach one of the greatest scenic wonders of North America in style. Diesel-powered (and a few steam) trains take riders from Williams on a 65-mile journey to the Grand Canyon's South Rim through high desert and pine forests. An exceptional ride, the trip is also a great value in saving you time in trying to find a parking space along the ever-popular South Rim.

CHOICES: The Grand Canyon Railway offers various levels of service including coach, first class, dome, luxury dome, and luxury parlor. Service and attention are hallmarks of this railroad. Coach passengers can enjoy the strolling musicians and tour guides, while those in cars with higher levels of service will have extra room, private bars, and fantastic views. Numerous all-inclusive packages are available, including lodging. Discounts (AAA, AARP, military/first responders, etc.) are available.

WHEN TO GO: Traveling this area any time of year can be rewarding. Christmas Day is the only day the railroad doesn't run. The summer's heat and winter's chill is kept at bay by air-conditioned and heated cars.

GOOD TO KNOW: The Arizona State Railroad Museum (not to be confused with the Arizona Railway Museum in Chandler) is in the process of being constructed on 20+ acres adjacent to the railroad. Watch for certain items of rolling stock on display around the area pending erection of the museum building.

WORTH DOING: At the South Rim, the train arrives at the original Santa Fe Railway log-cabin-style depot. Walk up the hill to El Tovar, the historic railroad-built hotel, and you'll stand in awe of nature at its finest. Shuttles travel to other rim points.

DON'T MISS: The railroad offers steam-hauled operations on first the Saturday of the month and selected special days during the year behind Burlington Route 2-8-2 No. 4960 and Lake Superior & Ishpeming 2-8-0 No. 29. The engines burn recycled vegetable oil.

GETTING THERE: Williams is 32 miles west of Flagstaff. Take I-40 to Exit 163 and follow Grand Canyon Boulevard to the depot.

LOCATION: 233 N. Grand Canyon Boulevard, Williams
PHONE: 800-843-8724
WEBSITE: thetrain.com

Verde Canyon Railroad

Alexander D. Mitchell IV

On the Verde Canyon Railroad, you'll travel 42 miles on a former copper mining spur, 1,800 feet below the red rock canyon rim where eagles often soar. The ride takes you across bridges, around rock formations, and through a 680-foot tunnel.

CHOICES: The 4-hour round trip from Clarkdale to the isolated Perkinsville Ranch and its now-deserted station and return travels between two national forests and into the Verde River Canyon, accessible only by rail. Narration and car attendants describe the history and point out the archaeology, geology, and wildlife of the area. Two levels of service are available: coach seating features vintage Pullman-style seats, with a snack bar; while First Class provides plush seating, complimentary appetizers, and a full-service cash bar. All cars access open-air viewing cars equipped with canopies. A caboose is available for small private parties, and a cab ride option is also offered. Package deals with local lodging are also available.

WHEN TO GO: Trains run year-round, but summer can be exceptionally hot with occasional monsoons. In winter, you can view nesting bald eagles.

243

GOOD TO KNOW: The railroad's pair of streamlined FP7 diesel locomotives from the 1950s (originally Alaska RR) features a unique eagle paint scheme.

WORTH DOING: Visit the Tuzigoot National Monument, just outside the railroad's entrance, where an ancient Sinagua pueblo was built. The "ghost town" of Jerome, now an artists' colony, and the historic town of Cottonwood are just a short drive away.

DON'T MISS: Adjacent to the depot is the John Bell Museum, a renovated former troop sleeper that contains railroad and mining history displays.

GETTING THERE: The railroad is about 30 minutes from Sedona and 2 hours from Phoenix. From Sedona, go toward Cottonwood on Highway 89A to Mingus Avenue. Turn right on Mingus Avenue and go 2 miles to Main Street. Turn right on Main Street and travel through Old Town Cottonwood. Look for the sign and turn right on Broadway. From Phoenix, take I-17 north to Exit 287. Go west on Highway 260 and then turn left at Main Street through Old Town Cottonwood. Look for the sign and turn right on Broadway.

LOCATION: 300 N. Broadway, Clarkdale
PHONE: 800-582-7245
WEBSITE: verdecanyonrr.com
E-MAIL: info@verdecanyonrr.com

COLORADO

Boardwalk Park Museum

Located in Boardwalk Park, an 1880s Colorado & Southern depot houses an exhibit of local steam-era railroading history. You can walk through a freight room, waiting room, and station agent's room. A caboose, schoolhouse, and church are also on site. The museum is open Thursdays through Sundays during summer.

LOCATION: 100 N. Fifth Street, Windsor
PHONE: 970-674-3521
WEBSITE: windsorgov.com
E-MAIL: lbrowarny@windsorgov.com

Castle Rock Museum

The museum is housed in a restored 1875 Denver & Rio Grande depot built of rhyolite stone. It retains original interior features, such as a ticket window and baggage area, with 125 years of graffiti on its walls. It displays exhibits of the D&RG and Continental Divide Raceways. It is open Wednesdays through Saturdays.

LOCATION: 420 Elbert Street, Castle Rock
PHONE: 303-814-3164
WEBSITE: castlerockhistoricalsociety.org
E-MAIL: museum@castlerockhistoricalsociety.org

Cripple Creek & Victor Narrow Gauge Railroad

The 4-mile, 45-minute trip takes you through Gold Country over a portion of the old Midland Terminal Railroad. Running south from Cripple Creek, the steam train crosses a reconstructed trestle and passes historic mines near the deserted mining town of Anaconda. The railroad operates three narrow-gauge locomotives, and trains operate mid-May to mid-October.

LOCATION: Fifth Street and Bennett Avenue, Cripple Creek
PHONE: 719-689-2640
WEBSITE: cripplecreekrailroad.com
E-MAIL: form on website, ccvngrr@aol.com

Limon Heritage Museum

This museum focuses on local history and the Union Pacific and Rock Island Railroads. Located in a restored 1910 depot, it features a restored office and rail exhibits. A saddle boxcar, dining car, and UP caboose are on display in the adjacent rail park. It is open Monday through Saturday Memorial Day to Labor Day.

LOCATION: 899 First Street, Limon
PHONE: 719-775-2346
WEBSITE: townoflimon.com

Moffat Railway Car

Tours of this 1906 Pullman car are available weekdays through the Moffat County Visitor Center, near where it is on display. The car originally belonged to rail magnate David Moffat and was named for his daughter Marcia. The nearby Museum of Northwest Colorado (590 Yampa Avenue) contains a display of Moffat Road memorabilia.

LOCATION: 360 E. Victory Way, Craig
PHONE: 800-864-4405 or 970-824-5689
WEBSITE: craig-chamber.com
E-MAIL: form on website

Pueblo Railway Museum

Concentrating on the golden age of railroading, the museum displays steam engines, diesel locomotives, rolling stock, and unique rocket cars in the yard behind Union Depot. Artifacts and rotating displays are housed in the Southeastern Colorado Heritage Center located across from the depot. Locomotive cab and caboose rides are offered during the year.

LOCATION: 201 W. B Street, Pueblo
PHONE: 719-251-5024
WEBSITE: pueblorailway.org
E-MAIL: in_dianajones@earthlink.net

Ridgway Railroad Museum

The Ridgway Railroad Museum focuses on local railroading history. It displays an assortment of restored railcars, and its indoor collection includes artifacts, photos, and tools. The museum is open daily except during winter months, when it is closed. It holds various special events and monthly work sessions.

LOCATION: Highway 550 and Highway 62, Ridgway
WEBSITE: ridgwayrailroadmuseum.org
E-MAIL: ridgwayrailroadmuseum@ouraynet.com

245

Rio Grande Southern Railroad Museum

The museum is located in a replica of the original Dolores depot. It is home to the restored Galloping Goose No. 5, which now operates several times during the year on the Cumbres & Toltec Scenic Railroad and the Durango & Silverton Narrow Gauge Railroad. The museum is open Mondays through Saturdays mid-May through mid-October and Tuesdays and Thursdays the rest of the year.

LOCATION: 421 Railroad Avenue, Dolores
PHONE: 970-882-7082
WEBSITE: gallopinggoose5.com
E-MAIL: gghs5@centurytel.net

Colorado Railroad Museum

Dave Crosby

When you think of Colorado railroading, you think of mountain-climbing, narrow gauge trains of the Denver & Rio Grande Western. And that is exactly what you'll see at this museum just outside Denver in the foothills near Golden. But that's not all—the museum includes 100 pieces of equipment from many other Colorado railroads.

CHOICES: The museum features narrow-gauge and standard-gauge equipment, from a steam locomotive once used on the Pikes Peak Cog Railway to a 317-ton Burlington Route 4-8-4 steam locomotive and even a set of streamlined 1950s passenger diesels from the Rio Grande. You'll see examples of the famous Galloping Goose self-propelled railbuses that ran on the narrow-gauge Rio Grande Southern in southwestern Colorado.

WHEN TO GO: The museum is open year-round, except for several holidays. On Ride the Rails days, most Saturdays April through October, some Sundays, and daily in July, you can a take a short ride around the 15-acre property. Most passenger trains are powered by a vintage diesel engine. On select days, you can ride aboard a Galloping Goose or behind steam locomotive No. 346.

GOOD TO KNOW: No. 687, a 2-8-0 built in 1890 and retired in 1955, is the only preserved standard gauge Rio Grande steam locomotive.

WORTH DOING: The MillerCoors Brewery is adjacent to the museum and offers tours on most days throughout the year. You can also explore historic downtown Golden or try tubing on nearby Clear Creek.

DON'T MISS: Visit the five-stall roundhouse that houses the museum's restoration shop and features an operating turntable. A viewing gallery gives you a peek at the work it takes to maintain the collection.

GETTING THERE: The Colorado Railroad Museum is located 12 miles west of downtown Denver and is easily reached from I-70. Take Exit 265 westbound or Exit 266 eastbound, and it is just off Highway 58 between I-70 and Golden.

LOCATION: 17155 W. 44th Avenue, Golden
PHONE: 800-365-6263 or 303-279-4591
WEBSITE: coloradorailroadmuseum.org
E-MAIL: form on website

Cumbres & Toltec Scenic Railroad

Jim Wrinn

If you have ever craved going back in time to the 1920s to see what railroading was like, here's your chance. The Cumbres & Toltec operates 64 miles of track through the San Juan Mountains. Steam locomotives still labor up steep grades, cross 100-foot-tall trestles, and hug narrow shelves above yawning gorges. For more than 125 years, passengers have ridden over Cumbres Pass on a 3-foot-gauge line that crosses the border between Colorado and New Mexico 11 times.

CHOICES: The railroad offers a choice of excursions. From either Antonito or Chama, N.M., you can take a full-day round trip to Osier, Colo., where a buffet lunch is provided. To see this scenic area in two different ways, you can ride the train one way and return by motor coach. Half-day trips take you from Chama to Cumbres with a return by motor coach. Seating options include a parlor car, a tourist car, a coach car, and an open-air gondola car. On many Saturdays, sunset dinner trains operate from Chama to Cumbres. Cinder Bear rides are designed for children.

WHEN TO GO: Excursion trains operate daily from the end of May until mid-October, with some special events taking place during the season.

GOOD TO KNOW: The Friends of the Cumbres & Toltec Scenic Railroad organization has installed two webcams that allow you to virtually visit the railroad's Chama yard. You can access them at railroad's website or at coloradonewmexicosteamtrain.org.

WORTH DOING: Ride Galloping Goose No. 5, which will make several appearances on the railroad in August and September.

DON'T MISS: At 10,015 feet elevation, Cumbres Pass is the highest pass reached by rail in the United States. At the summit is an old section house, one of the railroad's many historic buildings. As the train's steep descent begins, you'll see sweeping views of the Chama Valley.

GETTING THERE: The railroad is located between Colorado Springs and Santa Fe. Highway 285 takes you to Antonito. To reach Chama from Santa Fe, take Highway 285 to Highway 84.

LOCATION: 5234 B Highway 285, Antonito
PHONE: 888-286-2737 or 719-376-5483
WEBSITE: cumbrestoltec.com
E-MAIL: info@cumbrestoltec.com

247

Denver Trolley

Denver Trolley, Darrell Arndt

The Denver Trolley is often referred to as one of Denver's best-kept secrets. The trolley runs through the South Platte River Greenway Park linking several of the city's most popular attractions. The trolley is a faithful replica of a turn-of the-century, open-air breezer, which is ideally suited for enjoying the sightseeing trip.

CHOICES: The route starts at Confluence Park beside the REI store. The riverfront ride lasts 25 minutes. Stops are made at the Downtown Aquarium, Children's Museum, and Broncos Stadium at Mile High. The trolley only makes intermediate stops southbound, and runs end-to-end northbound.

WHEN TO GO: The trolley operates Thursday through Monday, Memorial Day weekend to Labor Day. It departs continuously every half hour from REI. For Denver Bronco home games, fans can catch a shuttle to the game.

GOOD TO KNOW: Confluence Park is the site of Denver's original settlement and is now a hub for paved bicycle trails that serve the city.

WORTH DOING: The Platte River area is a great place to take the family. Combine a trolley ride with nearby attractions, such as the Children's Museum, Elitch Gardens Theme Park, or the aquarium. You can also take a tour of Broncos Stadium and the Colorado Sports Hall of Fame.

DON'T MISS: In addition to serving Amtrak, Denver's renovated Union Station is now a hotel and transit hub for commuter rail operations. Shopping and dining options make it an ideal destination for enjoying urban Denver.

GETTING THERE: The route is located in downtown Denver. By car, take I-25 to Exit 211 (23rd Street), turn east on Water Street, and follow the signs to the Children's Museum or continue straight to the REI store for your best parking options. RTD buses and light rail operate within a short walk. The trolley is a 15-minute walk from Amtrak at Union Station.

LOCATION: 15th Street and Platte Street, Denver
PHONE: 303-458-6255
WEBSITE: denvertrolley.org
E-MAIL: info@denvertrolley.org

Durango & Silverton Narrow Gauge Railroad

Brian Schmidt

The Durango & Silverton is one of the most spectacular narrow gauge steam train rides in North America. Traveling through the Rockies, coal-fired locomotives pull trains 45 miles through the rugged Animas River Gorge on a railroad built in the 1880s to reach silver mines. The destination, Silverton, is a step into the past.

CHOICES: The Durango & Silverton offers several options for passengers. During summer, you can live like a railroad executive with Presidential class service on board the *Cinco Animas*, a private car that features plush seating and observation platforms. For great views, try first-class service on the *Silver Vista* or *Knight Sky*, glass-roofed, open-air observation cars with outdoor viewing platforms. First-class service is also available aboard an 1881 parlor car. Deluxe and standard service provide seating in a coach car or a covered gondola. During the winter off-season, the Cascade Canyon train travels 26 miles from Durango to the Cascade station.

WHEN TO GO: Winter provides incredible snowy vistas. Summer offers the excitement of up to three trains running each way, but it is also the busy season. September has the best color show when Aspen trees turn a brilliant yellow and quiver in the autumn breeze. Various events take place throughout the year.

GOOD TO KNOW: For a fee, yard tours are available to give you a chance to see the inner workings of the railroad.

WORTH DOING: Take part in the other activities that abound near Durango, such as whitewater rafting, hiking, and fly fishing. A visit to Mesa Verde National Park is a must.

DON'T MISS: There is a 2-hour layover in Silverton, which gives you time to visit the freight yard museum at the depot, which is open May through October and displays many pieces of rolling stock. The Durango museum, part of the roundhouse, is open corresponding to the passenger train schedule. There, a baggage car used in *Butch Cassidy and the Sundance Kid* is now a movie theater.

GETTING THERE: The station is located in downtown Durango. The drive to the Four Corners area on Highway 550 is a scenic delight, as long as you don't mind heights.

LOCATION: 479 Main Avenue, Durango
PHONE: 877-872-4607 or 970-247-2733
WEBSITE: durangotrain.com
E-MAIL: form on website

Colorado
Forney Museum of Transportation

Dave Crosby

What began as an antique automobile collection has become one of the nation's premier transportation museums. The museum's rail collection includes several locomotives, a rotary snow plow, passenger cars and a steam crane.

CHOICES: Union Pacific Big Boy locomotive No. 4005 is the centerpiece of the rail collection, but don't overlook other important rail vehicles such as Denver's only cable car, a Forney type locomotive, and a vintage live steam train.

WHEN TO GO: The Forney Museum is open year-round except for major holidays. Exhibits change often and special events are listed on the museum's website.

GOOD TO KNOW: The Forney Museum recently acquired Denver & Rio Grande Western No. 3006, a 1962 General Motors Electro-Motive Division GP30 diesel locomotive.

WORTH DOING: There are plenty of things to do in Denver within 15 minutes of the museum, such as touring the Capitol, the Firefighters Museum, the Botanic Gardens, and the Unsinkable Molly Brown's house. Within a couple of hours west and south, and 10,000 feet up, are Mount Evans and Pikes Peak, two driveable 14,000-foot-tall Rocky Mountains.

DON'T MISS: Also view highlights of the auto collection such as Amelia Earhart's 1923 Kissel Speedster, a 1967 amphibious car from Germany, a 1911 electric car, a Staver, and a Nyberg.

GETTING THERE: The Forney Museum is located northeast of downtown Denver, a short distance off I-70 via Exit 275B. Look for the vintage caboose in the museum's parking lot.

LOCATION: 4303 Brighton Boulevard, Denver
PHONE: 303-297-1113
WEBSITE: forneymuseum.org
E-MAIL: customerservice@forneymuseum.org

Fort Collins Municipal Railway

Bryan Bechtold

Fort Collins was the last city in the United States to operate the tiny four-wheel trolley cars known as Birneys, running its trolley system until 1951. A volunteer group of citizens rebuilt the original Mountain Avenue track and restored Car 21 to like-new condition, returning it to operation on its authentic tree-lined route in 1984. Car 21 turns 100 in 2019.

CHOICES: The 3-mile, round-trip trolley ride runs along Mountain Avenue from City Park to Howes Street, 2 blocks west of downtown. A round trip lasts 30 minutes. Other boarding stops are at Shields Street and Loomis Street. There are free rides on special days and for moms on Mother's Day and dads on Father's Day.

WHEN TO GO: The trolley operates on weekend afternoons and holidays from May to September.

GOOD TO KNOW: The original trolley barn is just two blocks north on Howe Street at the downtown end of the line. Inside is Birney Car 25, which is expected to complete its restoration in 2020. Car 25 is one of five remaining cars that ran in Fort Collins.

WORTH DOING: Both ends of the route are family friendly. Downtown Fort Collins has an outstanding variety of restaurants and shopping just a short walk from the trolley. You can also pack a picnic and enjoy the City Park end of the line. For outdoor enthusiasts, Rocky Mountain National Park is less than 2 hours away by car.

DON'T MISS: For railfans, BNSF freight trains run down the middle of nearby Mason Street for almost a mile providing an opportunity to view mainline action up close.

GETTING THERE: Fort Collins is 65 miles north of Denver on I-25. Exit I-25 at Colorado 14 and then drive west through town to City Park. A small depot is next to the tennis courts at Roosevelt and Oak Streets.

LOCATION: Roosevelt Street and Oak Street, Fort Collins
PHONE: 970-224-5372
WEBSITE: fortcollinstrolley.org
E-MAIL: fcmrs1919@gmail.com

Colorado
Georgetown Loop Railroad

Dave Crosby

This railroad shows how engineering overcame mountains when it came to reaching precious minerals in the Colorado Rockies. As the name states, the railroad's highlight is a full loop, where the tracks cross over themselves to gain elevation. The reconstructed Devil's Gate viaduct stands no less spectacular than when it was built in the late 1800s.

CHOICES: You can board at the Devil's Gate station in Georgetown or at Silver Plume. Either way, you experience the same trip, but riding up grade first is always the better show. As you ride the train, scan the mountain slopes for bighorn sheep. Both diesel and steam locomotives operate. There are three levels of service including open-air coach cars, parlor cars, and a presidential car.

WHEN TO GO: The operating season begins in May and continues to November. During much of the season, five trains run on a daily basis. Holiday trains operate in November and December. Beginning in October, the trains are made up of heated coaches pulled by a diesel locomotive.

GOOD TO KNOW: Steam locomotive No. 9, built in 1923 by the Lima Locomotive Works, is a rare Shay geared locomotive with three cylinders on one side. New to the loop is a Central American Railways 2-8-0 built in the U.S. and restored in 2016.

WORTH DOING: The town of Georgetown is quaint and quiet with little influences of the modern world—with the exception of nearby I-70. Its National Historic Landmark District features unique shops, restaurants, and small museums in restored Victorian buildings.

DON'T MISS: After riding the train, travel on I-70 between Georgetown and Silver Plume and watch another train tackle the mountain, with not only the loop but also with a series of zigzags. Accessible only by train, you can take a guided walking tour through the 1870s Lebanon Silver Mine.

GETTING THERE: The railroad is about 50 miles west of Denver off I-70. Exit 226 takes you to Silver Plume and, a few miles away, Exit 228 takes you to Georgetown.

LOCATION: 646 Loop Drive, Georgetown
PHONE: 888-456-6777
WEBSITE: georgetownlooprr.com
E-MAIL: info@historicrailadventures.com

Leadville, Colorado & Southern Railroad

Leadville, Colorado & Southern Railroad

In a state with many spectacular scenic railroads, this line doesn't disappoint. Leaving from the charming mining town of Leadville, the LC&S marches up the side of the Rockies near the tree line. Upon departure from the depot, the train leaves the 10,200-foot elevation for a 900-foot climb along the southern side of the upper Arkansas River Valley to a point close to Climax at Fremont Pass. The train passes through forests of lodgepole pine, spruce, and aspen.

CHOICES: On the 2.5-hour round trip, you can ride in an open car or a car with a roof. Especially for train fans, there are several seats available in the locomotive or in the caboose. If it's a beautiful day in Colorado, as it often is, stick to the open cars for unobstructed views. Stay on the right side of the train for spectacular views of the mountains and the molybdenum mine at the end of the line. Along the way, the conductor provides narration and answers questions.

WHEN TO GO: The trains run late May into October, when the aspen trees put on a magnificent show of yellow. In mid-summer, the Wildflower Special lets you view alpine flowers at their peak. Several barbecue specials also run.

GOOD TO KNOW: Incorporated in 1878, Leadville is the highest incorporated city in the continental United States at 10,152 feet above sea level. Downtown Leadville is home to many shops, galleries, restaurants, and lodging establishments and makes an easy base camp from which to explore the central Rockies.

WORTH DOING: Be sure to explore Leadville's National Historic Landmark District, which includes many buildings built between 1880 and 1905.

DON'T MISS: Raft and ride packages are available that combine a half-day rafting trip along Browns Canyon on the Arkansas River with a scenic train ride.

GETTING THERE: From Denver, take I-70 west and then Highway 91 south to Leadville. From Vail, take I-70 west to Highway 24 and then Highway 24 south to Leadville.

LOCATION: 326 E. Seventh Street, Leadville
PHONE: 866-386-3936 or 719-486-3936
WEBSITE: leadville-train.com
E-MAIL: form on website

253

Rio Grande Scenic Railroad

Jim Wrinn

The Denver & Rio Grande built an incredibly scenic route into the San Luis Valley and its biggest city, Alamosa, in the late 1880s. The standard gauge line of today replaced a much more difficult narrow gauge line but lost nothing as far as its engineering marvels or trackside splendor.

CHOICES: The railroad offers a variety of train rides. The regular excursion train crosses famous La Veta Pass to let you view the Rockies. On select summer weekdays, a diesel train winds through a variety of scenery, from flat farmland to mountains, on its trip from Alamosa to La Veta. Summer concert trains run to Fir on weekends. Fort Garland is another pick-up location.

WHEN TO GO: Regular excursions run late May through September. In addition to the summer concerts, other special events take place.

GOOD TO KNOW: Seating choices vary by route and train. They include dome, coach, and open-air cars. Diamond class seating is featured on restored club cars that ran on the fabled *City of New Orleans*.

WORTH DOING: Explore the Spanish Peaks country. It is filled with hiking trails, scenic roads, and natural wonders such as the tallest sand dunes in North America, which are found in Great Sand Dunes National Park.

DON'T MISS: Between June and August, the railroad presents its summer music festival in a mountain setting that is accessible by excursion trains. You can enjoy music under the stars, surrounded by aspen and pines, in a natural meadow amphitheater.

GETTING THERE: Located in south-central Colorado, Alamosa is about 200 miles south of Denver and 90 miles west of Pueblo. Highway 160 is the key route in and out of the San Luis Valley. The highway becomes Main Street in Alamosa, and the depot is just off Main Street on State Avenue.

LOCATION: 610 State Avenue, Alamosa
PHONE: 877-726-7245
WEBSITE: coloradotrain.com
E-MAIL: form on website

Royal Gorge Route Railroad

Royal Gorge Route Railroad

Nowhere else in America can you ride a train through a narrow mountain gorge with a fast-flowing river and look straight up at 1,000 feet of cliff. The railroad offers a range of services on its 24-mile round trip through the Royal Gorge.

CHOICES: Service classes on the 2-hour excursions begin with coach, which seats you in comfortable air-conditioned cars with access to an open-air car. Club class offers unobstructed views out large windows. Vista-dome class provides panoramic views under glass, food service, and a full-service bar. On the gourmet lunch and dinner trains, you can enjoy a three-course meal in a dining car or in the dome car. Cab rides in the railroad's GP40-2 locomotive are also available.

WHEN TO GO: Trains begin running daily in March through October, with service expanding during summer. Weekend trips are available during January, February, and November. Murder mystery trains, various specials, and holiday trains also run. Twilight is one of the best times to ride through the gorge.

GOOD TO KNOW: After looking up at the world's highest suspension bridge, 1,053 feet above the river, you can go up to Royal Gorge Bridge Park (admission required) and drive, walk, or tram across the gorge.

WORTH DOING: Rafting and kayak outfitters in the area offer half- and full-day trips for beginners and experienced paddlers alike. If you make it through Satan's Suckhole, watch out for the deceptively named Puppy Rapids.

DON'T MISS: On the popular Santa Express, children of all ages are encouraged to wear jammies and enjoy hot cocoa and a cookie on the way to the North Pole, which is decorated with more than 17,000 lights!

GETTING THERE: Cañon City is 115 miles from Denver and 45 minutes from Colorado Springs via Highway 115.

LOCATION: 330 Royal Gorge Boulevard, Cañon City
PHONE: 888-724-5748 or 719-276-4000
WEBSITE: royalgorgeroute.com
E-MAIL: info@royalgorgeroute.com

255

NEW MEXICO

Belen Harvey House Museum

Adjacent to the BNSF Division yard, the museum contains exhibits on Harvey Houses and the Santa Fe Railroad. Listed on the National Register of Historic Places, the Southwestern-style structure is one of state's few surviving Fred Harvey eating establishments. The museum is open Tuesday through Saturday.

LOCATION: 104 N. First Street, Belen
PHONE: 505-861-0581
WEBSITE: harveyhousemuseum.org
E-MAIL: harveyhousemuseum@gmail.com

Las Cruces Railroad Museum

The museum is housed in a 1910 AT&SF depot with a Mission Revival look. Its photographs, artifacts, and displays highlight the depot itself, railroad workers, and railroad communications. It also features a model railroad train room. The museum offers a variety of lectures and programs, including Railroad Days in May. It is open Tuesday through Saturday.

LOCATION: 351 N. Mesilla Street, Las Cruces
PHONE: 575-647-4480
WEBSITE: las-cruces.org
E-MAIL: rrm@las-cruces.org

UTAH

Tooele Valley Museum and Historic Park

Housed in the old Tooele Valley depot, built in 1909, the museum tells the story of the area's colorful mining and smelting years. Tooele Valley Railway steam locomotive No. 11 is the museum's No. 1 attraction. The 1910 Alco 2-8-0 Consolidation type engine is displayed with two wood cabooses and other rolling stock. The museum is open Tuesday through Saturday, Memorial Day through September.

LOCATION: 35 N. Broadway Street, Tooele
PHONE: 435-882-2836 or 435-843-2143
WEBSITE: tooelevalleymuseum.com
E-MAIL: form on website

Western Mining and Railroad Museum

Museum exhibits highlight the Denver & Rio Grande Western and other railways. Located in the old Helper Hotel, which was completed in 1914, the museum contains four floors of artifacts. The third floor contains a railroad office and two rooms of railroading artifacts. A 100-year-old caboose is also on display. Other exhibits, including a simulated coal mine, focus on the mining industry and its workers. It is open year-round Monday through Saturday summers and Tuesday through Saturday during winter.

LOCATION: 296 S. Main Street, Helper
PHONE: 435-472-3009
WEBSITE: facebook.com/Western-Mining-And-Railroad-Museum-135440466630696/
E-MAIL: wmrmuseum@helpercity.net

Utah

Golden Spike National Historic Site

Jeff Terry

The construction of the transcontinental railroad is one of the pivotal events in the nation's history. Completed May 10, 1869, at this remote spot northwest of Ogden, the National Park Service does justice to the event by running replica locomotives and conducting reenactments. 2019 is the 150th anniversary. See the website for special events.

CHOICES: Reenactments of the Last Spike Ceremony, complete with dignitaries in period dress, take place on Saturdays and holidays May through mid-September. The two steam locomotive replicas, the coal-burning Union Pacific No. 119 and the wood-burning Central Pacific *Jupiter*, are accurate reproductions and fully functional. The visitor center offers informative films and exhibits.

WHEN TO GO: The visitor center is open every day, except for Thanksgiving, Christmas, and New Year's Day. Between May and mid-October, the steam locomotives are on display and conduct demonstrations. During winter, when the locomotives are being maintained, engine house tours are available.

GOOD TO KNOW: The correct name for the location of Golden Spike National Historic Site is Promontory Summit, not Promontory Point, which is 35 miles to the south. The summit is the highest location on Promontory Pass. For some reason, the wrong location was reported in some records in 1869 and perpetuated throughout history.

WORTH DOING: The area is still very rugged. For an even more rugged adventure, go northwest of the park to Devils Playground, which contains granitic rock weathered into fantastic forms and eerie shapes.

DON'T MISS: Walk Big Fill Loop Trail (1.5-mile round trip), which takes you out on the original Central Pacific grade and back on the Union Pacific grade. You'll see the site of the Union Pacific's trestle, go through cuts, and see drill marks where workers blasted away rock. West and east auto tours allow you to see interesting elements of the original railroad.

GETTING THERE: Golden Spike National Historic Site is in northern Utah, 30 miles west of Brigham City. The site can be accessed from either I-15 or I-84. Highway 83 takes you to the entrance, which is Golden Spike Drive. Road signs help guide you to the park.

LOCATION: Golden Spike Drive, Promontory
PHONE: 435-471-2209
WEBSITE: nps.gov/gosp
E-MAIL: form on website

Heber Valley Railroad

Scott Hartley

This railroad offers a scenic ride beside Deer Creek Reservoir and into Provo Canyon with the Wasatch Mountains as a backdrop over a line that began operating in 1899.

CHOICES: Heber Valley offers several regular excursions in the shadow of 12,000-foot Mount Timpanogos aboard vintage coaches. The *Provo Canyon Limited* is a 3-hour round trip that runs to Vivian Park and back. The 90-minute *Deer Creek Express* goes to Deer Creek Reservoir and returns. The *Lakeside Limited* is a scenic 2-hour ride along Deer Creek Reservoir and the base of Mount Timpanogo.

WHEN TO GO: The railroad operates year-round. Regular excursions run on a varied schedule, usually four or five days a week, closed Sundays. Summer is especially beautiful in Utah, but winter excursions offer a unique look at a snowy wonderland. Summer excursion packages combine river rafting, horseback riding, or ziplining with a train ride. Numerous special events take place, from sunset barbecues to the North Pole Express.

GOOD TO KNOW: The railroad's main power are two diesel engines, an ex-Army EMD MRS-1 and a Baldwin switcher. Ex-Union Pacific GP9 No. 296 has been restored and is slated to be joined by two more GP9s in 2019. Two 2-8-0 steam locomotives, No. 618 and No. 75, are currently undergoing restoration for eventual return to service.

WORTH DOING: Take a scenic drive along the Provo Canyon Scenic Byway (Highway 189) that runs between Heber Valley and Provo. A short side trip on the Alpine Scenic Loop (Highway 92) takes you past Robert Redford's Sundance Resort.

DON'T MISS: For a high-flying adventure, try combining a wilderness zip line with a train ride. The adventure begins with a train ride through Heber Valley, and if you make it through without running into Black Jack Raven and his gang of train robbers, you'll be driven into the Wasatch Mountains to the zip line drop-off, where you'll zip over the scenery.

GETTING THERE: The railroad is located between Salt Lake City and Provo. From Salt Lake City, take I-80 east to Exit 148 and then follow Highway 40 into Heber City. Turn right on W. 300 South and then left on S. 600 West to the station.

LOCATION: 450 S. 600 West, Heber City
PHONE: 435-654-5601
WEBSITE: hebervalleyrr.org
E-MAIL: info@hebervalleyrr.org

Ogden Union Station

Scott Hartley

Built in 1924, Ogden Union Station now houses a variety of museums and galleries, including the Utah State Railroad Museum and Eccles Rail Center. The museum contains artifacts of Utah railroading, and the rail center displays historic pieces of equipment. Other museums in the station focus on history, firearms, gems, classic cars, and the arts.

CHOICES: You can browse an extensive collection of rolling stock that is displayed outside the station or go inside. You'll see locomotives and cars from the big Class I railroads that served Utah, including Union Pacific, Southern Pacific, and Rio Grande. Interactive exhibits bring to life the story of the first transcontinental railroad, which was completed nearby at Promontory Summit, just west of Ogden. You'll also pass under timbers used to construct the historic Lucin trestle across the Great Salt Lake. A model railroad depicts scenery from across Utah.

260

WHEN TO GO: The museum is open Monday through Saturday year-round, but the outdoor railroad exhibits are accessible anytime. Many special events take place at the station, some relating to railroading.

GOOD TO KNOW: UP 4-8-4 No. 833, representing the zenith of steam passenger and freight power, was one of the last big steam locomotives built in America.

WORTH DOING: There are numerous hiking trails in and around Ogden, on which you can see mountains, waterfalls, forests, and wildlife. In scenic Ogden Valley, you can ski on the same slopes as Olympic skiers did or just enjoy the scenery. In Ogden, you can take in a show or film at Peery's Egyptian Theater, with its restored Egyptian look.

DON'T MISS: View the Union Pacific cauldron car, which carried the Olympic flame during the 2002 Winter Olympics that were held in Utah and based in Salt Lake City. The unique car carried the flame more than 3,200 miles across 11 states.

GETTING THERE: From Salt Lake City, take I-15 north to Exit 341 and follow Highway 79 east. Turn left onto Wall Avenue. The museum is in downtown Ogden and directions are well marked.

LOCATION: 2501 Wall Avenue, Ogden
PHONE: 801-393-9886
WEBSITE: theunionstation.org
E-MAIL: museums@theunionstation.org

REGION 9

Yosemite Mountain Sugar Pine Railroad, page 287

REGION 9

CALIFORNIA

1 Cable Car Museum
2 California State Railroad Museum
3 Colma Depot
4 Edward Peterman Museum of Railroad History
5 El Dorado Western Railroad
6 Fillmore & Western Railway
7 Folsom Railroad Museum
8 Fort Humboldt State Historic Park
9 History Park
10 Knott's Berry Farm
11 Laws Railroad Museum
12 Lomita Railroad Museum
13 Millbrae Train Museum
14 Napa Valley Wine Train
15 National City Depot
16 Nevada County Narrow Gauge Railroad and Transportation Museum
17 Niles Canyon Railway
18 Niles Depot Museum
19 Orange Empire Railway Museum
20 Pacific Southwest Railway Museum
21 Placerville & Sacramento Valley Railroad
22 Poway-Midland Railroad
23 RailGiants Train Museum
24 Railtown 1897 State Historic Park
25 Roaring Camp Railroads
26 Roots of Motive Power
27 Sacramento RiverTrain
28 San Bernardino History and Railroad Museum
29 San Francisco Municipal Railway
30 Skunk Train
31 Society for the Preservation of Carter Railroad Resources

32 South Coast Railroad Museum
33 Tehachapi Depot Railroad Museum
34 Timber Heritage Association
35 Travel Town Museum
36 Western America Railroad Museum
37 Western Pacific Railroad Museum
38 Western Railway Museum
39 Yosemite Mountain Sugar Pine Railroad

NEVADA

40 Nevada Northern Railway Museum
41 Nevada Southern Railway
42 Nevada State Railroad Museum
43 Virginia & Truckee Railroad

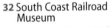

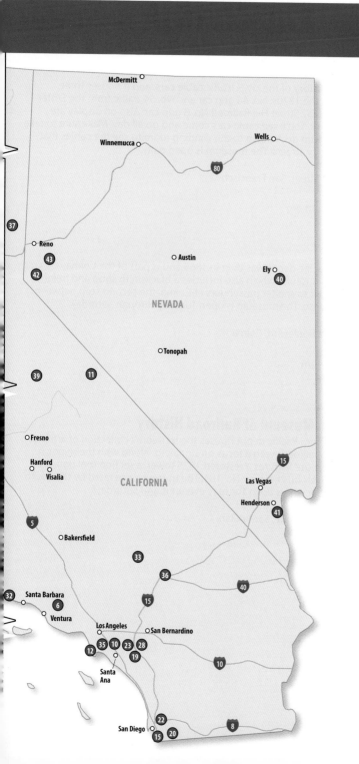

CALIFORNIA

Cable Car Museum

This museum tells the history of the city's iconic cable cars, and it houses three antique cable cars from the 1870s: No. 46 grip car and No. 54 trailer from the Sutter Street Railway, and the Clay Street Hill Railroad No. 8 grip car. Also on display are photos, tools, and models. You'll see cable cars come and go all day. Make sure to take the steps from the museum deck down to the winding room to see the cables that pull the cars along the city streets. The museum is open daily.

LOCATION: 1201 Mason Street, San Francisco
PHONE: 415-474-1887
WEBSITE: cablecarmuseum.org

Colma Depot

This former Southern Pacific depot was built in 1865 and is part of the Colma Historical Association's museum, which also includes a blacksmith shop and freight shed. The depot was built to shelter passengers at Colma, the second stop between San Francisco and San Jose. The museum is open Tuesday through Saturday.

LOCATION: 1500 Hillside Boulevard, Colma
PHONE: 650-757-1676
WEBSITE: colmahistory.com
E-MAIL: form on website

Edward Peterman Museum of Railroad History

A restored former Southern Pacific depot houses the museum's collection of artifacts that highlights western railroads with a focus on signaling. Along with the depot, which dates to 1863, the site features a restored 1926 tower, a section tool house, a speeder shed, and OWR&N business car No. 184. The museum, operated by the South Bay Historical Railroad Society, is open Tuesday evenings and Saturdays.

LOCATION: 1005 Railroad Avenue, Santa Clara
PHONE: 408-243-3969
WEBSITE: sbhrs.org
E-MAIL: form on website

El Dorado Western Railroad

For a different train ride, try the El Dorado Western. The railroad takes you on 35-minute round trips over the Placerville Branch of the Southern Pacific on historic gang cars. Rides leave from El Dorado and Shingle Springs on alternate Sundays. Some special trips last 90 minutes.

LOCATION: 4650 Oriental Street, El Dorado; 4241 Mother Lode Drive, Shingle Springs
PHONE: 530-409-8473
WEBSITE: museum.edcgov.us/el-dorado-western-railroad
E-MAIL: museum@edcgov.us

Folsom Railroad Museum

Located in a Santa Fe coach, the museum displays railroad artifacts and photographs. It features a reconstructed turntable and a Southern Pacific caboose. A handcar derby takes place in May. It is open Saturdays and Sundays. Johnny Cash fans can visit the nearby Folsom Prison Museum.

LOCATION: 198 Wool Street, Folsom
PHONE: 916-985-6001
WEBSITE: fedshra.org
E-MAIL: feds@fedshra.org

Fort Humboldt State Historic Park

The park includes a logging museum that displays historic, steam-powered redwood-logging equipment, including two 0-4-0 locomotives and a steam donkey. On select summer Saturdays, the Timber Heritage Association steams up the equipment and provides short train rides. The park also includes a historical museum on the site where Ulysses S. Grant briefly served.

LOCATION: 3431 Fort Avenue, Eureka
PHONE: 707-445-6547
WEBSITE: parks.ca.gov
E-MAIL: info@parks.ca.gov

265

History Park

History Park contains 27 original and reconstructed historic buildings including a trolley barn. Operated by the California Trolley & Railroad Corporation, the barn contains trolleys, a horse-drawn streetcar, and other historic vehicles. Buildings are closed during the week, and trolley rides take place on weekends. Southern Pacific steam locomotive No. 1215 and several railcars are also on display.

LOCATION: 635 Phelan Avenue, San Jose
PHONE: 408-287-2290
WEBSITE: historysanjose.org

Lomita Railroad Museum

This museum is a replica of the Boston & Maine station at Wakefield, Mass. You can climb into the cab of Southern Pacific No. 1765, a 2-6-0 Baldwin built in 1902, and look inside a 1910 UP caboose. Several freight cars and a wooden water tower are also displayed. The museum exhibits lanterns, china, and other artifacts. It is open Thursday through Sunday.

LOCATION: 2137 W. 250th Street, Lomita
PHONE: 310-326-6255
WEBSITE: lomita-rr.org
E-MAIL: lomitamuseumstaff@lomitacity.com

Millbrae Train Museum

The museum contains photos, artifacts, and documents related to the area's railroad history. Housed in a former Southern Pacific train station, the museum displays a 1941 Pullman sleeper from the *City of San Francisco* streamliner. The museum is one of 10 historical landmarks on a self-guided walking tour. It is open on Saturdays, as is the nearby Millbrae History Museum.

LOCATION: California Drive at Murchison Drive, Millbrae
PHONE: 650-333-1136
WEBSITE: millbraehs.org
E-MAIL: form on website

National City Depot

Still in its original location, the National City Depot, built in 1882, is the oldest railroad-related structure in San Diego County. Operated by the San Diego Electric Railway Association, it exhibits several trolleys, railroad items, and local historical displays. The depot is open Saturday and Sunday.

LOCATION: 922 W. 23rd Street, National City
PHONE: 619-474-4400
WEBSITE: sdera.org/depot.php
E-MAIL: messages@sdera.org

Nevada County Narrow Gauge Railroad and Transportation Museum

The museum's collection features NCNGRR engine No. 5. The 1875 Baldwin hauled timber, passengers, and freight. Other narrow gauge equipment and wooden railcars are on display as are a 1901 steam-powered automobile and other historic transportation pieces. Docent-led tours of the museum are available. It is open Friday through Tuesday during summer and on weekends in winter.

LOCATION: 5 Kidder Court, Nevada City
PHONE: 530-470-0902
WEBSITE: ncngrrmuseum.org
E-MAIL: form on website

Niles Depot Museum

The museum focuses on the Southern Pacific and Western Pacific, the early railroads of Fremont, Newark, and Union City. It also includes Union Pacific and Amtrak artifacts. Exhibits include railroad signals, model railroads, and a WP caboose. Housed in a passenger depot and a freight depot, the museum is open on Sundays.

LOCATION: 37592 Niles Boulevard, Fremont
PHONE: 510-797-4449
WEBSITE: nilesdepot.org
E-MAIL: tcsme@nilesdepot.org

Placerville & Sacramento Valley Railroad

Enjoy the scenery of Gold Country aboard the Placerville & Sacramento Valley Railroad. Rides vary in length and can range from 40-minute to 2-hour excursions aboard motorcars or on railcars pulled by a diesel switcher.

LOCATION: 155 Placerville Road, Folsom
PHONE: 916-597-0107
WEBSITE: psvrr.org
E-MAIL: info@psvrr.org

Poway-Midland Railroad

You can ride a variety of railroad equipment on this railroad. It operates a 1907 Baldwin 0-4-0 steam locomotive, a trolley car, an authentic San Francisco cable car converted to run on battery power, and a speeder. You'll also see historic buildings, restored rolling stock, and a gallows turntable. Equipment runs on weekends except for the second Sunday of each month.

LOCATION: 14134 Midland Road, Poway
PHONE: 858-486-4063, 858-391-0251
WEBSITE: powaymidlandrr.org
E-MAIL: info@pmrrv.org

Roots of Motive Power

267

Roots of Motive Power collects and restores rail and other equipment used for logging. The organization gets steamed up at various events during the year, both on and off the site, including the Roots of Motive Power Festival at the Roots facility and Frontier Days in Willits. Visitors can also tour the collection during scheduled work days each month.

LOCATION: 400 E. Commercial Street, Willits
WEBSITE: rootsofmotivepower.com
E-MAIL: mail@rootsofmotivepower.com

San Bernardino History and Railroad Museum

Located in a restored 1918 Santa Fe depot, the museum contains a replicated 1910 railroad station, a variety of railroad inspection and work vehicles, artifacts, and photographs. It also features objects of local historical value including antique vehicles. The museum is open Wednesdays and Saturdays.

LOCATION: 1170 W. Third Street, San Bernardino
PHONE: 909-888-3634
WEBSITE: sbdepotmuseum.squarespace.com
E-MAIL: allenbone@verizon.net

Society for the Preservation of Carter Railroad Resources

Visit Ardenwood Historic Farm on a Thursday, Friday or Saturday between April and November and ride the narrow gauge train pulled by a Plymouth diesel locomotive. The group collects and restores historic wooden cars from Northern California with an emphasis on Carter Brothers' products. On Labor Day weekend the farm holds a historic Rail Fair that includes operating Porter narrow gauge steam locomotives and operating model railroads, including live steam.

LOCATION: 34600 Ardenwood Boulevard, Fremont
PHONE: 510-544-2797
WEBSITE: spcrr.org
E-MAIL: info@spcrr.org

South Coast Railroad Museum

The museum's centerpiece is the historic Goleta depot, a Victorian-styled Southern Pacific country station. The museum features hands-on exhibits and an SP bay window caboose. Occasional train rides and special events are scheduled throughout the year, and handcar rides are offered. In the Gandy Dancer Theater, you can view railroading and travel films. It is open Friday through Sunday.

LOCATION: 300 N. Los Carneros Road, Goleta
PHONE: 805-964-3540
WEBSITE: goletadepot.org
E-MAIL: form on website

Tehachapi Depot Railroad Museum

Built as a Southern Pacific type 23 depot, the building replaced the 1904 depot, which burned down in 2008. Among the museum's artifacts is a collection of working railroad signals. The depot also schedules a variety of events during the year. It is open Thursday through Monday.

LOCATION: 101 W. Tehachapi Boulevard, Tehachapi
PHONE: 661-823-1100
WEBSITE: tehachapidepot.com
E-MAIL: info@tehachapidepot.com

Timber Heritage Association

Speeder car rides are offered every fourth Saturday, June through September. The 4-mile round trip travels from the town of Samoa, along the beautiful Humboldt Bay to Manila. On these Saturdays, the association's shops are open for tours, and you can see its collection of logging artifacts and locomotives. The rides board by the Samoa Cookhouse.

LOCATION: 930 Vance Avenue, Samoa
PHONE: 707-443-2957
WEBSITE: timberheritage.org
E-MAIL: thabruce43@gmail.com

Western America Railroad Museum

Housed in the restored Casa Del Desierto, a 1911 Harvey House, the museum features railroad art, artifacts, and memorabilia. Its outdoor displays include locomotives, cabooses, and other equipment. Highlights include Santa Fe FP45 No. 95 in classic warbonnet scheme, a 1938 horse car, and an experimental A-frame container car. It is open Fridays, Saturdays, and Sundays.

LOCATION: 685 N. First Street, Barstow
PHONE: 760-256-9276
WEBSITE: barstowrailmuseum.org

California State Railroad Museum

Dave Crosby

This is among the best interpretive museums about railroading. The museum mixes a magnificent large-artifact collection with plenty of details and a sense of drama that brings them to life. Displays, hands-on exhibits, and human interaction all combine to produce an excellent experience for everyone, from those with a passing interest in trains to those with a deep appreciation for railroading. And if you want the real thing, the museum operates its Sacramento Southern Railroad, a short train ride.

CHOICES: Made up of several buildings, the museum offers guided tours. The Railroad History Museum, at 100,000 square feet, is the largest exhibit space and contains 21 restored cars and locomotives. Be sure to climb the stairs that take you into the cab of one of the largest preserved steam locomotives, a rare Southern Pacific Cab Forward-type with its crew compartment in front of the boiler.

WHEN TO GO: Weekends, April through September, and select Tuesdays are when the museum offers its Sacramento Southern train rides behind Granite Rock No. 10, a rebuilt 1943 tank engine, or a vintage diesel locomotive. The 45-minute, 6-mile round trip travels over the levees of the Sacramento River. The museum also runs special events and excursions throughout the year.

GOOD TO KNOW: The museum is situated in the Old Sacramento district of the state capital near where the first transcontinental railroad was launched eastward in the 1800s. The district is a 28-acre National Historic Landmark District and state historic park.

WORTH DOING: The Old Sacramento State Historic Park contains a variety of museums, landmarks, and historical buildings.

DON'T MISS: When you board the Sacramento Southern, take a look at the reconstructed Central Pacific freight depot, where you'll see displays highlighting the freight transportation industry.

GETTING THERE: When driving to Sacramento, take I-80 from San Francisco or I-5 from Reno. If you want the full rail experience, take an Amtrak train. The station is adjacent to Old Sacramento. The museum is at the corner of Second and I Streets.

LOCATION: 125 I Street, Sacramento
PHONE: 916-323-9280
WEBSITE: californiarailroad.museum
E-MAIL: form on website

Fillmore & Western Railway

Dave Crosby

Operating over a segment of a former Southern Pacific branch line, the Fillmore & Western Railway is a well-run combination of weekend scenic excursion trains, murder mystery dinner trains, and special trains. It is also one of the premier movie location sets. Billing itself as the "Home of the Movie Trains," from wrecks to shootouts, Hollywood has used this scenic little Southern California line to represent Washington D.C., Florida, the Pacific Northwest, and just about every place in between.

CHOICES: On some passenger runs, the F&W operates ex-Duluth & Northeastern 2-8-0 steam engine No. 14. On weekend excursion trains, you can ride in an open-air railcar or in restored vintage passenger coaches. The train stops in downtown Santa Paula for an hour, letting you visit the historic Southern Pacific depot, the amazing rotating water ball in Railroad Plaza Park, the Santa Paula Art Museum, the California Oil Museum, or the Ventura County Agriculture Museum.

WHEN TO GO: Excursions run on Saturdays January through March, and on Saturdays and Sundays April through September and in November.

GOOD TO KNOW: The railroad hosts several different dinner train options for families including some murder mystery trains.

WORTH DOING: Farther north up the California coast is Santa Barbara, San Luis Obispo, and Hearst Castle, the ultimate in opulence and home of the man who ran the Hearst newspaper and radio empire.

DON'T MISS: Explore the healthy roster of passenger and freight equipment in various states of repair found on the property.

GETTING THERE: Fillmore is about 60 miles northwest of downtown Los Angeles and about 25 miles east of Ventura. From Highway 126 in Fillmore, turn on Central Avenue to Main Street.

LOCATION: 364 Main Street, Fillmore
PHONE: 805-524-2546
WEBSITE: fwry.com
E-MAIL: info@fwry.com

Knott's Berry Farm

Dave Crosby

Knott's Berry Farm is a Southern California theme park that has morphed from its 1952 western-style operation into a world-class attraction with rides and events designed for every age. Part of the theme park is the original 3-foot-gauge Calico Railroad.

CHOICES: The railroad is just one part of this large theme park operation that rivals any other attraction in the United States. Most trains are powered by one of two Denver & Rio Grande Western 2-8-0s, either No. 41 (former Rio Grande Southern No. 41 and originally Denver & Rio Grande Western No. 409) or No. 340 (also a former D&RGW of the same number). There is also a Rio Grande Southern Galloping Goose and a number of authentic narrow gauge coaches, a parlor car, and a caboose.

WHEN TO GO: Southern California is enjoyable almost any time of the year, although summers can get very hot.

GOOD TO KNOW: If you're bringing the family, plan to stay all day. Like other theme parks in the area—Universal Studios and Disneyland—this is a kid-friendly destination with everything you need in one giant arena to tucker out even the hardiest person by the end of the day. Look for new twists in the western-themed Ghost Town Alive interactive experience, and try the new Sol Spin thrill ride.

WORTH DOING: Southern California abounds in attractions, restaurants, and activities for everyone. Spend a week or a weekend.

DON'T MISS: Good news for the railroad fan is that, by carefully selecting your photographic spots, you can come away with images that make it look like you snapped them in Colorado 70 years ago.

GETTING THERE: Buena Park is part of the greater Los Angeles area in Orange County. If you have a vehicle, it is accessible by several freeways, and exits are clearly marked. You can also take shuttles, sightseeing tours, and public transportation.

LOCATION: 8039 Beach Boulevard, Buena Park
PHONE: 714-220-5200
WEBSITE: knotts.com
E-MAIL: form on website

Laws Railroad Museum

David Lustig

The 11-acre Laws Railroad Museum is home to the largest collection of equipment that operated on the Southern Pacific's narrow gauge empire, which at one time stretched almost 300 miles from Nevada to the Lone Pine area of Owens Valley.

CHOICES: Museum displays include SP 4-6-0 No. 9, one of the last three steam engines to operate on the line, various freight cars, a caboose, a turntable, and the original station. The museum has built a number of structures to show what Laws looked like in its heyday. A former Death Valley Railroad gas-electric doodlebug operates on select summer weekends. New to the museum are replicas of the mule team borax wagons used in Death Valley during the 1880s.

WHEN TO GO: The museum is open all year with a few exceptions. It is closed on several major holidays such as New Year's Day, Easter, Thanksgiving, and Christmas. It also may close due to severe weather, and some buildings close during winter.

GOOD TO KNOW: The nearest city with restaurants and accommodations is Bishop. If you drive up from the south on Highway 395, there are numerous towns with hotels and eateries, starting with Lone Pine, Independence, and Big Pine. During the ski season, Highway 395 is the main route to and from the various resorts north of Bishop, so you might consider making reservations well in advance.

WORTH DOING: Owens Valley is known for the many motion pictures, mostly westerns, that have been filmed there over the years. A number of small nonrail museums dot the area. The remains of the Manzanar Relocation Center, one of the places where Japanese-Americans were interned during World War II, is part of the National Park Service and open to the public.

DON'T MISS: The area from Keeler to Laws is littered with narrow-gauge artifacts, ranging from the remains of trestles and buildings to 4-6-0 No. 18 in Independence.

GETTING THERE: Laws is truly in the middle of nowhere, and the trip to the museum is half the fun. The museum is 4.5 miles north of Bishop on Silver Canyon Road, just off Highway 6.

LOCATION: Silver Canyon Road, Bishop
PHONE: 760-873-5950
WEBSITE: lawsmuseum.org
E-MAIL: lawsmuseum@aol.com

California

Napa Valley Wine Train

Scott Hartley

When you think of Napa Valley, you think of wine. And if you want a memorable wine (or beer) experience, take this ride through one of the world's most famous grape-growing valleys. You'll ride in elegant style on board a fashionable train on a 36-mile round trip while enjoying a gourmet lunch or dinner and a glass of wine.

CHOICES: Ride in a heavyweight passenger car or a Vista-dome for a 3-hour round trip from Napa to St. Helena and back, each with a different dining experience. Or you can choose one of four 6-hour "Tour" trains, which make stops to visit three wineries and offer an onboard gourmet meal as well. A new offering is the Hop Train, specializing in local craft beers served in an open-air car.

WHEN TO GO: Any time of the year is good, but the September grape-harvesting season is among the most popular. Daily service begins in March and goes through November, with Friday through Sunday service the rest of the year.

GOOD TO KNOW: Attire is generally casual depending on the time of year or type of event. Dinner tends to be more dressy, and cocktail-party attire is acceptable. A jacket and tie is not required, but may be a welcome addition for cool nights. One bit of advice: no blue jeans.

WORTH DOING: Napa Valley is filled with hundreds of wineries to visit as well as having numerous special events.

DON'T MISS: All entrees are prepared in the kitchen cars, and you are welcome to sneak a peek inside to watch the action.

GETTING THERE: From San Francisco, take I-80 east to Exit 33, CA-37 West, to Exit 19, CA-29/Sonoma Boulevard toward Napa. Take the CA-221 Napa/Lake Berryessa exit, which becomes Soscol Avenue. In Napa, turn right on First Street and then turn left on McKinstry Street. Ferry service and a bus connection from San Francisco also makes for a fun day.

LOCATION: 1275 McKinstry Street, Napa
PHONE: 800-427-4124 or 707-253-2111
WEBSITE: winetrain.com
E-MAIL: form on website

Niles Canyon Railway

Dave Crosby

This museum railroad, a project of the Pacific Locomotive Association, provides a magnificent ride through a dramatic canyon at the edge of the San Francisco Bay area. An outstanding collection of equipment and beautiful scenery make this an excellent day trip in central California.

CHOICES: The railway runs 75-minute round trips through scenic Niles Canyon between Sunol and Niles. Departures are scheduled at both stations. On all trains, you can select from open cars, covered cars, or enclosed coaches. Trains are powered by either a diesel or a steam locomotive from the railway's impressive collection, which also includes a wide variety of passenger cars, freight cars, and cabooses.

WHEN TO GO: The railroad operates Sundays, April through August, and on the first and third Sundays the remaining months, except November and December, when the holiday schedule for the nighttime Train of Lights offers rides four days a week. Look for special events, such as Steamfest, wine tasting trains, beer tasting trains, and Southern Pacific and Western Pacific days. No trains run in January. Caboose rentals are available for private parties.

GOOD TO KNOW: The line was the last completed link of the transcontinental railroad.

WORTH DOING: Walk around downtown Niles for specialty and antique stores and restaurants. The Niles depot offers a park and a train-viewing platform.

DON'T MISS: The restored Sunol depot was originally built in the 1880s, and the Niles depot, which features colonnade-style architecture and houses railroad exhibits, was built in 1901.

GETTING THERE: The Niles Canyon Railway is situated between Oakland and San Jose. From San Jose, you can take I-880 to Fremont and exit on Highway 84 east. Turn left onto Mission Boulevard and continue 3 blocks west to Sullivan Street, and the Niles station is on the left. To reach the Sunol depot from San Jose, just take I-680 to Highway 84. Travel west on Highway 84 1 mile and turn right onto Main Street to Kilkare Road. From Oakland, take I-880 to Highway 84 east to get to either location.

275

LOCATION: 6 Kilkare Road, Sunol
PHONE: 510-996-8420
WEBSITE: ncry.org
E-MAIL: form on website

California

Orange Empire Railway Museum

Dave Crosby

The Orange Empire Railway Museum was organized in 1956 by trolley and electric railway enthusiasts to preserve a fast disappearing way of transportation. Visitors can ride on classic trolleys, passenger trains, and other railroad equipment from Southern California's past.

CHOICES: Two trolleys run on a half-mile loop line, and one is usually an early Los Angeles streetcar. Another train, pulling freight or passenger cars, operates on the 1.5-mile standard gauge main line. On the freight train, you can ride in either a caboose or open gondola. The cars and locomotives are rotated from the museum's collection, which contains more than 180 vintage pieces. You also have the opportunity to run a locomotive.

WHEN TO GO: The museum is open 363 days a year and special events occur during the year. Trains run on weekends and some holidays. The weather is usually bearable during most of the year; however, summertime temperatures can reach triple digits.

GOOD TO KNOW: The museum, situated on 100 acres, is about 20 miles south of Riverside. It has preserved, and is restoring, an eclectic mix of more than 225 pieces of railroad equipment that includes electric, steam, and diesel power as well as a variety of freight and passenger rolling stock. A Fred Harvey museum is on site.

WORTH DOING: The surrounding area, from Riverside to Temecula, is well developed with all the amenities a traveler would expect. For military aircraft fans, the March Field Air Museum has an extensive collection of aircraft adjacent to March Air Reserve Base in Riverside.

DON'T MISS: A 1922 oil-burning 2-6-2 steam engine, Ventura County Railway No. 2, operates excursions the third weekend of every month from September to May and during certain special events and major holidays.

GETTING THERE: Perris is about an hour's drive from either San Diego or Los Angeles. In Perris, exit at Route 74. Follow Route 74 (Fourth Street) west for 1 mile and turn left onto A Street.

LOCATION: 2201 S. A Street, Perris
PHONE: 951-943-3020
WEBSITE: oerm.org
E-MAIL: info@oerm.org

Pacific Southwest Railway Museum

Pacific Southwest Railway Museum, John Wright

The Pacific Southwest Railway Museum operates in two locations near San Diego. The main collection is at Campo, just north of the U.S.–Mexico border. The other location is at La Mesa, about 10 miles east of downtown San Diego.

CHOICES: At Campo, visitors can enjoy several train-riding options, including a 12-mile, diesel-powered trip on a mountain railroad to Tunnel No. 4, and locomotive cab rides are available on the trip. The 40-acre site displays more than 80 pieces of equipment including diesel locomotives (among them, several interesting military switchers), steam locomotives, freight cars, passenger cars, and cabooses. Also featured is a fully restored "Jim Crow" passenger car. The La Mesa site displays railroading exhibits, freight cars, and a steam locomotive.

WHEN TO GO: The Campo facility is open most weekends throughout the year. The museum offers a variety of special events, including some tailored to kids, such as pumpkin and North Pole trains. The La Mesa site is open on Saturday afternoons.

GOOD TO KNOW: The restored La Mesa depot is the only surviving San Diego & Cuyamaca Railway station.

WORTH DOING: The greater San Diego area is brimming with places to visit, including Old Town. Sea World is just north of the city, and the coastline is tourist friendly. If you have always wanted to tour a U.S. Navy aircraft carrier, the decommissioned USS *Midway* is open to the public, with many types of aircraft positioned on its flight deck.

DON'T MISS: Now a history museum, the nearby Campo Stone Store was also a military outpost, bank, and post office. Another Campo museum to visit is the Motor Transport Museum with its large collection of vehicles and industrial equipment.

GETTING THERE: The Campo site is 50 miles east of San Diego. From San Diego, take Highway 94 to Campo and turn right onto Forrest Gate Road and then left onto Depot Street. Take the Spring Street exit off Highway 94 into La Mesa to reach the La Mesa depot, which is at 4695 Nebo Drive.

LOCATION: 750 Depot Street, Campo
PHONE: 619-465-7776 or
619-478-9937 (weekends)
WEBSITE: psrm.org
E-MAIL: form on website

277

RailGiants Train Museum

Jim Wrinn

The RailGiants Train Museum houses an outstanding collection of significant locomotives and rolling stock. The site is on the grounds of the Los Angeles County Fairgrounds. The collection includes locomotive No. 9000, the only UP 4-12-2 in existence, locomotive No. 5021, the only Southern Pacific 4-10-2 in existence, rare Santa Fe 4-6-4 No. 3450, and UP Centennial diesel No. 6915. The center of museum activities is the former Santa Fe Depot from Arcadia, Calif., built in 1895 and preserved in 1969.

CHOICES: You can wander among the exhibits, various locomotives, a heavyweight Pullman lounge, a Santa Fe wood caboose, a refrigerator car, a Santa Fe horse express car, UP diesel locomotive SD40-2 No. 3105, UP caboose No. 24567, and much more.

WHEN TO GO: The exhibit is open one weekend every month and daily during the Los Angeles County Fair in September.

GOOD TO KNOW: This is one group with roots. A part of the Railway & Locomotive Historical Society, the Southern California Chapter began in 1953 and opened its first exhibit with Climax geared locomotive No. 3, a donation of Sunkist Growers.

DON'T MISS: Look for U.S. Potash 2-8-0 No. 3. It is the museum's only 36-inch-gauge locomotive.

GETTING THERE: Suburban Los Angeles is the location. The site is easily accessed off Interstate 10. When the fair is open, you can even take a Metrolink commuter train to the grounds.

LOCATION: 1101 W. McKinley Avenue, Pomona
PHONE: 909-623-0190
WEBSITE: railgiants.org
E-MAIL: form on website

Railtown 1897 State Historic Park

Dave Crosby

Railtown 1897 State Historic Park is considered by many as the premier place for seeing California railroad history. It was originally part of the Sierra Railroad, arguably one of the best-known railroads in the world due to its extensive use in movies and television shows. You can also enjoy a train ride over these historic rails.

CHOICES: The historic shops and roundhouse have been operating as a steam locomotive maintenance facility for more than 100 years. One of the highlights of any visit is taking the roundhouse tour and experiencing for yourself what a working facility looks, feels, and smells like. On the 6-mile, 45-minute round trip through California's Gold Country, you can ride in coaches or open-air observation cars. Special theme trains also run during the year.

WHEN TO GO: The park is open daily year-round (except Thanksgiving, Christmas, and New Year's Day). Guided roundhouse tours take place each day of the summer schedule but are more limited during the rest of the year. Excursions run every weekend April through October with limited service in November and December. Steam-powered train rides behind Sierra No. 3 usually take place on Saturdays and with diesel locomotives on Sundays.

GOOD TO KNOW: The state of California purchased the station, shops, and roundhouse facilities in 1982 to create Railtown 1897. With more than 200 credits, it is one of the most-filmed railroad locations. The first known filming was in 1919 for a silent movie, and scenes for *High Noon, Back to the Future Part III,* and *Unforgiven* were filmed here.

WORTH DOING: This area, up through Sutter's Mill, is where people settled during the gold strikes, so history abounds. If you like the outdoors and learning western history, this is a great place to explore.

DON'T MISS: On the guided tour of the roundhouse, be sure to examine the props that were used in the movies filmed on the railroad.

GETTING THERE: From any direction, you have to drive to get to the Jamestown area, but California's Gold Country is almost universally seductive, so you'll enjoy the trip. It is about a 90-minute drive from Stockton.

LOCATION: 18115 Fifth Avenue, Jamestown
PHONE: 209-984-3953
WEBSITE: railtown1897.org
E-MAIL: form on website

279

Roaring Camp Railroads

Dave Crosby

Located in coastal wooded mountains, Roaring Camp runs two unique trains that offer the best of California scenery and vintage railroading. The Roaring Camp & Big Trees operates steam-powered narrow gauge trains through redwood forests, while the Santa Cruz, Big Trees & Pacific runs diesel-powered trips down a scenic river gorge to the ocean.

CHOICES: The Roaring Camp & Big Trees operates a fleet of 1880s-era Shay, Heisler, and Climax locomotives on a winding route up Bear Mountain. The route passes through Welch Big Trees Grove. The 75-minute excursions feature open-air coaches, and passengers can detrain at the summit to tour the forest or take a guided walk back. Santa Cruz boardwalk trains employ 1920s-era passenger coaches and open-air cars pulled by ex-Santa Fe CF7 diesels. The 3-hour round trip runs through Henry Cowell Redwoods State Park, down the San Lorenzo River Gorge, and through an 1875 tunnel before arriving at the historic Santa Cruz boardwalk. The Santa Cruz trains don't run January through March.

WHEN TO GO: Despite heavier crowds, summer is a great time to visit as Roaring Camp operates the most daily trains. The higher altitude and marine climate bring moderate temperatures; cool and foggy days are typical in summer. Seasonal trains include moonlight steam trains and dinner parties, days with Thomas and Percy, children's ghost trains in October, and a holiday lights train in November and December.

GOOD TO KNOW: In nearby Santa Cruz, the century-old seaside boardwalk is a historic gem and features a 1924 wooden roller coaster. Monterey, Pacific Grove, and Pebble Beach are only a short drive away on California Highway 1.

WORTH DOING: Roaring Camp re-creates an 1880s logging town and features historic buildings, a depot, engine house, antique cabooses, and picnic grounds. Access to the grounds is free, and picnicking is encouraged, but there is a charge for parking.

DON'T MISS: Seasonal events in Roaring Camp include Civil War reenacts, mountain men gatherings, harvest fairs, and steam festivals.

GETTING THERE: Roaring Camp is located 6 miles north of Santa Cruz off Route 17. Take Mount Hermon Road to Graham Hill Road. Turn left on Graham Hill Road and drive a half mile to Roaring Camp.

LOCATION: 5401 Graham Hill Road, Felton
PHONE: 831-335-4484
WEBSITE: roaringcamp.com
E-MAIL: form on website

280

Sacramento RiverTrain

Sacramento RiverTrain

Just outside of Sacramento, you'll find a uniquely scenic and relaxing train ride through rich farm country and a sprawling wildlife refuge. Operating over a 1911 electric interurban route, the Sacramento RiverTrain rolls between the cities of West Sacramento and Woodland, traveling along the banks of its namesake river and through the Yolo Wildlife Area, which is home to nearly 200 species of birds.

CHOICES: The railroad operates dinner, brunch, and lunch trains year-round, mostly on weekends. Passengers can board in either Woodland or West Sacramento for a leisurely 28-mile round trip that lasts up to 3 hours. The recently remodeled train is powered by GP7 No. 136, sporting new blue and gold colors, and includes vintage coaches, diners and open-air cars. Special events include train robberies, wine and beer trains, zombie trains, murder mystery excursions, and sunset dinner trains.

WHEN TO GO: Trains run year-round and are climate-controlled. Those who enjoy riding open-air cars might prefer to visit during spring or fall, instead of the sweltering summer months. Seasonal trips include pumpkin trains, valentine specials, a New Year's Eve express, and a popular Christmas train that runs from late November through December.

GOOD TO KNOW: The route is rich with history, originally built by the Woodland & Sacramento Railroad and operated by the Northern Electric Railway. Later owners included the Sacramento Northern, Western Pacific, Union Pacific, and Yolo Shortline.

WORTH DOING: Woodland features a charming historic downtown, surrounded by museums and wineries. Sacramento, only 15 minutes away, is home to the state capital, the California State Railroad Museum, and many other historic attractions.

DON'T MISS: Look for the 8,000-foot Fremont Bridge over the Sacramento River, which the railroad claims is the longest wooden trestle in the western United States.

GETTING THERE: From San Francisco, take I-80 East to West Sacramento and continue on I-80 to Reno (right lanes). Go 2 miles north and exit at Reed Avenue. Drive east and turn left on North Harbor Boulevard. The station is almost underneath the I-80 overpass.

LOCATION: 400 N. Harbor Boulevard, West Sacramento
PHONE: 800-866-1690
WEBSITE: sacramentorivertrain.com
E-MAIL: form on website

San Francisco Municipal Railway

Elrond Lawrence

Of all the transportation systems in the United States, one—the cable car—is forever linked to the City by the Bay, San Francisco. The San Francisco Municipal Railway operates the cable cars and historic streetcars as well as light rail and buses. Many of the city's attractions are easily accessible by the cable cars or streetcars.

CHOICES: Cable cars run on three lines: Powell-Hyde, Powell-Mason, and California. The Powell-Hyde Line ends near Ghirardelli Square, and the Powell-Mason Line ends at Bay Street in Fisherman's Wharf. The California Street Line runs east-west from Van Ness Avenue to Market Street. To board a cable car along a route, just look for the brown and white signs. Streetcars run regularly along Market Street and the Embarcadero on the F Market & Wharves line that connects the downtown area with Fisherman's Wharf.

WHEN TO GO: Cable cars run every day of the year, and there is never a bad time to visit San Francisco. Just be sure to take a jacket—even in summer!

GOOD TO KNOW: In San Francisco's diverse and historic streetcar fleet, some of the restored streetcars are more than 100 years old and originally ran in other U.S. cities as well as those in countries such as Italy, Australia, and Switzerland.

WORTH DOING: There is always plenty to see and do in San Francisco. You can walk through the Presidio, visit Chinatown, explore Fisherman's Wharf, and take a tour to Alcatraz Island and its prison. Great food and culture abounds.

DON'T MISS: The San Francisco Railway Museum, which features a replica of a motorman's platform of a 1911 streetcar and other interactive exhibits, is located at the F Market Steuart Street stop, just across from the Ferry Building.

GETTING THERE: Both the Powell-Hyde and Powell-Mason Lines begin at Market Street, and the California Street Line has a terminal at Van Ness Avenue.

LOCATION: 1145 Market Street, San Francisco
PHONE: 415-701-2311, 311 inside SF
WEBSITE: sfmta.com or streetcar.org
E-MAIL: form on website

Skunk Train

Sierra Railroad

The Skunk Train continues a grand tradition of transporting passengers into redwood forests that dwarf even the giant diesel locomotives and cars that traverse this route.

CHOICES: The Skunk Train offers two different excursions from its depots in Fort Bragg and Willits. Departing the Willits depot offers passengers the experience of a 40-mile round trip aboard the *Northspur Flyer* on board one of the rail line's famous "Skunk" motorcars or a full-sized diesel-powered train. The shorter 7-mile round trip known as the *Pudding Creek Express* departs from the coastal town of Fort Bragg and offers a bite sized hour-long round trip behind a diesel locomotive.

WHEN TO GO: Trains and motor cars operate year-round from both depots with the most frequent departures taking place in the summer months. Special Christmas runs take place each December and also depart both locations.

GOOD TO KNOW: The Skunk Train got its nickname from the motor cars first deployed by the California Western Railroad in the 1920s. The original gasoline engines inspired bystanders to note that "You could smell them before you see them."

WORTH DOING: The Fort Bragg depot is located on the scenic Pacific Coast Highway, which offers stunning views of the Pacific Ocean, while Willits is located deep within the redwoods less than an hour from the Mendocino National Forest.

DON'T MISS: The Skunk Train is now offering railbike departures from the Fort Bragg Depot. These four-wheel, two seat carts are pedal powered and offer an up-close look at the natural wonder of the redwoods.

GETTING THERE: Just over 3 hours north of San Francisco, the scenic drive to Fort Bragg starts on Highway 101. At Cloverdale, exit onto Highway 128 west, which turns into Highway 1, and continue north to Fort Bragg. The depot is at the foot of Laurel Street. Willits is 2.5 hours north of San Francisco on Highway 101. The depot there is at 299 East Commercial Street.

LOCATION: 100 W. Laurel Street, Fort Bragg
PHONE: 707-964-6371
WEBSITE: skunktrain.com
E-MAIL: form on website

Travel Town Museum

David Lustig

Travel Town is a good place to enjoy a couple of hours looking at equipment that has been preserved nowhere else. The museum, part of the Griffith Park complex in Los Angeles County, has a collection of small- to medium-sized steam, diesel, and electric locomotives and a surprisingly diverse roster of rolling stock.

CHOICES: Operated by the Department of Recreation and Parks, the museum is free and kid-friendly. Nevertheless, the diversity of the saved equipment makes Travel Town worth stopping at if you're in the area. Steam equipment includes tank locomotives, 0-6-0s, 2-8-0s, a 2-6-2, a 2-8-2, a Shay, and a Heisler. Other equipment to view includes an operating EMD Model 40 diesel, a Baldwin RS12, a Santa Fe gas-electric, a Pacific Electric freight motor, plus various pieces of rolling stock.

WHEN TO GO: The museum is open every day except Christmas. On the second Saturday of each month, docent-led tours through several historic railroad passenger cars take place. In October, Depot Day features special exhibits and activities.

GOOD TO KNOW: A food concession is inside, but eating and picnic areas are nearby in other parts of Griffith Park. If you would like to have lunch at a historic eatery, you can grab a chili dog at Pink's, which is 15 minutes away on La Brea Boulevard and has been operating since 1939.

WORTH DOING: Explore Griffith Park, a quiet oasis in busy LA, and especially take the time and visit the park's other sites including the famous observatory and world-class Los Angeles Zoo, which is right next to Travel Town.

DON'T MISS: If you want to take a break from walking, a rideable scale train encircles the collection.

GETTING THERE: Travel Town is near the confluence of I-5 and the 134 Freeway. Freeway exits are clearly marked.

LOCATION: 5200 Zoo Drive, Los Angeles
PHONE: 323-668-0104
WEBSITE: traveltown.org
E-MAIL: form on website

Western Pacific Railroad Museum

Western Pacific Railroad Museum

Here at one of the Western Pacific's last diesel locomotive shops is a great collection of rolling stock. The focus is on one of the West's most beloved railroads, Western Pacific, which traveled through beautiful mountain scenery and hosted the legendary *California Zephyr*. The setting couldn't be more appropriate.

CHOICES: This 37-acre site displays more than 100 pieces of equipment. Three former Western Pacific streamlined diesels call the museum home, as do locomotives from the Union Pacific and the Southern Pacific. Western Pacific 0-6-0 No. 165, a steam switcher currently being restored, is the only steam locomotive in the collection. Rolling stock includes passenger cars, boxcars, cabooses, and maintenance-of-way equipment. The museum is hands-on, so you can climb into cabs and hop onto cars.

WHEN TO GO: The museum is open daily April into September and select days after that. On summer weekends, caboose rides through a pine forest on a 1-mile loop of track make for a fun train trip. Pumpkin trains run in October and Santa trains in December.

GOOD TO KNOW: Visit in August for the annual Portola Railroad Days festival, which includes train rides, food, music, and a parade.

285

WORTH DOING: Close by is Lassen Volcanic National Park, where you can see hydrothermal features such as boiling mud pots, steaming ground, and roaring fumaroles.

DON'T MISS: Run a locomotive through the museum's program that puts you in the engineer's seat.

GETTING THERE: Portola is located in the Feather River Canyon between Sacramento and Reno. From the west, take I-80 to Highway 89 and go north to Highway 70, which runs into Portola. From the east, take I-80 to Highway 395 to Highway 70.

LOCATION: 700 Western Pacific Way, Portola
PHONE: 530-832-4131
WEBSITE: wplives.org
E-MAIL: info@wplives.org

California

Western Railway Museum

Western Railway Museum

The Western Railway Museum gives visitors the opportunity to ride historic streetcars and interurban electric trains that once served California and other western states. There are more than 50 cars on display.

CHOICES: A trip to the Western Railway Museum begins in the mission-revival inspired visitor center. After purchasing admission tickets, explore Cameron Hall, a large display and exhibit hall designed in the grand railroad station style. The museum offers 15-minute, 1-mile-long streetcar rides around the grounds. Its interurban ride over the former Sacramento Northern Railway main line runs to Birds Landing Road and features views of Suisun Marsh and Mount Diablo.

WHEN TO GO: The Western Railway Museum is open weekends. From Memorial Day through Labor Day, the museum expands its schedule and is open Wednesday through Sunday. It is closed on some holidays.

GOOD TO KNOW: You can look through Car House 1, and the museum offers guided tours of Car House 3. It also features a shaded picnic area.

WORTH DOING: During October, special Pumpkin Patch Trains take visitors on a scenic 5-mile journey to a pumpkin patch, complete with a hay-bale fort, hay rides, live music, animals, and, of course, pumpkins. In April, Scenic Limited wildflower trains and wine-tasting trains also run.

DON'T MISS: Visitors can stroll through the museum's large car house or take a guided tour of the building on weekends.

GETTING THERE: The museum is about 45 miles northeast of San Francisco, 12 miles east of I-80 on Highway 12. Public transportation is an option in reaching the museum by train and bus service.

LOCATION: 5848 Highway 12, Suisun City
PHONE: 707-374-2978
WEBSITE: wrm.org
E-MAIL: form on website

Yosemite Mountain Sugar Pine Railroad

Jim Wrinn

The Yosemite Mountain Sugar Pine Railroad is a 1-hour, 4-mile narrated railroad excursion at Yosemite National Park's south gate. The ride allows you to see what it was like when geared steam locomotives hauled massive log trains through the Sierra Nevadas. It is a restored segment of the old narrow gauge Madera Sugar Pine Lumber Company Railroad, with a portion of the original right-of-way reconstructed using the same techniques as 100 years ago.

CHOICES: Two geared Shay steam locomotives, Nos. 10 and 15, formerly used on the West Side Lumber Company, power the excursion trains. A unique experience is riding a Jenny railcar powered by Model A Ford automobile engines, which operate beginning in March. The Moonlight Special, which operates Saturday nights in September and Saturday and Wednesday nights during the summer, begins with a steak dinner and features masked bandits, moonlight, and campfire sing-alongs.

WHEN TO GO: The Yosemite Mountain Sugar Pine Railroad operates daily March into October. At close to 5,000 feet elevation, it can get chilly at Fish Camp, even in the summertime. At the height of summer tourist season, Yosemite National Park gets extremely crowded.

GOOD TO KNOW: Refurbished railcars, once used to transport logging crews, now carry excursion passengers.

WORTH DOING: You can easily spend an entire day or longer in the area. Other activities in the Fish Camp area include fishing, backpacking, hiking, camping, and mountain biking. You can even try your hand at panning for gold.

DON'T MISS: For a fun evening, try the moonlight melodrama, which starts with a steak dinner, continues with music and a steam train excursion, and finishes with a play and music in the woods.

GETTING THERE: Fish Camp is 40 miles north of Fresno and 60 miles east of Modesto on Highway 41.

LOCATION: 56001 Highway 41, Fish Camp
PHONE: 559-683-7273
WEBSITE: ymsprr.com
E-MAIL: info@ymsprr.com

287

NEVADA

Nevada Northern Railway Museum

Dave Crosby

The Nevada Northern is often hailed as the best-preserved standard-gauge railroad in the country. The operating railway museum is headquartered on a 56-acre complex with 66 historic buildings, set amid the vastness of the Great Basin. The Nevada Northern was completed in 1906 to haul copper, and most cars and locomotives have been on the railroad since the first day of their service lives.

CHOICES: The Nevada Northern offers something for everyone. Its 90-minute excursion goes through two tunnels and up mountain grades on the way to Ruth. Steam locomotives usually run on weekends and vintage diesels on weekdays. The railroad also operates a variety of special and seasonal trains, including Wild West trains, geology trains, and a Halloween ghost train that features stories from the region's colorful past.

WHEN TO GO: Regular excursions run March through October. The railway is open daily except for Tuesdays, Labor Day through Memorial Day, and several holidays. Summer is busy, with trains running daily. Ely is mile-high, so the weather can be unpredictable.

GOOD TO KNOW: The Nevada Northern offers guided tours of the shops and grounds after excursions. If you want an even more up-close look at the railway, you can stay overnight in a caboose or a bunkhouse.

WORTH DOING: Visit Great Basin National Park, which is 60 miles from Ely. In this diverse environment, you can see 13,000-foot mountains and 5,000-year-old bristlecone pines and explore Lehman Caves.

DON'T MISS: At the railway, you can view steam locomotives, wooden passenger cars, and a steam-powered rotary plow. Structures include the original depot, engine house, freight shed, coaling tower, and water tower. Diesels include everything from an SD9 to a Baldwin VO1000 and a trio of Alco RS-model road switchers.

GETTING THERE: Ely is in east-central Nevada at the junction of Highways 6, 50, and 93.

LOCATION: 1100 Avenue A, Ely
PHONE: 866-407-8326 or 775-289-2085
WEBSITE: nnry.com
E-MAIL: form on website

Nevada Southern Railway

Nevada Southern Railway

Nevada Southern Railway

The railway offers a train ride with a historical twist. This was part of the construction railroad from Las Vegas to Hoover Dam, with tracks having been laid in 1931. It's a nice ride in the desert and a break from the hustle of Las Vegas.

CHOICES: Along the 35-minute round trip, you get an up-close look at desert plant life, especially when riding in the train's open-air car. The other cars are air-conditioned, restored Pullman coaches dating back to 1911. A generator car behind the locomotive supplies power to the coaches. Operated by the Nevada State Railroad Museum, the railway's outdoor interpretative area displays a variety of equipment, including Union Pacific steam locomotive No. 6264 with its unusual Vanderbilt tender.

WHEN TO GO: The railway operates on weekends with four trips each day. Summer in Nevada can be hot, with temperatures hitting triple digits. Santa, train robbery, and other special trains run. It is closed in December. The museum pavilion is open daily.

GOOD TO KNOW: A 7.5" gauge steam train operates the second and fourth Saturday each month except for January, July and August.

WORTH DOING: Take a trip to nearby Boulder Dam and tour this technological wonder. Boating on Lake Mead is a popular activity any time of the year.

289

DON'T MISS: Ride a train pulled by a historic diesel. One of the locomotives used, UP No. 844, is one of the last GP30 diesel locomotives—an early 1960s diesel that replaced the first generation of diesel locomotives that had themselves replaced steam power.

GETTING THERE: Boulder City is a 30-minute drive from Las Vegas and McCarran International Airport. It is an easy drive from Las Vegas along Highway 93 into Boulder City. Once there, turn left on Yucca Street to the museum and railway.

LOCATION: 601 Yucca Street, Boulder City
PHONE: 702-486-5933
WEBSITE: nevadasouthern.com
E-MAIL: webmaster@nevadasouthern.com

Nevada State Railroad Museum

Dave Crosby

The Nevada State Railroad Museum maintains one of the nation's most geographically significant collections of railroad cars and locomotives with many of the pieces being operational.

CHOICES: The museum operates steam train and motor car excursions on specific dates throughout the spring, summer and fall. Virginia & Truckee 4-6-0 No. 25 powers most steam trains, while 1926 Edwards Motor Car No. 10 operates most other times. On special occasions the museum will operate its rare streamlined McKeen motorcar No. 22, built in 1910 for the Virginia & Truckee Railroad.

WHEN TO GO: The museum building is open Thursday through Monday year-round with the exception of Thanksgiving, Christmas and New Year's Day. Rides are offered most weekends May to October with Christmas trains offered late November and December.

GOOD TO KNOW: The museum is preparing to exhibit Coach 17, the sole remaining piece of railroad equipment that was present at the Golden Spike ceremony that marked the completion of the first Transcontinental Railroad. 2019 is the 150th anniversary of the Golden Spike ceremony.

WORTH DOING: Carson City is the Nevada state capital and features an array of shops and restaurants. Nearby, the rebuilt Virginia & Truckee Railroad operates steam and diesel excursions from the outskirts of Carson City to Virginia City.

DON'T MISS: Every July 4th weekend the museum operates some of the more significant steam locomotives in its collection such as the *Inyo* of the Virginia & Truckee, and the narrow-gauge *Glenbrook*, both built by Baldwin in 1875.

GETTING THERE: The museum is on Highway 395 (Carson Street) on the south side of Carson City. Carson City is within a day's drive of most major cities on the West Coast.

LOCATION: 2180 S. Carson Street, Carson City
PHONE: 775-687-6953
WEBSITE: museums.nevadaculture.org/nsrmcc
E-MAIL: amichalski@nevadaculture.org

Virginia & Truckee Railroad

Dave Crosby

The Virginia & Truckee Railroad was born of the silver and gold trade of the famous "Comstock Lode." Today's steam and diesel-powered excursions traverse both untamed lands and tiny outposts left over from the golden days on mining.

CHOICES: Two different trips are offered over the route of the famous Nevada shortline. Those wishing for a short but memorable experience may opt to ride the 35-minute trip from Virginia City to Gold Hill and return. For those who wish a longer ride, the "Sisters in History" route carries passengers between Carson City and Virginia City on a 24-mile round trip that affords passengers a 3.5-hour layover in Virginia City.

WHEN TO GO: The Carson City to Virginia City train operates weekends only, Memorial Day through October, while the Virginia City to Gold Hill excursion operates daily during this period. During November and December the famous Polar Express operates on the Carson City route.

GOOD TO KNOW: Each year, more track is relayed on the original Virginia & Truckee roadbed. On select Saturdays, trains operate from Carson City's Eastgate Station into the Carson River Canyon on new trackage not travelled by other excursion trains.

WORTH DOING: Virginia City, founded in 1859, is now a National Historic Landmark District with restored buildings and cemeteries that recall the glory days of mining in the area. Numerous restaurants, shops and museums are located near the railroad.

DON'T MISS: Be sure to visit the Nevada State Railroad Museum in nearby Carson City with its impressive displays or artifacts and restored locomotives and cars.

GETTING THERE: Virginia City is on Highway 341, 25 miles south of Reno and 15 miles north of Carson City.

LOCATION: 165 F Street, Virginia City
PHONE: 775-847-0380
WEBSITE: virginiatruckee.com
E-MAIL: info@virginiatruckee.com

REGION 10

ALASKA

1 Alaska Railroad
2 Museum of Alaska Transportation & Industry
3 Tanana Valley Railroad Museum
4 White Pass & Yukon Route

HAWAII

ALASKA

Museum of Alaska Transportation & Industry

The museum is home to the trains, planes, and other machines that helped develop the state. It features a train yard with locomotives, railcars, and a renovated section house. The museum is open daily mid-May to September.

LOCATION: 3800 W. Museum Drive, Wasilla
PHONE: 907-376-1211
WEBSITE: museumofalaska.org
E-MAIL: form on website

Tanana Valley Railroad Museum

The museum runs a restored 1899 Porter 0-4-0 steam locomotive around the perimeter of Pioneer Park on select days during the year. The museum is open daily Memorial Day through Labor Day, and visitors may see restoration activity as well as learn about the railroad. Pioneer Park contains several other interesting museums and operates a narrow-gauge train through the site.

LOCATION: 2300 Airport Way, Fairbanks
PHONE: 907-459-7420
WEBSITE: tananavalleyrailroad.com
E-MAIL: ftvrr.inc@gmail.com

Alaska Railroad

Frank Keller

© Frank Keller Photography 2018

Completed in 1923, the Alaska Railroad was built to link the Pacific seaport of Seward with the resource-rich interior long before there were highways. Passenger service offers breathtaking excursions into rugged back-country terrain that is often inaccessible by car.

CHOICES: The flagship *Denali Star* operates daily between Anchorage and Fairbanks with stops at Wasilla, Talkeetna, and Denali National Park. A local favorite, the *Coastal Classic* goes to Seward, where boat tours provide access to Kenai Fjords National Park and Resurrection Bay. The *Hurricane Turn* provides flag-stop service for campers and fishermen along the Susitna River. The *Glacier Discovery* runs from Anchorage to Whittier for glacier cruises and to Spencer Glacier and Grandview whistle-stops for kayaking, rafting, and hiking.

WHEN TO GO: Most trains operate mid-May to mid-September when the weather is warm and the days are long. The best time to visit is early in the season, when there is still snow on the mountains and little rain. Winter service is provided by the *Aurora* winter train operating between Anchorage and Fairbanks on weekends and midweek from mid-September to mid-May. Special trains also run.

GOOD TO KNOW: The railroad works closely with major cruise lines, offering cruise passengers Grandview service to connect the ports of Seward and Whittier with the Anchorage airport. The cruise lines also operate their own train with double-decker domes between Anchorage and Denali Park.

WORTH DOING: The *Hurricane Turn* provides an escape from sightseeing and tourism overload and a chance to visit with friendly Alaskans on their way to remote cabins. It operates Thursday through Monday and features a dome coach.

295

DON'T MISS: Try either the *Coastal Classic* or *Glacier Discovery*. The scenery south of Anchorage is more varied and breathtaking than most of the Denali route.

GETTING THERE: Airlines fly to both Anchorage and Fairbanks. Cruise ships from Vancouver and Seattle are another option.

LOCATION: 411 W. First Avenue, Anchorage
PHONE: 800-544-0552 or 907-265-2494
WEBSITE: alaskarailroad.com
E-MAIL: reservations@akrr.com

White Pass & Yukon Route

Karl Zimmermann

The White Pass & Yukon's 67.5 route miles make it the longest operating narrow-gauge railroad in North America. More importantly, virtually every one of those miles is knockout beautiful—a potpourri of lakes, rivers, and snow-capped mountains. Completed in 1900, the railroad was built to link the Yukon and other booming gold-mining districts with tidewater at Skagway.

CHOICES: The most popular trip is the half-day, 40-mile round trip to White Pass Summit. Best of all are 8-hour runs along the full length of the line, Skagway to Carcross, riding the train one way and a motor coach the other. A brief layover at Bennett allows a visit to the museum there. Additional train-motor coach combinations are available, and the trains will drop off and pick up hikers at certain locations, including Laughton,14 miles from Skagway, or Denver, 6 miles distant.

WHEN TO GO: The White Pass & Yukon operates from early May through September, and any time in that window is fine for a visit—though it is likely to be bracingly chilly early and late. As compensation, the snow-capped mountains will be more scenic.

GOOD TO KNOW: Mikado No. 73, pride of the White Pass fleet, has been undergoing a major overhaul, putting the usual steam excursions to Fraser Meadows in abeyance, but an early return is expected. Unique and colorful diesels—modernized, shovel-nose General Electric units and newer low-nose road switchers—handle all the other trains.

WORTH DOING: The few hotels and handful of B&Bs in Skagway are best booked in advance. You can tour Skagway, the Yukon, and other scenic areas by Jeep, raft, horseback, or dogsled.

DON'T MISS: Although the entire line is spectacular, pay particular attention to the first 20 miles to White Pass Summit. Here, the railroad uses grades of up to 3.9 percent to climb 2,865 feet. For the best views, grab seats on the left side of the train.

GETTING THERE: Most passengers arrive at Skagway by cruise ship, but you can get to Skagway from Bellingham, Wash., or Prince Rupert aboard the comfortable ferries of the Alaska Marine Highway. For motorists, Skagway is 110 miles south of the Alaska Highway via the South Klondike Highway.

LOCATION: 231 Second Avenue, Skagway
PHONE: 800-343-7373
WEBSITE: wpyr.com
E-MAIL: info@wpyr.com

HAWAII

Lahaina Kaanapali Railroad

The Sugar Cane Train travels around the historical whaling town of Lahaina on the Hawaiian island of Maui. Narrow-gauge steam engines transport visitors in open-air cars through golf courses, along the ocean, and across a scenic railroad trestle.

LOCATION: Pu'ukoli'i Road, Lahaina
PHONE: 808-667-6851
WEBSITE: sugarcanetrain.com
E-MAIL: form on website

Laupahoehoe Train Museum

The musem is located on the Big Island along the Hamakua Heritage Coast. It is housed in a station agent's home, which has been restored and furnished to its early 1900s appearance. The museum contains photos and artifacts of the Hilo Railroad and displays a standard-gauge caboose, narrow-gauge boxcar, and diesel switcher.

LOCATION: 36-2377 Mamalahoa Highway, Laupahoehoe
PHONE: 808-962-6300
WEBSITE: thetrainmuseum.com
E-MAIL: laupahoehoetrainmuseum@yahoo.com

Hawaiian Railway Society

Hawaiian Railway Society

The Hawaiian Railway Society operates the only active train on the island of Oahu. It offers regularly scheduled 90-minute, fully narrated rides over 6.5 miles of track. Along the way, you'll pass a variety of interesting and historical sites, including Fort Barrette. The train stops at Kahe Point, so you can take in the extraordinary ocean views.

CHOICES: Regular excursions take place Saturday and twice on Sunday. On the second Sunday of each month, parlor car No. 64 is added to the regular train of open cars, and reservations (and an additional fare) are necessary for riding in this beautifully restored car. Three side-rod diesel locomotives have been restored to operation, and several steam locomotives have been cosmetically restored. The society also has a collection of railcars and other equipment on display.

WHEN TO GO: The 3 p.m. Saturday and Sunday rides are ice cream rides on which the train stops at Two Scoops in Ko'Olina, where ice cream can be purchased.

GOOD TO KNOW: Parlor car No. 64 is the luxurious parlor car that Benjamin Dillingham, founder of the Oahu Railway & Land Company, had built for his personal use in 1900. Restored by the Hawaiian Railway Society, No. 64 is worth the ride, and the fare for riding the car goes toward its upkeep.

WORTH DOING: No trip to Oahu would be complete without a heart-rending visit to Pearl Harbor. You can also wander over Oahu and other islands and literally discover pieces of Hawaii's railroading past, which included sugar plantation, military, and common carrier railways.

DON'T MISS: The society's site, which is situated on what was part of the Oahu Railway & Land Company main line, is north of Pearl Harbor. The scenery is incredible. Wear comfortable shoes and wander through the train yard and then relax with lunch in the picnic area.

GETTING THERE: The operation is minutes from Honolulu by bus or car. If you drive, take H1 west and exit on 5A Ewa. Then take Highway 76 south for 2.5 miles, turn right at Renton Road, and continue for 1.5 miles to the entrance.

LOCATION: 91-1001 Renton Road, Ewa
PHONE: 808-681-5461
WEBSITE: hawaiianrailway.com
E-MAIL: info@hawaiianrailway.com

Kauai Plantation Railway

David Lustig

The Kauai Plantation Railway operates daily on a genuine Hawaiian plantation. Experience plantation life and learn about Kauai agriculture as the train travels through more than 100 acres of unspoiled Hawaii on a 3-foot-gauge train. Passengers enjoy a 40-minute journey through fields of sugar cane, pineapple, banana, papaya, coffee, tropical flowers, and hardwood trees.

CHOICES: Train rides leave from a Hawaiian train depot, and you can ride in a reproduction of a railway car from the time of King Kalakaua or an open-sided excursion car. In addition, there is a ride-hike-lunch-orchard tour. Motive power is a pair of small diesels, including a restored 1939 Whitcomb engine.

WHEN TO GO: The train operates daily, and there are up to five runs a day. Hawaii is in the tropics, and any day is a beautiful day.

GOOD TO KNOW: The 3-foot-gauge railway was the first railroad built on Kauai in almost 100 years. More than 2.5 miles of roadbed was constructed with rails hand-spiked onto 6,000 wooden ties. More than 50 varieties of fruits and vegetables can be found on the plantation, from avocado and bananas to rambutan and sugar cane. The plantation also features a restaurant and shops as well as a tasting room for Kōloa Rum, which is produced on the island with sugar cane.

WORTH DOING: A train and luau package is available for Tuesday and Friday evenings in which you can experience a Hawaiian feast and entertainment.

DON'T MISS: On the tour package, after riding the train, you can hike in the rain forest and sample fresh fruit picked right off the tree. You also have the opportunity to feed goats, sheep, and pigs.

299

GETTING THERE: The Kauai Plantation is just off Route 50 (Kaumualii Highway) approximately 1 mile south of Lihue, which is the main city on Kauai. The railway is located at Kilohana Plantation next to Kauai Community College. Just look for the white picket fence.

LOCATION: 3-2087 Kaumualii Highway, Lihue
PHONE: 808-245-7245
WEBSITE: kauaiplantationrailway.com
E-MAIL: train@hawaiilink.net

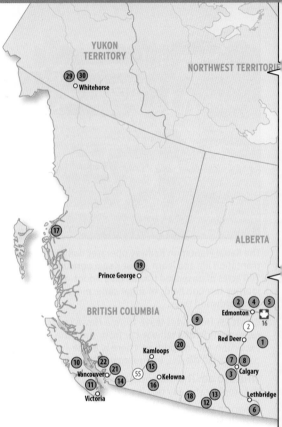

ALBERTA

Alberta Railway Museum

The museum's collection of railway equipment and buildings focuses on the Canadian National Railway and the Northern Alberta Railway. It includes more than 75 locomotives and cars, three stations, a telegraph office, and a water tank. The museum is open weekends from Victoria Day through Labor Day. You can take a walking tour, ride a speeder, and on long holiday weekends, ride a passenger train.

LOCATION: 24215 34th Street NW, Edmonton
PHONE: 780-472-6229
WEBSITE: albertarailwaymuseum.com
E-MAIL: form on website

Edmonton Radial Railway

The Edmonton Radial Railway operates streetcars in Fort Edmonton Park and in Old Strathcona. Streetcar operation at Fort Edmonton Park is suspended while the fort undergoes a two-year renovation program. In Old Strathcona, the trolley crosses High Level Bridge over the North Saskatchewan River to downtown Edmonton. The Strathcona streetcar barn contains a museum with exhibits on streetcar history. Streetcars operate from May into October, and the museum is open Saturdays.

LOCATION: 103 Street and 84th Avenue, Edmonton
PHONE: 780-437-7721 or 780-496-1464
WEBSITE: edmonton-radial-railway.ab.ca
E-MAIL: info@edmonton-radial-railway.ab.ca

Fort Edmonton Park

Nestled in Edmonton's river valley, Fort Edmonton Park is a living history museum that represents four historical periods between 1840 and 1920. It contains more than 75 buildings. A 1919 steam train takes you through the park, and caboose rides are available. A streetcar also travels along the historic streets. The park is currently undergoing a major enhancement, please visit FortEdmontonPark.ca for attraction availability.

LOCATION: Fox Drive and Whitemud Drive, Edmonton
PHONE: 780-496-7381
WEBSITE: fortedmontonpark.ca
E-MAIL: info@fortedmontonpark.ca

Galt Historic Railway Park

The park exhibits artifacts from the steam and coal eras in southern Alberta, focusing on the Galt Railway system. It includes the restored 1890 depot that straddled the Canada–U.S. border near Sweetgrass, Montana. Speeder rides are offered during special events. The park is open Tuesdays through Saturdays, June through August.

LOCATION: 65032 Range Road 19-4C, Stirling
PHONE: 403-756-2220
WEBSITE: galtrailway.com
E-MAIL: gcprs@telus.net

Royal Canadian Pacific

The Royal Canadian Pacific, an arm of the passenger department of Canadian Pacific Railway, offers chartered all-inclusive luxury-train ride packages on CPR's route through the spectacularly scenic Canadian Rockies. Ride aboard vintage, heavyweight CPR sleeping, observation, and dining cars with lavishly restored interiors.

LOCATION: 7550 Ogden Dale Road SE, Calgary
PHONE: 403-319-4690
WEBSITE: royalcanadianpacific.com
E-MAIL: rcp_info@cpr.ca

Alberta Prairie Railway Excursions

Alberta Prairie Railway Excusrsions

A trip aboard the Alberta Prairie conjures up visions of what a central Alberta wheat line must have been like 100 years ago. Traveling from the well-developed community of Stettler, it passes through stands of trees and fields before reaching Big Valley, where the ruins of a roundhouse and a restored depot remain.

CHOICES: The railroad offers an extensive schedule of excursions and specials throughout the year. All excursions include a buffet meal, which is served in Big Valley, onboard entertainment, and possibly a train robbery. Specially themed rides include live dinner shows, steak barbecues, country dinner trains, Polar Express rides, and teddy bear trains. The trains are pulled by Baldwin 2-8-0 steam engine No. 41, or by General Motors Diesel No. 1259. Several times a year, usually for special events, such as on Canada Day, historic steam engine No. 6060 is in operation.

WHEN TO GO: Summer excursions begin in May and continue until mid-October each year.

GOOD TO KNOW: The railway was once part of a vast grain railroad network belonging to the Canadian Northern. Be sure to chat with the train crew. Many of the veteran railroaders on this line have great stories. And if you get the right conductor, he might just sing you a song or recite a poem for you en route.

WORTH DOING: In Big Valley, the restored station and several railcars display railroad and local history artifacts. You can take a self-guided tour of the five-stall roundhouse remains and former rail yards, view a wooden grain elevator, and visit the Jimmy Jock Boardwalk, which is modeled after a frontier town's street.

DON'T MISS: For an added prairie experience, you can take a 20-mile covered wagon trip along historic rail rights-of-way.

GETTING THERE: Stettler is about 3 hours northeast of Calgary on Highway 12.

LOCATION: 4611 47th Avenue, Stettler
PHONE: 800-282-3994 or 403-742-2811
WEBSITE: absteamtrain.com
E-MAIL: info@absteamtrain.com

Aspen Crossing Railway

This railway takes you back to a simpler time. Along a 28-mile, 3-hour round trip, passengers get to enjoy serene prairie views, pass historic wooden elevators, learn about the area's agriculture and the railroad—or simply relax to the soothing sounds of the rail.

CHOICES: In addition to regular Sunday excursions, there is a large variety of special event trains, including twilight departures, elevator tours, wine tasting trips, or brunch trains. Many of the trains include musical entertainment and/or a train robbery.

WHEN TO GO: Trains run from May through September. During May, June, and September, trains operate on Saturdays, Sundays, and most Fridays. July and August see trains Fridays through Sundays, with the addition of a circus train on Wednesdays. October weekends and the days before Halloween are dedicated to the Train of Terror. The Polar Express runs in December.

GOOD TO KNOW: Some 1-hour mini excursions are available during the season. In August, look for the Southern Alberta Music Festival to take place at Aspen Crossing.

WORTH DOING: While at the station, you can dine in a restored 1887 Pullman railcar. The restored car was once the private business car of former Prime Minister John Diefenbaker. If you want to make your visit an extended stay, you can stay in the railway's 85-site modern campground or one of three caboose cabins. The cabooses are from the Union Pacific, Canadian Pacific, and Northern Alberta Railway.

DON'T MISS: On the Prairie Tour, you'll see the Mossleigh grain elevators, some of the rare original elevators left in Canada. In the 1930s, there were more than 5,000 grain elevators, and now less than 350 remain across the prairie provinces.

GETTING THERE: Aspen Crossing is located about an hour's drive southeast of Calgary. It is 1 mile west of Mossleigh on Highway 24.

LOCATION: Highway 24, Mossleigh
PHONE: 866-440-3500 or 403-534-2129
WEBSITE: aspencrossing.com
E-MAIL: info@aspencrossing.com

Heritage Park

Heritage Park

Discover what life was like in the Canadian West between 1864 and 1914 by visiting this re-created village framed by the Rockies. More than 150 exhibits, including many buildings transplanted from Calgary and other locations throughout Alberta, bring the past to the present.

CHOICES: The park includes a roundhouse and turntable along with 30 locomotives and cars. A train ride is an excellent way to see the park. Make a day of your visit and wander from building to building, paying particular attention to the transplanted railway stations, rolling stock, and re-created carbarn. If it's too hot, take a cruise on the water aboard the replica sternwheeler SS *Moyie*. Heritage Town Square represents a street scene from the 1930s to '50s, complete with an automobile museum and a replica train station.

WHEN TO GO: All of Heritage Park is open daily from mid-May through mid-October. Historical Village is open weekends during September through mid-October. Then over the winter, Gasoline Alley Museum is open Tuesday through Sunday.

GOOD TO KNOW: A short streetcar line connects the outer parking area to the main entrance. It's well worth it to park out there, view ex-CPR 2-10-4 No. 5931 and S2 No. 7019, and then ride over to the gate in a replica Calgary or Winnipeg trolley.

WORTH DOING: Calgary's 10-day annual Stampede, which can draw more than one million people, is the world's largest rodeo. The event also features chuck wagon racing, agricultural exhibits, entertainment, and a parade.

DON'T MISS: During Railway Days in September, the park celebrates Canadian railways and rolls out much of its collection. You can also take a caboose ride, ride a handcar, and tour a steam locomotive cab.

GETTING THERE: Heritage Park is approximately a 20-minute drive southwest from downtown Calgary. A shuttle service operates during park hours from the Heritage light rail stop.

LOCATION: 1900 Heritage Drive SW, Calgary
PHONE: 403-268-8500
WEBSITE: heritagepark.ca
E-MAIL: info@heritagepark.ca

VIA Jasper-Prince Rupert Route

VIA Rail

The VIA Rail Canada train between Jasper and Prince Rupert, British Columbia, is one of the scenic highlights of any trip to western Canada. The 2-day, 725-mile trip, which includes an overnight stop in Prince George, takes you from the Rocky Mountains in Jasper National Park to the Pacific coast.

CHOICES: Travelers can opt for either economy or touring class. Budget-minded vacationers can relax in the leg-rest seats found in economy class. Those with a voracious appetite for scenery may want to spend a little more for touring class, which puts you in a dome car with its upper observation deck and panoramic views. Touring class also provides meals. Economy class has access to the dome during the off-peak months of October through May.

WHEN TO GO: The train operates Wednesday, Friday, and Sunday year-round. The shorter days and deep snows of winter give way to a plethora of spring flowers in May. Hot summer days morph into colorful, cool fall days by October. Economy class is offered year-round, and touring class is available only from mid-June through September.

GOOD TO KNOW: Don't forget to book a hotel room for your overnight stay in Prince George. When arriving in Prince George, you may want to take a taxi, even though accommodations are a few blocks away as the area around the VIA station may be considered rough. Prince Rupert is a port of call on the Alaska Marine Highway.

WORTH DOING: In Jasper, you can explore Jasper National Park, the northernmost park in the Rocky Mountains, and leave feeling hot or cold. You can experience a glacier close up and soak in a hot spring. In Prince Rupert, you can visit the Kwinitsa Railway Museum and the First Nation Carving Shed, where artists produce works in wood and metal.

DON'T MISS: Just west of Jasper, Mount Robson, the highest peak in the Canadian Provinces, is visible from the train for only a few cloudless days a year. You may also see moose, bear, elk, wolves, seals, and eagles along the way.

GETTING THERE: VIA Rail operates the Vancouver-Toronto *Canadian* three times a week during summer and twice a week the rest of the year. Shuttle services are available between Jasper and Edmonton.

LOCATION: 607 Connaught Drive, Jasper
PHONE: 888-842-7245
WEBSITE: viarail.ca/en/explore-our-destinations/trains/rockies-and-pacific
E-MAIL: form on website

BRITISH COLUMBIA

BC Forest Discovery Centre

The most relaxing, and most scenic, way to take in this 100-acre site is by riding the train, which is pulled by a steam-powered 1910 locomotive or a gas-powered locomotive. Speeder rides are also offered. The site's collection features Shay, Climax, and Vulcan locomotives. A two-truck, 24-ton Shay is being rebuilt and should be in service sometime in 2019. Other exhibits include an operating sawmill, a lookout tower, and antique logging trucks. The site is open April into October, daily June to September, and for special events.

LOCATION: 2892 Drinkwater Road, Duncan
PHONE: 250-715-1113
WEBSITE: bcforestdiscoverycentre.com
E-MAIL: info.bcfdc@shawlink.ca

Fort Steele Heritage Town

Fort Steele Heritage Town is a restored 1890s pioneer town complete with railway. A Montreal Locomotive Works 2-6-2 Prairie type locomotive takes you on a 20-minute scenic ride that includes a stop at a viewing platform. You can also examine a variety of rail equipment and steam engines displayed by the enginehouse. Fort Steele is open year-long, and the railway operates daily during summer.

LOCATION: 9851 Highway 93/95, Fort Steele
PHONE: 250-417-6000
WEBSITE: fortsteele.ca
E-MAIL: info@fortsteele.bc.ca

Fraser Valley Heritage Railway

The railway runs heritage interurban cars No. 1225 and No. 1304, and speeders on the original BC Electric Railway route. Cars leave from the replicated Cloverdale station along the line through Surrey. For 2019 and 2020, the Sullivan Station will be operational for passenger pickup and drop off. The railway operates weekends from May to October.

LOCATION: 176A Street and 56th Avenue, Cloverdale
PHONE: 604-574-9056
WEBSITE: fvhrs.org
E-MAIL: info@fvhrs.org

Kwinitsa Railway Station Museum

Located in Prince Rupert's waterfront park near the Museum of Northern BC, this restored station house is an excellent example of the small stations once found along Canada's northern railway line. Photographs, videos, and detailed restorations depict the life of station agents and linemen who worked for the Grand Trunk Railway at the turn of the 20th century. It is open daily June through August.

LOCATION: Bill Murray Way and First Avenue, Prince Rupert
PHONE: 250-624-3207
WEBSITE: museumofnorthernbc.com

Nelson Electric Tramway

Streetcar 23 runs from the park to Prestige Lakeside Resort along the beautiful west arm of Kootenay Lake. The 2.5-mile round trip takes about 20 minutes and includes some street running. The streetcar operates from May into October. Car 23 ran in Nelson more than 60 years ago and was restored after being turned into a dog kennel (and a chicken coop). The trolley barn contains historical exhibits.

LOCATION: Rotary Lakeside Park, Nelson
PHONE: 250-352-7672
WEBSITE: nelsonstreetcar.org
E-MAIL: info@nelsonstreetcar.org

Railway & Forestry Museum

The museum displays historic railway and forestry exhibits in a park-like setting. The extensive rail collection dates to 1899 and includes two stations and a turntable. It also contains both steam and diesel locomotives and more than 40 pieces of rolling stock. The museum is open daily May to September and Wednesday through Saturday the rest of the year.

LOCATION: 850 River Road, Prince George
PHONE: 250-563-7351
WEBSITE: pgrfm.bc.ca
E-MAIL: trains@pgrfm.bc.ca

Revelstoke Railway Museum

This railway museum focuses on the history of the Canadian Pacific Railway in western Canada. You can walk through Business Car No. 4 and view steam locomotive No. 5468, various railcars, and artifacts. You can also try a train simulator. The museum also operates a small facility at Craigellachie, 28 miles west of Revelstoke, where the last spike of the Canadian Pacific Railway was driven. The museum is open year-round.

LOCATION: 719 Track Street West, Revelstoke
PHONE: 877-837-6060 or 250-837-6060
WEBSITE: railwaymuseum.com
E-MAIL: railway@telus.net

Alberni Pacific Railway

Alberni Pacific Railway, Ken Rutherford

The Alberni Pacific offers passengers a chance to visit the former McLean Paper Mill, 6 miles east of Port Alberni over the former Canadian Pacific Railway Port Alberni Subdivision. The mill is a National Historic Site that commemorates the history of logging and milling in British Columbia.

CHOICES: Trains to the mill are pulled by a 1929 Baldwin 2-8-2T steam locomotive or vintage diesel locomotive, and passengers ride in converted former Canadian National transfer cabooses, three of which are open and two are covered. The 35-minute trips leave (and return) from a restored 1912 CPR station. Cab rides in No. 7 are also available.

WHEN TO GO: Runs are made over this scenic trackage Thursdays through Sundays between the end of June until September. Special events occur throughout the year including special steam trains in fall as well as wine trains, train robberies, and Santa trains.

GOOD TO KNOW: The McLean Mill is the only steam-operated sawmill in Canada. This historic site and the railway are part of the Alberni Valley Heritage Network that celebrates the area's history and culture. Also included are the Alberni Valley Museum and Maritime Discovery Centre.

WORTH DOING: Visit Port Alberni's quaint harbor, which offers a mix of restaurants, galleries, tours, and shops. You are also within minutes of numerous outdoor activities including seeing Delta Falls, the tallest waterfall in Canada.

DON'T MISS: At the mill, you can explore the site on your own or take a guided tour. It has been laid out as an early 20th century logging camp with restored buildings and original pieces of logging equipment, including an operating steam donkey.

GETTING THERE: Bus service is available from Vancouver to Port Alberni. Ferry service operates between the mainland and various points on Vancouver Island including Port Alberni.

LOCATION: 3100 Kingsway Avenue, Port Alberni
PHONE: 250-723-6161
WEBSITE: albernisteamtrain.com
E-MAIL: info@alberniheritage.com

Cranbrook History Centre

Cranbrook History Centre

The centre's rail collection is a magnet for anyone interested in Canadian passenger rail travel as it once was. The centre is home to the only surviving train set of equipment from the 1929 *Trans Canada Limited* as well as the beautifully reconstructed Royal Alexandra Hall.

CHOICES: Visitors can choose from several different guided tours that examine the trains in the museum's collection, including the *Soo-Spokane Train Deluxe* and *Trans Canada Limited*. Various business cars, cars of state, and historic structures are also included. Guides explain the history of the equipment and bring to life the beautifully restored railcar interiors. Be prepared to walk. Depending on the tour, you could cover a half mile or more.

WHEN TO GO: The museum is open daily July and August. During the remainder of the year, it is open Tuesday through Saturday.

GOOD TO KNOW: Cranbrook is a gateway to the Canadian Rockies, which are a short drive away. Enjoy the sun and a hot soak. Situated at an elevation of 3,000 feet, Cranbrook also is one of the sunniest spots in Canada. After a walking tour of the museum, you can soak in several hot springs in the area.

WORTH DOING: Fort Steele is less than 20 minutes away. Once a thriving mining town, Fort Steele became a ghost town when the railroad bypassed it for Cranbrook. It is now a heritage town, where visitors can experience its boom-town history.

DON'T MISS: Visit the exquisitely re-created Royal Alexandra Hall from the Canadian Pacific Railway's Royal Alexandra Hotel that once stood beside CPR's Winnipeg Station. The hall was the grand cafe of the hotel and features Edwardian architectural style. Other exhibits are located on the lower level of the original CPR freight shed, including working model railway displays.

GETTING THERE: Air service to Cranbrook is available with direct flights from Vancouver and Calgary. Greyhound also operates daily scheduled service to the city. It is about a 3.5-hour drive from Spokane, Wash.

LOCATION: 57 Van Horne Street South, Cranbrook
PHONE: 250-489-3918
WEBSITE: cranbrookhistorycentre.com
E-MAIL: info@cranbrookhistorycentre.com

Kamloops Heritage Railway

John Godfrey

This steam-powered tourist line's regular excursion is a 7-mile round trip on the Canadian National's Okanagan Subdivision that features mountain vistas, lakeside scenery, and an occasional train robbery.

CHOICES: On the Spirit of Kamloops' 70-minute excursion, you can ride in a restored 1930s air-conditioned coach or in an open-air car. Along the way, masked riders reenact the famous 1906 train robbery by the Bill Miner gang. The train departs from a restored 1927 CN station and crosses the South Thompson River over a 1927 steel trestle bridge, where the train stops and allows you to photograph the scenery.

WHEN TO GO: The Spirit of Kamloops operates Thursday and Friday evenings and during the day on Saturdays in July and August. Illuminated with hundreds of lights, the Spirit of Christmas is a 1-hour holiday special, complete with candy canes, hot chocolate, and caroling. Halloween trains also operate.

GOOD TO KNOW: The former courthouse in Kamloops, where train robber Bill Miner was tried and convicted, is now a popular hostel.

WORTH DOING: At the Secwepemc Museum in Kamloops, you can discover the history of the Shuswap people. Visit Heritage Park and go through the incredible 2,000-year-old winter village and the summer pit houses.

DON'T MISS: Railway Heritage Park is the base of operations for the passenger train, and you can view equipment on display in the yard and take a guided tour of the backshop. You may even get an up-close look at locomotive 2141.

GETTING THERE: Kamloops is about a 3.5-hour drive from Vancouver. You can follow the Trans Canada Highway east or take the scenic Fraser Canyon route, but allow time for viewing the vistas along the way. The ticket office is located just outside the main door of the station building at Station Plaza.

LOCATION: 510 Lorne Street, Kamloops
PHONE: 250-374-2141
WEBSITE: kamrail.com
E-MAIL: info@kamrail.com

Kettle Valley Steam Railway

Kettle Valley Steam Railway

The Kettle Valley Steam Railway operates over the only preserved portion of the famed Kettle Valley Railway, which was completed in 1915. Passengers can enjoy the rural landscapes of Summerland's Prairie Valley, and take in the mountains and views of Okanagan Lake from the Trout Creek Bridge, a major feature of the original line.

CHOICES: The KVR offers regular excursions over a 6-mile route. The 90-minute trip winds through Prairie Valley and its scenic vistas. A century-old steam locomotive, No. 3716, or a backup diesel engine supplies the power. You can ride in two 1940s vintage passenger coaches or three open-air cars. Special events are scheduled throughout the year and include Easter, Mother's Day, and Christmas trains. About a dozen train robbery and barbecue events take place.

WHEN TO GO: The KVR operates on a varied schedule. In May and June, and during September and October, regular excursions run Saturday through Monday. In July and August, they run Thursday through Monday.

GOOD TO KNOW: Summerland is situated in the Okanagan Valley amid lush orchards and vineyards, and the valley is home to more than 50 wineries.

WORTH DOING: Take a side trip into nearby Penticton and tour the former CP ship SS *Sicamous*. This steel-hulled sternwheeler was built in 1914 as a multipurpose vessel that provided first-class passenger service as well as delivering cargo and daily mail.

DON'T MISS: The Trout Creek bridge, at the current turnaround point south of Summerland, sits 238 feet above the canyon floor and provides spectacular views.

GETTING THERE: The Prairie Valley station is located off Highway 97 from either Rosedale Avenue or Prairie Valley Road. It is about a 10-minute drive from the highway.

LOCATION: 18404 Bathville Road, Summerland
PHONE: 877-494-8424 or 250-494-8422
WEBSITE: kettlevalleyrail.org
E-MAIL: reservation@kettlevalleyrail.org

313

Rocky Mountaineer

Rocky Mountaineer

This premier rail tour company offers more than 65 unique rail experiences through the wild beauty of the Canadian Rockies and the Pacific Northwest. In addition to its signature destinations of Banff, Jasper, and Lake Louise, the company offers service to Seattle on its Coastal Passage route.

CHOICES: Rocky Mountaineer offers 2-day (or longer) all-daylight journeys over four routes. On First Passage to the West, you follow the route of early explorers over the Rockies from Vancouver to Banff or Lake Louise in Alberta. On Journey through the Clouds, you experience coastal mountains, Fraser Canyon, Hell's Gate, Pyramid Falls, and Mount Robson on the journey from Vancouver to Jasper, Alberta. The Rainforest to Gold Rush route takes you from Vancouver to Whistler through Gold Country to Quesnel for an overnight stay and then along the Fraser River to Jasper. The Coastal Passage route provides passengers with a 3-day trip from Seattle to the Canadian Rockies (or the opposite direction).

WHEN TO GO: Service begins in April and runs to October.

GOOD TO KNOW: The Jasper and Banff/Lake Louise trains are combined between Vancouver and Kamloops. Trains operating on the former British Columbia Railway north of Greater Vancouver arrive and depart from the vicinity of the former BCR station in North Vancouver.

WORTH DOING: Go for the gold and take advantage of the fancy digs and pampering with GoldLeaf service. It is a luxury train, after all. GoldLeaf service features bi-level dome coaches with full-length windows above, and gourmet cuisine served in the exclusive dining room below. You can also try SilverLeaf service, which is featured in a single-level, glass-domed coach.

DON'T MISS: All trips run both eastbound and westbound, and either direction offers spectacular scenery.

GETTING THERE: Scheduled motor coach service connects Jasper, Banff, and Whistler to the outside world. VIA Rail Canada provides rail service to and from Jasper, Kamloops, and Vancouver. Seattle is a stop on the Amtrak rail network.

LOCATION: 1755 Cottrell Street, Vancouver
PHONE: 877-460-3200 or 604-606-7245
WEBSITE: rockymountaineer.com
E-MAIL: reservations@rockymountaineer.com

West Coast Railway Heritage Park

West Coast Railway Heritage Park

Heritage Park provides a home to the West Coast Railway Association's large collection of locomotives and rolling stock. Located in a beautiful 12-acre mountain valley setting, the museum offers visitors a chance to learn about railway history from 1920 to 1960 in Canada's westernmost province.

CHOICES: The park features a variety of railway stations and other buildings. You are also able to see railway equipment in various stages of restoration in the 1914 PGE car shop. The collection of more than 90 vintage railway cars and locomotives includes cabooses, snowplows, a restored 1890 business car, and the only surviving Pacific Great Western steam engine. A mini train ride circles the park.

WHEN TO GO: The park is open year-round, with a shorter schedule during winter. Summer months provide the least likelihood for an encounter with the area's famous "wet sunshine." The park holds various special events including days out with Thomas the Tank Engine and the Polar Express.

GOOD TO KNOW: The West Coast Railway Association also operates the Locomotive 374 Pavilion in Vancouver, which houses historic CP locomotive 374. The locomotive, built in 1886, brought the first transcontinental passenger train into the city.

WORTH DOING: Incorporate a visit to the museum with a scenic drive along the Sea to Sky Highway for a nice day-long family outing. The Sea to Sky Highway travels through five different biogeoclimatic zones, from coastal rain forest to mountain forest. This predominantly two-lane road goes from Vancouver to Whistler.

DON'T MISS: The park's 21,000-square-foot roundhouse displays various exhibits including Royal Hudson No. 2860, one of the last Royal Hudson locomotives built for the Canadian Pacific Railway by Montreal Locomotive Works in June 1940.

GETTING THERE: From Vancouver, it is about an hour's drive north on Highway 99 along spectacular Howe Sound, North America's southernmost fjord, to Squamish. Turn left on Industrial Way until Queens Way and then turn right and follow the signs.

LOCATION: 39645 Government Road, Squamish
PHONE: 604-898-9336
WEBSITE: wcra.org/index.php/heritage-park
E-MAIL: info@wcra.org

MANITOBA
Prairie Dog Central Railway

Mark Perry

This railway's round trip over the former CN Oak Point Subdivision from the north side of the Manitoba capital to the towns of Grosse Isle or Warren offers a glimpse into prairie railroading of the past.

CHOICES: The train takes a leisurely trip through rural Manitoba, and you can travel in either open-vestibule or closed-vestibule coaches. The wooden coaches, built between 1901 and 1913, are fully restored and air-conditioned—when the windows are open. Power is provided by ex-CPR 4-4-0 steam locomotive No. 3, ex-BNSF GP9 No. 1685, or diesel No. 4138. Special events, including train robberies, take place throughout the season. You can also ride in an ex-CPR wood caboose or be an engineer for a day on a diesel. Vintage equipment can be seen around the shops, notably two ex-CPR G5 steam locomotives and a GE 35-ton diesel.

WHEN TO GO: Trains operate on Sundays during May and June, on Saturdays and Sundays July through September, and on weekends in late October for Halloween trains. Special runs also operate on Victoria Day, Canada Day, and other holidays.

GOOD TO KNOW: Ex-Winnipeg Hydro 4-4-0 No. 3 was built in 1882 by Dubs in Scotland and is one of the oldest operable engines in North America. The railway's station, constructed in 1910 by the Canadian Northern Railway, is a Canadian Heritage Railway Station. It was moved from St. James Street and renamed Inkster Junction Station.

WORTH DOING: During the stopover at Grosse Isle, take time to examine the displays of local crafts and home-baked goods and tour the old school. Grosse Isle is home to the 72-mile Prime Meridian Trail, a recreation trail built on an abandoned rail line.

DON'T MISS: Secure a ticket in either combine No. 103 or coach No. 105. These beautifully maintained relics are rolling time machines to another century.

GETTING THERE: Inkster Junction Station is located immediately north of Winnipeg's airport on Prairie Dog Trail. It is on the north side of Inkster Boulevard between Route 90 and Sturgeon Boulevard.

LOCATION: Prairie Dog Trail, Winnipeg
PHONE: 204-832-5259 or 866 751 3248
WEBSITE: pdcrailway.com
E-MAIL: info@pdcrailway.com

Winnipeg Railway Museum

Mark Perry

The Winnipeg Railway Museum takes visitors back to the historical first days of railroading across the vast western Canadian prairies. The museum's two tracks, located under the train shed at VIA Rail Canada's Union Station, host a variety of equipment, exhibits, and displays for all enthusiasts to enjoy.

CHOICES: The museum operates in the train shed of the grandiose Canadian Northern 1911-built Union Station. It contains various displays of both vintage steam and diesel locomotives, railbuses, passenger coaches, freight cars, cabooses, and many other Canadian Railway artifacts. A pair of restored vintage fire trucks that came from nearby CNR and CPR backshops are displayed. Various spreaders, snow dozers, and other equipment round out the collection.

WHEN TO GO: The museum is open year-round. It is open daily April through October. During the rest of the year, it is open Monday, Thursday, Saturday, and Sunday.

GOOD TO KNOW: Located in the heart of downtown Winnipeg, Union Station is still actively used by VIA Rail Canada's passenger trains. The CN's busy two-track Rivers Subdivision runs right next to the train shed.

WORTH DOING: A historic gathering place for centuries, the fantastic shopping, dining, and entertainment development is Winnipeg's number-one tourist attraction. Formerly, The Forks was a CNR rail yard, and the remaining historic railway buildings have been well preserved and upgraded. Railway equipment is preserved on the grounds, and a pristine CNR F unit is displayed inside the Children's Museum.

DON'T MISS: The museum features some notable railway equipment on display including the first steam engine in Manitoba, Canadian Pacific's wood-burning Baldwin *Countess of Dufferin*, and the unique CN GMD-1 No. 1900, a steam generator equipped GMDL diesel that switched passengers cars around Union Station.

GETTING THERE: Winnipeg is 60 miles north of the North Dakota border on Highway 75. VIA Rail operates a cross-country passenger train from Vancouver and Toronto that stops in Winnipeg. Union Station is at the corner of Main Street and Broadway Avenue in downtown Winnipeg.

LOCATION: 123 Main Street, Winnipeg
PHONE: 204-942-4632
WEBSITE: wpgrailwaymuseum.com
E-MAIL: wpgrail@mts.net

SASKATCHEWAN

Rusty Relics Museum

Rusty Relics Museum portrays pioneer life in Saskatchewan. Housed in Carlyle's 1909 station, its collection features several buildings, machinery, and artifacts. Railway items include a caboose, a jigger, a tool shed, and a working telegraph. It is open Monday through Friday, June through August.

LOCATION: 115 Railway Avenue West, Carlyle
PHONE: 306-453-2266 or 306-453-2363
WEBSITE: rustyrelicsmuseum.com
E-MAIL: rustyrelicmuseum@sasktel.net

Saskatchewan Railway Museum

This 7-acre museum contains more than 10 buildings, including a station, express shed, interlocking tower, and tool sheds from the Canadian National, Canadian Pacific, Canadian Northern, and Grand Trunk Railways. On display are a variety of freight cars, passenger coaches, streetcars, cabooses, and locomotives, including CPR Alco S3 No. 6568. You can take a guided tour or explore the museum on your own. It is open Fridays through Sundays and holiday Mondays late May to September.

LOCATION: Highway 60, Saskatoon
PHONE: 306-382-9855
WEBSITE: saskrailmuseum.org
E-MAIL: srha@saskrailmuseum.org

Western Development Museum

The WDM in Moose Jaw focuses on transportation, and it displays a passenger coach, Canadian Pacific station, and CPR locomotive 2634. It also offers train rides pulled by a Vulcan steam engine, the only operational steam locomotive in the province. The museum is open daily year-round, except for Mondays January through March.

LOCATION: 50 Diefenbaker Drive, Moose Jaw
PHONE: 306-693-5989
WEBSITE: wdm.ca
E-MAIL: moosejaw@wdm.ca

Southern Prairie Railway

Southern Prairie Railway

Located in southern Saskatchewan, this railway offers excursions across the prairies, not unlike the ones early settlers would have taken. The train features a 1922 Pullman passenger coach and a 1945 GE diesel locomotive.

CHOICES: Trains leave from a restored Canadian Pacific station, and several uniquely themed excursions are available. The 2.5-hour round-trip Heritage Train runs west along an old CP branch line to Horizon, where tour guides take you through a 1920s grain elevator. On the fourth Saturday of the month, you can ride to Pangman for a trip to a farmers market.

WHEN TO GO: Heritage Trains operate Saturdays and Sundays from mid-June through September. On select dates, you can sample a one-of-a-kind pitchfork fondue meal or a turn-of-the century settler's supper. Other specials include brunch trains, train robberies, 1920s rum runner trains, and an all-day train.

GOOD TO KNOW: The CP train station was built in 1912 and moved 150 miles from Simpson, Saskatchewan, to Ogema.

WORTH DOING: About an hour's drive south of Ogema, you'll find the Big Muddy Badlands, which features cone-shaped hills, steep cliffs, caves, and unique weathered formations, highlighted by Castle Butte.

DON'T MISS: The nearby Deep South Pioneer Museum features 30 buildings that re-create a pioneer village. The museum also includes more than 150 tractors and pieces of farm equipment. You can also take a stroll down Ogema's historic Main Street.

GETTING THERE: Ogema is about 90 minutes south of either Moose Jaw or Regina and about 4 hours northwest of Minot, N.D.

LOCATION: 401 Railway Avenue, Ogema
PHONE: 306-459-7808
WEBSITE: southernprairierailway.com
E-MAIL: info@southernprairierailway.ca

YUKON

Copperbelt Railway & Mining Museum

Located in copper country, the museum's exhibits focus on the area's mining and rail history. You can take a ride through the 10-acre park on a passenger car pulled by a diesel mining engine. The museum is open daily mid-May until the end of August, and the train ride runs every 30 minutes.

LOCATION: Mile 919.28 Alaska Highway, Whitehorse
PHONE: 867-667-6198
WEBSITE: macbridemuseum.com
E-MAIL: copperbelt@yukonrails.com

Whitehorse Waterfront Trolley

In downtown Whitehorse, you can ride a restored 1925 trolley along the city's waterfront. The trolley departs from Rotary Peace Park and travels to Spook Creek. Along the way, you can stop at the MacBride Museum of Yukon History, White Pass & Yukon depot, visitor information center, and SS *Klondike* National Historic Site. You'll also hear stories about the area's history. The trolley operates daily mid-May into September.

LOCATION: 1127 First Avenue, Whitehorse
PHONE: 867-667 6355
WEBSITE: macbridemuseum.com
E-MAIL: trolley@yukonrails.com

REGION 12

The iron horse

La ruée vers l'ouest

Go west young man!

713 713

Exporail, page 336

LABR

QUEBEC

ONTARIO

28
Quebec ○

40

27

Montreal ○
26

Ottawa ○

Thunder Bay ○

Sudbury ○ **17**

16

9

19

Sault Ste.
Marie ○

8

24

21 **22**

(401) ○ Kingston

20 **23** **14** ○ Toronto

13

15 ○ London

10 **12**

11 **18**

NEW BRUNSWICK

1 McAdam Railway Station

2 New Brunswick Railway
   Museum

3 Shogomoc Historical
   Railway Site

NEWFOUNDLAND

4 Railway Coastal Museum

5 Railway Society of
   Newfoundland Train Site

NOVA SCOTIA

6 Museum of Industry

7 Sydney & Louisburg
   Railway Museum

ONTARIO

8 Agawa Canyon Tour Train

9 Canada Science and
   Technology Museum

10 Canada Southern Railway
   Station

11 Chatham Railroad
   Museum

NEW BRUNSWICK

McAdam Railway Station

Built in 1900, the McAdam Railway Station has been restored and is a heritage railway station that contains a telegraph office, rail artifacts, and photos. Guided tours are available July through September. You'll hear about German spies, early rail travel, and a shooting in the waiting room. Also be sure to try a slice of railroad pie.

LOCATION: 96 Saunders Road, McAdam
PHONE: 506-784-3101
WEBSITE: mcadamstation.ca
E-MAIL: info@ mcadamstation.ca

New Brunswick Railway Museum

The museum contains more than 20 pieces of rolling stock that includes locomotives, passenger cars, freight cars, maintenance-of-way equipment, and cabooses. Some of the cars are open for viewing. The museum also displays a speeder car, telegraph office, and smaller artifacts. It is open June through September.

LOCATION: 2847 Main Street, Hillsborough
PHONE: 506-734-3195
WEBSITE: nbrm.ca
E-MAIL: nbrailway@nb.aibn.com

Shogomoc Historical Railway Site

In the French Fry Capital of the World, you can take a guided tour of a 1914 restored CPR train station, which contains railway artifacts and displays. Three renovated CPR passenger cars are on site. One displays additional artifacts and another is a restaurant. The station is open June to September, and the dining car is open all year.

LOCATION: 9207 Main Street, Florenceville-Bristol
PHONE: 506-392-8226 or 506-392-6763 (off season)
WEBSITE: florencevillebristol.ca
E-MAIL: tourism@florencevillebristol.ca

NEWFOUNDLAND

Railway Coastal Museum

The Railway Coastal Museum is housed in the restored 1903 Riverhead station and contains a large collection of items relating to Newfoundland's rail and coastal boat services. You can walk along the platform where passengers boarded the *Newfie Bullet* and examine the rolling stock displayed in the train park. The museum is open year-round, daily during summer.

LOCATION: 495 Water Street West, St. John's
PHONE: 866-600-7245 or 709-724-5929
WEBSITE: railwaycoastalmuseum.ca
E-MAIL: info@railwaycoastalmuseum.ca

Railway Society of Newfoundland Train Site

The society maintains a collection of narrow-gauge rolling stock from the Newfoundland Railway. Several trains are displayed including the *Newfie Bullet*, once Newfoundland's fastest passenger train. Steam locomotive No. 593 is displayed with a representative selection of cars. A snowplow train is also featured. You can walk through all the railcars. The museum is open daily during the summer.

LOCATION: Marine Drive and Station Road, Corner Brook
PHONE: 709-640-8685 (in season)
WEBSITE: facebook.com/Railway-Society-of-Newfoundland-Museum-623797571321603/

NOVA SCOTIA

Museum of Industry

Through its artifacts, big and small, the museum tells the story of how Nova Scotia changed through industry and technology. It features demonstrations of a steam engine, printing press, and sawmill. On display are nine locomotives, including *Samson* and *Albion,* two of the oldest surviving locomotives in the world. *Samson* was built in 1838 by Thomas Hackworth. It is open daily May through October and weekdays November through April.

LOCATION: 147 N. Foord Street, Stellarton
PHONE: 902-755-5425
WEBSITE: museumofindustry.novascotia.ca
E-MAIL: industry@novascotia.ca

Sydney & Louisburg Railway Museum

The museum features rolling stock, artifacts, and photographs relating to the Sydney & Louisburg Railway. Housed in an 1895 S&L station, the museum also contains historical exhibits about Louisburg. An original freight shed and roundhouse also contain displays. You can also view Nova Scotia's oldest passenger coach. It is open weekdays in June and daily during July and August.

LOCATION: 7330 Main Street, Louisbourg
PHONE: 902-733-2720   902-733-2214
WEBSITE: facebook.com/slrailway
E-MAIL: slrailwaymuseum@gmail.com

ONTARIO

Canada Science and Technology Museum

The museum reopened in November 2017 and features 80,000 square feet of new exhibition space and contains five galleries. The museum's rail collection features 1,000 artifacts ranging from photos to locomotives and dates back to the early days of Canadian railway history. The museum is open daily from May to September, closed Mondays starting in September through April.

LOCATION: 2421 Lancaster Road, Ottawa
PHONE: 866-442-4416 or 613-991-3044
WEBSITE: cstmuseum.techno-science.ca
E-MAIL: contact@techno-science.ca

Canada Southern Railway Station

Built in the 1870s, this restored Italianate-style station houses the North America Railway Hall of Fame, which features exhibits on its various inductees. It also includes artifacts from the station's history. Rail-related and other events take place at the station throughout the year. Tours are available weekdays.

LOCATION: 750 Talbot Street, St. Thomas
PHONE: 519-633-2535
WEBSITE: casostation.ca
E-MAIL: tourismandevents@narhf.org info@casostation.ca

Chatham Railroad Museum

Housed in a retired 1955 Canadian National baggage car, the Chatham Railroad Museum includes interactive exhibits and photos on local as well as national and international railroad history. Located across from the VIA rail station, the museum is open Tuesdays through Saturdays during the summer.

LOCATION: 2 McLean Street, Chatham
PHONE: 519-352-3097
WEBSITE: chathamrailroadmuseum.ca
E-MAIL: crms@mnsi.net

Fort Erie Railway Museum

This museum site features the restored Grand Trunk Ridgeway station, which houses historic furnishings, telegraph equipment, tools, and other artifacts. Canadian National Railway steam engine No. 6218, a 4-8-4 Northern type, is the museum's centerpiece. Also on display are a fireless engine, a CN caboose, and other equipment. The CN's B-1 station that monitored traffic over the International Railway Bridge is also on site. It is open daily Victoria Day weekend to Labor Day.

LOCATION: 400 Central Avenue, Fort Erie
PHONE: 905-894-5322
WEBSITE: forterie.ca/pages/museum

Komoka Railway Museum

Komoka's restored Canadian National station houses a collection of artifacts and photos dedicated to rail history in the area. It includes tools, lanterns, and a tiny flag stop station. Also on display are a 1913 Shay locomotive and a steel-sided baggage car. The museum is open every Saturday morning from the first Saturday in April to the last Saturday in November. For additional summer hours, see the website. The museum is closed from December through March.

LOCATION: 131 Queen Street, Komoka
PHONE: 519-657-1912
WEBSITE: komokarailmuseum.ca, facebook.com/komokamuseum/
E-MAIL: station-master@komokarailmuseum.ca

Muskoka Heritage Place

Muskoka Heritage Place contains the Muskoka Museum, Pioneer Village and the narrow-gauge Portage Flyer, which has the restored equipment from the world's shortest commercial railway, the Huntsville & Lake of Bays Railway. Ride in ancient restored open-air streetcars pulled by a restored 0-4-0 steam locomotive or a GE 25-ton diesel locomotive. After boarding at the train station, you travel along the Muskoka River to Fairy Lake. Watch the crew turn the locomotive on a tiny turntable from the platform on the restored Purser's Cabin that was moved from Norway Point on Lake of Bays. The train station doubles as a museum with outstanding exhibits focusing on local steamships and locomotives.

LOCATION: 88 Brunel Road, Huntsville
PHONE: 705-789-7576
WEBSITE: muskokaheritageplace.org
E-MAIL: form on website

Northern Ontario Railroad Museum & Heritage Centre

This museum emphasizes railroading history in northern Ontario and includes additional exhibits on mining and lumbering. Artifacts are displayed in the Museum House, which was used by the Canadian National as a superintendent's residence. In nearby Prescott Park, it displays a U-1-f bullet-nosed steam locomotive, Temiskaming & Northern Ontario steam locomotive No. 219, a wooden CNR caboose, and other equipment.

LOCATION: 26 Bloor Street, Capreol
PHONE: 705-858-5050
WEBSITE: normhc.ca
E-MAIL: info@normhc.ca

Port Stanley Terminal Rail

Excursion trains depart from a historic station next to the King George lift bridge. Early GE and CLC diesel locomotives pull open and closed coaches, some that have been converted from cabooses. Regular 1-hour excursions run to Whytes Park. A variety of special trains run during the season, and some travel the entire line into St. Thomas. You can view the fleet of equipment in the yard just north of the station. Excursions operate April through December (including Santa Trains just prior to Christmas), with an expanded schedule during July and August. Trains travel along the entire line to Parkside on Saturdays in July and August.

LOCATION: 309 Bridge Street, Port Stanley
PHONE: 877-244-4478 or 519-782-3730
WEBSITE: pstr.on.ca
E-MAIL: info@pstr.on.ca

Railway Museum of Eastern Ontario

This museum is housed in a restored 1914 Canadian Northern Railway station that contains artifacts relating to the Canadian Pacific, Grand Trunk, Canadian National, and other railways. The national historic site displays a 1912 steam locomotive, a CP diesel, passenger cars, a CN snowplow, and a unique dental car. You can spend a night in a caboose, take a train ride, or partake in other activities. The museum is open daily mid-May through mid-October.

LOCATION: 90 William Street West, Smiths Falls
PHONE: 613-283-5696
WEBSITE: rmeo.org
E-MAIL: info@rmeo.org

School on Wheels Railcar Museum

This car was one of seven railway schools that served children and adults along
northern Ontario railways. When touring the car, you will walk through the classroom
and living quarters and view historical videos, children's activities, artifacts, and
photos. It is open Thursdays through Sundays and holiday Mondays, Victoria Day
weekend through September.

LOCATION: 76 Victoria Terrace, Clinton
PHONE: 519-482-3997
WEBSITE: museumsontario.ca
E-MAIL: cnrschoolonwheels@gmail.com

Toronto Railway Museum

The museum features a variety of railroad components including the John Street
roundhouse, an interlocking tower, and operational turntable. In addition to
viewing historic rail equipment and displays, visitors can check out the cab of a
steam locomotive, tour Roundhouse Park, and ride on a miniature railway, weather
permitting. It is open Wednesdays through Sundays.

LOCATION: 255 Bremner Boulevard, Toronto
PHONE: 416-214-9229
WEBSITE: trha.ca
E-MAIL: info@torontorailwaymuseum.com

Waterloo Central Railway

The railway operates excursion trains through southern Ontario behind a 60-ton
diesel locomotive. The railway's restored steam engine may also run. You can take the
entire 12-mile round trip or detrain at St. Jacobs, where you can look around, visit the
railway museum, and take a later train back. Market trains run Tuesdays, Thursdays,
and Saturdays April through October. The railway also operates various special trains
throughout the year.

LOCATION: 10 Father David Bauer Drive, Waterloo
PHONE: 888-899-2757
WEBSITE: waterloocentralrailway.com
E-MAIL: form on website

York-Durham Heritage Railway

Celebrating over 20 years of operation, the York-Durham Heritage Railway is a
nonprofit association run by volunteers. The railway offers excursions on Sundays,
June to October. Ride in one of its heated/air conditioned heritage coaches from the
1950s. Visitors are encouraged to experience the open-door baggage car. The train
is equipped with a wheelchair accessible washroom, snack car and souvenir stand.

LOCATION: 19 Railway Street, Uxbridge
PHONE: 905-852-3696
WEBSITE: ydhr.ca
E-MAIL: ydhr@ydhr.ca

Agawa Canyon Tour Train

Steve Smedley

Based out of Sault Ste Marie, Ontario, the Agawa Canyon Tour train draws visitors from around the world for a 114-mile ride into the hardwood forests of Northern Ontario. The one-day tour train departs from the former Algoma Central Railway station in downtown Sault Ste. Marie.

CHOICES: The tour train takes you to Agawa Canyon and back on a one-day round trip. In the canyon, you'll have 90 minutes to explore: take a scenic walk on trails to several waterfalls, climb 300 stairs to the inspiring lookout perched 250 feet above the canyon floor, or enjoy a picnic lunch. Packages with Sault Ste. Marie accommodations are available.

WHEN TO GO: The most popular time is during the fall season. Some highlights of the trip are the Montreal River trestle at the hydroelectric dam, and finally the Agawa Canyon Wilderness Park, at Milepost 144 and only accessible by train. The canyon was carved out by the Agawa River, much of the area is sparsely populated and not accessible by vehicle.

GOOD TO KNOW: Aboard the train, a GPS-triggered narration, available in five languages, highlights points of interest and shares some of the rich history of the region. Also, locomotive-mounted cameras provide an "engineer's eye view" on monitors installed throughout the coaches.

WORTH DOING: There's much to do in Sault ste marie, such as strolling along the boardwalk, visiting a casino, or touring the locks.

DON'T MISS: The Canadian Bushplane Heritage Centre, located a few blocks away, is a wonderful visit. Across the bridge, the Soo Locks are a must-see.

GETTING THERE: Sault Ste. Marie is located at I-75 and Highway 17. The train leaves from the depot downtown, and signs will point the way to the depot.

LOCATION: 129 Bay Street, Sault Ste. Marie
PHONE: 800-242-9287
WEBSITE: agawatrain.com
E-MAIL: agawacanyontours@cn.ca

Elgin County Railway Museum

Elgin County Railway Museum

The railroad has been a part of life in St. Thomas since 1856. Over the years, a total of 26 railways have passed through town, helping it garner the moniker of the Railway Capital of Canada. Located in the former Michigan Central locomotive shops, the Elgin County Railway Museum helps preserve and display the railway heritage of St. Thomas and the surrounding area.

CHOICES: As a working museum, equipment restoration is ongoing, and you can occasionally catch a glimpse of the volunteers in action. The museum displays a variety of equipment including locomotives, cabooses, and passenger cars. Highlights are a CP diesel locomotive, a CNR Hudson, a Grand Trunk Western caboose, a Pullman sleeper, and an electric-powered car that transported children to school in the 1920s. In St. Thomas, the BX interlocking tower is available for touring during special events.

WHEN TO GO: The museum is open year-round. It is open Tuesday through Sunday between Victoria Day and Labor Day weekends. From September to Canadian Thanksgiving, it is open Wednesday through Saturday. The rest of the year, it is open Saturdays only. Thomas the Tank Engine stops by several weekends in July, and the museum hosts various events during the year.

GOOD TO KNOW: A short drive from the regional center of London, St. Thomas is a small town with all services. Its Iron Horse Festival takes place in August.

WORTH DOING: Combining a visit to the museum along with a ride on the nearby Port Stanley Terminal Rail makes for an interesting day of exploring the preserved rails of southern Ontario.

DON'T MISS: Climb aboard the legendary 1930 CN Hudson 5700 steam engine that is on display.

GETTING THERE: VIA Rail Canada offers scheduled passenger service through London to the north. If driving, the museum is 2 hours from Toronto, 2 hours from the U.S. border at Detroit, Buffalo, or Niagara Falls, and 1 hour from Sarnia and Port Huron. Once in St. Thomas, you will find the museum on Wellington Street between Ross Street and First Avenue.

LOCATION: 225 Wellington Street, St. Thomas
PHONE: 519-637-6284
WEBSITE: ecrm5700.org
E-MAIL: thedispatcher@ecrm5700.org

Halton County Radial Railway

Halton County Radial Railway

Canada's pre-eminent trolley museum brings the streetcar era to life with the help of the largest collection of operable streetcars in the country. Its streetcars, radial cars, and work cars operate over a rebuilt portion of a long-abandoned interurban railway.

CHOICES: Streetcars, such as Toronto Transit Commission No. 2894, travel over a short track on a 20-minute ride through a hardwood forest. The railway features four display barns filled with 75 pieces of equipment that, in addition to streetcars, includes freight cars, passenger coaches, buses, and a locomotive or two. Most of the streetcars were built in the early 20th century.

WHEN TO GO: Streetcars operate on weekends and holidays from May to October and daily during July and August. A number of special events are incorporated into the operating season.

GOOD TO KNOW: Admission includes unlimited streetcar rides and access to the exhibits displayed in the carbarns and Rockwood Station, which was built in 1912 for the Grand Trunk Railway. You can also enjoy a picnic lunch on the railway's grounds.

WORTH DOING: On Labor Day weekend, steam fans can take in Milton's steam-era event that features steam-powered equipment in action, a parade of tractors and antique autos, and tractor pulls.

DON'T MISS: Take a break on your trolley ride with a stop at the ice cream shop at the outer loop and return to the main grounds on a different car.

GETTING THERE: Milton is 25 miles west of Toronto on Highway 401. From Highway 401, take Exit 312 and go north on Guelph Line until you reach the museum. It is also the the terminus of Toronto's Milton commuter train line.

LOCATION: 13629 Guelph Line, Milton
PHONE: 519-856-9802
WEBSITE: hcry.org
E-MAIL: streetcar@hcry.org

South Simcoe Railway

South Simcoe Railway

The South Simcoe Railway operates over 4 miles of former Canadian National trackage through rolling countryside north of Toronto. Excursions are powered by a 1948 diesel locomotive or steam locomotive No. 136, which was built in 1883.

CHOICES: Regular excursions from Tottenham to Beeton and back take about an hour. As the train rolls through Beeton Creek Valley, the conductor provides an informative commentary. Passengers ride in restored 1920s steel heavyweight coaches. Special trains include the Easter Express, Haunted Halloween Adventure, and Santa Claus Express.

WHEN TO GO: The railway runs multiple trips on Sundays and on holiday Mondays between Victoria Day weekend and Canadian Thanksgiving. It also operates on some Mondays and Tuesdays in July and August and weekends in October for viewing the fall colors.

GOOD TO KNOW: The town of Tottenham has a variety of quaint shops and eateries. Across the road from the railway is Tottenham Conservation Area, a park that offers swimming, camping, fishing, and hiking.

WORTH DOING: For a unique combination rail-water excursion, the RMS *Segwun*, the oldest operating steamship in North America, sails July and August on the Muskoka Lakes, about a 2-hour drive north to Gravenhurst.

DON'T MISS: Take one rail trip and then follow another for some great photos. The engine faces south into the sun, and the relatively slow pace of the train makes it easy to follow.

GETTING THERE: No public transit is available to this neck of the woods. Tottenham is about an hour's drive north from Toronto. From Highway 400, take Highway 9 west 9 miles to Tottenham Road and turn right. Continue into downtown Tottenham and turn left onto Mill Street to reach the station.

LOCATION: Mill Street West, Tottenham
PHONE: 905-936-5815
WEBSITE: southsimcoerailway.ca
E-MAIL: info@southsimcoerailway.ca

PRINCE EDWARD ISLAND

Elmira Railway Museum

The museum offers a look at railroading on the island in the early 1900s. It features a station house with a re-created station master's office and waiting room as well as displays and artifacts. A miniature train operates around the museum, and various special events take place on the outdoor stage, which was built from the base of a flatcar. The museum is open weekdays June and September and daily during July and August.

LOCATION: 457 Elmira Road, Elmira
PHONE: 902-357-7234 or 902-368-6600 (off season)
WEBSITE: peimuseum.com
E-MAIL: elmira@gov.pe.ca

Exporail

Exporail

The largest collection of railway equipment in the country is well worth a stop for anyone interested in Canadian railways and rail transit. Locomotives, rolling stock, and streetcars from many parts of the country tell of the evolution of both industries.

CHOICES: The museum's collection boasts 160 railway vehicles. Special events and exhibits are scheduled throughout the year geared toward modelers and transit enthusiasts. The museum has several train ride options. A streetcar runs daily between May and October. On Sundays May to October, you can take a short ride on a passenger train. The main building contains only a portion of the collection, and you can explore the rest of the site from stops along the streetcar loop. You'll be able to see Barrington Station, a restored, rural flag stop station from southwestern Quebec.

WHEN TO GO: The museum is open daily between mid-May and early September. During September and October, it is open Wednesday through Sunday. The remainder of the year, the museum is open on weekends, for spring break, and around Christmas.

GOOD TO KNOW: Stop, Look, Listen: Incoming Train? is a new permanent exhibition on railway safety that provides an interactive, educational, fun and preventative railway safety experience for young visitors and their parents.

WORTH DOING: There is much to see and do in Montreal. You can discover centuries of history in Old Montreal, explore Olympic Park and Mount Royal, or take in one of its many festivals and international events.

DON'T MISS: Walk through an inspection/observation pit to gain a new perspective on locomotives and rolling stock in the Grand Gallery of the Angus Pavilion.

GETTING THERE: The museum is located 12 miles from downtown Montreal. Amtrak's *Adirondack* connects the city with the rest of its network in Albany, N.Y. CIT Roussillon provides bus service near the museum, and EXO provides commuter rail. On Saint-Pierre Street, a locomotive marks the entrance to Exporail's parking lot.

LOCATION: 110 Saint-Pierre Street, Saint-Constant
PHONE: 450-632-2410
WEBSITE: exporail.org
E-MAIL: info@exporail.org

Orford Express

Scott Hartley

Enjoy the eye-catching scenery of Quebec's eastern townships from the only dinner train in the province as it travels Central Maine & Quebec rails between Magog and Sherbrooke.

CHOICES: The dinner train is made up of a pair of converted RDCs and a dome car led by either an FL9 or a unique M-420 TR locomotive. Service options include dining in the main car, the salon section of the lounge, and the panoramic section of the lounge car. In addition to dinner outings, brunch and lunch excursions are also offered. Trains run May through December, and on summer days, Wednesday through Sunday, you'll find at least one type of train in operation.

WHEN TO GO: While the long days of summer offer the maximum daylight viewing, the often spectacular fall colors in the surrounding hills are a delight to behold.

GOOD TO KNOW: A variety of packages including local accommodations is available, lessening the chance of nocturnal large wild-life encounters after evening trips.

WORTH DOING: You can incorporate the dinner train into a long weekend of exploring the region, while including stops at Exporail in suburban Montreal or the hot air balloon festival in St Jean that takes place each August.

DON'T MISS: Upper level dome seating offers an unparalleled view of the surrounding countryside, not regularly seen since the days when the Canadian Pacific's *Atlantic Limited* traveled these same rails.

GETTING THERE: Located at the head of Lake Memphramagog, the Orford Express station in Magog is 75 miles from greater Montreal via Highway 10 and is also served by intercity bus. Magog can also be reached from upstate Vermont across the lake by private boat.

LOCATION: Quai MacPherson Pointe Merry, Magog
PHONE: 866-575-8081 or 819-575-8081
WEBSITE: orfordexpress.com
E-MAIL: info@ orfordexpress.com

Train de Charlevoix

Scott Hartley

Train de Charlevoix offers passengers 78 miles of scenery on this former Canadian National line along the north shore of the St. Lawrence River, and passing through two tunnels in the Charlevoix and Capitale-Nationale regions of Quebec.

CHOICES: Trains to and from Montmorency Falls, about 10 miles east of Quebec City, and La-Malbaie meet near the line's midpoint (and headquarters) at Baie-St.-Paul, with both trains also making stops at two intermediate locations. It is possible to make a round trip over the entire line in just one day, but most passengers opt for shorter rides, or spending a night at one or more at one of the stops. Train seating is assigned; seats on the "river side" cost slightly more than being on the "mountain side." Be sure to make your choice known when you purchase your tickets. Bicycles may be brought on board for a fee.

WHEN TO GO: Fall foliage season is the most popular time of year, but scenery is beautiful through the June to October operating season. Space on the two-car German-built trains sells out quickly, so make your reservations early.

GOOD TO KNOW: Train de Charlevoix and VIA Rail Canada have partnered to allow visitors to ride VIA to Quebec City's magnificent Palace Station and be transferred by shuttle bus to Charlevoix's station at Montmorency Falls. Watch for seals and beluga whales in the river.

WORTH DOING: The train's Quebec City-area station is adjacent to 272-foot-high Montmorency Falls. Take the cable car to the top. A suspension foot bridge lets you walk over the top of the falls, and then walk down a long set of stairs to the base.

DON'T MISS: Visitors should spend at least a day and night in Quebec City, a year-round tourist destination.

GETTING THERE: The southern terminal is in the outskirts of Quebec City on the St. Lawrence River. Quebec City is about 150 miles northeast of Montreal.

LOCATION: (Quebec City area) 5300 Boulevard Sainte-Anne, Beauport. Other main stations are at Baie-Saint-Paul and La Malbaie
PHONE: 418-240-4124, 844-737-3282
WEBSITE: traindecharlevoix.com
E-MAIL: form on website

Index

G

H

I

J

K

L

M

Advertiser Index

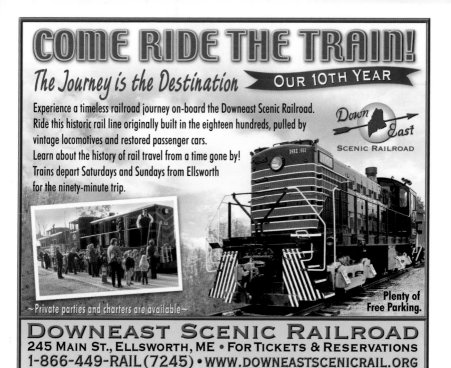

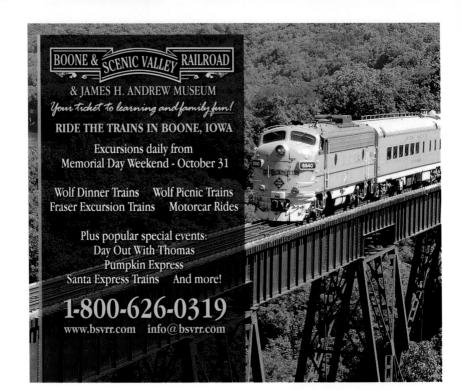

MODERN DAY RAIL ADVENTURES FOR THE HISTORIC TRAIN LOVER

ALASKA RAILROAD PHOTO CREDIT: GLEN ARONWITZ

RAILROAD MUSEUM OF PENNSYLVANIA

REAL TRAINS. REAL HISTORY. REAL EXCITEMENT!

Experience the awe-inspiring power of trains and the fascinating heritage of our nation's railroading!

- 100 historic locomotives and railroad cars
- Steinman Station passenger depot and telegraph office
- Stewart Junction railway education center
- 1915 street scene
- Working restoration shop
- Extensive library and archives, by appointment
- Whistle Stop Shop museum store
- Unique special events and exhibits

Open year-round. Free onsite parking, free WiFi.
Group tours and facility rentals.

RAILROAD MUSEUM OF PENNSYLVANIA
Real Trains. Real History. Real Excitement.
300 Gap Road, PA Route 741, P. O. Box 125
Strasburg, Lancaster County, PA 17579
(717) 687-8628 • www.rrmuseumpa.org

Smithsonian Affiliate

Pennsylvania
Historical & Museum
Commission

Administered by the Pennsylvania Historical & Museum Commission, with the active support of the nonprofit Friends of the Railroad Museum of Pennsylvania.

YouTube

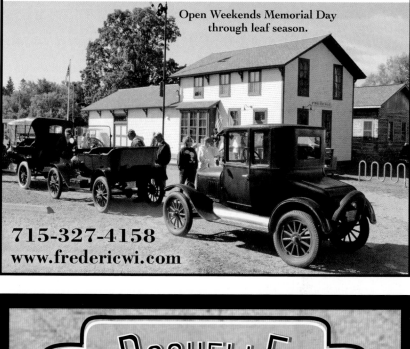

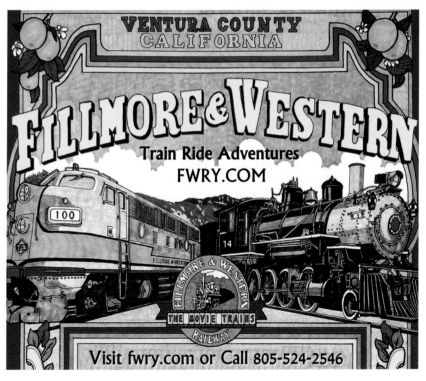

RIDE THE RAILS
NEXT TO THE WHALES

ALL ABOARD THE OREGON COAST SCENIC RAILROAD!

Forge full-steam ahead along the beautiful Tillamook Coast. Watch beaches and hills roll by your window, on this delightful 2-hour journey. The train stops in Garibaldi and Rockaway Beach, so you can shop, snack and explore before hopping back onboard. Be sure to check out our special excursions, too.

Plan Your Trip
oregoncoastscenic.org

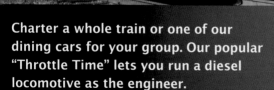

GOLDEN SPIKE TOWER

A panoramic view of the world's largest rail yard.

OPEN DAILY

1249 N HOMESTEAD RD · NORTH PLATTE, NE

GOLDENSPIKETOWER.COM

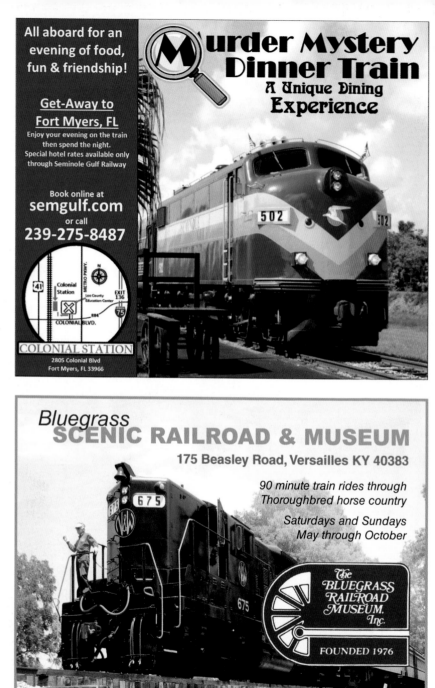

Travel Through Time On Indiana's Most Scenic Railroad

Whitewater Valley Railroad
Grand Central Station
455 Market St., Connersville, IN 47331

765-825-2054

Ride the train, rain or shine, as it departs Grand Central Station in Connersville, IN at 12:01 pm every Saturday, Sunday and Holidays between May and October. Two hour layover in Metamora.

Celebrating over 40 years of Operations. The Whitewater Valley Railroad is an operating railroad museum dedicated to the preservation of a historic branch line railroad, to the restoration of railroad equipment, and to the conduct of railroad educational programs operated by trained volunteers.

The Whitewater Valley Railroad is a Not For Profit 501c3 Organization.

Find us on **Facebook**   You Tube

FOLLOW US ON twitter

Come and see where the Red Diamonds still work the rails. Ex Cincinnati Union Terminal #25, the last remaining 750 hp unit in existence and only one of four Lima-Hamilton diesels to survive.

Train Excursions and Special Events are available throughout the year. Our trains are also available for charter. contact us for more information.

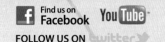

www.officialbestof.com

BEST SCENIC RAILWAY
THE **OFFICIAL BEST OF**
INDIANA 2013

All Aboard For Fun!

STEP ABOARD the Grapevine Vintage Railroad. Travel in authentic 1920s Victorian-era coaches between Grapevine's Cotton Belt Depot and the Fort Worth Stockyards for an afternoon of fun. Or hop on the Grapevine One-Hour Train Excursion. It's a perfect way to spend a day in Grapevine, Texas.

705 S. Main St., Grapevine, TX 76051
130 Exchange Ave., Fort Worth, TX 76106

For tickets, schedules and train information, visit
www.GVRR.com or call **817-410-3185**

BRANSON SCENIC
Ozark Zephyr
RAILWAY®

March through Mid - December
Regular Excursions
Mon - Sat
11:30 am, 2 pm, 4:30 pm (seasona

Dinner Train
(April - October) Saturdays at 5 p

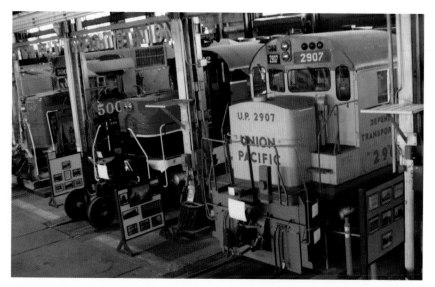

Arkansas
RAILROAD MUSEUM

Featuring Engine 819

Steam locomotive 819, the last 4-8-4 built in Pine Bluff is one of seven items on the National Register of Historic Places that can be seen here. Several rare diesel locomotives, a complete steam wrecker train, cabooses, a snow plow and railroad memorabilia are on display.

**OPEN WEEKDAYS
AND SATURDAYS
9:00 AM-2:00PM**
Museum Phone
870-535-8819

PINE BLUFF
ExplorePineBluff.com

1700 Port Road, Pine Bluff 71601
LOCATED JUST OFF U.S. HIGHWAY 65B

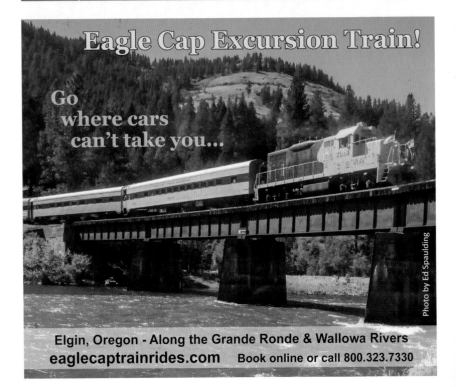

CONWAY SCENIC RAILROAD

Experience old-fashioned train rides, all departing from our 1874 Victorian Station in North Conway Village.

Choose from Coach, First Class, or Dining Car seating. Whether you choose one of the Valley Train routes to Conway or Bartlett, or the legendary Crawford Notch excursion, this is a journey back in time the whole family will enjoy!

ConwayScenic.com • (603) 356-5251

38 Norcross Circle | North Conway Village

Children under 4 ride FREE in Coach on the Valley Trains!
Well-behaved dogs are alway welcome.

Colorado RAILROAD Museum ®

LOSING TRACK OF TIME — SINCE 1959 — **60** YEARS

MINUTES FROM DOWNTOWN DENVER
OPEN DAILY • Train Rides Every Saturday
303-279-4591 or 800-365-6263
Join us online to discover all our new events happening throughout the year

Colorado RAILROAD Museum.org

YOU'LL COME OUT DIFFERENT.

Steal away a day on the Cumbres & Toltec Scenic Railroad. It's a 64-mile journey that zig zags through steep mountain canyons, the high desert, and lush meadows between Antonito, Colorado and Chama, New Mexico. Begin your adventure in either town. The trip includes a hearty lunch buffet and luxury motor coach shuttle back to your car. You'll take home the unspoiled West inside of you.

BOOK NOW AT CUMBRESTOLTEC.COM   1-888-286-2737

Cumbres & Toltec
AMERICA'S MOST HISTORIC SCENIC RAILROAD

Share the fun of train travel and relive our country's oil history as you ride the OC&T 'through the valley that changed the world.'

Vintage 1930's Pullman Coach Cars, 1925 Wabash Cannonball - our First Class Car, only operating Railway Post Office car in the USA, Museum, Gift Shop, Concessions

Regular season June - October

June & Sept: Saturdays & Sundays leaving at 11 am

July & August: Wednesdays, Thursdays, Saturdays & Sundays 11 am
Except August 10th & 11th at 1 pm

Many Special Events including Peter Cottontail Express, Santa Trains, Speeder Rides and Murder Mystery Dinners.

Oil Creek & Titusville Railroad

Perry Street Station
409 S. Perry St., Titusville, PA 16354
814-676-1733 • www.octrr.org

The Galveston Railroad Museum

www.galvestonrrmuseum.org

2602 Santa Fe Place • Galveston, Texas 77550
(409) 765-5700

Location of the original Gulf, Colorado, and Santa Fe Passenger Union Depot in Downtown Galveston, Texas. The museum features five acres, including 50 pieces of rolling stock, model trains and numerous exhibits. Home of the Santa Fe Warbonnets, the largest railroad museum in the Southwest.

- Open Seven Days A Week
- Hours: 10AM - 5PM Daily
- Train Rides Saturdays
  11AM - 2PM
  Weather Permitting
  Check website for details

CLIMB ABOARD

Take a scenic train ride through Cuyahoga Valley National Park!

CUYAHOGA VALLEY SCENIC RAILROAD

- Dining excursions
- Beer and wine tastings
- Murder mystery dinners

Visit **CVSR.com** for Schedule and Tickets

- Family programs
- Group outings
- Private car rentals

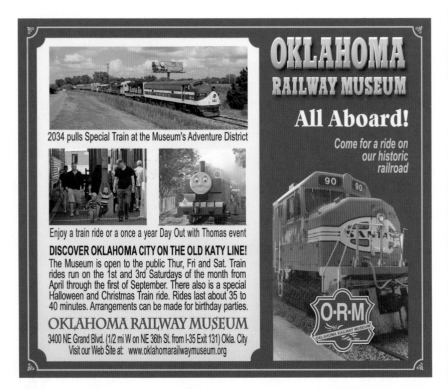

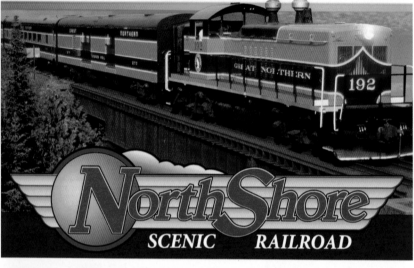
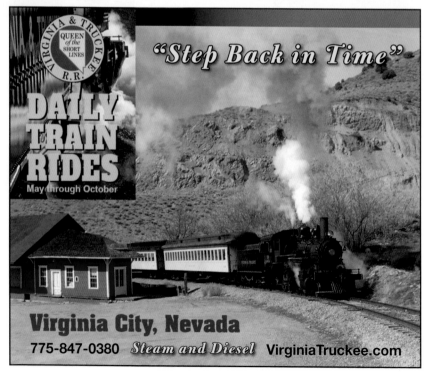

HISTORY COMES IN ALL FORMS
OURS JUST HAPPENS TO BE MADE OF STEEL

Discover the Western Pacific Railroad Museum, where you can experience hands-on railroad history. Home to North America's largest and most complete collection of Western Pacific trains, the museum has over 150 pieces of rolling stock. Tour the vintage passenger cars, climb aboard to ride the trains and even operate a locomotive.

Located in California's beautiful Feather River Country, the Western Pacific Railroad Museum offers train rides each weekend from Memorial Day to Labor Day, features Pumpkin Trains in October and Santa Trains in December. Reservations are recommended for Run-A-Locomotive.

For more information, call 530-832-4131, or visit www.WPLives.org.

ADMISSION

Adults 19 & up	$ 8.00
Youth 4-18	$ 4.00
Children 3 & under	FREE
Family Pass	$20.00

*Train Rides Extra Fare

MUSEUM HOURS

Shop the museum store and visit the museum

April	Thursday – Sunday 10 AM – 5 PM
May – Sept	Daily 10 AM – 5PM
Oct	Thursday – Sunday 10 AM – 5 PM

WPRM
Western Pacific Railroad Museum
PORTOLA

www.wplives.org

700 Western Pacific Way near Old Town, Portola, California
Western Pacific Railroad Museum is operated by the Feather River Rail Society

·1880 TRAIN·

The best vacations are

POWERED BY STEAM.

It's A New Day

At the Western Maryland Scenic Railroad, we have two priorities: To preserve America's rich railroad heritage, and to provide a one-of-a-kind immersive experience that takes you back to the **"Golden Age of Railroading."** We invite you to visit us and see what we have to offer.

Allegheny Mtn. Express

Steam engine No. 1309 - **the largest articulated steam locomotive in service in the United States** - debuts in the summer of 2019. Ride behind No. 1309 in standard coach and relax in the Allegheny Mountains.

Cumberland's Crescent

Imagine yourself **back in the days when service mattered**. Ride the diesel-powered Cumberland's Crescent and treat yourself to the most unique dining experience in Western Maryland.